To my Mother, Evie, ‘S’, Crystal, Vicky, Kihyuk, Shirley, and ‘SA’(Katherine)

CONTENTS

An Invisible Fear

Joel Collins Pacheco

ISBN: 978-1-7377463-1-7

'I will either find a way or make one.'

—Hannibal

1 THE ENIGMA MACHINE

Gemma—An Invisible Fear—The Empty Box

LONDON

It was a bright and sunny day in London—a rare sunny day. It was autumn and there was a slight chill in the air. The natural light that morning had a quality of light that only appeared in autumn. Yes, it was a perfect day.

A beautiful woman, with blonde hair and pale blue eyes, smiled. As she glided effortlessly down the pavement, her reflection was captured in one of the large store windows which lined the cobblestone street. The woman's smile was as beautiful as she was.

'Gemma!' said the woman happily.

Gemma, standing at the edge of the street, and bundled up in her blue, red, and purple All Saints scarf, a pair of faded blue jeans, and her blue quilted jacket, turned and looked in the direction of the woman's voice. Gemma smiled.

The woman crossed the street. She was holding a small empty cardboard box. She smiled. When she reached Gemma, she hugged her tightly. 'Thank you for the box, Gemma. The kitties will love it,' the woman said happily. The woman radiated love, kindness, goodness, wholesomeness, and an almost ethereal beauty.

'I'm glad you like it. And, I'm sure the kitties will too,' said Gemma happily. It was such a small gift. Such a simple little thing, yet it made the woman happy.

'I love you, Gemma.'

THE APARTMENT

Gemma awoke in the dark. The dream was retreating; like a sash window closing quickly; she had to speak immediately while the portal was still open. She wanted to respond to the woman in the dream. She wanted her to hear what she was going to say. Was it only just a dream? Or was it a form of communication?

'I love you, Mummy.'

The portal closed. Yes. It was closed. Yes. Gemma's mother had heard her.

Gemma, alone in the dark and shrouded in white cotton sheets and a white duvet, looked around the small room. There was only silence.

What time was it? It didn't matter. Gemma's mother had communicated with her. Gemma was grateful.

'Yes, I love you, Mother. I always have, and I always will. I'm sorry that I wasn't with you when you passed away. I should have been there. I miss you every day. I'm sorry. I love you. Thank you for visiting me. Please pet the kitties for me and tell them that I miss them and that I love them too.'

Gemma started to cry.

'I'm sorry, Mummy. I took you for granted. I should have appreciated you more. I didn't. I'm sorry.'

A moment more of reflection and Gemma, looking in some Cosmic direction and with tears streaming down her face said, 'I love you.'

Gemma—An Invisible Fear—Louise Percival

LONDON
Louise lay unconscious under white cotton sheets and a dark blue wool blanket. Louise was now in a private room at an NHS hospital. Natural light filled the white walled room. She had yet to regain consciousness.

Aurelia had found her lying on the hardwood floor of their room in the girl's residence hall at their university in London. It had been a terrible shock for her. Aurelia had frantically telephoned for an ambulance, and while still on the line with the Emergency Dispatcher, had run across the hall and knocked furiously on Teuta's door. The slender twenty-one-year-old Albanian undergraduate, in a pair of navy blue pyjamas and with her dark hair tied back with a white ribbon, had answered sleepily. Aurelia, badly shaken, had led her by the hand across the hall.

Teuta helped Aurelia carefully and gently placed Louise in the bottom bunk. Teuta's roommate, a blonde Kosovar Albanian girl named Albana, looked into the room briefly and then ran down the hall to awaken the Resident Advisor.

'The ambulance will be here in a few minutes, Aurelia,' said Teuta, in an attempt to calm her. The effort, while well intentioned, didn't work. Aurelia tapped on the glowing screen of her smartphone. A moment later her mother answered.

'Is everything alright, Aurelia?' asked Alexa.

Upon her hearing her mother's voice, Aurelia began to cry.

THE HOSPITAL
The dark-haired and surprisingly (relatively) young doctor, in a dark blue blazer, a white dress shirt, a dark blue wool tie, and dark grey wool trousers, looked at the medical chart on the clipboard. The relatively young doctor looked more like an office worker than a neurosurgeon. Yes, the NHS had jettisoned the white lab coat in favor of having its doctors look like bank branch managers in Luton.

LORD MAUD
'Do you have any idea what has happened to Louise?' asked the elderly

baron in his clipped Mayfair accent. The 4th Baron, in a dark grey business suit, pale blue dress shirt, and a dark blue neck tie, had been on his way to a meeting when his daughter-in-law, Violet, had telephoned from the Lake District and told him about Louise. He had immediately directed his driver to take him to the hospital.

'No, My Lord. We won't know what has happened to her until we can complete an MRI. I have scheduled one for 11am,' said the doctor from Surrey.

Standing in the hallway of the hospital ward with the doctor were Alexa, the tall, white-haired 4th Baron, Külli, and Gemma. Aurelia was seated in a waiting room down the hall with Teuta. Aurelia had been so upset that Alexa had asked her to wait in the room with Teuta while she spoke with the doctor. Gemma, Alexa, and Külli were all wearing pencil skirts and blouses. While Alexa and Gemma wore pumps, Külli wore a set of high heels, which meant she almost matched the 6'4" baron in height.

'Does Miss Percival have any family?' asked the doctor.

'Yes, we have been trying to contact her father in East Anglia all morning,' replied the baron.

EAST ANGLIA
'Yes. This is Harold Percival,' replied a clear and concise voice over the phone.

'Mr Percival, my name is Bran Maud. Louise is a close friend of my granddaughter Freya. I am calling because Louise is in the neurological ICU in London. She was found unconscious in her residence hall this morning. She is still unconscious.'

'What?' replied Louise's father quietly.

'Louise was found unconscious in her room this morning. She is in the neurological ICU.'

There was a brief silence on the line, and then Louise's father replied. 'Thank you for calling, Mr Maud. Is Louise expected to live?' asked Louise's father calmly.

'I am afraid I can't answer that question. Louise is now undergoing an MRI downstairs. We will know soon.'

The other end of the line went quiet. The 4th Baron listened carefully for a minute, trying to detect the sound of breathing, or, well, anything. Had Louise's father hung up?

'Mr Percival? Are you there?' asked the elderly 4th Baron.

'Yes. I'm here,' said Louise's father. 'Please text me the name of the hospital, Louise's doctor, and the phone numbers I will need. Thank you, Mr Maud. Please tell the doctors I will arrive there sometime today. I will board the first available train to London.'

'Louise has many people here in London who care about her. We will stay here with her for as long as necessary. I could pick you up at the train station, if you like. Please, we would like to assist you and Louise as much as we can, Mr Percival.'

'Thank you, sir. Yes, I will text you after I board the train today.'

THE DOCTOR'S OFFICE

The two young doctors looked at the glowing computer screen. The doctor in coat and tie studied the images carefully. A second doctor, a blonde woman in a dark blue surgical smock, spoke quietly with the other doctor from Surrey. The neurosurgeons nodded in agreement.

Seated in the small white walled office were the 4th Baron, Gemma, Alexa, and Külli.

Gemma stared out the window of the office. It was a grey overcast wintery day. She wished none of this had happened. Why now? Why were so many things going wrong now? Gemma felt like she was standing on the beach and being slowly submerged in a Cosmic tide. What would the next few days and weeks bring? Gemma hoped that Louise would be alright. Please, God, let Louise be alright.

'Louise has had a mild stroke. We will keep her in the hospital for a few days and monitor her. There is the possibility of another stoke occurring in the next few hours or days. Oh, Louise was slipping in and out of consciousness during the MRI. She was asking for someone named Gemma,' said the young woman doctor.

'That's me,' said Gemma. 'Is Louise awake yet?'

'I don't know, Mrs Ripley. She is in her hospital room. Louise was asleep the last I saw her being rolled down the corridor in a gurney,' replied the dark-haired neurosurgeon.

'How long do you expect Louise to stay in the ICU, doctor?' asked Külli.

'At least a week. Hopefully we will be able to release her before Christmas. If there are no complications,' said the young woman doctor.

'She will be required to take medication on a daily basis for the foreseeable future. Preventing another stroke is paramount,' said the young man as he adjusted his wool necktie.

The doctors then volunteered to show the MRI images to the visitors assembled in the office. While the baron, Külli, and Alexa listened to the doctors explain what they were seeing on the computer screen next to a large modern desk, Gemma remained seated and stared out the window. Yes, more was on the way. The Cosmos was stirring. Gemma could sense that something sinister and dark was moving towards them. Gemma closed her eyes and prayed to God to protect them from the coming storm which would undoubtedly envelop them all.

THE HOSPITAL ROOM

Aurelia and Teuta, both in faded blue jeans and white cotton blouses, sat at the edge of Louise's bed. Louise, tiny and fragile, stared at both of them sleepily from the large white pillow.

'I'm sorry,' said the diminutive and strawberry blonde Louise softly.

'No need to apologize, Louise. I'm glad you're alright,' said Aurelia quietly.

'How do you feel?' asked Aurelia.

'I have a strange headache. The top of my head feels like a flame is dancing on it, and there are little bolts of electricity striking at my brain.'

'Have you told the doctors about it?' asked Aurelia.

'Yes. They gave me some medication. They say it's common among stroke patients,' replied Louise quietly.

Aurelia reached out and gently grasped Louise's small soft hand. 'You'll be alright, Louise. You will be.'

Teuta decided it was best to leave the two friends alone. She smiled and said, 'I am heading back to the university now. Can I bring you anything from your room, Louise?'

'No. No, thank you. Teuta, thank you for your help this morning. Aurelia told me that Albana helped me too. Please tell her how grateful I am for her helping me.'

Teuta smiled. She was worried about Louise. A stroke at nineteen. How terrible. 'Please telephone me if you need anything.'

'Thank you, Teuta,' said Louise.

The dark-haired and attractive Teuta put on her grey wool jacket, and the undergraduate from the ancient city of Vlorë quietly left the room.

Aurelia, alone with Louise, gently caressed Louise's small hand in hers.

Louise, in a loosely fitting pale blue hospital gown, stared out the window of the hospital room for a moment. It was snowing. Louise, her brain swirling with painful sparks and jolts, turned to look at Aurelia.

'Aurelia. I had a strange dream last night. I remember it quite clearly. I think it is important.'

Gemma—An Invisible Fear—Muddy Hills

THE MIDLANDS

December 15th, 2019

Freya put down her pen and looked out the window. The grass quad, stone domes, and ornately carved cloisters were covered in a fresh white blanket of snow. It was overcast. More snow was forecast to fall before night fell. Freya loved snow. She loved the winter and the cold wintery air. Snow was comforting to Freya. It usually calmed her nerves. But not today. Freya had been at Suga's desk in her room—the boilers at school were still undergoing extensive repairs and undergraduates were still camping out in the warmer rooms—when she received a phone call from her godmother Gemma.

Louise had collapsed sometime in the middle of the night. Aurelia had found her unconscious on the floor of their room in their dormitory in London. Louise had been taken to the hospital in an ambulance. Louise, Freya's closest friend in the world, had apparently suffered some kind of stroke and now lay in a bed in the neurological ICU in a hospital in London. Gemma had calmly explained the situation. She also mentioned that Aurelia was extremely upset by what had happened. Gemma was at the hospital with Külli, Alexa, Aurelia, and Freya's paternal grandfather, the 4th Baron.

Freya had wanted to board a train for London immediately, but Gemma told her that she should wait for news. Louise was now downstairs having an MRI. Gemma would telephone her after speaking with the doctors.

'Freya, Louise is in good hands. I will keep you informed.'

VIOLET

'Yes, Freya. I know you are upset. I am upset, too, but we have to be calm.

Your grandfather is at the hospital right now. Aurelia is there too. Poor Aurelia. She is really upset. You have to be strong for Louise, alright?' said Violet over the telephone.

'Yes, Mummy. Will Louise be alright?' asked Freya.

'I am afraid Louise had had a minor stroke, but she is now awake. Your grandfather telephoned me a few minutes ago. The doctors are going to keep her in the ICU for the rest of the week.'

'A stroke? How can this be? Louise is only nineteen, Mummy,' said Freya while starting to cry.

'I don't know. The doctors are trying to determine what happened. But Louise is awake. She was talking with Aurelia when your grandfather looked into Louise's hospital room. Freya, please don't cry.'

'I'm going to travel to London this afternoon. I want to be with Louise, Mummy. Louise needs me. I need Louise, Mummy. I need her too,' said Freya choking back tears.

'Oh, Freya, I feel the same way. Louise is a daughter to me. She is your sister. Please, be calm. Gemma and Külli are both with her now. First it was Gemma, then Poppy and the twins, and now poor Louise. This year has been hard on everyone. I will be glad when this year is over,' replied Violet.

'Mummy, I can purchase a train ticket online right now and be in London in three hours.'

'Freya, you have exams today. This is Exam Week. Louise would not want you to miss your exams.'

EXAM WEEK

This was Exam Week. Unlike other universities in England that had their exams in January, ~~Rhodes~~ Midlands-Hasegawa, at some point in the past, had adjusted its schedule of school terms and exam times. Some said that it had been done to accommodate the foreign students, who usually made up about eighty percent of the students. Yes, Michaelmas started a month early, in September. Yes, it was strange, but one got used to it. And Freya liked the idea of having a fresh start at the beginning of each term. Yes,

Muddy Hills was unique in England for many different reasons. Muddy Hills was not drowning in Political Correctness and Wokedom. That the schedule and character of a long-forgotten university in the Midlands was out of sorts with the rest of the country had failed to register with anyone beyond the University's ornate stone gates.

Freya studied her reflection in the mirror. Stay calm, Freya. She felt herself starting to tremble. Freya's only desire at that moment was to be at her friend's side. Louise would have rushed to her side without the slightest hesitation, for sure.

In May, Finals Week required the undergraduates to wear their black Russel Cord academic gowns (sub fusc), white dress shirts, white bow ties, and carry their black mortar boards. (Carry, not wear, not yet.)

In December, the undergraduates were required to dress formally (as they normally did for their classes). For women, that meant a skirt, blouse, and formal shoes (not trainers or sandals). That unnerving morning had found Freya wearing a dark grey pleated skirt, a white blouse, a knee length dark blue wool overcoat, her red, blue, and purple All Saints scarf, and a pair of black patent leather pumps.

Freya's smartphone had rung after she had returned from breakfast and everyone else in Suga's room, Jinx, Suga, Pasha, and Wren, had left for their exams. Freya's first exam started an hour later than the others. Freya had decided not to tell Jinx about Louise. Jinx had exams and the play to prepare for. Jinx was fragile, sensitive. Freya didn't want to derail her with such terrible news. Freya, however, was a wreck.

LONDON

When Gemma entered Louise's hospital room, she found Külli, her long glossy brown topped by a pair of transparent framed reading glasses, sitting at her bedise alone. Alexa had driven Aurelia back to her university after Louise had fallen asleep. Aurelia had calmed down a lot and Louise had insisted before she fell asleep that Aurelia return to school. Louise assured her that she would be alright. Külli had taken Aurelia's place. Külli sat near in a wooden chair near the window of the hospital room shrouded in the greyish gloom of a wintery afternoon in December. Külli had been left somewhat disoreinted by the events of that morning. She couldn't help but think of her own father dying in a hospital room in London almost two decades earlier. She loved her father—and her mother. It had injured Külli that she had not been at either of her parent's bedsides when they passed away. Her parents had both died alone. She did not want that to happen to Louise. Where was Louise's father? How could he ignore his only child at this point in her life? Külli despaired. Unbeknowst to her, Louise's father was enroute to London from East Anglia.

Gemma opened the door quietly and carefully. She walked in, a slight click of her heels on the floor of the room announced her. Külli looked away from Louise and directly at the diminutive and slender Gemma. Külli nodded slightly in acknowledgement. Gemma walked over and stood next to the hospital bed. Yes, tiny, fragile, sweet, little Louise had been left injured.

Gemma walked over to Külli and sat down in the wooden chair next to her.

'How are you?' asked Gemma quietly.

'I'm alright. Louise is sleeping,' replied Külli in a near whisper.

'Alexa gave me the day off. I will stay with her. I know you are in the middle of sorting through Christmas orders at Vahtra. I'll telephone if anything happens, okay?'

Külli nodded slightly. Yes, it was true. Külli had a lot of work to do. Gemma understood that. Külli knew that Gemma had lost her mother, and had not been there for her passing. It had saddened Gemma as much as Külli being away when her own parents had passed away in the hospital. Gemma also knew that Külli had to attend to her outfitters. Yes, Gemma understood the situation clearly. Yes, she would call Gula immediately if anything happened. Okay. Külli, confident that Gemma would not leave Louise alone, nodded.

'Thank you, Gem.'

MIDLANDS-HASEGAWA UNIVERSITY
Freya's first exam that morning had been Latin. She had sailed through it.

Afterwards she walked out into the corridor and turned on her smartphone: no messages. Okay. Everything is alright. Louise was in ICU. The slender, flaxen-haired Freya walked down the corridor, buttoning her blue wool overcoat as she did. She reached the wooden double doors and exited the stone building. A blast of cold air greeted her as she stepped outside.

Freya looked up at the grey overcast sky. Flakes of snow were falling. One landed on her soft warm cheek. And then another. Freya took out here smartphone from her coat pocket. She taped out a text and then touch the screen.

How is Louise?

A minute later, an answer.

She's sleeping. How are you, Freya?

Freya quickly tapped out a response.

I'm worried about Louise, Godmother. Can Louise talk normally? Is there any paralysis?

Ping.

So far, she seems alright. I haven't spoken to her yet. Aurelia said she seemed alright. I will text you immediately after I speak with her and whenever there is any news on her condition. Say a prayer for Louise. I have. Find solace in God, Freya.

Yes. Gemma was right. Freya, her long glossy blonde hair held up with silver hair pins, walked down one of the cloisters, stopped, and then folded her hands in prayer. Freya closed her eyes, and she said a prayer for her dearest friend in the world: the fragile and gentle soul named Louise.

Gemma—An Invisible Fear—The Dream

LONDON

It was while the nurse was checking Louise's IV that she stirred awake. Louise's eyes opened and then closed. And then opened again. 'Gemma?'

'Yes. I'm here, Louise.'

Louise smiled. She extended her small soft hand towards Gemma and Gemma grasped it gently.

'I'm happy you are here, Gemma. I'm sorry for everything. I have made a mess during Freya's Exam Week.'

'Freya sent me several text messages this morning. She is really worried about you. Freya and I have been praying for you, Louise. Everyone has been. How do you feel?' asked Gemma quietly.

'I have a strange headache. Like the top of my head is burning and electricity is zapping my brain. I have never experienced anything like it. The doctor said that it is common among people who have had a stroke. He said it should go away in a few days.'

'Would you like me to ask the doctor for some more medication?' asked Gemma.

'Yes. Thank you. But. Gemma. I have to tell you something. Privately.'

'Of course.'

'Gemma. I had a dream last night. I think it was the cause of my stroke. It was so real. It wasn't a normal dream. I remember it perfectly,' said Louise quietly; her voice a mixture of pain and anxiety.

Gemma nodded slightly.

'Yes, Louise. I understand. My dreams are often quite important. I think that sometimes they can be a form of communication. Supernatural communication. Whatever you tell me, I will believe.'

Louise exhaled slowly. Okay. Louise had not told Aurelia about her dream. She wanted to tell Gemma first. Louise knew that Gemma would understand. For some reason, Louise knew that.

'Last night I dreamt that I was walking through the snow in East Anglia…'

LIVERPOOL STREET STATION

The British Rail Class 755 engine slowed to a complete stop. The tall middle-aged man looked out the window of the train carriage. Yes, it was snowing. The glass roof of the Gothic train station filled the station with the natural, albeit, grey light of the overcast sky. The passenger looked at his silver Omega watch: 2:33pm. Yes, soon he would see his only child, a daughter, a little over a year after their very brief last meeting.

HAROLD PERCIVAL

Major Harold Algernon Percival (Ret'd), formerly of the Coldsteam Guards, had only seen Louise twice since she was eight years old. Now, at nineteen, Louise had grown into a beautiful young woman. Louise, in fact, looked exactly like her late mother. And that was a problem for Harold.

Yes, Harold had loved Louise's mother more than words could describe. He had always had a rather distant personality, but Edith, Louise's late mother, had been able to break through that iron wall and capture his heart. Edith had been as kind and affectionate as Harold was reserved. It had been difficult for the young subaltern to show emotion. Harold's father had been a strict disciplinarian. Harold's childhood had been harsh. For the young Harold, the army had been an escape. Edith had been his salvation.

When Louise was born, the strawberry blonde and diminutive Edith felt complete. Edith had made Harold feel whole for the only time in his life. Harold had considered Louise an extra, but a truly loved addition to the family. He had loved Louise as much as he had Edith. However, it had always been difficult for Harold to show Louise much affection. Harold had been taught that children were meant to be seen and not heard. The lively Louise and her gentle and affectionate mother would often run around the house playing games. Edith would drive Louise to the local school and pick her up every day. Louise had had a lot of friends at the village school.

Louise loved attending it. Edith would greet Louise at the gates of the school with a gentle hug. Louise was a happy and good-natured little girl.

Louise had viewed her father with some degree of affection. He was, after all, her father. Harold was on active duty throughout most of Louise's life. He would take the train home from London whenever he had leave. Sometimes Edith and Louise would take the train and stay at the family's modest terraced house in London (which the family still owned) while Harold protected the Sovereign. Louise could remember holding her mother's hand while they walked among the crowds outside Buckingham palace to watch her father parade with his regiment. These were happy memories for Louise.

Any memory of her mother was a happy one for Louise.

There was one memory that Louise sometimes wished she could forget: the rainy day her father told her that her mother was dead. Edith had been returning home in her car when a sudden rain storm had caused her to slide off the road and into a tree. Edith had been found barely alive by a local farmer and his son. They had telephoned for an ambulance, but it was too late. The farmer had attempted to stem the bleeding, but it was hopeless. Edith's injuries were too severe. Louise's mother died before the ambulance could arrive.

Harold had been left completely shattered by Edith's death.

When he gazed upon the young Louise, Edith stared back at him. It was crushing. Louise was an innocent child. It hurt Harold to send her away to his sister's family, but he couldn't bear to look at Louise. She was a constant reminder of what he had lost. It tore at him to send his daughter away, but it was for the best. Yes, it was for the best.

No one had ever bothered to ask Louise what she had wanted.

Now, eleven years after the death of his beloved wife, Harold Percival found himself facing the loss of his only child; a gentle teenage girl that he had completely neglected since she was eight years old. Had it been for the best? Really?

THE TRAIN PLATFORM

The white-haired 4th Baron, in a pike grey overcoat (with a black bear fur collar) and highly polished black leather Oxfords, spotted Louise's father as he stepped down from the train. Yes, he looked just like the photo that Violet had found online and emailed him. Yes, Major Harold Percival had been an extremely handsome young army officer. The photo of him in the pages of Tatler as a young subaltern had drawn a lot of attention when first published in the 1990s. Today, almost fifty, he looked remarkably the same, save for his white hair, which was cut like a British army officer's.

Harold Percival, in a charcoal grey wool overcoat, dark blue suit, a pale blue dress shirt (with a Windsor collar), and a dark blue silk necktie, was easily one of the *smartest* looking men the baron had ever laid eyes on. Was this paragon of military virtue really Louise's father? Louise, the gentle soul, the fragile young girl that now lay in a hospital bed, and brain damaged from a stroke. How could this man have neglected her for so long? How could he have practically abandoned his own daughter? The elderly 4th Baron could only guess. However, his very own daughter-in-law, Violet, had done much the same with his granddaughter Freya. The baron hoped that one day, somehow, Louise's father would come to the same realization that Violet had. But, perhaps, that was too much to ask?

The baron's tall (though at 6'2" still two inches shorter than the baron) and menacing bodyguard stood next to him in a black overcoat, black suit, white dress shirt, and black silk necktie. The young man, formerly of the Parachute Regiment, scanned the crowd around him.

'Mr Percival?' asked the baron.

'Yes. I am Harold Percival.'

'My name is Bran Maud. I am here to take you to see Louise.'

'Thank you, Your Lordship.'

Yes, Louise's father had searched online for the identity of the man who had telephoned him. Bran Maud was a baron and a hereditary member of the House of Lords.

LONDON

The drive to the hospital in the baron's glossy dark blue Range Rover had been a rather quiet one. Louise's father seemed lost in thought. He had shown no emotion as he listened to the baron discuss Louise's medical situation.

THE HOSPITAL ROOM

'Gemma, I think the dream was something supernatural. I am sure it was. The dragon looked towards the Lake District. I don't know how I know that, but I do. Gemma, I am scared. For you. For Poppy. For everyone.'

Gemma had listened in silence. Yes, Louise was right. Gemma was sure of it. This had been no ordinary dream.

'Thank you for confiding in me, Louise. Yes, I think you're right. I think this dream means something *quite* real.'

'What should we do, Gemma?' asked Louise quietly.

'Let me think about this. Louise, would you mind if I shared this dream with Poppy, Külli, and Violet? They might have some insight into it?' said Gemma.

'Yes, if you think it will be helpful. I am worried about you, Gemma.'

Gemma caressed Louise's hand gently and said, 'Don't worry Louise. I'll be alright. I'm worried about you. Please get some rest. I want you to get better.'

Gemma.'

'Yes?'

'I want to see Freya perform in the play on Saturday. It's important to me,' said Louise quietly. Louise looked as if she would cry.

Gemma was worried that any more bad news would prove dangerous to Louise. What could Gemma say?

'Louise, let's see how you feel on Friday. Let's see what the doctors say. If they feel it is safe to discharge you from the hospital, then you can take the train with me and Enoch to Muddy Hills. Okay? But please don't worry about this. Freya wants you to recover as soon as possible.'

The strawberry blonde Louise gently nodded her head. 'Of course, you are right, but I have been looking forward to this. It is a once in a lifetime event, Gemma. Please talk with the doctors for me.'

'Alright, Louise. I will talk to them, but your health and well-being are what is important now.'

'Okay,' replied Louise quietly.

Gemma gently hugged Louise. Louise started to cry as she hugged Gemma.

'Why did this have to happen now?' asked Louise.

'I don't know, Louise. Why do so many good people suffer reversals so often? I can't answer that question, but please, get some rest. I will do everything within my power to get you to Muddy Hills.'

'Okay,' said Louise quietly.

When Gemma leaned back in the wooden chair, Louise wiped her tears.

'You have been through worse than this, Louise. You are brave. You and Freya were so brave that night at All Saints. You made it through that; you will make it through this, alright?'

Louise smiled. 'Yes, you are right, Gemma. I have experienced much more dangerous situations than this.'

Louise looked out the window of the hospital room at the falling snow.

'Gemma?'

'Yes?'

'Could you smuggle in some thin crust pepperoni pizza for me?'

'Sure,' replied Gemma, and she smiled.

There was a knock on the white hospital door. Gemma and Louise looked in the direction of the door. Through the narrow glass window, they could see the 4th Baron. And another sharply attired and handsome white-haired man.

'Father?' said a clearly ~~surprised~~ shocked Louise.

Gemma knew that it was time to step out into the hallway. She stood up, adjusted her blouse, and said, 'I'll be in the hallway if you need me.'

'Thank you, Gemma.'

The door opened and Louise's father entered. Gemma had never met him before. What she had heard had not been good. So, this was Louise's father? Gemma nodded slightly.

'I'll wait outside, Mr Percival,' said Gemma.

'Thank you,' replied Louise's father quietly. The baron noticed that the sharpness in Harold's voice had all but disappeared.

Gemma walked past Louise's father and exited the hospital room. She gently closed the door behind her.

Louise, tiny and fragile, had been crying just a few minutes before, and she looked like it. Her strawberry blonde hair, cut into a chin length bob, framed her pale face. Louise's mother's brown eyes stared at her father. It was uncanny. Louise was a carbon copy of her mother. Beautiful and gentle. Pure and innocent. It was unsettling for Louise's father. Memories came flooding back to him, much the way they had over a year ago when Louise had arrived for the Christmas holidays. At that time, he had pushed her away, but now, Louise lay broken in a hospital, perhaps unable to survive the month. Would he walk away from Louise, his only child, again?

Louise's father, tall, slender, and handsome, approached Louise's bed slowly. He stopped. He looked at one of the wooden chairs.

'Please be seated, father,' said Louise quietly.

'Thank you.'

Louise's father, in a dark blue bespoke suit, sat down next to Louise's hospital bed.

Suddenly, the fierceness seemed to vanish from her father's face.

Louise didn't know what to say.

Her father spoke first.

'I'm sorry, Louise. There is no excuse for the way I have treated you. None. It wasn't until this morning when Lord Maud telephoned me that I realized the enormity of what I had done to you. I'm sorry, Louise. You didn't deserve what I have put you through. I am ashamed of myself. I have treated you cruelly. A cruelty that I will never forgive myself for. I will never forgive myself for any of it. You were always such a good little girl, Louise. Always kind and sweet, just like your mother.'

And with those words, Louise broke down sobbing.

And for the first time, since his wife's death, Harold Algernon Percival broke down and cried.

Gemma—An Invisible Fear—The New Inseparables

THE MIDLANDS

Freya had been able to stay focused long enough to pass her Ancient Rome exam that afternoon. Freya was confident that she had done more than that—she had passed it with flying colors. Yes, history was something Freya loved. But she loved Louise even more, and Louise had occupied her mind during the exams that day.

Freya was walking down one of the stone cloisters that afternoon after her history exam when she stopped and looked out across the snowy quad towards the Girl's Residence Hall. Icicles had formed along the edge of the cloisters; a freezing wind chilled Freya to the bone. Freya had to tell Jinx what was happening. It would be distressing for her, but it would also be unfair to keep her in the dark about it.

Ping.

Freya took her smartphone out of her coat pocket and looked at it. There was a message from Gemma. Freya tapped the screen.

Louise is awake. She has a bad headache and is on medication, but she speaks normally and there is no sign of paralysis. I have more good news: Louise's father is with Louise now in her hospital room. They have been talking for the last twenty minutes. I hope something good comes out of this. Try not to worry too much, Freya. Pray for Louise. I am. Louise wants to attend the play this weekend. She wants to see you on stage playing Cleopatra. It depends on what the doctors say, but, if possible, I will bring Louise with me to Midlands-Hasegawa.

Freya sighed with relief. No, Louise wasn't out of the woods yet, but Louise was talking normally. And shockingly, her father had travelled to London to see her. Part of Freya was angry. Louise's father had treated the gentle and sweet Louise terribly. Most of poor little Louise's life had been spent alone in cold boarding schools bereft of family affection. It was only three and half years ago that Louise had met Freya—someone who truly loved her. It wasn't fair. Louise had been left emotionally scarred by it all. Freya had had Gemma, Karmen, and the rest Freya's family to love and protect her when her mother, Violet, had had little interest in her. Louise had had no one for years, most of her life. Freya despaired when she thought of what Louise had been through.

Dear kind Louise. Please be ok. Please recover quickly. I want you to have a happy life. And I promise, when I leave England, I will take you with me, wherever I go. I need you, Louise. You are my truest friend in the world.

And not for the first time that day, Freya clasped her hands in prayer and asked God to save Louise.

THE RESIDENCE HALL

Jinx and Suga sat in wooden chairs in front of the large stone fireplace. The fire was warm and both girls were illuminated in the orange glow of the flames. Jinx was wearing a long, pleated, navy blue skirt, a white blouse (with open cuffs and a large collar), and her Borders School cricket sweater. The v-neck of the beige sweater was a band of dark blue with a white stripe in the center and blue and white striped cuffs. Jinx had not played very much cricket while at her school in Wales, but she liked the cricket sweater and so she bought one at the school store just before she graduated. It looked nice on her, and the sweater was quite warm. Suga, having completed both of the days' scheduled exams, had changed into a set of red, blue, and purple tartan flannel pyjamas. Suga's long glossy blonde hair was piled onto of her head and held in place with silver hairpins. Suga, curvaceous and beautiful, smiled.

'You know, I wouldn't mind if the boilers were out all winter. I enjoy having you, Freya, and Wren camping out in my room,' said Suga in her gentle Scottish lilt.

Jinx smiled. 'Yes. I will miss this. I will definitely miss baking potatoes in the fireplace. It's fun living like this. When we get older, we will have families to take care of. I wonder if we will have time to do this?'

'Of course, we will!' said Suga happily. 'I plan to have at least three children. I want to have as much fun as I can. We have a large stone fireplace back home in Scotland. We grill meat in it. I'm going to raise my children to be Border Reivers like their Mummy.' Suga burst out laughing. 'Yes, I will also teach them how to fight with a claymore and ride horses before they even know how to walk.'

Jinx laughed. 'Please invite me to visit from Surrey. I will introduce my children to yours.'

A skeleton key could be heard turning in the Edwardian lock of the dorm room. The glossy white wooden door opened and Freya appeared in the doorway. Freya looked cold. She turned and quietly shut the door.

'Come over and sit next to the fire, Freya. It's quite warm,' said Jinx happily.

'Thank you, Jinx,' said Freya in a tired and detached tone of voice.

Jinx tilted her head to one side. She had never heard Freya talk like that. Surely, something was wrong. Jinx decided it was best to let Freya warm herself by the fire before asking her about anything. Jinx stood up, took a few steps, and then lifted up a wooden chair and placed it next to hers.

'Please have a seat, Freya,' said Jinx.

'Thank you, Jinx.'

Suga, unaware that anything was wrong, turned to Freya and said, 'Tonight they are serving lasagna. And that always includes garlic bread. I love garlic bread.'

Freya didn't respond. She just warmed her hands by the fire and stared into the flames.

Suga decided that Freya was too cold and tired to pay much attention to what was being said to her. She must be really exhausted after a day of exams. Suga didn't take it personally. Suga looked at her watch: 3:45pm. It would be dark in a few minutes. Suga decided that now would be a good time to return some books to the library before dinner.

'I'm going to the library. Does anyone have any books that need to be returned?' asked Suga.

'No, thank you, Suga,' replied Jinx.

Freya snapped out of her trance and looked over at Suga, and said, 'No. But thank you for asking.'

Suga smiled. She put on a long dark grey wool overcoat over her tartan pyjamas and buttoned it up. She went to her desk, picked up her book bag, and left for the library. The second Suga closed the door behind her, Jinx, her pale smooth face framed by a chin length bob of glossy black hair turned to Freya.

'Is everything alright?'

Freya started to slowly shake her head. 'No, things are not alright. This morning Aurelia found Louise unconscious on the floor of their dorm room. Louise has had a stroke. She is now in the neurological ICU. Apparently, the stroke was a mild one. I don't know what that means. Louise can talk and she hasn't been left paralyzed.'

'When did you find this out?' asked a visibly upset Jinx.

'This morning, after you had left for your first exam. I didn't tell you because I didn't want to upset you. I'm sorry. Louise's condition was unknown at the time. I wanted to wait and find out more before I told you anything. Please don't be angry with me.'

'I'm not angry. Will Louise be alright?' asked Jinx.

'I don't know. Gemma is with her. So is my grandfather, Alexa, and Külli. Aurelia was at the hospital with her, but she is now back at school. She has another week of class before the Christmas holidays. They have exams in January. Louise wants to attend the play this Saturday,' said Freya quietly.

'Have you spoken with Louise yet?' asked Jinx.

'No. Gemma spoke with her for a few minutes, but then Louise's father showed up at the hospital. Gemma left them alone to talk. I haven't heard anything since. Louise has a really bad headache.'

'Louise's father is at the hospital?' asked Jinx.

'Yes, he is there with her. I hope they can reconcile.'

'This is terrible. A stroke at nineteen? I didn't think it was possible,' said Jinx quietly.

Freya was numb. She couldn't believe any of this was happening.

'Just as everything was turning around. Louise and Aurelia were hoping to attend here after the holidays,' said Freya.

Suddenly Freya's phone rang. She looked at the glowing screen. It was Louise. Freya's eyes widened. Freya tapped on the screen.

'Hello? Freya,' said Louise. She sounded tired and weak.

'Yes. It's me, Louise. I love you,' said Freya starting to cry.

'I love you too, Freya,' said Louise choking back tears. 'I can't believe this has happened to me.'

'I can't either, but I will travel to London on Saturday and stay with you in the hospital, okay?'

'I want to attend the play, Freya. I want to see you on stage. It's important to me,' said Louise through tears.

'Louise, please don't be upset. They are going to film the play. I will bring a copy of it and play it for you in the hospital,' said Freya quietly.

'I want to see the play in person, Freya. Gemma said that if the doctors allow me, she will take me with her to Muddy Hills.

Louise's sounded so fragile over the phone. Freya was worried that she would have another stroke.

'Don't worry, Louise. Gemma will move heaven and earth to help you. Right now, please just focus on getting better, okay?'

'Alright, alright,' said Louise weakly.

'Louise, is anyone there with you?' asked Freya.

'Yes. Gemma is here with your grandfather. They have both been so kind. My father came to see me, Freya. He told me how sorry he was for…everything. He wants to be my father. I don't know what to think of all of this. He just stepped out in the hall a minute ago. He is talking with Gemma and the baron. I had a moment alone, so I called you.'

'I love you, Louise. That's all you have to know, okay?

'I love you, Freya. I always will. No matter what happens,' said Louise, and she started to cry.

Freya started to cry too. She tried to muffle the sounds of her crying, but she quickly realized she didn't know where the microphones were on her smartphone.

'Nothing will happen, Louise. You will get better. And you will attend Muddy Hills with Aurelia next term. I will make sure of it. Okay?'

'Okay,' said Louise through tears. Louise was scared. Freya could hear it in her voice, and it scared Freya.

'I wish I were there. I would bite your fingers,' said Freya while trying not to cry.

Louise suddenly burst out laughing. 'You remember that? asked Louise.

'Yes, I do, you little imp. I will never forget that New Year's in the Lake District by the fountain. You surprised me.'

Louise could be heard laughing gently over the phone.

'Louise, just get some sleep. Is anyone going to stay with you in your room tonight?' asked Freya.

'Yes. Gemma said she would. She is going to smuggle in a thin crust peperoni pizza for me tonight,' said Louise sleepily.

'Louise, please go to sleep now. You need rest. I will call you later, okay?'

'Okay,' replied Louise weakly. Suddenly Freya felt another burst of fear move through her very soul. Would this be the last time she would ever speak to Louise? No, don't even think that. Freya couldn't help it.

'Louise, I love you. I have loved you from the first day we met. I am glad we became friends. I would have been completely lost without you. Completely lost.'

'I have always felt the same, Freya. Always,' said Louise weakly.

'And I'll let you have the bed closest to the fireplace, Louise. The boilers won't be working, so that will be important.'

Silence. Louise did not answer.

'Louise?'

Nothing.

'Louise?'

Only silence.

Louise!' shouted Freya over the phone.

The next voice that Freya heard was Gemma's.

Gemma—An Invisible Fear—The Carthaginians

LONDON

Carter Holland, blond and blue-eyed, in a bespoke black Savile Row suit, white dress shirt (with a Londoner collar), and a light grey silk necktie, stood looking out of one of the windows on the top floor of his Edwardian merchant bank building in The City. It was winter in England, which meant nightfall came early. Outside of the large pane glass windows of the building the darkness was broken only by the bright lights of London. Carter looked at the platinum watch which glinted on his wrist: 5:03pm.

The once ornate interior of the building and been gutted decades ago and replaced with smooth white minimalist walls and a complex lighting system of recessed lighting and wall mounted lamps (minimalist discs of glass) from Germany and Japan. The top floor of the building had very little in the way of furniture. In the very center of the vast cavernous room was a long table of minimalist design. The table, a symmetrical collection of glass, aluminum and titanium, had been made in Germany. There were ten arm chairs on either side of it. Each chair was of a utilitarian design and made of steel and polished aluminum. The chairs had not been designed for comfort. At the head of the table was a large black leather, high back, minimalist arm chair. That is where Carter Holland presided over meetings. There would be no doubt who the Lord of the Giants was here.

Carter stood in the shadows of the room. Only the lamps on either side of the stainless steel elevator doors partially illuminated the top floor. Well, that and the bright lights of the city outside.

It had been three days since the incident in the Medieval church. And still

Declan had remained silent. Where was he? Was he dead?

The Revenant was somewhere in the east. He was scheduled to return to London tomorrow. Carter had already sent a typed note to the Revenant's office instructing him to meet him in the tomb tomorrow night. The letter had been stamped in red ink with the symbol of the Carthaginian goddess Tanit (which meant it was to be shredded and incinerated after being read). Yes, Enoch Tara's Special Unit was now on the prowl. It would not take long for them to find those responsible for the death of Brigada. Was the Revenant aware of what had happened in London in his absence? Of course, he was.

Carter Holland had doubled the size of the security teams which surrounded him. Most of the men around him were now armed (illegally).

The project had been scheduled to enter its final phase with the New Year. And now this complication. All of Carter's own doing. Yes, he had miscalculated. Yes, Carter's momentary recklessness and impatience was now threatening to derail everything. Carter knew that.

When the Revenant returned to London, Carter would breathe easier. At least he hoped he would. It would be left to the Revenant to lock horns with Tara's Special Unit and protect him. That was, after all, what the Revenant was paid for.

THE ELEVATOR

Carter's smartphone glowed brightly for a moment and then went dark. Carter looked at the screen. Someone was coming up in the elevator. Security had let the person through automatically. The number of people on that list was very few. Was it the 11th Baron? No, he was now dying in a private clinic in London. Was it the Revenant? No. He would never break cover and show up at the offices of Quadriga Investments. It wasn't Declan; Carter had not cleared him for immediate access. There was only one person left on the list: **her**.

Carter looked in the direction of the elevator doors just as they opened. Fully illuminated in the interior of the stainless steel elevator was a slender, blonde, and beautiful young English woman. She stepped out of the lift and stood motionless in the light of the two wall mounted lamps on either side of the elevator doors. She flashed a white smile—a smile like a Siberian winter.

'What do you have to report?' asked Carter; his voice echoing softly across the room.

'Everything is going just as you said it would,' replied the strikingly beautiful young woman who was clad in a dark grey pencil skirt, a white blouse, a blue blazer (with white edging), and knee length black leather boots.

'Then why are you here?' asked Carter.

'There has been a change of plans. Perhaps.'

'What do you mean?'

'Gemma Ripley might not spend Christmas in the Lake District. One of her goddaughter's friends has suffered a stroke. She is in the neurological ICU in a hospital in London. Gemma might stay in London over the holidays.'

'Which hospital?' asked Carter.

'The one in Queen Square,' replied the young woman.

'This will complicate things,' said Carter.

'Nothing has been confirmed. If her plans change, I will be among the first to know.'

'Have you done what I asked?'

'Not yet. The opportunity hasn't arisen,' replied the young woman.

'Alright.'

Carter was not upset. He knew that she would do what he had asked. Carter believed in her. The young woman walked towards him, casting shadows across the cavernous room as she approached him. She stopped just a step away, and then she embraced him. Carter received her coldly.

'Long day?' asked the young blonde woman. She understood Carter's moods. This kind of behavior was not unknown to her.

'Yes. Very long.'

The young woman took a step back, her glossy blonde hair and bangs framing her smooth, flawless, pale face. 'The night is still young,' said the young woman, and she smiled.

Carter crossed his arms. **Yes, the night was still young.** Carter turned his back on the young woman and walked to one of the large white pane glass windows overlooking the City. He took out his smartphone and tapped the screen.

'Come to London tonight,' said Carter.

A voice hissed back over the phone and then the line went dead.

Gemma—An Invisible Fear—Egyptian Art Deco

THE LAKE DISTRICT

The sterling silver Egyptian Art Deco bracelet glinted in the sunlight. Poppy tilted her wrist one way and then another. The bracelet flashed each time as the metal caught and reflected the light. The slender, blonde, blue-eyed, and diminutive Poppy, in pair of dark khaki cotton trousers and a white blouse with open cuffs and an open collar, looked out the window of the drawing room.

The fiery sun, a pulsating burning orb, peeked out from behind large white clouds. The night before there had been a heavy snow and the grounds around the country house were now an endless ocean of white snow. It was freezing cold outside, but not cold enough to deter Poppy from taking her morning walk.

Yes, the telephone call from Alexa the day before had been deeply distressing. Louise had had a stroke. She was now brain damaged and lying in the hospital. The last year and a half had been harsh for The Inseparables. And just when everyone thought the worse was behind them, this happens. Poppy had prayed for Louise that morning. Undoubtably, Violet had too.

Freya had telephoned her mother yesterday morning crying. It had been hard for Violet to bear. Yes, Louise was more like a sister to Freya. Yes, Louise was more like a daughter to Violet. Yes, Violet loved Louise. Yes, the next few hours and days would be dangerous for Louise. Another stroke could leave her paralyzed or dead. Violet had telephoned Hughie, who was staying with Violet's family in Northumberland, and cried softly over the phone. Hughie had been in contact with his father, the 4th Baron, in London. Violet's family was making arrangements to have Louise stay with them in Mayfair for Christmas. Violet now planned to return to London after the play with Hughie and Freya in Enoch's private rail carriage along with Gemma and Enoch. Yes, Gemma was now staying with Louise in her hospital room. Louise wanted to attend the play at Muddy Hills. Wouldn't that be dangerous for her? Violet's Rhodesian mother-in-law, the baroness, had telephoned that morning. She told Violet not to worry, she would telephone the hospital and speak with a dietician and find out what kind of diet Louise should follow. Hughie had telephoned again, yes, he had spoken with a neurosurgeon. Yes, the surgeon would consult with the doctors at the hospital in Queen Square.

Poppy had told her family the night before. Yes, it was a shock. Everyone in Poppy's family loved Louise. She was part of the family now. Yes, Louise had been practically abandoned by her own family, but she was now part of so many others.

THE CASTLE RUINS

Poppy, in her dark purple wool cashmere cape (with a mink collar and hood), entered the castle through the gate house with Violet, the snow crunching underfoot. Violet, in a pair of dark grey wool trousers, a white blouse (with a large collar), and navy blue frock coat (with a wide light brown fur collar), adjusted the white silk scarf which shrouded her long, glossy, blonde hair. The courtyard, a vast blanket of white snow, unfurled before them.

Poppy breathed in the cold country air. It was refreshing and strengthening. Poppy could see her breath materializing in the cold wintery air. She stopped and looked at Violet.

'Do you know what Louise's father said to her?' asked Poppy.

'Louise told Freya that her father had apologized to her for everything. "Everything"—that was the word Louise used. Louise had a terrible headache and was very weak when she telephoned Freya. They only talked for a few minutes. Louise fell asleep on the phone. Freya was afraid that Louise had had another stroke. Gemma picked up Louise's smartphone. She had been standing outside in the hallway watching Louise talk on the phone in her hospital bed when Louise dozed off. Gemma entered her hospital room and could hear Freya shouting Louise's name over the phone. Poor Freya. Gemma spent the night sleeping on a cot next to Louise. She telephoned Freya this morning and told her not to worry. Poor little Louise. She is such an angel, and this happens?' said Violet, her voice breaking with emotion.

Poppy stopped and looked at Violet. Yes, the openly emotional Violet still took some getting used to. However, Poppy was glad that Violet had changed for the better. Violet stood ramrod straight in the middle of the snowy courtyard; her long glossy blonde hair partially concealed under a white silk scarf. Yes, Freya bore a strong resemblance to her mother. Violet's new found sensitivity was not a weakness. **Humanity is a strength.** Humanity requires courage and unselfishness. And at that moment, humanity was needed more than ever.

'I wish I could travel to London to see Louise. The doctors want me to rest for at least another week. I am not even sure if they will release me to travel to see the play. I think, however, right now, Louise needs rest, not a flood of visitors.'

'Yes, you are right. Louise is in good hands. Gemma and Külli will be staying with her at the hospital,' said Violet. 'Louise's father is staying in London right now. He hasn't said much to anyone except for Louise.'

'I hope they can reconcile. He has a lot to make up for,' said Poppy.

'Yes. He does. *And so do I.* I don't pretend to understand him, but I hope he does change—for the better,' said Violet.

'Yes, I hope so too,' said Poppy. 'I want Louise to be happy. She deserves to be after so much misfortune.'

Poppy, of course, had not missed Violet's pointed self-criticism. Yes, Violet was still processing everything. Violet had changed for the better. She was trying. Violet was trying to make amends.

Poppy walked forward and grasped Violet soft manicured hands in hers and smiled. 'We all have done things we regret, Vava. That we try to change for the better is important, that matters. Most people never even try.'

Violet did not respond. She simply held Poppy's hands and looked into her pale blue eyes.

'Vava. You have always been a good person. It just took you a little longer to find yourself. You are now a better person for it,' said Poppy. 'Freya telephoned and cried over the phone with you because she knew that she could and that you would understand her. Freya would not have felt that way a year ago. Now she does.'

Violet nodded ever so slightly and said, 'You always know what to say, Poppy. Thank you.'

Poppy smiled. 'Let me show the cistern, then we can walk back to the house for a nice cup of tea, alright?'

Violet smiled. 'Alright.'

THE TEMPORARY BEDROOM

Poppy leaned back in the brown leather club chair. She was breastfeeding her infant daughter Waverly. The infant's glossy blonde hair matched Poppy's perfectly. Poppy, content and happy, smiled.

Arthur, Poppy's infant son and Waverly's twin brother, slept quietly in his modern crib, under a pale blue wool blanket and shrouded in layers of expensive white Japanese bedding (a gift from Akiko). Arthur's blond hair, glossy and shiny, had grown considerably in the last few weeks. The beautiful and angelic Arthur always slept soundly.

Holly, the blue uniformed nanny, was now having lunch in the kitchen.

Violet sat on the narrow camp bed near one of the leaded glass windows of the former office. Violet, comfortable on a wave of white bedding, observed the gentle scene. Violet had never breastfed Freya. She had refused. Pregnancy and childbirth had been enough. It was left to Gemma and Karmen, the Croatian nanny, to bottle-feed Freya. Yes, breastfeeding her daughter was just one more thing Violet had deprived herself of.

Freya.

Violet took out her phone and tapped out a message and sent it.

MIDLANDS-HASEGAWA

Freya was walking down the hall to her dorm room when her smartphone pinged. Freya had been on the way to her room to retrieve some clothing from the wooden wardrobe when she had received her mother's text message.

How are you, Freya?

Freya looked at the message on the glowing display of her smartphone. Yes, her mother was worried about her. Yes, a year ago she would not have bothered to ask. Freya's soft tapered fingers gently touched the screen. This short digital message meant a lot to Freya. She wished that it had been written on a small of piece of paper and mailed to her, so she could keep it forever. Freya stared at the image of the screen for a moment more and then tapped out a reply and sent it.

I am alright. I love you, Mummy.

THE DORM ROOM
Freya unlocked the door to her and Jinx's room. The boilers had been out for over two weeks. Freya's room was freezing cold. Stacked in boxes in the center of the room were a few cardboard boxes filled with the belongings of the students next door whose room had been flooded when a frozen water pipe had burst. Frost covered the pane glass white sash windows. Natural light filled the room. Freya missed sharing this room with Jinx. Freya wished that they could move back in that day.

Suddenly a quiet knock came from one of the iron radiators. The another. And another.

Could it be true?

Freya walked across the room and touched the radiator near the window. *It was warm.*

Freya smiled. She looked up at the Heavens (well, the white plaster ceiling) and said, 'Thank you, God.'

THE DINING HALL
'Rise!'

Hundreds of young undergraduates stood and faced the wooden podium which stood in front of the large gilt framed portrait of Cecil Rhodes. An elderly, white-haired man in a dark blue suit, white shirt, and Rhodesian regimental neck tie, addressed the students.

The PA system was still broken, so the students stood in silence and listened carefully.

'As most of you should now be aware, the boilers have been repaired. I would like to thank the staff at the Physical Plant for all of their hard work. I apologize for the delay. Some of the parts had to be manufactured by bespoke order in order to make the repairs. However, I can assure you that the boilers have had their lives extended by several years. Today, for lunch, the staff well be serving honey biscuits as a special treat.'

The President of Midlands-Hasegawa University turned to speak with a member of the white-uniformed kitchen staff. The elderly Rhodesian smiled and then turned back to the assembled students and said, 'Lunch today will be, of all things, pizza. I am sure that it will be quite good. I would like to take this opportunity to thank the kitchen staff for all of their dedication. And now, let us bow our heads in prayer and give thanks.'

The entire student body of Midlands-Hasegawa University, most of them not even Christians, bowed their heads—some in devotion to God, others out of respect for the Christian nation that had welcomed them.

LUNCH

Freya, Jinx, Wren, Suga, Wallis, and Pasha sat at the table closest to the large double doors next to the entrance of the dining hall. Suga, in a beige cable knit sweater, dark blue wool trousers, and with her long glossy blonde hair tied back with a white silk ribbon, held the small honey biscuit in her soft hand.

'You actually can smell the honey. And the raisin on top is a nice touch. These biscuits are beautiful.' Suga smiled. She then nibbled on the biscuit. 'They're delicious.'

'Yes, they are. And they are popular among Rhodesians,' said Wren happily, the strikingly beautiful Wren's honey blonde bangs partially obscuring her blue eyes as she spoke.

'Do you bake honey biscuits often,' asked Pashay, the petite Laotian undergraduate.

'Yes, all the time,' replied Wren. 'Jinx, have you ever baked any honey biscuits?'

'What?' replied Jinx. Jinx (Or Jane, as she was known to her grandparents), had been lost in thought. Just adjusted the large collar on her white cotton blouse as she turned her head towards Wren.

'Have you ever baked any honey biscuits?' said Wren.

'Oh, yes. With my mother.'

'Are you alright, Jinx?' asked Wren.

'Yes, I'm fine. Just a little tired.'

'After the play, I'm going to board the train for Scotland. It will be nice to spend the Christmas holidays with the family. I plan to sleep a lot too,' said the blonde Suga in her gentle Scottish lilt.

'I'm going to spend Christmas in London with my parents,' said Pashay, her long glossy black hair tied into two long braids with white ribbons.

'Just for the holidays, Pasha? Or does your family live in London?' asked Wren.

'We own in a tiny terraced house in Covent Garden. We like the house because of the beautiful Edwardian lamp above the glossy blue front door and that our neighbors are quiet. What are you doing for the holidays, Wren?' asked whippet thin and attractive Pasha.

'I'm going home. I can't wait. My parents set up the Christmas tree a few days ago. The Christmas tree looks beautiful with all of the decorations and lights. Christmas in the village means an endless round of caroling, hot drinks and wonderful biscuits in different homes, and a beautiful church service,' replied Wren happily.

'Mummy is going to take the train up from Surrey and see the play. She is looking forward to meeting all of you. After the play, we are going to drive back to Surrey in the Bristol,' said the flaxen-haired Wallis.

'What are you doing for Christmas, Freya?' asked Suga as she picked up another slice of thin crust pepperoni and green pepper pizza from her white porcelain plate.

'I'm going to stay in Mayfair with my family,' said Freya quietly.

THE DORM ROOM

'Thank you, Jinx,' said Nara, the South Korean undergraduate. 'We really appreciate being able to store our things here while the ceiling pipes were repaired.'

'We were happy to do it. Your room looks great. The Physical Plant repainted the room and even replastered the ceiling perfectly,' said Jinx happily.

The raven-haired, teenage Nara, in a pair of faded blue jeans, a white cotton blouse, and a dark blue v-neck sweater, picked up the last of the cardboard boxes, smiled, and left the room.

A few minutes later, Freya, clad in faded blue jeans, and white cotton blouse, and a blue quilted jacket, entered carrying her large white pillow. 'Alright. That's everything. It's good to be back in our own room again.'

'Yes,' said Jinx as she carefully closed the white door to their room.

Jinx's demeanor changed as soon as the she closed the door. Louise's fate pressed down on them both.

Freya sat down on the white duvet (which was embroidered with purple lavenders) which covered her bed. Freya exhaled and looked out the window. It was already dark. Yes, Louise lay in a neurological ICU in a hospital in London a few hundred miles away. The next few days and weeks would be pivotal. Ninety percent of stroke patients die within a month after their stroke. For some reason, this fact seemed to pre-occupy Freya. If Louise could survive the month, then she would be alright.

Jinx walked over to her wardrobe and started to undress. 'I'm not going to dinner tonight. I'm going to study for my mathematics exam and then go to bed early,' said Jinx quietly.

'Yes. I'm not going to dinner either. I going to review my class notes and then go to bed. I am exhausted,' said Freya.

'What exam do you have tomorrow?' asked Jinx and she took a pair of blue and red tartan flannel pyjamas out of the wooden wardrobe.

'Early Medieval Literature' replied Freya.

Freya started to undress next to her bed. After carefully undressing, Freya walked over to the wardrobe and took out a pair of flannel pyjama bottoms and a white t-shirt. She put on the dark blue pyjama bottoms (with a white piping and a white draw string) and white t-shirt and then walked back to the bed. She picked up her faded blue jeans, white Egyptian cotton blouse, and blue quilted jacket and carefully hung them up in the wardrobe.

Jinx was seated at her worn wooden desk when Freya climbed into bed. Jinx carefully studied her class notes and text book while Freya read through her class notebook.

Ping.

Freya's smartphone glowed momentarily on her nightstand. Freya reached over and pick up her cell phone. There was a text message from Gemma.

Louise is asleep. Octavia brought her a thin crust pepperoni pizza for lunch. Louise was happy to see Octavia and have pizza with us. Louise only took a few bites and then went back to sleep. I put the pizza in the small refrigerator I have had installed in the corner of the room. I keep bottled water in it for Louise. Tomorrow she will have cold pizza for breakfast. Louise is doing well. The doctors come by and check on her several times a day. Louise sleeps a lot. I think that is for the best. She needs to rest. Louise's father came by this

morning and spent around a half an hour speaking with Louise. I went for coffee. When I returned, Louise seemed rather pensive. I didn't ask her what they talked about.

Freya put down the phone down on the night stand, unable to decide how to respond. A few minutes later there was another text.

Ping.

Külli just arrived. She will spend the night with Louise. Louise talked about seeing you in The Ptolemies this evening. I hope she will be well enough to see it. Louise really wants to see you on stage. Please don't worry, Freya. Everything that can be done for Louise is being done. Your father has also brought in a neurologist to consult with the doctors here. Before Louise went to sleep tonight, we prayed together. Louise prayed for your continued protection and happiness. I thought you should know that.

Freya felt emotions bursting inside of her. Louise had prayed for her protection and happiness. Even in Louise's fragile condition, she had thought of Freya. She had prayed for her. Freya felt tears welling up in her eyes.

'Is everything alright?' asked Jinx.

'I hope so, Jinx. Louise seems to be alright. Gemma spent the day with her. And Louise's father visited her. Külli is staying with her tonight.'

'That's good,' said Jinx quietly.

Freya clasped her hands in prayer and closed her eyes. She began to pray in silence. Freya prayed that Louise would recover and be able to see the play at school. Freya prayed for her family. She prayed for her godmother Gemma and all of The Inseparables (both the originals and the new), and she prayed for her friends and for England. When Freya opened her eyes, she looked over at Jinx and saw that she was quietly praying at her desk.

Gemma—An Invisible Fear—The Ptolemies

THE MIDLANDS

Wren, her long honey blonde hair held up with silver hair pins, studied her notes carefully. Only two more exams remained: Roman History and English Literature. It was Wednesday. Wren looked at her inexpensive quartz watch: 3:43pm. It would be dark soon. Yes, the sun went down early this far north in the winter.

The boilers having been repaired, Wren had returned to her small dormitory room a few doors down from Freya and Jinx. She lived alone. The bare white walls reflected the natural light which poured in through the pane glass window which looked out onto the snow-covered grass quad. Beyond the quad, Wren could see the gloriously ornate stone cloisters of Midlands-Hasegawa. Yes, the university was beautiful.

Next semester, she hoped to move into an upstairs alcove room with Freya, Wallis, and Jinx. Well, perhaps not Wallis. She seemed bird happy sharing an alcove with her Japanese roommates in 'Little Tokyo'. Wren was grateful to have such good friends. Wren was glad to be back in her own room and sleeping in a proper bed. She did, however, miss sharing the floor in front of Suga's fireplace with the others.

Saturday would mean the end of the term. Her parents would drive up Muddy Hills to pick her up in the Riley. They would have lunch together in the dining hall and afterwards watch Freya and Jinx perform on stage in the school play. Freya and Jinx would both shimmer on stage. Wren looked forward to spending the Christmas holidays with her parents in the family pile. Yes, the Medieval manor house, now partially restored, was worthy of the name. Wren smiled. Things were finally looking up.

There was a gentle on the door.

'Yes, just a minute,' said Wren as she stood up. Wren, in red, purple, and grey tartan pyjama bottoms, a heavy beige cable knit sweater, and a pair of white cotton sippers, walked over to the door. Wren opened the wooden door. It was Wallis.

'Hello, Wren,' said Wallis happily. The flaxen-haired Wallis was wearing a dark grey pleated wool skirt, a white blouse (with a large collar), a blue blazer (with white edging), and a pair of black patent leather pumps. Wallis entered. Wren carefully and quietly closed the glossy white door.

'Please have a seat,' said Wren, pulling up one of the two wooden chairs in her small room. Wallis sat down. Wren sat down on the white duvet of her narrow bed. Wallis, bathed in the natural light of an overcast winter day, was beautiful. A gentle beauty. A serene beauty. Wren had never really observed Wallis so carefully. Yes, Wallis was truly beautiful.

'Latin wasn't as difficult as I had expected,' said Wallis. 'Freya has been tutoring me. I studied it in boarding school, but Freya has really helped me get a feel for the language. I feel like a Roman when I speak it with her.'

'How is Freya?' asked Wren.

'What do you mean?' replied Wallis.

'I mean, she seems so distant the last few days. I wonder if something is wrong?'

'Yes, I have noticed. Jinx too. I don't want to pry. Maybe it is just the pressure of the school play?' said flaxen haired Wallis in her posh and Sloaney intonation.

'Yes, that's probably it,' replied Wren.

'Mummy is taking the train to Muddy Hills. We will drive back to Surrey in the Bristol motorcar. I've told Mummy about the castle ruins—but not about the secret tunnel—and the ghost in the Jacobean library. Mummy is looking forward to meeting you, Wren,' said Wallis.

'It will be nice to meet her. I feel like I know her already after all of the stories you have told me about her,' said Wren happily.

THE HALLWAY

Freya and Jinx, both in pleated skirts, white blouses, and blue blazers, walked down the hallways together in silence. They had both just completed an exam. Both were worried about Louise. Freya opened the door to their room and they both entered. Jinx closed the glossy white door behind them.

Freya's smartphone rang. She hastily pulled it out of coat pocket and looked at the glowing screen. It was Louise. Louise! Freya tapped on the glowing screen.

'Hello?'

'Yes, Hello, Freya. How are you?' chirped Louise.

'I'm alright. The real question is: How are you, Louise?' replied Freya.

Jinx stood near her bed. She wanted news of Louise too.

'I'm feeling much better. My headache is almost gone, and I feel a bit dizzy sometimes, but, otherwise, I am alright,' said Louise happily.

Freya spoke in a shaky emotional voice. 'I'm happy to hear that, Louise. I have prayed for you every day. So has Jinx. We have both been so worried about you. Please rest.'

'I have slept more in the last five days than the last month at school. I had cold pizza for breakfast this morning with Külli and Octavia. I have been completely spoiled, Freya,' said Louise happily.

'Who is with you now?' asked Freya.

'Külli. She down the hall getting a cup of tea from the vending machine. She is really sweet. Octavia left an hour ago. She had to return to her office. Gemma is going to a concert tonight with Enoch.'

'I'm really happy to hear that you are you feeling better, my dear Louise. I miss you. And I love you,' said Freya through tears.

'Oh, thank you, Freya. I miss you too. And I love you. I love Jinx too. How is she?'

'She's right here. Would you like to speak with her?'

'Yes, please.'

Freya handed Jinx the phone.

'Hello, Louise. How are you feeling?' asked Jinx.

'Much better, Jinx. Please don't worry about me too much. I'll be alright. How are your exams going?' asked Louise.

'Good. I think. I only have one left. Tomorrow morning. It's good to hear your voice, Louise.'

'It's good to hear yours, Jinx. I miss you. I will see you soon,' said Louise.

'I miss you, too, Louise. Please take care,' replied Jinx.

'Thank you, Jinx. I will get better. I promise.'

'I'm going to hold you to that, Louise. I'll give the phone back to Freya now. I know she wants to talk with you. I'll speak to you later.'

'Alright. It was nice talking to you, Jinx.

You, too, Louise.'

Jinx handed the phone back to Freya.

'Louise?'

'Yes. Oh, Külli just came in with the doctor. I'll call you back in a few minutes, ok?'

'Sure. I love you, Louise.'

'I love you, Freya.'

THE HOSPITAL ROOM

The neurosurgeon, in a pair of dark khaki trousers, a white dress shirt, and a blue and purple tartan neck tie, looked at the clip board. Louise and Külli stared at him in silence. Was everything alright?

'How do you feel today, Louise?' asked the doctor.

'Much better, Doctor.'

'How are the headaches?'

'Almost gone, Doctor. The medication works well.'

The doctor smiled. 'Well, do you think you are ready to be discharged?'

'Yes, sir. Doctor, could I see a play in the Midlands this weekend? I would like to take the train up with some friends to see my best friend perform in a play.'

The doctor exhaled and looked through the documents and charts on the clipboard. He looked up at Louise. 'Well, I suppose a train trip should be alright.'

'Louise will travel in a private rail carriage with several of us,' said Külli. 'If you think it will be alright, Doctor.'

'Yes, just don't overtax yourself. Take the medication and get plenty of rest. When will Louise return to London?'

'The same day, Doctor,' replied Külli.

'Alright.'

MUDDY HILLS
Freya, now sitting on her bed, started to cry softly as Louise told she would be able to attend the play that Saturday. An enormous weight had lifted from her shoulders. Louise would be alright. Wouldn't she? Please, God. Let Louise be alright.

'I'm going to take the train up from London with Gemma, Külli, Octavia, Enoch, and Jubal Wyatt on Saturday morning. I will meet you after the play,' said Louise happily. 'It feels like I haven't seen you in a hundred years, Freya.'

With those words, Freya started to cry.

'Take care of yourself, Louise. I love you, and I need you. And I am glad that you will be able to see me and Jinx in the play.'

'Yes. I am looking forward to seeing you both on stage. And getting out of the hospital,' said Louise happily.

Freya felt almost dizzy.

'Oh, and after the play I will be returning with everyone to London. I'm going to stay at your grandparent's house in Mayfair this Christmas. And Freya, my father will be in London for Christmas too. Your grandparents have invited him to spend Christmas with us. I would like you to meet him. I think he is trying. I don't really understand him or know him very well, but I think he is trying.'

Freya felt her emotions churn at the mention of Louise's father. He had neglected Louise so badly throughout most of her life. He had left Louise badly injured emotionally. Freya hoped that Louise's father would change. Louise had done nothing wrong. Freya hoped that her father fully realized that.

'I'm glad you will be staying with us, Louise. And, as promised, we will have pizza.'

'Thank you, Freya.'

THE RHODES THEATRE

Elfie, the blonde Rhodesian undergraduate and director, checked the costumes carefully. The actors all stood in a line on the stage. Some of the glittering backdrops stood behind them. A minor adjustment here. One there. Yes. Perfect.

'Alright, everyone. The play is only three days away. On Friday night, we will have our final dress rehearsal. Are there any questions?' asked the slender blonde Elfie.

No one said a word.

'Alright. Good luck on your exams. I'll see everyone on Friday night.'

The actors started to disperse; the men to their dressing rooms, the women to theirs. Jinx, resplendent in her Egyptian costume and pharaonic crown, remained standing in the center. Rex, wearing the armor of a Macedonian general, walked over to her. 'You look fantastic, Jinx,' said Rex.

Rex, blonde and lithe, beautiful and sweet, smiled. 'I haven't seen you in the last few days. How have your exams been going?'

'Good. How have your exams been going?' asked Jinx.

'Good. I am nervous about the play. My mother would like to meet you. I have told her all about you,' said Rex.

'I'm looking forward to meeting her. My parents are going to attend the play. I haven't told them that much about you yet,' said Jinx, and she smiled.

'I will miss you over the Christmas holidays, Jinx.'

'I'll miss you too. I love you, Rex.'

'I love you, too, Jinx.'

2 THE SCHOOL OF CORPSES

Gemma—An Invisible Fear—The School of Corpses

LONDON

London, a polyglot boarding house for the world. London, once the center of the world, had changed beyond all recognition. The London that he had grown up in in the 1930s and 40s had vanished. The changes had not been limited to demographics, even the architecture of the city had changed radically. London had once been an imperial city—the center of a vast global empire; now it was a strange witches' brew of hostile peoples, religions, and languages. London had been left disfigured by architectural aberrations. Modern London was not a shadow of its former self; it was an entirely different city built on the ruins of the old one.

The white-haired 11th Baron, in his 95th year, had recently developed a bad cough—which soon turned into a lung infection. Still, he had trudged on, like a weary soldier marching through frozen and mud choked trenches. Yes, victory was within their grasp.

And then, a few days ago, the elderly baron had awoken and realized he was too weak to get out of bed. His breathing had become labored. His left side was partially paralyzed. He had suffered a stroke and now had double pneumonia. Yes, the end was near. One of the servants had discovered him gasping for breath and struggling to move when she had knocked on the glossy white door of the bedroom in the house in Mayfair with the baron's morning cup of tea.

THE PRIVATE CLINIC

Carter Holland had arranged to transfer the 11th Baron to a private clinic in London that was staffed with some of England's most highly qualified medical staff. The rooms in the clinic were all private. The clinic offered a wide array of medical procedures—from (illegal) organ transplants to providing a place for the illegitimate offspring of billionaires to be secretly brought into the world. Yes, the powerful could be brought into the world, have their lives extended, and die, all away from the prying eyes of the public in such a place as this. Carter Holland had had this well-equipped and secure clinic constructed for himself and his allies.

And the 11th Baron was his greatest ally.

The 11th Baron, the scion of an ancient English noble family, could hardly be considered a friend. Carter Holland, born into a middling middle-class family, was but a mere mortal compared to the 11th Baron. The societal gap between the two men was chasmic. The baron had never extended his hand in friendship. It had never bothered Carter. Carter had exceeded his grasp and (secretly) become one of the world's wealthiest men. Carter had transcended his modest origins, like the shedding of a layer of cosmic skin. It was Carter's innate talents and ambition which had drawn the 11th Baron to him. The time and place where they had first met was now irrelevant. They had met and become allies.

And now, after decades of struggle, their plans were about to be put into motion.

THE PRIVATE ROOM

Carter Holland had received a typed note on a small piece of paper folded and placed in a small white envelope which had been handed to him by one of his security team while he was reviewing a financial report in the offices of Quadriga Investments.

The end is near.

Yes, Carter had been expecting this for the last few days. Carter Holland, in the back seat of his privately owned and bullet proof glossy black London cab and shadowed by four other vehicles loaded with heavily armed members of Carter's security unit, headed through the snowy streets of London that night to the private clinic where the baron was now fading away.

Yes, the man he had summoned from East Anglia a few hours ago would be arriving in London at any moment. The visitor could wait.

THE PRIVATE ROOM
Carter, in a black bespoke Savile Row suit, white dress shirt, and a silver neck tie, entered the sterile hospital room—a collection of white walls and a large plate glass window. Outside the door were two tall, powerfully built, and menacing members of Carter's security team in dark Savile Row suits.

Near the window of the private hospital room was the baron's large hospital bed. The baron's snow-white hair had been freshly cut like a City banker's. Machines flickered and pulsed with lights and glowing digital screens. The frail, slender, and aged baron looked like a skeleton shrouded in white sheets. An IV was attached to his bony arm. The baron appeared to have lost half his body weight in the last three weeks. A tall, slim, and blonde nurse in a white uniform stood next to the bed with a tablet computer. She was carefully monitoring the baron's vital signs. The only sounds in the room which could be heard came from the medical machinery which encompassed the baron's bed. And yes, that included the sharp sounds of the baron's heart beat monitor.

'Please leave us,' said Carter quietly as he approached the hospital bed.

The nurse, slightly startled, turned to face Carter Holland. She had no idea who the blonde, blue-eyed, handsome and svelte man was standing before her. She didn't know that he owned the clinic and was her employer. She knew—yes, knew—that this man standing in front of her was important. She nodded slightly in Carter's direction, and without saying a word, she left the room, being careful to close the door quietly behind her.

Carter walked to the edge of the bed. Yes, the doctors had told him that the baron would not survive the night. It was as if he had given up. The aged baron had had only one request: to see Carter Holland before he died. The baron's eyes were closed. A small transparent plastic oxygen mask covered his mouth.

'No. I'm not asleep, Mr Holland. Not yet,' said the frail baron as he slowly opened his eyes. 'I've been waiting for you.'

Carter could have taken a seat in one of the two silver aluminum chairs next to the hospital bed, but he decided to remain standing, out of respect for the 11th Baron.

'I came straight away, Your Lordship.'

The baron pulled off the oxygen mask and beckoned Carter to lean in. The Baron had something to tell him. Carter leaned forward.

'How goes our plans?' asked the baron as he gasped for air.

'Like clockwork. All is in order. All is moving forward. The war will begin in less than a month,' replied Carter.

'Mr Holland. I leave this broken, miserable, spent world an exhausted…old man. All has gone against us and our people. So few listened to me…so…few,' gasped the baron. 'You…cannot…fail, Carter. You cannot. Everything now depends on you. I regret that I will not live to see…the…Carter.'

The pale, gaunt, and white-haired baron gasped for air. Carter attempted to put the small plastic triangular oxygen mask back on the aged man's face; the baron pushed the transparent plastic mask away.

'How difficult it is to die,' whispered the baron.

The baron looked out the window. Outside, the London skyline flickered in the darkness. The white-haired Baron's gaze then slowly shifted back to the hospital room. He looked towards the ceiling and suddenly the 11th Baron's blue eyes glazed over.

'It's darkness,' gasped the baron.

And then the elderly 11th Baron, a graduate of Eton and Christ Church, Oxford, a veteran of the Second World War, the Malaysian Emergency, and the Mau Mau Uprising, slowly closed his eyes and departed the broken world he had despaired of.

Gemma—An Invisible Fear—The Evil Spirit

LONDON

Carter Ajax Holland stood in motionless silence as the elevator ascended. He could see his murky reflection in the stainless steel walls of the elevator. An hour ago, his closest ally had closed his eyes for final time. Carter would never speak with the baron again. And this bothered Carter. The 11th Baron had been the closest to a real father as he had ever had. When Carter's biological father passed away in 2016, it hadn't bothered Carter at all. Major A.N. Holland (Ret'd) had departed this world without so much as a ripple. Had Carter Holland's father ever meant anything to him? No. The 11th Baron, however, had.

It was at this moment that Carter Holland realized how important the baron had been to him both in terms of useful connections and emotionally. The 11th Baron had believed in him. It was the baron who had told Carter that it could be done. Carter could create a new country and save a few shards of Western Civilization. It was the baron that had introduced Carter to the people he needed in order to carry out his plans. It was, in fact, the 11th Baron, who had assured Carter that it was truly Carter's destiny to rule. And now this man that had been so pivotal to Carter Holland's life was gone forever. Carter would never see the baron again. Carter's mentor—for that is what the baron had truly been—was gone. Forever.

The smooth steel elevator doors opened and a long shaft of bright electric light spilled out of the lift. The top floor of Quadriga Investments was dark, save the light from the elevator. Carter Holland, blonde, svelte, blue eyed, and resplendent in a black Saville Row suit, stepped out of the lift. The doors closed behind him. Now only the modern wall lamps illuminated the area around the elevator landing in the long cavernous room. Carter stood in the dim light of the lamps; his eyes adjusting to the twilightish light of the top floor.

And then a dark shape in the darkness moved towards him. Carter reached for the straight razor in his coat pocket; in an instant there was a flash of cold Solingen steel in the dim crepuscular light.

'Who are you?' asked Carter.

'Thy evil spirit, Brutus,' replied the dark shape.

Carter, still pointing the glinting cut throat razor in the direction of the dark shape, exhaled.

'How did you get up here? You're not on the list for immediate access,' said Carter.

'You invited me. Or have you forgotten?' replied the Evil Spirit.

Carter, still pointing the straight razor at the dark shape, tilted his right hand one direction, and then another. The steel blade glinted in the light cast by the wall lamps behind him. He studied the figure for a moment. It would be so easy to lure the man forward and slash his throat.

'Who let you come up here?' asked Carter.

'Your security chief was waiting for me. He escorted me to the lift himself.'

Carter stood motionless in the darkness.

'Is something wrong, Mr Holland?' asked the dark shape.

'I have a problem that needs to be dealt with swiftly and decisively. And quietly. Secretly,' replied Carter while still holding the cut throat razor.

'That is the only reason you ever summon me, Mr Holland. And I am here.'

Carter slowly lowered the straight razor, folded it, and placed it back in his coat pocket. The dark shape took a few more steps forward and then stopped at the edge of the illumination of the electric light. The dark shape now appeared as a rail thin man in a dark suit, white dress shirt, and dark necktie. The white-haired man appeared to be quite old. The wrinkled visage smiled.

'What are your orders, Mr Holland?'

'I want you to kill.'

3 THE LORD OF TEN THOUSAND YEARS

Gemma—An Invisible Fear—The Orchestra

LONDON
The concert hall, a concrete Brutalist structure—dreary, draining, and ugly—that evening, was filled with the most beautiful music Gemma had ever heard. Was it really the most hauntingly beautiful music that she had ever heard? One reason Gemma felt that it was because that night she was seated next to the love of her life: Enoch Tara. However, that was not the only reason.

The Honourable Gemma Ophelia Ripley, in a black velvet dress that almost shimmered in the dim light of the hall, listened carefully to every note of music that swept over the audience in gentle waves. Gemma knew this piece of music well. Her mother had had a vinyl record of it and used to play it on the old record player in the drawing room of the country house in Sussex (which was now owned by a vulgar Russian oligarch).

Yes, Gemma's mother had loved music. Gemma's mother had played the violin in her youth—a happy and idyllic youth growing up in her parents' Edwardian house in Primrose Hill in the 1950s and 60s—a now vanished world. Once, when the radio was playing in the nursery in the Georgian country house in Sussex, the eight-year-old Gemma had watched as her mother stood near one of the windows, and as if playing an invisible violin, had moved her long delicate fingers attempting to remember how to play that particular piece of music. And tonight, the same composition was being performed by the orchestra (in white tie and tails). Gemma could feel her mother's presence next to her. Yes, she was here with her beloved daughter Gemma (or, more accurately, 'Ophelia'—Gemma's mother had usually called her by her middle name). Gemma and her mother were both enjoying the concert together. Gemma wanted to reach out in the vast semi-darkness of the concert hall and grasp her mother's hand. It was a happiness tinged with sadness.

The music swirled and eddied about the silent audience like a gentle stream. And then an oboe could be heard: Clear, bright, penetrating, acerbic, keen, biting, rasping, reedy, powerful, robust, full, and insistent. Gemma could feel the music flowing through her. It was powerful and soothing. And then, after a moment, a single French horn sounded. The French horn, an instrument that sounded so distinctly different from any other brass instrument: first full, then velvety, gently transitioning from warm to soft, then to bright and metallic, sometimes all within less than a minute. Yes, this had been her mother's favorite piece of music, and now she was able to experience it while seated next to her fiancé Enoch Tara.

Was it really just luck or coincidence that Gemma found herself listening to her mother's favorite composition on that wintery night in December in London? No. It was God that had made tonight possible. Gentle God. Merciful God. Loving God. And Gemma was grateful to God for everything and this moment—yes, this gentle moment.

Enoch, in black tie and shrouded in the demi-darkness of the concert hall, stared straight ahead. Enoch, lost in thought, only heard parts of the music emanating from the orchestra. He was struggling to comprehend all that had been happening: the shadowy assault on global finance, the attempts by unknown enemies to uncover the Special Unit, and the brutal murder of the Brigada a few days before. Yes, the brutal murder of the Spanish Legionnaire was exceptionally troubling for him. The Comandante, the leader of the Special Unit, was now moving against the people that had been pursuing him and his soldiers. Enoch would not be receiving up to the minute reports from the Special Unit; the Comandante was now operating on his own—with a free hand. The Comandante and his men would find the people responsible for the Brigada's murder and kill them. Enoch had let the Special Unit off the chain.

Louise's well-being was also deeply troubling to Enoch. Poor Louise. A stroke at nineteen. Gemma had spent the last few days at Louise's bedside. This evening, Külli had volunteered to stay the night at the hospital with Louise while Gemma attended the concert with Enoch. Octavia was staying with her in Louise's hospital room too. Enoch would visit Louise at the hospital the next day with Gemma. Enoch wanted to do a lot for Louise: buy her a house, a car, even a horse, if she wanted one. But Louise would have never accepted any of it. Enoch's friendship was all that she had ever wanted of him. Enoch knew that. Enoch had decided earlier that day that after he had married Gemma, that he would talk with her about what they could do for Louise. Surely there must be something.

Tonight, Gemma would attempt to escape her worries for an hour or two. Gemma also hoped to calm Enoch's nerves too. Gemma was worried about Enoch. She had been left in the dark about what had happened with the Brigada and the activities of the Special Unit. Gemma couldn't even begin to fathom what was really going on with Enoch. He would tell her one day, but for now, he was shielding her from whatever was going on. Gemma trusted Enoch to make the right decisions. She trusted him—absolutely.

MARBLE ARCH

Gemma and Enoch had been driven back to Enoch's house in Marble Arch in the silver S60 Volvo. Next to the Volvo's driver was another member of Enoch's regular security team. Neither of the men were armed. The four other men who shadowed Enoch in two other vehicles were. The situation had changed.

Enoch and Gemma were both tired after the concert. Enoch had asked Gemma to stay with him at the house in Marble Arch. She agreed to. Gemma guessed that something was going on and Enoch wanted her there.

After they arrived at home, Gemma made her way upstairs to a guest room two doors down from Enoch's room. Gemma had changed out of her velvet dress at Enoch's earlier in the day. A pair of faded blue jeans, a white Egyptian cotton blouse, and a blue quilted jacket hung in the closet. Gemma's red, blue and purple wool All Saints scarf had been carefully folded and placed in the empty box the dress had come in. There was also a dark blue canvas overnight bag with some of Gemma's other belongings. After changing out of the dress, she carefully returned the black velvet dress to the glossy white box filled with white tissue paper. She then took a hot shower.

Afterwards, Gemma, in a white cotton Turkish bathrobe and with her damp (slightly longer than) shoulder length brown hair wrapped up in a white cotton towel, laid down on top of the white duvet which covered her bed. Much better.

The only light in the room came from the plasma screen television. The volume had been turned down and images from the evening news illuminated the bedroom in flashes of light. Gemma wasn't interested in watching television. She closed her eyes.

Gemma was about to reach for the TV remote when there was a gentle knock on the glossy white bedroom door. She opened her eyes.

'Yes?'

'Gemma, it's me,' said Enoch. 'Could I come in?'

'Just a minute.'

Gemma got up, turned on the small lamp on the night stand, and walked over to the bedroom door. She opened the door and light from the hallway flooded into the room. Enoch, in the blue and red tartan pyjamas, white waffle patterned spa bathrobe, and the pair of white cotton slippers she had given to him the week before, stood in the doorway. Enoch, though obviously tired, smiled.

'Please, come in,' said Gemma, and she smiled.

'I'm sorry to disturb you, Gem. I know you are tired. But I won't be able to get to sleep if I don't talk with you about this now.'

Gemma, slender and shapely at the same time, walked into the bedroom and sat down on the edge of the bed. Enoch walked into the room behind her and sat down in a white upholstered high back arm chair opposite of Gemma.

Yes, Gemma was as beautiful as she had ever been. The few silver hairs that glinted in Gemma's hair (which was now wrapped up in a white cotton towel) hadn't detracted from her looks at all. Gemma's clear, pale, and smooth complexion, illuminated in the flashes of light given off by the television screen, radiated youthful vitality. Gemma, starkly beautiful, exhaled.

'What's wrong, Enoch?'

'Gemma, could we get married in January?'

Gemma arched an eyebrow. What was going on? Gemma knew that, as an employee of Millennium Investments, Enoch was not allowed to disclose anything to do with his financial investments, but the last few days of emotional outbursts were not related to finance. Something terrible had happened and things were still happening. What it could be, Gemma couldn't even begin to guess. But, whatever it was, it was terrible.

'I am with you, Enoch. I am here. I will always be with you,' said Gemma. Gemma paused for a moment. Enoch looked drained and pale. Gemma, after a lifetime of abuse and reversals, hated to see anyone else suffer. And Enoch was suffering. And Gemma loved Enoch.

'Enoch, let's wait until June. I want everyone to be able to attend. If we get married next month, half the guests won't be able to make it. Alright?'

Enoch seemed to reflect on Gemma's words for a moment. He then started to nod slightly. 'Alright. Yes. You are right, Gemma.'

'Besides, I'd be afraid to drive the Lagonda in heavy snow,' said Gemma and she smiled.

Enoch smiled. He then leaned forward in the chair and spoke. 'Gemma. I have something to tell you. I want you to know that I bought the rest of the Royal Airforce training center. The land and buildings. I was worried about troublesome neighbors. I want you to have that place all to yourself. I have the necessary documents here with me. I was going to surprise you at the wedding reception, but I want to transfer ownership of the land and buildings over to you now. Tomorrow morning, I'd like you to sign the documents. Please consider it an early wedding gift.'

Gemma was stunned. This had caught her entirely off guard. And this had raised other questions for her.

'Thank you, Enoch. This means a lot to me. It really does. Yes…but why…not wait…alright.'

Yes, Enoch was worried about something. Was signing over the training center now a consequence of those worries? Was Enoch facing financial ruin? Did he want Gemma to be in a sound financial situation before his conglomerate collapsed around him? Was that it?

'Thank you, Enoch,' said Gemma as she stood up and took a few steps towards him. She reached down and grasped Enoch's hands in her small soft hands. She smiled. 'Don't worry, in the spring, the raspberry bushes around the house will bear fruit and I will make raspberry jam and can the rest. Also, I'll plant sweet potatoes and a few Arran Victories. We will have plenty to survive on.'

Enoch smiled. Gemma had no idea what Enoch was facing. She really was in the dark. Enoch had decided it was best not to tell her. Not yet. Now, the threats to Enoch were not only financial, but existential. Enoch's life was in danger. Sweet Gemma. She thought he was facing financial ruin alone. If only it was just that, Enoch wouldn't be worried. He could start over and make enough money for both of them to live comfortably, at the very least. But if Enoch was murdered, he wanted Gemma to be financially secure. Yes, he had already set aside a sizable fortune for her, in gold, in a Swiss bank account. She would receive the money upon his death. If Enoch were murdered, and his conglomerate survived, Gemma would inherit most of it, with some of it going to his mother and a few of his closest friends and loyal employees. Yes, contingency plans were already in place. The situation had changed.

And then a thought flashed through Enoch's mind: Gemma seemed to have had a premonition of trouble ahead that night on the train when he had given Gemma her engagement ring. Yes, Gemma, so attuned to the supernatural, had felt the approach of something terrible. Enoch would not add to her anxieties; what good would that do?

'It's a good thing that I love Arran Victories, Gem,' said Enoch and he smiled.

'Freya mentioned that she had been having a lot of them lately, so I decided to plant some. We can bake them in the fireplace.'

Your house has a fireplace,' asked Enoch.

'No, but we can build a fireplace in the annex near the house,' replied Gemma.

'Ah, well, I have turned that into a guard post, Gem. I hope you don't mind.'

'Really? I hadn't noticed. Well, then we can build one in one of the other buildings. I would like to restore the auditorium. It would be perfect for plays. Maybe the center could operate as a children's summer camp? Yes, I would like that,' replied Gemma happily.

Ping.

Gemma's smartphone glowed momentarily.

'I'd better check that,' said Gemma as she walked over to the nightstand.

Enoch leaned back into the chair. Gemma had plans. Just listening to her talk about them made Enoch forget his troubles, if only momentarily.

'It's Isolde. She just emailed me. She has attached tomorrow's itinerary. She has really proven herself quickly. I'm going to ask Alexa about giving her a raise and a bonus,' said Gemma as she tapped out a quick reply.

Enoch, much calmer than he had been a few minutes before, suddenly felt sleepy.

'I'll see you tomorrow at breakfast, Gem. Thank you for inviting me to the concert. I really enjoyed it.'

'I'm glad you liked it. The last piece of music they played **is** my mother's favorite. It's my favorite too,' said Gemma quietly.

Yes, at that moment Gemma was speaking of her mother in the present tense. She missed her mother and felt that she was always with her. That subtle use of the verb had not gone unnoticed by Enoch. He smiled.

'It's my favorite piece of music too, Gem.'

Gemma—An Invisible Fear—The Revenant

LONDON
The Revenant leaned back in the backseat of the black cab as it made its way down the M4 motorway. The flight from Istanbul had been a long one. But that was good; it gave the Revenant time to think. A war had started.

The Sun was coming up; an orange light filled the interior of the cab. The Revenant could see himself reflected in the rear passenger window of the car. The Revenant was svelte, of average height, and with brown hair that had been cut like a City bankers. The Revenant studied his reflection in the glass for a moment. Yes—he looked like his mother.

The traffic was light on the M4 that morning. The Revenant looked at the silver dive watch which adorned his wrist: 8:03am. He adjusted the natural black rubber strap on his wrist. He reached into the coat pocket of his dark grey wool overcoat and took out his encrypted smartphone. He turned it on. The smartphone slowly came to life.

The black cab moved forward at an increasing rate of speed.

No messages.

The Revenant was sure that a typed letter would be waiting for him at the office that morning. Carter Holland had made a mess. Undoubtably, it had been left to the Revenant to clean it up. The Revenant tapped out a message on his encrypted smartphone and sent it.

THE CITY

The Revenant, in a charcoal grey suit, white dress shirt (with a Londoner collar), and black silk neck tie, entered the modern 10th floor office which overlooked the Square Mile. Today, the Revenant looked a CEO of a large international conglomerate. A few dark grey clouds loomed in the distance. A gentle morning light illuminated the City. Within a few hours it was forecast to snow. The Revenant looked at the utilitarian desk and modern high back leather chair. He pulled out the chair, sat down, and swiveled the chair in the direction of the large plate glass window. The London that appeared before him was silent, bleak, and cold.

There was a gentle knock.

'Come in.'

'Good morning, sir,' said the young blonde secretary. She smiled 'I was given this letter for you just a moment ago.' The slender young woman extended her hand; a single white envelope appeared before the Revenant.

'Thank you,' replied the Revenant as he gently took the envelope from her hand.

The man without a country broke the seal and opened the envelope. Inside was a single white sheet of paper with the symbol of the Carthaginian Goddess Tanit stamped on it.

Meet me at the tomb tonight at 1am.

SURREY

Jem Wilfred Lloyd, six feet tall and powerfully built, placed the ceramic tea cup on the white saucer. He looked out of the pane glass window of his house. The Thames quietly flowed by. It was winter. A vast ocean of white snow blanketed the village. The middle-aged Englishman, in a pair of dark grey wool trousers, a black leather belt, and a white dress shirt, lifted the white tea cup to his lips and inhaled the steam which rose gently from it. Yes, a nice cup of tea was just what the former corporal (Caporal) Lloyd needed.

As requested via encrypted email, Jem, a former member of the Parachute Regiment *and* the French Foreign Legion, had continued to oversee preparations for the coming war in the East. Yes, Jem would continue to meet with the squad leaders and platoon commanders of his battalion. There were fifteen men to a squad in the Core Army, three squads to a platoon, three platoons to a company, and five companies to a battalion, plus auxiliaries. Jem was in command of over 700 battle hardened men. He had been meeting 12-15 soldiers at a time (the NCOs and officers of each company) and briefing them on the particulars of the mission. Each time he held a briefing, it was in a different location.

The Texan, a former senior corporal (Caporal-Chef) the French Foreign Legion, commanded over four hundred mercenaries.

Bash, a South African exile and a former Atlas Cheetah jet fighter pilot, would command the entire fleet of combat drones.

A highly experienced Hungarian hussar, known to all (but the Revenant, who knew his real name) as 'Attila', would command over a hundred foreign mercenaries (mostly former hussars and other cavalrymen from various foreign armies) in a special Hussar Group. The Hungarian hussar, like all **true cavalrymen**, was as brave as he was impatient and reckless. These were the qualities that would be needed to destroy Enoch Tara's Special Unit. It would require celerity, intelligence, courage, and cunning to accomplish the mission. And in the imminent campaign in Eastern Europe, the Hussar Group would act as shock troops.

An Estonian mercenary and a small cadre of foreign mercenaries (all from Eastern Europe) would command the thousands of local, lightly armed, soldiers of the Potemkin rebel army.

The General would oversee the entire operation.

The Revenant had selected twenty battle-hardened and highly trained soldiers from the Hussar Group to assist him in the coming war in London. Yes, the General was right, Carter Holland had made a mess and now it would be left to the General and his men to clean it all up. The General, a man without biography and from a country that no longer existed, had assured Jem that twenty cavalrymen would be enough to take down Enoch Tara's Special Unit. Jem would have brought in at least a twenty more, but if the General said that would be enough, then it would be.

One of those men (a Crimean Tatar) was now retrieving a cache of weapons from a vacant house an hour's drive from London. Attila would be meeting everyone at the safe house this weekend. The Hungarian had served with the Revenant before. The Revenant knew the Hungarian to be highly professional as well as extremely intelligent and highly cunning. The Hungarian was also vicious—but in an emotionally detached way. He was not a psychopath; merely a man of iron will and with a determination to accomplish the mission at whatever cost.

War was upon them.

The General had decided to exclude Jem and all of the Westerners in the Core Army from the coming clash with Tara's Special Unit in London. The Revenant knew that few, if any, British citizens (or other Westerners) would agree to participate in combat actions on British soil. These men were soldiers, not gangsters. (Well, most of them were not gangsters.) They would balk at such a mission. No, this part of the operation was best left to foreigners, who, if necessary, could flee England and never return. The foreign mercenaries that the Revenant had selected to lock horns with the Special Unit were all from the wilds of Eastern Europe.

Jem would much rather be spending December with his elderly mother. He had neglected her for so long, and now aged and frail, Jem found himself needing her more than she needed him. She would be gone soon—never to speak again; never to reassure him; never to smile gently at his approach.

Jem clinched his fists. They were as hard as iron.

War was upon them.

THE GHERKIN
Gemma, in a white Egyptian cotton blouse and dark blue cotton pencil skirt, checked the email carefully one last time. Good. She tapped on the keyboard and the email was on its way to Singapore.

Gemma looked at her silver Cartier wristwatch: 12:03pm. She looked out through the curved glass walls of the office. The panorama of London that appeared before her was slowly darkening. It would begin to snow soon.

'Gemma. Would you like to have lunch with me today?' asked Alexa. Gemma had been so absorbed in her work that she had not noticed Alexa exit her office and approach her.

'What?' asked Gemma as she swiveled the ultra-modern leather chair to face her.

'Would you like to go to lunch with me?' asked Alexa as she adjusted the collar of her pale blue cotton blouse. Alexa, slender, blonde, and attractive, smiled.

'Yes. Alright,' said Gemma in a seemingly distracted tone of voice.

'Are you alright, Gemma?'

Gemma smiled. 'Yes. I'm alright. Where would you like to go for lunch?'

'How about we take the elevator to the roof?' asked Alexa.

THE HELIX RESTAURANT
A 360-degree panorama of London swirled around them. The sky was overcast and a pale slightly gloomy natural light filled the glass domed restaurant. London, however, remained beautiful. At least to the two people seated at the table near the window. Here, high above the City, the two All Saints alumni could relax. Kind of.

Alexa, seated across from Gemma, studied her office manager carefully while Gemma looked at the menu. Yes, in a year Gemma's life had been transformed. The tiny, frail, and forlorn figure that had appeared at Alexa's office a year ago had been replaced with a confident and radiantly beautiful woman. This was the beautiful and happy Gemma that Alexa remembered from All Saints. Gemma's smooth pale complexion glowed with health and vitality. Whatever had gone on in the past had, most likely, left its mark. Gemma had, apparently, overcome it all. At least Alexa hoped so. Alexa's renewed friendship with her former classmates from All Saints and Oxford had revitalized her as well. Alexa knew that she was surrounded by friends who loved her. And Gemma had introduced Alexa's daughter Aurelia to Louise. And through Louise, Aurelia had made friends with Freya and Jinx.

Gemma's glossy brown hair had grown much longer, seemingly overnight. Or, had the last few weeks been so much of a whirlwind that Alexa hadn't noticed? Alexa's blonde hair had also grown much longer. Neither of them had been to a hair salon since the hidden financial crisis had started. Alexa liked her long glossy blonde hair. Yes, she would let it grow longer.

One of Gemma's soft manicured hands carefully turned a page of the menu. Gemma's clear blue eyes scanned the menu through her glossy tortoise shell reading glasses. Yes, Gemma Ophelia Ripley, the truest beauty to ever walk the halls of All Saints, was now safe in the protective embrace of those who loved her. But did Gemma feel safe?

'Are you ready to order?' asked the waitress.

Alexa, deep in thought, looked up with a jolt.

'Could we have another minute, please?'

'Certainly,' replied the young waitress.

'I'm not that hungry today. I think I'll just have a salad,' said Gemma. 'And a fantastic dessert.' Gemma smiled.

Alexa smiled and said, 'Yes, that sounds about right, Gemma.'

Alexa then made eye contact with the young waitress, and she walked back over to the table to take their order.

'How is Louise?' asked Alexa.

'She seems to be getting better. She still has headaches, but there doesn't appear to be any paralysis, thank God.'

'Will she be able to attend the play?' asked Alexa.

'Yes. She will go with us in Enoch's private rail carriage on Saturday morning. She will share a cabin with Aurelia. Louise has been looking forward to it for months. Jubal Wyatt is going with us too. He'll be arriving in London tomorrow. After the play, he will come back to London with us. He's going to stay with friends in Covent Garden. I'm glad that Louise will be able to see the play. It will mean a lot to her and Freya. And everyone else.'

'Louise calls Aurelia every day. Aurelia doesn't want to wake her up if she is asleep. Louise understands that, so she usually calls Aurelia in the evenings. Aurelia told me that the instructors had given her Louise's class assignments. Louise is planning to take the final exams in January. She wants to transfer to Midlands-Hasegawa with Aurelia,' said Alexa.

'Yes, Louise is determined to take the final exams. She is strong willed. I admire her resilience. I guess she has had to be strong to survive all that she has been through,' said Gemma quietly, her voice trailing off.

Yes, Gemma had been through a lot too. Alexa didn't know everything that Gemma had had to endure; she had never asked and never would. Perhaps that was why Louise had connected so deeply with Gemma?

'Aurelia loves Louise. Thank you for arranging for them to room together at uni, Gem.'

'I'm glad that everything worked out so well for them,' replied Gemma.

'Have you spoken with Louise's father? Aurelia told me that he visits her every day.'

'Not really. Louise's father visits her every day in the hospital. He says very little to me. Or anyone else. He usually spends an hour with her in her hospital room. I hope they can reconcile.'

MAYFAIR

Carter Holland, after a very long and trying night, had come home and crawled into bed exhausted at 5am that morning. Carter's sleep had been filled with strange dreams. Carter awoke with a shock. He gasped for air. What had he been dreaming about; he couldn't remember; the dreams had vanished the moment he opened his eyes. Carter, after a long sleep, however, was still exhausted. His sleep had not been restful.

Natural light filled the large, white walled, Georgian bedroom.

Carter climbed slowly out of bed. Carter, in a pair of pale blue cotton pyjamas (with a white drawstring) walked across the hardwood floor of the bedroom and turned on the light to the white tiled bathroom. The florescent lamps flickered and Carter stared into the mirror. Carter's muscular, but slender body appeared in the reflection. The dark circles around Carter's eyes were also apparent. Carter walked to the sink; he turned on the water and let the hot water steam up the mirror. In under a minute, Carter could see only his blond hair and fleshy image in the condensation of the mirror above the sink. Carter wiped away the condensation with his bare hand. He stared into the blue eyes which stared back at him.

Stay focused.

Carter closed the tap and stepped back into the bedroom. He walked over to the birch nightstand and picked up his platinum wristwatch: 3:23pm. Carter returned the watch to the nightstand. He picked up his smartphone. He quickly scanned through the text messages and email. Nothing that interested him. He placed the phone back on the nightstand next to his watch.

The Revenant had returned. Carter wanted to see him immediately, but that would be too risky. Carter would have to wait. They would meet in the tomb after midnight. Carter had much to say, but he was struggling to find the words to say it. The Revenant, of course, knew—he must know—that Carter had made a mess of things in London. Had The Revenant already devised a plan of attack? Carter's mind swirled with possibilities. He felt suddenly dizzy.

Carter climbed back into bed and pulled the white duvet over his head.

Gemma—An Invisible Fear—The Honourable Wren Talbot

THE MIDLANDS

Wren, the future baroness, seated at the small worn wooden desk in her small, white walled dorm room, looked out the window onto the snow-covered grass quad of Midlands-Hasegawa. On the opposite side of the quad, Wren could see young undergraduates walking through the stone cloisters of the university. Yes, the term was all but over now. And this term had been transformative.

Wren, her blue eyes partially hidden behind her honey blonde bangs, looked at her quartz wristwatch. It was inexpensive, unlike Freya's silver Cartier watch. Wren had purchased it online. It looked rather nice—from a distance. Well, no, that's not fair. It was a nice watch. Wren had noticed how inexpensive Jinx's watch was when they first met at a Rhodesia Club meeting. Even now, after Jinx's modelling success in Japan and the release of her first film, Jinx still wore it.

Freya had more money than most of the undergraduates at Muddy Hills combined, yet she seemed unaffected by it. Perhaps that was because Freya had never had to worry about money?

Wren didn't really want money. She needed it. She wanted to save what remained of the family's inheritance: the house, the castle ruins, and the land. Beyond that, Wren had learned to go without luxury. Wren, beautiful, intelligent, and posh, had had a hard life. Yes, you could be a member of the English nobility and still have a hard life. Keeping up appearances could be brutal. It had been for Wren. It had warped her too. Wren, at nineteen, was already heavily scarred on the inside.

Yes, transformative. That was the only way Wren could explain the first term at Midlands-Hasegawa (Muddy Hills to the undergraduates of the school). Yes, her late-night talk with Freya had changed everything. Wren had become much more open; she was willing to reveal more about herself than ever before. And she had found here, at Muddy Hills, what she had always yearned for: true friends.

In a couple of days, Wren would be driving home with her parents in the freshly repainted (glossy dark blue) Riley back to the ancient family pile in Mercia. Wren's mother had telephoned her the night before and told her that plans were now moving forward quickly. The village was putting together the money to turn the castle into a tourist attraction. It wouldn't take that much money, and the villagers were happy to help. Also, the prospect of tourists flooding the town on weekends to visit the castle would benefit almost everyone. Yes, soon the family castle would be Merica's newest tourist attraction.

'Your father recommend we produce a line of t-shirts to sell to tourists,' said Wren's mother in her Rhodesian accent.

'T-shirts? Oh, Mummy. No. How about pennants with the family coat of arms?' replied Wren.

'Then I don't think you would like the wool scarves,' replied Wren's mother laughingly.

'Scarves?' asked Wren.

'Yes, three stripes, colors to be determined later, and the family coat of arms embroidered at one end.'

'Some castles sell three-dimensional paper models. I think that would be nice. Let's not turn the family castle into an amusement park, Mummy.'

Wren's mother laughed gently, her laughter resonating over the phone line (or rather through the ether channeled through a collection of cellphone towers).

'Some castles have a farm shop. Maybe we could sell tangerines, oranges, and lemons grown in the orangery?' asked Wren's mother in a rather posh Rhodesian intonation.

'That would be a good idea. But they would sell out quickly and then what would we have for lunch?'

'You have a point, Wren. Your father says the village below the castle will be the castle shop. Yes, that's a good idea. It's important our Mercians benefit from it too.'

'Yes. Father is right., well, except for the t-shirts,' said Wren and she laughed.

'Yes, well, the pennants do sound rather nice. Do you think they would sell?' asked Wren's mother.

'They sell them at the Deveraux castle in the Lake District. Freya told me the family also sells a history book. It was written by a local historian. Surely, you and Father could write one.'

'Yes, I suppose we could.'

'And I think we should use the painting in the drawing room for the book cover. The Elizabethan painting with all the arcane runes and symbols on it.'

'Yes, that would make a striking cover,' replied Wren's mother.

'Mummy?'

'Yes.'

'I love you.'

'I love you, too.'

4 THE CHEKA'S SMILE

'There is no greater joy, nor better music,
than the crunch of broken lives and bones.'

— Aleksandr Vladimirovich Eiduk

Gemma—An Invisible Fear—The Tomb

HIGHGATE CEMETERY
It was freezing cold. This winter was a harsh one. A thin layer of snow blanketed the ground and icicles hung from the tree branches in the vast cemetery that night. A northern cold front on this wintery December night had made London feel more like Tallinn. A full moon illuminated the graves of the departed in a bluish white incandescent lunar light. If it wasn't already cold enough, the occasional gust of wind made it even colder, icier.

A slender figure, of average height, brown hair (with the odd silver hair), in a charcoal grey wool suit, a white dress shirt (with a Windsor collar), black silk necktie, a dark blue wool overcoat (with a light brown fur collar), and a pair of black Chelsea boots, made his way carefully through the graveyard, past hundreds of graves, both marked and unmarked, the snow crunching underfoot. He stopped under a large tree and observed the Moon through thick barren branches that were weighed down under snow and ice. The moonlight illuminated the ice and icicles which hung from the branches.

Yes, the luminous Moon was truly beautiful.

When he was young, he would sit under a tree in the courtyard of the house with his mother and gaze at the Moon. The Revenant's mother had taught him to appreciate the little things in life. His mother was grateful for any time she could spend with her beloved son. The Revenant also remembered how he had taken his mother for granted; how he had sometimes been cruel to her over a selfish trifle. Regret gripped him like a pair of strong hands around his throat. How he wished he could go back and relive his life. He would change so much; he would appreciate every moment he spent with his mother as much—he was sure of this—as she had with him. He would always be kind, patient, and considerate. He would not say some of the things he had said to her and others. Yes, he would be a much better person and son. Yes, dear beloved mother. I'm sorry I failed you. I'm sorry for everything. He breathed hard; his breath materializing around him in the cold air. He placed a black leather gloved hand up against the tree to steady himself.

Be calm.

THE EGYPTIAN AVENUE

The Revenant made his through the large stone Egyptian Revival gates and walked down the long Egyptian Avenue. He walked carefully down the rarely visited avenue of catacombs. **So much death.** The Revenant stopped at the square stone entrance to the Gothic catacombs. In front of the entrance to the catacombs stood two dark figures—Carter Holland's men. No light could be seen coming the catacombs; only darkness awaited the Revenant. One of the suited men stepped forward, his blond hair and broad shoulders illuminated in the moonlight.

'Mr Holland is waiting for you inside, sir.'

THE GOTHIC CATACOMBS

The Revenant said nothing. He walked forward, turned, and entered the catacombs through the large iron doors. He stopped, turned on the lamp of his smartphone, and stepped into the darkness. He walked down the stone tunnel. The lamp illuminated the area ahead. Stone walls, ceilings, and floors surrounded him. He walked down the hall until he reached a large iron door that was partially open. Light was coming out from behind the door; it flooded into the hallway. He pulled the iron pull ring and door creaked open.

Beyond the black iron door was a large and very cold stone room. In the center was the large and ornately carved stone sarcophagus. An electric lantern sat on the floor next to it; the light this small lamp gave off was enough to illuminate the entire tomb in a pale white light. The Revenant entered, turned off the lamp and put the smartphone in the pocket of the blue wool overcoat.

Inside the tomb stood Carter Holland.

The handsome, svelte, and blond Carter, in a black bespoke Savile Row suit. a white dress shirt (with a Londoner collar), black silk tie, and black wool overcoat (with a coyote fur collar), was leaning against the large stone sarcophagus. He looked exhausted. As Carter looked into the Revenant's eyes, the Revenant saw something in them: fear. No. Not fear. **Something other than fear.** Carter was now the enigmatic one.

And then the Revenant noticed something else: the 11th Baron was absent.

'Where is the baron?'

'Dead. He had a stroke a week ago. He died a day and a half ago. I was with him,' replied Carter quietly.

The Revenant felt a shock go through him.

Carter Holland had never spoken in such a forlorn manner. The Revenant found it unsettling. Carter Holland was not a weak man. Or was he?

The 11th Baron had been the only person in England that the Revenant had ever trusted. It was the aged and white-haired baron who had found him working in a kitchen in a hotel in Mayfair almost two decades ago. The baron had taken a short cut through the kitchen late one evening and stopped when he noticed the Revenant washing dishes. Yes, the moment the baron had laid eyes on him, he knew the rather ordinary looking and easily forgotten (and relatively young) man washing dishes alone in the large stainless steel sink in the large white tiled hotel kitchen was different. The baron could sense it.

'Good evening,' said the 11th Baron, in white tie, a crisp white waist coat, and tails.

The Revenant, in a pair of cotton khaki trousers, a white t-shirt, and a white apron soaked with soapy water, stopped washing dishes and turned to face the aged Englishman in white tie and tails. Yes, the whited-haired baron radiated power.

The Revenant had bowed slightly and replied, 'At your service, sir,' in his indeterminable accent.

The aged baron took the measure of the man before him. He then nodded slightly and said, 'Yes, I believe you will be.'

It was the 11th Baron who had rescued the Revenant from a life of poverty and hopelessness. Within a month, the Revenant had a British passport and a small flat in North London. Within six months, he had completed his first overseas assignment. The baron would guide his life for much of the next two decades. Had the 11th Baron used him? Yes. Of course, he had. But the Revenant, at that point, was good for only one thing: war. And the baron had known that from the very first. The baron had always been fair to him. Yes, the path he had sent the Revenant on was a harsh one, but, after all he had been through, it was the only one he knew. News of the 11th Baron's death had been a shock. Yes, the baron was extremely old and frail, but, none the less, it had come as a shock.

'Will there be a funeral?' asked the Revenant.

'I suppose. The baron outlived all of his children, and he was not close to any of his grandchildren or great grandchildren, but I am sure that the baron's grandson will make all of the arrangements.'

'And he will be buried here? In one of these tombs?' asked the Revenant.

'Yes. Probably. Well, I really don't know. I've never met any of the baron's family. I know the baron's grandson lives in London. A member of my staff telephoned him and told him of his grandfather's death. I will look into it and let you know,' replied Carter in a quiet and disconnected voice.

The rage inside of the Revenant over the murder of the Brigada had dissipated completely with the news of the baron's passing. The Revenant exhaled and stared at Carter Holland. Carter's steely visage had vanished. The air of contempt had gone too. Carter Holland, the demigod, had fallen back to Earth.

'What do you know about Enoch Tara's Special Unit?' asked the Revenant.

'Very little. Less than you, I'm sure,' replied Carter quietly. Carter was now avoiding eye contact with the Revenant. Carter now stared blankly at the ornate stone sarcophagus before him in the stone tomb and did not bother to look up.

'Have you assigned anyone else to locate Tara's Special Unit?' asked the Revenant.

Carter hesitated. He looked up and turned to face the foreigner, the refugee, the exile, that stood before him in the white light given off by the electric lantern which had been placed on the floor next to the stone sarcophagus. The Revenant was so ordinary and average looking. His brown hair had been cut like a City banker, and if he walked among them in the City, no one would have given him a second look—or even a first look. This inscrutable man from a country that no longer existed was now probably the only obstacle standing between Carter Holland and Tara's Special Unit. The Evil Spirit that Carter had summoned from East Anglia was now moving against Declan's men, but he was like a blind man grasping for things in the dark. Declan and his men had seemingly vanished.

'No,' replied Carter.

'The team that killed the Spaniard. Where are they now?' asked the Revenant.

'I don't know. I have heard nothing from them since the day before the incident.'

'Why did you move without me? Why couldn't wait for me to return?' asked the Revenant.

'Enoch Tara moves so openly in London society, yet I know virtually nothing about him. When the Brigada was identified by my security team, I decided that I had to act immediately. The plan was to capture and interrogate him. If the plan had succeeded, I would now have all the information on Enoch Tara's security arrangements that I needed,' said Carter Holland, the frustration and exhaustion evident in his voice and demeanor.

Yes, Carter Holland was a man with a blazing intellect and of unbridled imagination; however, there was an undercurrent of crude brutality underneath Carter Holland's glossy appearance. And that was a weakness that could derail everything. Carter's iron will and formidable self-discipline were also breaking down as the culmination of the project approached.

'The plan failed, and now we have a huge mess,' said the Revenant.

'What are you going to do next?' asked Carter.

'Tell me about the team that killed the Spaniard. Who are they? Tara's Special Unit will be looking for them now. We could use them to draw out Tara's Special Unit,' said the Revenant.

Carter could feel his inner strength returning. The Revenant was now here. Yes, the Revenant was ruthless and highly cunning. He would know what to do.

'The leader was a former para named Declan Bailey, but he has disappeared along with his younger brother Colin and his gang. From what I've read in the newspapers, Declan may well be dead. All I know is that they have gone silent. I suspect they have all fled the country.'

'Why do you think that?' asked the Revenant.

'Declan is not the type to go silent—unless he is dead. I only dealt directly with Declan. The rest of the unit is a mystery to me,' said Carter.

The Revenant doubted Carter's words. Carter Holland micromanaged everything. The very idea that Carter would rely on a violent and secretive security unit and know almost nothing of its composition strained credulity. This was not the first time that Carter had withheld information from him. The Revenant had expected as much would happen before even boarding the British Airways Airbus A318 in Istanbul for the flight back to England. But what could the Revenant do about it? He had agreed to work for Carter Holland knowing full well how paranoid Mr Holland was. Yes, his employer's reticence had meant that Revenant was fighting with one hand tied behind his back. (Or was it both?) What had really happened to Declan and his men?

'Without Declan, what will you do?' asked Carter, his handsome face illuminated in the white light which radiated from the small electric lamp.

The Revenant took a moment to observe Carter up close. Carter had a clear and flawless complexion. His blond hair was glossy and not a hair was out of place. Carter, the princeling, appeared to have never done a day of physical labor in his life. Carter was roughly the same age as the Revenant, but Carter looked ten or fifteen years younger than him. What a different world Carter lived in. Yes, the 11th Baron had reached into the depths of humanity and retrieved the Revenant. It was men like the Revenant who protected men like Carter—who guarded them and allowed them to live their lives anyway they chose. Carter had always had options that the Revenant had never had. At least, that is how it appeared. Carter had climbed out of England's middling middle class and made himself what he was today.

Enoch Tara had come from an upper-middle class background, and yet he did not aspire to rule a country of his own creation. What Tara's true goals were remained unknown to the Revenant. The Sphinx had offered him his own analysis—opinion—of Mr Tara, but how accurate was it? The Revenant really didn't know. The mysterious Mr Tara had remained a mystery. The Revenant suspected that billionaire financier Enoch Tara possessed a level of self-discipline that Carter Holland did not. The Revenant wondered what Enoch Tara was up to now. Of course, Mr Tara was aware that someone was pursuing him. Of course, he was. Tara's Special Unit had been unleashed. And all of this could have been avoided if Carter had just listened to the Revenant and not ordered the abduction of the Brigada.

'What will you do you next,' asked Carter for the third time.

'I have another lead. I have the identity of another member of Enoch Tara's Special Unit. This person will lead me to the Special Unit,' said the Revenant in his indeterminable accent.

Carter nodded slightly in the pale white light.

'Mr Holland.'

'Yes.'

'Go back to your office and focus on finance, Mr Holland. You have already thrown a span into the works. Do not throw another.'

Carter Holland's blue eyes became as hard as bullets. 'Who was this exile from a defeated nation, this war refugee from a country that no longer existed, to tell me anything?' thought Carter. Carter felt a wave of savage energy move through him. No, he had not told the Revenant of the unit from East Anglia and the Evil Spirit who led it. Carter knew that he had to eliminate Declan and his men before any of them could be captured and interrogated by Tara's Special Unit. A cordon sanitaire had to be created around Carter Holland to protect him; to protect his identity. If Enoch Tara discovered who was behind the murder of the Brigada, Tara would put two and two together and link him to the global upheaval that was upending the markets. Tara was a dangerous opponent. Carter knew that. Carter doubted the Revenant really understood Tara's true nature. Carter would not defer to an underling. The Evil Spirit would move ahead and eliminate Declan and his men while the Revenant destroyed the Special Unit.

'Alright,' said Carter quietly.

The meeting now at end, the Revenant turned to leave the tomb. Of course, he knew Carter would do what he wanted anyway. The Revenant, integral to the project, could not back out now. It was too late.

The Revenant's fate was tied to Carter Holland's.

Gemma—An Invisible Fear—The Comandante

LONDON

The Comandante was of average height, slender, but muscular. He had light brown hair (with the occasional silver hair) and blue eyes. And at forty-five, he was still physically fit and handsome. The Comandante, in a pair dark khaki cotton trousers, a dark blue mock turtle neck, and a pair of brown leather Chelsea boots, looked through a pair of military grade binoculars. Yes, from this small flat across the street he could see the facade of the pebbledash semi-detached clearly.

The small flat on the top floor of a three storey building the Spaniard was standing in had been rented out under an alias from a website which specialized in short term stays. The bottom floor of the three storey building was a used bookstore. The bookstore was staffed by a middle-aged woman and her slender blonde daughter, a recent university graduate. Neither of them seemed to take any notice of the men who entered and left the building at regular intervals. They had grown used to short stay tourists that occupied the top floor for a few days at a time. A single weathered wooden door led to a set of worn wooden steps which led to the third floor walk-up. The second floor was empty and would soon be undergoing renovations. The entrance to the red brick building was on the other side of the building. That was good. No one in the small semi-detached under surveillance could see the men entering and leaving the building.

Inside apartment on the top floor of the building were four men.

The apartment was sparsely furnished. There was a queen sized bed, a battered nightstand, and wooden wardrobe in the bedroom. There was also a sitting room, a small tiled kitchen, an entry hall, and a white tiled bathroom (with a white acrylic bathtub). The sitting room had a cheap worn-out sofa that had been upholstered in dark blue fabric, a shabby orange arm chair, and a small wooden coffee table. And this being England, the walls of the flat had been decorated with the ugliest wallpaper known to man. The dark blue curtains that decorated each of the four windows in the flat were badly faded. A gauzy white curtain shielded the men in the room from being observed from the outside. Yes, this was a budget rental.

The Comandante looked at the silver watch attached to his wrist with a natural rubber strap: 11:53am.

It was an overcast wintery day in December. A light layer of fresh snow blanketed London. The other men in the apartment sat uncomfortably on the rundown and shabby furniture. The other men in the main room all spoke to each other in Afrikaans.

Yes, the man identified in the CCTV footage owned the semi-detached across the street. It was a rather nondescript house for such an interesting man like Colin Bailey. He had been convicted of numerous petty crimes, going back to his teens. He had been arrested, but never convicted of far more serious offenses. Colin seemed to have a knack for evading justice. Yes, the official files in Scotland Yard had made for interesting reading. He had been on Scotland Yard's radar for almost two decades, but nothing had ever stuck. Colin owned a pub and pizza shop in London and a small construction company which specialized in renovations. The pub was usually crowded with ne're do-wells and their chavvy girlfriends. The pizza shop was rather popular and had earned four stars (out of four) on most online reviews. Of course, these businesses were was nothing but a front for laundering money. And Colin Bailey was making a lot of money. He declared less than a quarter of it to Her Majesty's Revenue and Custom's.

Colin Bailey had an older brother named Declan, a highly decorated and recently retired British Para. Declan Bailey owned a security company; however, it had no known ties to Carter Holland. Of course, it didn't. But of course, *it did.* Yes, the pieces were all falling into place now. Declan Bailey lived in a rather large Edwardian semi-detached in North London. He was unmarried. Declan's house was also under surveillance by the Special Unit. No movement had been detected in either house for the last twenty-four hours. There were lights on in some of the rooms of Declan's semi-detached, but there was no noticeable movement inside. Declan's black Audi A7 was nowhere to be seen. Nor was Declan.

The Comandante knew that at least one man had been killed in the attack on the Brigada. Most likely, from the blood splatter in the church, several men had been badly wounded. Was Declan dead? Was his brother dead? Were they both badly wounded? The Comandante had to take one of them alive. He needed to know who was behind the attack on the Brigada. He couldn't just kill them—at least not yet. That would come later. Yes, Declan and his younger brother would **not** be turned over to the police to stand trial. England's judicial system no longer functioned properly. The courts would likely sentence them to fifteen years for the brutal murder of the Brigada and they would both be out in five and a half. **That was not justice.** No, after one or both of the brothers had given them the information they needed, they would be killed—or rather, executed.

The Comandante, formerly of the Spanish Foreign Legión, looked at his Omega dive watch: 11:59am.

The first flakes of snow began to fall. The Comandante increased the magnification on the binoculars. Yes, there was someone in the house. The second floor window. The Comandante increased magnification—the digital screen inside the binoculars recalibrated and the image became clearer. It was a strikingly beautiful, young, blonde woman. She had stayed in the house for the last 24 hours without turning on the lights. She had been actively trying to conceal herself.

Okay. Get ready.

'Someone is in the house. On the second floor,' said the Comandante in his mildly accented English.

The South Africans sprang to life. The men did not approach the windows of the main room; they carefully adjusted their body armor and put their coats on. The blond Afrikaner, in a pair of faded denim blue jeans, a white button-down Oxford dress shirt, and a blue quilted jacket, buttoned up the coat as he uttered something in Afrikaans to the others. One of the other Afrikaners, a middle-aged man with dark brown hair, picked his 40mm pistol from the coffee table. The third Afrikaner, a young man of slender build and confident demeanor walked quietly over to the door and looked at a tablet computer that had been hung from the wall. The tablet's screen glowed with live video feed of the hallway outside the door of the apartment. No one was in the hallway or the stairwell. All was clear. So far.

Alright. Get ready.

Declan was a former Para—a professional soldier. His brother was a highly cunning and violent criminal. Proceed with caution.

The young woman in the semi-detached put a cellphone to her head and began speaking. Someone had telephoned her.

Alright. Focus. You have been through this a hundred times. Remember: One of the brothers had to be taken alive. The Comandante studied the young woman carefully. She was shapely and attractive—a gangster's girlfriend. She was wearing a pair of faded blue jeans and a beige sweater that clung to her every curve. Her long blonde hair was in two long braids, like the tails of horses. She looked around nervously as she spoke on the phone. Yes, either she would soon leave the house or someone would arrive to pick her up. The Spaniard was sure of that.

'Jonny, head downstairs and start the car. Clement, go with him,' ordered the Spaniard.

The two Afrikaners looked at the makeshift CCTV screen, checking to see that the hallway and stairwell were clear, and then they opened the door and headed down the stairs. The last one out closed the door behind him.

The young blonde woman suddenly moved to the window and looked to her right. The Comandante followed her gaze to the white Citroën hatchback that had just stopped in front of the semi-detached. The young woman darted away from window and disappeared from sight.

The Comandante focused the binoculars on the white hatchback. Yes, there it was, the license plate. He read the license plate number out loud; the remaining South African wrote the number down on a notepad on the coffee table.

The front door of the semi-detached opened and the attractive young woman emerged. She locked the door behind her and walked quickly to the waiting automobile. She opened the door, climbed in, and the hatchback sped away.

'Have them follow the white hatchback,' the Spaniard said to the blond South African standing behind him. The young man immediately tapped on his phone and spoke in Afrikaans.

Downstairs, a dark blue Audi A6 was already moving in the white Citroën's direction. A minute later, they were following the white hatchback two car lengths behind.

And a few seconds after the Audi had driven by, a white 2017 Volkswagen GTI hatchback, which had been parked three blocks away, started and followed the South Africans into the afternoon London traffic.

Gemma—An Invisible Fear—Aurelia

LONDON
Aurelia, in faded blue jeans, a white cotton blouse, and a heavy beige cable knit sweater, walked down the white walled hallways of the hospital. The nineteen-year-old Aurelia, her long blonde hair held in place by a blue velvet headband, stopped and looked through the narrow window of the white door to Louise's hospital room. She could see Louise lying in bed, shrouded in white cotton sheets and a large white pillow. Louise, her

strawberry blonde hair framing her smooth pale face, was talking with someone. Aurelia looked through the window at a different angle, and Gemma, in a white cotton blouse and dark blue pencil skirt, appeared.

Yes, Gemma, beautiful, well-educated, posh, and kind—most of all—kind, was happily talking with Louise. Aurelia observed the forty-one-year-old Gemma carefully. Yes, Gemma was a bit of a mystery to Aurelia. Yes, a lot had happened to Gemma, much of it terrible, but Gemma had survived all of it. Alexa, Aurelia's mother, had spoken quite a bit about her time at All Saints with Gemma and the other Inseparables, but had always been circumspect when it came to discussing other aspects of Gemma's life. Alexa had showed her several photos from her days at All Saints and Oxford University. Gemma had been radiantly beautiful, and so had Aurelia's mother. But what good had Gemma's beauty been to her? Her beauty had drawn misery to Gemma. It was only within the last year that Gemma's life had finally turned around.

Alexa, in the last few months, had become rather slim and regained much of her youthful appearance. Alexa was beautiful. Aurelia's younger sister Sarah had inherited her mother's beauty. In fact, she was a carbon copy of her mother as a teenager. And Aurelia? She had always been plain looking. Aurelia had compensated for it by excelling at sports. Aurelia had the build of an Olympian. Yet, she envied the other girls for their beauty, especially the extreme beauty of Freya and Jinx.

Louise had suffered a stroke, and now lay brain damaged in the hospital. The extent of the damage was unknown. On the surface, Louise appeared unaffected, but the brain operates in mysterious ways. Aurelia, deeply worried about her dear friend Louise, it had found it difficult to focus on her studies or even get a good night's rest.

After a couple of minutes as the door, Aurelia knocked gently on the door and entered.

'Good afternoon, Louise,' said Aurelia happily as she entered the room.

Louise and Gemma both looked in Aurelia's direction and smiled.

'Aurelia. It's good to see you,' said Louise and she smiled.

Aurelia felt a wave of emotion sweep through her. The nineteen-year-old Louise beamed with happiness as Aurelia approached. Louise was still here, still alive. Aurelia placed the canvas book bag she was carrying on the table next to the hospital book and then leaned down to hug Louise. The moment Aurelia felt her warm embrace, electricity seemed to race through her.

'How are you?' asked Aurelia as tears began to well up in her eyes.

'I'm getting better. The headaches have almost disappeared. I'm going to see the play this weekend.'

Aurelia gently released Louise from her embrace and slowly stood back up.

'The doctors said it would be alright?'

'Yes. I'm going to take the train up to Muddy Hills with everyone,' replied Louise.

Aurelia exhaled. 'I'm happy to hear that. But please don't push yourself too hard, Louise. I worry about you,' said Aurelia.

Louise smiled. 'Don't worry. I'll be alright. I have more novels to write.'

Aurelia suddenly remembered something. 'In addition to your notebooks and homework assignments, I also have your mail. I collected it from the school post office. There is something from your publisher.'

Aurelia unzipped the blue canvas bag on the table and took out a large white thin cardboard envelope with several stamps and post markings on it. She carefully handed it to Louise.

Louise opened it carefully. She pulled out a white piece of paper.

Dear Miss Percival,

Enclosed is a copy of the preliminary book cover for your novel. As requested, we took the photos you supplied us of the Devereux House in the Lake District and had a water color of it painted by an artist in Sussex. We have also formatted the cover in the manner you suggested and used the font which you requested. Please let us know what you think. We can have another water color produced if you are unsatisfied with this one.

Sincerely,

M.C. Sayers
Contract Manager
Occidental Prometheus Publishing

Louise placed the letter on the bed and picked up the large envelope. She carefully pulled out thin piece of cardboard. Printed on it was a water color of Poppy's country house along with the title and Louise's name across the bottom of the cover. Louise's gentle brown eyes widened slightly. Here was the cover of her first novel—just as she had imagined it. No, it was even better than she had imagined. Louise's eyes drifted over the gentle greys and sharp black lines which defined the stone house that had witnessed Louise's gentle transformation. Yes, the artist had captured the spirit of the house perfectly. It was amazing. Louise's hands started to tremble. Was this really happening? Yes. Soon Louise would hold the book her hands. People would read her words.

Louise gently turned the thin cardboard print towards the girls so that they could see it. Gemma and Aurelia both studied it carefully. Yes, Gemma recognized the large country house immediately. Aurelia, having yet to visit Poppy's family pile, did not. Yes, the house was shrouded in snow; that was how the house looked when Louise had visited it last January with Freya. Obviously, that holiday had made a deep impression on the gentle and wounded Louise. That Christmas holiday had also been a turning point for Gemma. The water color of the house was beautiful.

And then Gemma noticed the title: **The Undaunted**

'The cover is beautiful, Louise,' said Gemma quietly, softly.

Louise could detect the emotion in Gemma's voice. Yes, Louise had survived Grey along with Gemma, Freya, and Poppy. What had gone on between Grey and Gemma remained a mystery; a secret that Louise did not want to know. Grey had tried to kill them all. He had failed. And today, almost a year later, Gemma was with her. They had both survived so much. And they had each other. The Inseparables had each other.

Louise did not respond to Gemma verbally. The look in her eyes spoke for her.

'I will have to email the publisher and give my approval immediately,' said Louise quietly.

'I will buy the first copy,' said Gemma happily. 'I'm curious to read it,' said Gemma as she arched an eyebrow.

Louise smiled impishly.

'I'll take that as a yes,' said Gemma and she smiled.

'Well, then, I'm going to buy the second copy,' said Aurelia happily.

'Oh, and all of the instructors told me to say hello and they all wished you a speedy recovery. I think all of them are worried about your taking the exams in January.'

'I want to take the exams. I'm alright. I will be. The only exam I am worried about is chemistry. And I will pass it with flying colors. I'm sure,' said Louise and she smiled gently, very gently.

'I'm sure you will,' replied Aurelia.

Gosh, I can't believe I almost forgot,' said Aurelia suddenly. Aurelia reached into the blue canvas book bag and took out two white envelopes. Each bore a stamp with the Sovereign on it. Each was also sealed with an embossed stamp of Midlands-Hasegawa University. 'I picked them up at the school post office just before I came over,' said Aurelia excitedly. She handed one of them to Louise.

'Now we find out if we have been accepted,' said Louise somewhat nervously. Their acceptance was not a sure thing. Mid-year transfers like this were unusual at Muddy Hills. Louise held the white envelope in her hands. She turned it over in her hands and looked at her name and school post office box address that had been typed—yes, typed—out on the envelope. A simple yes or no would decide if Louise would be reunited with Freya next term. Louise's heart started to beat a little faster.

'You go first, Louise,' said Aurelia.

Louise opened the envelope and took out the white letter. She unfolded it; the university letter head blazed at the top of the letter. This was it. Louise carefully read the letter in silence. Gemma and Aurelia, their eyes fixed on Louise, waited patiently.

'I have been accepted into Muddy Hills.'

Louise's statement was met with silence. It was now Aurelia's turn. Yes, it would not be good news unless Aurelia had also been accepted. Aurelia was an Inseparable now. Louise wanted Aurelia to come with her—or rather—escape with her from the unbearable wokeness which was smothering their university in London. Midlands-Hasegawa would be a respite, albeit a temporary one, but nonetheless a respite from the brutal and unforgiving Political Correctness that was rapidly destroying England. The next two and a half (or three) years would be one last gulp of fresh air before they would all have to re-emerge into the modern world. Aurelia would, undoubtably, return to Singapore. Freya would leave England too. Where she would go, Louise doubted even Freya really knew for sure. Jinx would stay in England. As would Louise. She would return to East Anglia. The idea that Louise would be separated from Freya hurt her. At least they would have a couple of more years together before they parted. Muddy Hills would be the last redoubt. And, Louise knew, the girls would be happy there, if only for a brief moment.

Aurelia opened the envelope and took out the letter. She unfolded it and began to read. Aurelia exhaled. She looked up from the letter.

'I've been accepted too.'

Gemma—An Invisible Fear—Modernity

LONDON
The white Citroën hatchback slowed as it approached the intersection. Was the driver aware of the dark blue Audi A6 following him? Probably not. If he was, he was almost certainly not aware of the white VW that was following both cars at a distance through London traffic that afternoon.

The South African behind the wheel of the Audi slowed. He was two cars behind the Citroën now. Easy. Relax. The white hatchback isn't going anywhere fast. Traffic wouldn't allow for a sudden escape. Be patient. If he you lose him now, he might disappear forever. You need the information. The driver shifted and the dark blue Audi accelerated as it moved through the intersection.

The young woman, clad in a pair of faded blue jeans and a dark blue quilted Burberry jacket, and driving the white Volkswagen, peered at the cars ahead through clear ceramic framed glasses—the kind that a movie star would have worn in the 1960s. This pair of glasses, however, was worn to disrupt facial recognition software. She wore her light brown hair in a short chin length bob. Her complexion was pale, smooth, and flawless. She was not the type to smile. People only glimpsed her white (and slightly crooked) teeth when she spoke, which she rarely ever did. She was, at 5'9", tall for a woman. She was also athletic.

She had worked for withered man in East Anglia for two years. Three years before, she had been at the end of her tether. The Evil Spirit had spotted her working out in a boxing gym. Yes, The Evil Spirit recruited people in places such as that because the people training there had nothing to lose and could fall no further. The withered old man—who really wasn't as old as he appeared—had made her whole. He had given her purpose.

'The Audi is registered to a bakery in Sussex,' said the young man, in a Bristol accent, seated next to her in hatchback as he tapped on a tablet computer.

'How about the Citroën?' asked the young woman.

The young man tapped on the computer screen and the information appeared.

'It belongs to someone named Paige Wight. She lives in a council estate in North London with her mother. Twenty years old. Last place of employment, a hair salon. She's quite the looker.'

'She must be Colin Bailey's girlfriend. And he drove her car over to pick her up. Alright. Let's see where Colin takes us,' said the young woman.

'The Audi must belong to Tara's Special Unit,' said the slender young man in faded blue jeans and a dark grey hoodie (which had pieces of clear tape attached to it that also disrupted facial recognition software—somehow).

'Yes. They are the ones we have to keep our eyes on,' said the young woman as she slowed the white hatchback in the heavy afternoon traffic. 'Contact the others. Send them the information you have.'

'Already done,' said the young man.

THE BANK
Brian Atherton, svelte and handsome, studied the computer screen in front of him carefully. Yes, funds were still being shifted. To where? The movements were subtle. The funds had left no wake as they moved. How was that possible?

Brian, in a dark blue suit, pale blue dress shirt, and dark blue necktie, stood up and walked across the office. He looked out of the large pane glass window. The City stirred below him. He looked to his right; the Gherkin loomed up before him; it's red aviation lights glowing in the wintery gloom.

In a couple of days, he would take the train to the Lake District and then board Violet's private train carriage to Midlands-Hasegawa. He would be reunited with his wife Poppy and they would watch Freya on stage in The Ptolemies. Gemma and Enoch would take Tara's private rail carriage to Muddy Hills. It would be filled to capacity: Jubal Wyatt, the playwright and screen writer, would also be accompanying them. Yes, Külli, Octavia, Louise, and Aurelia would be travelling with them too.

Poor Louise.

Of course, Brian was curious about what Mr Tara knew about the current financial upheaval—an upheaval that had remained largely hidden to most of the world. Of course, Brian would not ask. Confidentiality had to be respected.

After the play, Freya, and Louise would travel in Violet's private rail carriage with her back to London. Hughie would also return to London with them. It had been decided that Louise would spend Christmas in Mayfair in order to be near the hospital. And, yes, Louise's father would be joining her in London for Christmas. Brian hoped that things would work out between Louise and her father. Brian (and Poppy, if she had been able to attend) would travel by train (in a private British Railways cabin) back to the Lake District. Enoch would be staying with Gemma at her house near Poppy's country house. Or was that still the plan? Perhaps Gemma and Enoch would spend Christmas in Surrey with Enoch's mother? Holiday plans seemed to be shifting daily now.

Yes, it was almost hard to believe: in the midst of one of the world's (potentially) worst financial disasters, everyone was heading north to watch a school play.

Brian, now the vice president of the bank, barely slept at all. The only time he really did sleep was when he took the train to the Lake District to see his wife and children. And the one or two nights he stayed with Poppy at the family pile. Brian was looking forward to spending the Christmas holidays with Poppy and the twins. Brian had never looked forward to Christmas this much. Yes, whatever the future brings, Brian, Poppy, and their children would be together.

Gemma—An Invisible Fear—Colin Bailey

LONDON

The white Citroën took a left turn at the intersection. The driver, a relatively unknown English gangster, looked into the rearview mirror as the hatchback made its way through the intersection. Colin exhaled.

The last four days had been very difficult—very, very difficult. Even for a hardman—tough, ruthless, and, violet—like Colin Bailey. The Brigada had been a far tougher an opponent than anyone had expected. One of Colin's best mates had been shot in the Anglican church along with one of the Paras. Jas, the Para, who had served three tours in Afghanistan and Iraq with Declan, had died instantly; the Spaniard's bullet shattering his forehead. 'Biscuit'—Colin's best mate since childhood—had been shot in the neck. 'Biscuit' (his real name had been Eddie) had bled to death in the backseat of the car within minutes of being wounded. Mason, another one of Colin's mates, had been slightly wounded, but managed to help Colin carry Biscuit out of the church and place him in the car. Mason had started crying in the backseat of the stolen silver BMW when Biscuit died; Biscuit's head resting on Mason's shoulder. It had all been so chaotic: shouting, struggling, the echoing of the gun fire, the reverberation of the pistol fire had been deafening, shapes and shadows moving through the dim illumination of the church, bullets ricocheting off of the Medieval stone walls, the flash of a cut throat razor, and blood. So much blood. The Brigada, though mortally wounded, had kept on fighting. The Spaniard had managed to kill two and wound three. Worst of all? Colin's older brother, Declan, had been shot twice.

The rest of the gang (because that's really the only way to describe them) had fled the church pell-mell. Without Declan's leadership, the gang became a wild and disorganized mob. Someone, Colin really didn't know who, had helped Declan climb into the backseat of the Audi. Someone had driven off with Declan. The last thing Colin remembered clearly from the night was the sound of the snow crunching underfoot as he ran to the car. It was all darkness and headlights. The gang had escaped, but badly mauled.

The cars had sped through the darkness, down backstreets and narrow alleyways. Yes, try to avoid the CCTV. Impossible! The loud static over the two-way radio was interrupted by occasional shouts. Colin snapped out of his state of shock and regained his senses.

'Everyone! Shut up! Listen!' Colin's voice crackled over the two-way radio. 'Everyone to the warehouse! Now!'

There was more static, some voices, and then silence. Colin turned off the two-way radio. Stay calm. Okay. Drive.

THE WAREHOUSE

Colin had been the last to arrive at the warehouse. The rundown red brick warehouse, on the edge of London, was located behind a large recycling plant that operated 24/7. The plant was almost entirely automated. The large plant was now staffed with around a dozen workers. The noise inside the plant was deafening. The workers rarely ventured onto the factory floor unless shrouded in protective gear. Though the plant was heavily insulated and soundproofed, the sounds of metal being shredded, torn, ground up, and crushed was still loud enough to disturb the neighbors—if there were any; which there were not.

There weren't any neighbors to report five cars arriving within minutes of each other that night.

Colin's warehouse, which itself was surrounded by a three-meter-high red brick wall, housed a bulldozer, forklift, two lorries, a white transit van, and a flatbed trailer. All of the vehicles were battered and older than Colin (who was in his early-thirties). All of the equipment and vehicles were illuminated in the fluorescent light of the industrial ceiling lamps of the brick structure. There was also a large tool shed at one end of the warehouse that was secured with a padlock. The warehouse was kept in military order.

There was a makeshift office at one end. Outside of the office (which consisted of three plywood walls attached to the building and a cheap wooden door) were three old sofas. Colin spotted his brother Declan, badly wounded and bleeding profusely, lying on one of them.

Declan was being attended to by an older man, a corpulent Romanian doctor. Declan had hired the Romanian doctor (a former member of the Securitate—Departamentul Securităţii Statului) to assist with the interrogation (torture) of the Brigada. Now the fifty-nine-year-old surgeon, surrounded by bandage rolls, pharmaceuticals, and an odd number of canvas and leather medical bags, was attempting to save Declan's life. Declan had been shot through the chest and shoulder. The bullets had caused extensive internal injuries.

Colin, his faded blue jeans and a light grey hoodie splattered with blood, walked quickly across the warehouse floor.

'Will he be alright, doctor?' asked Colin in a mixture of agitation and panic.

The craggy faced and grey-haired Romanian, in blood-soaked surgical gloves, without looking up from what he was doing, answered in heavily accented English while holding a scalpel and some other kind of surgical instrument. 'We need to get him to a hospital.'

'That's not an option, doctor. If we show up in casualty now, the police will arrest us. Scotland Yard is just wanting for people like us to show up. We can't go. You have to work on my brother here. Tell me what you need and I will get it,' said Colin, trying to contain his emotions.

'If we can move him to my clinic, I can treat him there,' said the doctor while continuing to work on the unconscious patient.

'Where is your clinic exactly?' asked Colin.

'On the other side of London.'

The young men (some only teenagers) around Colin were a collection of hoodies, leather jackets, denim blue jeans, and track suits. Colin Bailey, at thirty-three, was the oldest. Two of the men stood bandaged, their clothes splattered with blood. Of the eight men surrounding Colin, only one of the young men made any sound at all: Mason. The twenty something Mason, clad in blood smeared faded blue jeans and a grey hoodie, was leaning against the stolen BMW and quietly sobbing. The door to the silver sedan was open; the dome light illuminating the bloodied corpse of 'Biscuit'. Yes, the slender and wayward Biscuit's life had ended violently at twenty-three. But, given Biscuit's demographic, it was to be expected. Still, Biscuit had been Mason's friend. Biscuit had been Colin's friend too. This brutalized and depraved group of Hollow Men had known no other life nor seen any other way out. Biscuit was not the first in the gang to die violently. There had been others, but this time it felt different. This time the gang knew they were out of their depth. Declan had been badly wounded; 'Jas', the other former Para, lay dead in the backseat of the stolen Audi. With Declan incapacitated, Colin would be in charge.

Colin Bailey was no rank amateur. He was a highly experienced, extremely cunning, violent, and dangerous criminal. Declan had trained everyone in the gang on how to handle weapons and even walked them through the basics of squad tactics. But that would not be enough to lock horns with Enoch Tara's Special Unit and survive. Declan Bailey employed dozens of ex-military men for his legitimate security operations, who were unaware of Declan's criminal activities. And Declan Bailey, formerly of the Parachute Regiment, had a few more men like him who had served in special forces units and were gangsters, just like him. Colin Bailey knew these men, and he would have to summon them immediately. They would be needed now more than ever.

But, first things first. Declan would have to be moved to the private clinic if he were to survive the night.

'Alright,' said Colin, in a grating working class accent, to two of the men standing next to him. 'Put Biscuit and Jas in the trunk of the BMW. Take the M25. Find a quiet place. Park and burn the car. Aiden. You follow them and drive them back to the pub. Wait upstairs. Enter through the back. I don't want anyone seeing any of you.'

The three Hollow Men; their eyes cold, their faces sunken and scarred, all nodded slightly, but wordlessly. All three turned and started to walk in the direction of the dark blue Audi and silver BMW. The outline of the skinny twenty-year-old Aiden's pistol could be seen bulging slightly under his black leather jacket.

Mason, tears streaking down his face, looked in Colin's direction and through trembling lips said, 'You're just going to burn them to ash? Biscuit's mum would want to give him a proper send off.'

'We can't risk returning the bodies. The police will be looking about. Biscuit would understand,' replied Colin quietly.

Mason could only stare. Yes, this was just part of the life that they had all chosen. Colin was right. He was. Mason nodded in agreement.

Colin walked back and stood next to the white Ford transit van. This vehicle would transport Declan, the doctor, and two teenage members of the gang to the doctor's private clinic. Davie would drive. Mason was too upset to do much of anything. He would stay at the warehouse and wait for the others to arrive. The others would stay with Declan at the clinic until further notice.

After Declan had been carefully placed in the back of the van (on a thick army surplus sleeping bag which had been put on top of three carefully folded grey wool blankets), the men climbed in. Two other members of the gang pulled the large warehouse door open and the white van drove out into the darkness of a cold winter night, the vehicle's headlights illuminating the area ahead.

Gemma—An Invisible Fear—Michaelmas Term

THE MIDLANDS

The blonde and blue-eyed Freya, in a pleated navy blue skirt, white cotton blouse (with a large), and a grey blazer (with white edging), had collected her exam results from her mail box in the main hall. Yes, the small bronze door with an even smaller glass window that was opened by a simple combination lock. Year of installation: 1923. The white envelope was sealed. Freya stood in the afternoon light of the university post office surrounded by dozens of other undergraduates. Had Freya taken the time to look around her, she would have noticed that most students did what she had done the moment before: carefully remove the white envelope, look at it for a moment, pause, and then carefully open it. Yes, the Michaelmas term at Midlands-Hasegawa had ended. Freya had studied extremely hard; harder than she ever had. And now, the results.

Breathe.

Freya opened the envelope.

She unfolded the white sheet of paper and carefully read through the results.

Yes, Freya had excelled! She had done well in all of her classes, even mathematics. (Wallis had tutored her). Yes, Freya. You are an intelligent girl. Away from the misery of All Saints, you have excelled. Freya felt tears welling up in her eyes. Her first impulse had been to telephone her Godmother Gemma. A year ago, she would have. However, things had changed. Her mother, Violet, had changed, and she had become her mother because Violet had really wanted to be Freya's mother. Violet was trying. Okay. Reward your mother by telephoning her and sharing the good news with her first.

THE RESIDENCE HALL
'How did you do, Jinx?' asked Suga a moment after Jinx opened the door to her room. Suga, in a grey and dark blue tartan wool skirt, white blouse, a navy blue blazer, and a grey wool scarf (with two white stripes down the center), entered. Suga's long glossy blonde hair was worn over one shoulder. Suga, starkly beautiful, curvaceous, and sultry, entered the room and spun around to face Jinx.

Jinx, in a dark blue wool skirt and white cotton blouse, smiled. 'Very well. Well, I didn't do that well in mathematics, but I did very well on my Literature exam and Latin test. And, I had some trouble with Chemistry and

Mathematics. Jane Austen is one of my faves, so the exam was rather easy, *yah*. Well, not that easy,' replied Jinx.

Suga smiled. 'I did well in everything but French. Such a *beastly* language,' replied Suga in a rather posh—almost Sloaney—Scottish lilt.

'How did Pasha do?' asked Jinx.

'I haven't spoken with her yet. I think she did alright. I saw her talking happily with someone on her smartphone in one of the cloisters. Couldn't understand a thing she said. What language do they speak in Laos?'

There was a gentle knock.

Jinx took a few steps and then opened the door. It was Wren. Wren, honey blonde and radiant, posh and beautiful, stood in the doorway. Wren was clad in a mostly blue and slightly orange tartan skirt, white cotton blouse, and a blue blazer (with white edging). Wren, her blue eyes partially hidden by her honey blonde bangs, smiled.

'Yes, I passed all of my exams. I have the highest grade in my Literature class. Thank you, Jane Austen, for being perfect,' said Wren.

'Congratulations, Wren,' said Jinx happily.

'Thank you, Jinx,' replied Wren.

'Yes, congratulations. I'm sure Jane Austen is *quite* proud of you, Wren,' said Suga.

'Thank you, Suga.'

'Please, have a seat, girls,' said Jinx as she walked to the end of the room and turned the two wooden chairs around in front of the worn wooden desks.

'Has anyone heard from Freya yet?' asked Wren.

'No, not yet. She should be here soon. We have to go to rehearsal at 4pm.'

THE RESIDENCE HALL ENTRY HALL
'Yes, Mummy. I wanted you to be the first to know,' said Freya into her smartphone.

Violet became quiet for a moment, and then said, 'Thank you, Freya.'

Freya smiled. Yes, her mother had understood the significance of it completely. There was a brief pause and then Freya said, 'Is Louise really up to all of it, Mummy? I'm worried about her.'

'Louise is doing well, Freya. Wild horses couldn't keep her away. Louise is positively angelic. She will take the train with Enoch Tara and Gemma. Oh, Gemma has decided to return to London after the play. She is going to spend Christmas with Enoch's mother in Surrey. Afterwards, she will head up to the Lake District. Enoch has to stay in London. He is working on some kind of project. Gemma will spend some time with Poppy. Louise's father is coming to the house in Mayfair for Christmas. He will stay at his house in London, but spend time with Louise at the house in Mayfair. I telephoned Louise last night. Louise didn't mention him. I didn't ask. I hope they can work through things. Whatever happens, Louise will always be part of our family.'

'Have you told Louise that? That you consider her to be part of the family,' Mummy?'

'Yes, I told Louise last night when I telephoned her in the hospital. Louise started to cry. Poor little thing. She made me cry too.'

'I love you, Mummy.'

'I love you, too, Freya.'

THE RHODES THEATRE
The fair-haired Rex, linen-breasted in his Macedonian linothorax armor,

stood in the wings and watched the nineteen-year-old Jinx perform on stage. Jinx shimmered under the lights. Her golden Vulture Crown and glittering pharaonic costume had transformed Jinx into a true Ptolemy. Yes, she was her sister Cleopatra's most dangerous rival. This upstart rival claimant was now fighting for her very life. Rex, as Lord Antipater, the Macedonian, would attempt to save her.

Jinx and Rex were now a couple. Yes, Jinx had declared her love for the gentle and fragile Rex. And Rex had declared his. Without a doubt, they would marry. Rex could feel his heart beating in his chest. How long would it continue to beat? Please, God, give me a lifetime with Jinx. Please.

THE STAGE

Elfie, the twenty-one-year-old blonde Rhodesian director, stood in the center of the stage surrounded by the fully costumed cast, stage hands, and backstage crew.

'Alright, everyone. Tonight's rehearsal was perfect. I've decided to cancel Friday's rehearsal. We all need a break and I am sure some of you will have family arriving tomorrow. I want you all to know how proud I am of all of you. Thank you, Freya for bringing this play to us. Oh, and I received an email from Jubal Wyatt. He is in London and will be taking the train to Muddy Hills on Saturday.'

The news of the playwright's arrival in England caused a bit of commotion.

'Don't panic. Mr Wyatt is as human as the rest of us. He seems really nice. At least in his emails. He is looking forward to seeing us perform his play. The Ptolemies is that play that launched his career. He wants to see what we will do with it,' said Elfie happily and she smiled. 'Any questions? Comments?'

Silence.

Elfie, in a dark grey pleated skirt, a white cotton blouse, and a beige v-neck cricket sweater (banded in pale blue and navy blue stripes), smiled and said, 'Alright. Everyone. I'll see you on Saturday.'

THE DINING HALL

That wintery night in December, the nine hundred and eighty undergraduates of Midlands-Hasegawa ('Muddy Hills' to the students) dined in the large (once) ornate hall. After a long week of exams, the students were both exhausted and relieved. Yes, it was the end of the Michaelmas term.

Tomorrow, Friday, would be spent signing up for the Hilary term classes and packing for the Christmas holidays. There would also be a Formal Hall—a rather formal dinner—in the dining hall. A Formal Hall meant the undergraduates would attend dinner in full academic robes of Russell cord while carrying (but never wearing) their mortarboards. As a 'Hon', Freya's mortarboard would be adorned with a gold silk tassel, as opposed to the commoners whose mortarboards were adorned tassels of black silk. Wallis and Wren, also 'Hons', would don their black Russell cord subfusc (of noble cut) and sporting mortarboards with gold silk tassels, be seated next to Freya. Yes, Wren would be thrilled. Wren, in the presence of other noblewomen, would make a glittering entrance. (And yes, everyone would notice.) The other girls, commoners all, would file in behind them. (Or so thought Wren.)

Freya, however, had a million of things on her mind—the most important being Louise. Freya just wanted to hug Louise and tell her how much she loved her. Freya was terrified of losing her. Though a week had passed since the stroke, Louise was far from out of danger. How could God allow this to happen? Freya would see Louise in two days' time.

The play was part of a series of events on Saturday. Students would attend chapel and then have breakfast. There would be an assembly at noon and the President of the university would give a brief speech. The undergraduates would then be allowed to show their parents around the university (if they were there) and, if they chose to, make their way to the Rhodes Theatre to watch the end of term play at 2pm. End of term mid-year meant that very few foreign parents would be present. The large Rhodes Theatre would be filled with students and the families and friends of the few native British undergraduates that attended Midlands-Hasegawa.

Freya should have been both nervous and excited about the play, but given Louise's condition, Freya could feel only trepidation.

'Rise!'

Hundreds of weary undergraduates rose from their old wooden chairs. And then, miraculously, there was the loud high-pitched sound of a Public Address system. Muddy Hills had *finally* repaired the PA system. The elderly, white-haired, Rhodesian University President appeared behind the podium in a dark coat and stripped Rhodesian regimental tie.

'Yes, the PA system has been replaced. How very nice. I would like to congratulate all of you for completing the Michaelmas term at Midlands-Hasegawa.'

While the President was speaking, Freya noticed a slender elderly woman with shoulder length grey and white hair seated at the high table. She wore a dark blue cotton jacket over a white Egyptian cotton blouse. She looked quite posh. Next her was an elderly Asian man in a black suit, white shirt, and a light grey silk necktie. He had snow white hair. For a split second, Freya wondered who they could be. And then she knew who they must be.

'It is my great pleasure to introduce one of our university's most prominent alumnus, Mr Tōhaku Hasegawa and his wife Lara. Both are graduates of the university. Mr and Mrs Hasegawa have travelled from Japan to meet with the students and faculty and attend the school play. I will make this introduction brief and invite Mr Hasgawa to speak to you.'

The university president stepped away from the podium and Mr Hasegawa made his way to the wooden podium. The Japan billionaire walked rather gracefully to the podium, adjusted the microphone, and looked out on the assembled students. Mr Hasagawa, Freya guessed, was around 5'7'—at best. Though in his seventies, Mr Hasegawa was rather handsome.

'It is a great honour for me to address you all today,' he began in a surprisingly Rhodesian accented English. (Or perhaps not, considering that his wife of almost five decades was Rhodesian.) 'I can still remember the day I arrived at Midlands University. I was a shy and scared eighteen-year-old undergraduate from Japan. My first year at school had a profound impact on my life and future. It was at Midlands University that I found purpose. I remember having lunch for the first time in this very hall, and, as I can clearly see, at the exact same tables and chairs.'

A wave of laughter spread through the dining hall. Yes, most of the long dining tables had been purchased in the 1920s.

'Midlands University has always been an excellent school. It has always prided itself on offering a sterling education to its undergraduates. And, most importantly, the university has always been a place of free speech and free expression. And it will continue to be so.'

Now applause filled with hall; the loudest coming from the native English (and Scottish and Welsh) undergraduates who appreciated the freedom of speech and thought that Midlands-Hasegawa offered, unlike the other 'woke' universities in England. The native undergraduates at Midlands-Hasegawa were part of a new generation that did not appear to understand even the most basic principles of free thought and free expression. The young undergraduates of Muddy Hills, however, were an exception.

'I hope that all of you will find your niche at the university. For me, it was the Drama Club, where I met my wife, Lara. Remember: Excellence in all things. Thank you.'

Applause filled the dining hall once more.

A few moments later, in the women's section of the dining hall, the slim raven-haired Jinx, half way through a lunch of lasagna, and seated next to Freya, said, 'Mrs Hasegawa is from Bulawayo. Did you know that?'

'No, I didn't,' said Wren. 'No wonder she is so beautiful.'

'Do they have any children?' asked Wallis. The blue-eyed Wallis, the future 12th Baroness, wore a pale blue cashmere top and a dark blue wool skirt. Her long blonde hair held in place by a white velvet head band. Wallis, even in the gloomy natural light of a wintery day in the Midlands, looked hauntingly beautiful. Wallis, in this brief, fleeting moment of youthful beauty, seemed completely out of place in the vulgarity and vapidity that was modern England.

'No. None,' replied Jinx. 'Lara used to act in all of the school plays. I found heaps of photos of her online from the early 70s in the school plays. I also found a few of Mr Hasegawa. They acted in a play together,' said Jinx in her Rhodesian Sloaney intonation.

'Yes, the stage does seem a good place to meet people,' said Wren teasingly.

Jinx blushed.

'I'm looking forward to seeing you in all of your Ptolemaic splendor, Freya,' said Wallis.

'What?' asked Freya.

'I'm looking forward to seeing you in the play.'

'Oh, yes. Well. I think you'll like our performance. I hope you do,' replied Freya. Freya's thoughts were now of Louise. She would feel better once she saw her in person on Saturday. Freya had to see Louise and see with her own eyes that she was really alright.

Wren, serenely happy, glanced across the table at Wallis and asked, 'I'm looking forward to meeting your mother, Wallis.'

'Yes, I have told Mummy all about you and the Riley. And the ghosts,' replied Wallis and she smiled.

Gemma—An Invisible Fear—Mars in Winter

THE LAKE DISTRICT
The country house, built in 1897, and constructed of medieval stone, was veiled in ice and snow. The occasional barren tree, its branches weighted down with snow, dotted the wintery landscape around the house. Each

season dramatically transformed the Lake District, so much so that it appeared to be another country with the change of seasons. In winter, the family pile and the lands surrounding it underwent a dramatic transformation. Frost carpeted the ground, when it wasn't covered in a fresh blanket of snow. The fells, a complex collection of low hills and high ground, were topped with white snow against the sky; whether it was clear blue or a foreboding grey. The lakes and ponds around the house were frozen and shimmered in the wintery light like sheets of glass. And in the mornings, a white mist swirled and shrouded everything.

Winter, for the Barons Devereux, brought a peace and serenity borne of isolation. The castle ruins, which the family had owned for almost a millennium, were closed to visitors. The family's ancestral lands, were theirs alone in winter. And it was into the splendid isolation that the ancient noble family invited their most loved.

MARS RUPERT ARTHUR NOEL

Lord Mars, the 13th Baron, in grey wool trousers, a black leather belt, and a white (Egyptian cotton) dress shirt (with a St James collar), glanced at the silver Omega watch which adorned his wrist. He studied the silver hands and observed how the second hand glided smoothly over the indices. **Time: life's most precious commodity, and often its least valued.** Time: as beautiful as it is unforgiving. Mars wondered if he had enough of it left to start over. He had made so many mistakes. Now, at 47, was it too late?

Mars had never been handsome, attractive to some, yes. Mars was actually rather plain looking; it was his posh manner that many had found attractive. That aristocratic insouciance that Mars moved through life with; the way he wore his clothes; the subtle gestures that revealed his noble background to the observant; the effortlessness in which he carried on a conversation, regardless of its complexity, had marked Mars as a man cut from a different cloth. Mars, his brown hair peppered with grey and silver hairs, pondered his future.

Mars, seated in a purple velvet Art Deco armchair in the drawing room, looked out one of the windows. It was snowing again. The sterling silver

Asprey clock on the stone mantle of the 900-year-old fireplace chimed: 2:00pm. It would be dark soon; nightfall came early this far north in the winter. Mars leaned back in the velvet armchair. Three of the walls of the drawing room were polished Circassian walnut; the remaining northern wall was made of grey stone (constructed of stone taken from the ruins of family castle) and held three leaded glass windows. Behind him were a pair of highly polished Circassian walnut double doors set in a stone door frame. The Bauhaus door handles were made of sterling silver and gleamed in the grey mid-day winter natural light that filled the room. The hardwood floor, partially covered by a dark Persian rug, was warmed by the fire that glowed and crackled in the stone fireplace.

It was only here, in Poppy's country house, that Mars felt calm. Here, faraway from London and the ghosts of Hong Kong, Mars felt safe.

The double doors opened and James, the future 13th Baron, blond and blue eyed like his sister Poppy, entered. James, clad in a pair of khaki cotton trousers and a white Oxford button-down dress shirt, looked tired. It was also obvious that he had lost weight.

'Good afternoon, Mars. I heard you had arrived an hour ago.'

'Good afternoon, James. And yes, I did. I'm in the room at the end of the hall. Quite comfortable. It's good to be back with the family for the holidays.'

James sat down in the other Art Deco chair closest to the fireplace. He leaned back into the soft velvet chair. The James that appeared before Mars, though still attractive, was pale and had dark circles around his eyes. Mars had known James for over thirty years and couldn't remember seeing him in such a state.

'How long will you be staying at the house this winter?' asked Mars.

'I have been given twelve days off. I have never needed a holiday more than I do now. Work has been exhausting. The situation…is getting worse.'

Yes, 'the situation' James was referring to was the financial disruption that was still convulsing through the City.

'I understand. I have suffered my share of financial upheavals,' replied Mars.

'Mars, if you don't mind. May I ask what you make of all this?'

'Well, I don't know exactly who is behind it all, but I have some ideas.'

THE TEMPORARY BEDROOM

'Ah, here it is. I rarely wore my school scarf until last year. Now, I don't like to go out without it,' said Poppy as she carefully wrapped her red, blue, and purple wool All Saints scarf around her slender neck and shoulders. 'Gemma has always worn hers. Now Gula wears hers all the time too.'

'Yes. I have even pulled mine out of the top drawer recently,' said Violet. 'I never thought Freya would wear hers, but she does now,' said Violet as she searched through the drawers of an antique wooden dresser that had been placed near the glossy white bedroom door.

'When Waverly turns thirteen, she will be sent to All Saints. I want the line to continue unbroken,' said Poppy.

Poppy's words made Violet pause her search for the right cable knit sweater to wear on the train to Muddy Hills. Did Poppy really think All Saints would still be functioning thirteen years from now? Violet did not look in Poppy's direction; Violet simply stared into space, deep in reflection. Yes, England's fate was deeply troubling to her. Violet could sense that something horrible would soon befall the country. Violet could sense it.

'Gemma has decided to spend Christmas Day with Enoch and his mother in Surrey. She will take the train here afterwards. She'll stay here with us. It will be good to have Gemma back with us.'

'Louise wants to spend time with you and the family here over the holidays too. She wants to meet Arthur and Waverly. So does Freya,' said Violet.

Ping.

Poppy's smartphone glowed momentarily. Poppy walked around the bed (where her leather box suitcase lay), and picked up the phone.

I'm almost there. My train should be arriving at the station in twenty minutes.

'It's Brian. He'll be here soon. I'll pick him up at the station,' said Poppy happily.

'I'll drive you in the Range Rover. Brian probably has too much luggage for the Citroën to hold,' said Violet.

'Thank you, Vava.'

THE ENTRY HALL
The large glossy black doors opened The Honourable Hugh, in a dark blue wool overcoat (with a fur collar) entered. Hugh, blond, and at 6'4', towered over the young black-uniformed housemaid that had allowed him in. The local girl (one of two temporary replacements for the Croatians), nodded slightly as he entered the house.

'Good afternoon, sir. The baron has been expecting you. I'll escort you to the drawing room.'

'Thank you.'

THE DRAWING ROOM
'I'm afraid you just missed them. Violet has driven Poppy to the train station to pick up Brian,' said the 12th Baron. The elderly baron, his white hair cut like a British army officer's, got up from the chair to greet him. The baron, in a white dress shirt, dark grey wool trousers, and a pair of black brogues, extended his hand. Hugh shook it firmly.

'How could I have missed them? I just left the station. The rail carriage is now being unhitched from the train. It will be hitched to another at 10:30 tomorrow morning. It will only take about an hour to get to Muddy Hills.'

'It is nice of you to offer your private rail car to take everyone to see Freya in the play,' said the baron.

'I'm happy to do it, Your Lordship. Poppy means the world to us. The entire family does,' said Hugh.

The baron smiled. 'Please, join me for a cup of tea while we wait.'

THE TRAIN STATION

Poppy, in a pair of dark khaki wool trousers, a heavy beige knit sweater, a pair of brown leather Chelsea boots, and wrapped in her red, blue, and purple All Saints scarf stood next to Violet on the railway platform. Poppy's silver Egyptian Art Deco bracelet flashed against the grey wintery gloom. The train had pulled up to the station just a minute before. Poppy had been waiting in the glossy 2019 Blue Range Rover with Violet in order to stay warm. Now, after not seeing Brian for almost two weeks, Poppy decided she couldn't wait a moment more. The blonde Violet, in dark blue wool trousers, a white cotton blouse, and a dark grey overcoat (with a large fur hood and collar) had followed after her.

The entire village was blanketed in snow; the train station was no exception. The passengers exited the rail carriages and hastily made their way to waiting cars. The parka clad Brian, carrying two leather box suitcases and a laptop shoulder bag, was one of the last to step onto the platform.

'Brian!' said Poppy happily as she approached Brian on the railway platform. Brian looked at Poppy with dismay.

'Poppy. What are doing out in the cold?' asked Brian, his breath materializing around him in the cold air.

'I just got out of the car a moment ago. I'm alright, Brian.'

At that moment, Violet appeared walking down the platform while buttoning up her dark grey wool overcoat.

'Please tell Brian that have only been her for a brief moment, Vava.'

'Yes, that's true. Brian,' replied Violet.

'Well, please. Let's get to the car. I would like Poppy to be out of the cold as soon as possible,' said Brian.

'Hand me the laptop case, Brian,' chirped Poppy and she smiled.

THE COUNTRY HOUSE

It was snowing when the Range Rover arrived at the house. Violet parked in front of the house and everyone entered through the large glossy black double doors. Brian left his luggage in the Range Rover. The servants would retrieve it for him later and take it to his room.

THE TEMPORARY BEDROOM

Brian, in a pair of faded blue jeans and a thin beige cricket sweater (with dark blue and white bands around the v-neck and cuffs), held the infant Arthur in his arms. Yes, the tiny fragile infant was his son. Brian, now at the family pile in the Lake District, felt completely relaxed. Outside, it was snowing lightly and the grey wintery light of a snowy day flooded through the paned windows of the temporary bedroom. Brian was seated in an old leather armchair that had been moved into the bedroom. Arthur, content in his father's arms, studied Brian with his blue eyes as Brian gently caressed Arthur's soft blond hair.

'I wonder what he is thinking?' asked Brian quietly.

'He's probably happy to have you back, Brian. I'm sure Arthur missed you,' said Poppy quietly and she smiled.

'Not as much as I missed you and the children,' said Brian. 'I really don't want to even be away from them for the day tomorrow, but I want to see the play with everyone else. After we return, I don't want to spend a moment away from any of you until I have return to London on the third.'

There was a barely audible knock on the glossy white door of the bedroom. Poppy walked over to the door and carefully, quietly, opened it. It was Holly, the uniformed nanny.

'Sorry to bother you, ma'am,' said Holly politely and quietly. Lord Devereux asked me to inform you that new bathtub would be installed tomorrow while you in the Midlands.'

Poppy smiled.

'Thank you, Holly. Please tell my father how happy I am to hear that.'

'Yes, ma'am.'

Holly nodded slightly and walked back into the great hall.

Gemma—An Invisible Fear—The Ptolemaic Hons

MIDLANDS-HASEGAWA UNIVERSITY
The flaxen haired Freya, her long glossy hair separated into two long braids which cascaded down each shoulder, looked at her silver Cartier wrist watch: 3:03pm. Outside, the sky was overcast and Freya's white walled dorm room was filled with a pale grey natural wintery light. Freya was impatient. She wanted to see Louise. She wanted to see Louise in person and make sure that she was alright. Freya also missed her terribly. She hadn't seen her in almost two months. Both of them had been busy at school. Freya had also been rehearsing for the play; Louise had been editing her novel and plotting her escape from London to Muddy Hills with Aurelia. And then Louise had had a stroke.

The last week had been exhausting and emotionally draining. The events of the last year had changed everyone. They had been transformative. The Inseparables had all been transformed. It seemed as if a final hurdle was coming into view; one that everyone would have to clear. If one of them faltered, then all of them would.

Freya walked across the hardwood floor to one of the white sash windows and looked out on the snowy fields which surrounded the university. Here, in a forgotten school, in a forgotten town, Freya was safe. Freya would, however, not feel complete until Louise was safely installed in Muddy Hills with her. Please, God, protect Louise.

A skeleton key turned in the lock of the door, it opened, and Jinx stepped into the room. Jinx, in a dark grey pleated skirt, a white cotton blouse, a dark blue v-neck sweater, and carrying a brown leather portfolio, smiled.

'Rex gave me the nicest Christmas card,' said Jinx happily. Jinx took a white envelope out of her portfolio and held it up. She walked over to her desk and placed the portfolio on it. She turned and carefully took the card out of the envelope. She opened it read it to herself. No, it was too personal to share with anyone, even Freya. After reading Rex's sweet words, Jinx looked up at Freya.

'Are you alright?' asked Jinx. And then Jinx nodded slightly. 'Yes, I am worried about Louise too, but she is doing well. We will see her tomorrow. Everything will be alright,' said Jinx.

'I hope so, Jinx. I have to be honest with you. I'm worried about Louise. She is pushing herself too hard. She plans to take her exams after Christmas and then transfer immediately to Muddy Hills. Louise needs time off to recover from the stroke.'

'Yes. You're right. Louise just wants to be here with us. With you, Freya. I think that once she has settled into Muddy Hills with you, she will be happy. She will feel safe. And she will be out of her university and have escaped 'Woke London'.

'Yes. You're right, Jinx. Louise will arrive tomorrow. And in a few weeks, Louise will be here, with us, in an alcove room.'

Jinx put the Christmas card on the desk and then turned back to face Freya. 'One small problem, Freya. An alcove room is for four. What about Wren? She has lived all alone here and I know Wren is *all jolly hockey sticks* about sharing an alcove with us next term,' said Jinx in her Sloaney and posh Rhodesian intonation.

Freya sighed. 'I haven't even thought about that. We can't exclude Wren. She would be devastated, truly. Oh, no. It seems that life has become one problem after another,' said Freya.

'There is one possibility,' said Jinx.

'What?'

'We could have two desks removed from the alcove and have a fifth bed replace them. We would have to share two desks between the five of us, but I wouldn't mind. Do you think the other girls would?'

'No. I wouldn't. I volunteer to keep all of my notes, books, and textbooks on the bookshelf. I can study on my bed. I prefer that. Louise likes to study in bed too. She rarely sat at her desk at All Saints. There. A solution! Jinx, you are a genius! For sure.'

Jinx smiled and said, 'Crisis averted. Have you seen Wren this afternoon?'

'No. I've had too much on my mind to venture out of the room,' replied Freya.

THE ROOM AT THE END OF THE HALL

Wren, the honey blonde future baroness (by Writ), carefully adjusted the black Russell cord subfusc (of noble cut) while standing in front of the mirror.

Wren, at nineteen, had finally found her place, her *niche.* Finally. Wren had found friends that accepted her completely. And, just as importantly, she had found *Hons* that accepted her. Yes, Wren's nobility was as important to her as always. That Freya, the granddaughter of a baron and a viscount, and Wallis, the daughter of a baroness (and a future baroness by Writ, like Wren) were part of this circle of friends *mattered.*

Tonight, Wren would make a grand entrance to the Formal Hall flanked by fellow *Hons* in subfusc (of noble cut) and, like her, carrying black mortarboards with silk tassels of gold, not black silk like the others. Wren was special. Wren was from an ancient noble line. **Wren was England.**

There was a gentle knock on the glossy white door of her room.

'Just a minute,' said Wren as she walked over to the door. She opened. It was Freya. Freya, in a dark blue pleated skirt, pale blue blouse, and a pair of black patent leather pumps, smiled.

'Freya. So good of you to visit.'

'It has been decided that five of us will share a room next term. We will have to share two desks in order to fit a fifth bed into the alcove, but it will be necessary. We are a set after all.'

Wren smiled. Yes, Wren was part of the set. And now Freya was acknowledging it. Wren was elated. It had not occurred to her that someone might be excluded from an alcove meant only for four. Would the university allow it? Of course, they would. Freya shone far too brightly to be ignored by the administration now. The request for the alcove had already been accepted; an extra roommate would be approved too.

'I'll come by with Jinx and Wallis tonight. We'll go to the dining hall together,' said Freya.

Yes, just as she had hoped. The Hons of Muddy Hills would make a grand entrance at the Formal Hall. The gold tassels would glint in the candle light.

And Wren smiled.

THE ALCOVE ROOM ON THE SECOND FLOOR

The flaxen haired Wallis, in a pair of blue tartan pyjamas, lay on top of her white duvet. She was happy. She had done well on her exams—well, well enough. Tomorrow her mother, the 11h Baroness (by Writ), would visit her, watch the play, and then drive home in the Bristol Mark II with Wallis to the family pile in Surrey.

The door to the alcove opened and the nineteen-year-old Masako, tall and pale, entered. The Kyoto born Masako looked like she had stepped out of an ancient Japanese woodcut. Slender and elegant, every time Wallis looked at her, she couldn't help but imagine her in kimono. Masako, a noble descendant of one of Japan's ancient daimyos, glided into the room.

Wallis, her head propped up on two large white soft pillows, looked in her direction.

'What are your holiday plans, Masako?'

'I'm going to stay here at Muddy Hills over the holidays. That's what a lot of the foreign students usually do,' replied Masako.

'What about Kokoro and Sakura? Are they staying too?' asked Wallis.

'No, they are both flying back to Tokyo.'

Wallis didn't ask Masako why she wasn't flying to Japan. Most likely it was financial. Masako's family, while ancient and noble, was not particularly wealthy.

'Masako. I would like to invite you to stay with me and my mother in Surrey. We would love you to spend Christmas with us. And you could see the house. It was built in 1789—the year the French Revolution started.'

Masako looked at Wallis for a moment.

'Thank you for inviting me, Wallis, but I couldn't impose.'

'You wouldn't be imposing at all. We're friends, and Mummy would love to have you as a guest. I insist. And besides, I need a caroling partner who can actually sing, *yah*.'

Wallis then climbed out of bed, her long blonde hair flowing down her back and shoulders. Wallis took a couple of steps and stood before Masako, who was couple of inches taller than Wallis and said, 'Please, say yes.'

Masako smiled—just a little—and nodded slightly. 'Thank you, Wallis.'

Wallis smiled. 'I'll show you around the village. I'm sure everyone will love you.'

And Masako smiled.

Gemma—An Invisible Fear—The Family Pile

THE DINING ROOM

The dining room of the family pile in the Lake District had large pane glass windows on one side, and the other side of the dining room was paneled in polished Circassian walnut. The crown mold that ran along the top of the walls was dark mahogany imported from colonial India in the 1890s.

The plaster ceiling that hovered above the dining room was an ornate Victorian design and no less than three small crystal chandeliers hung from it. The chandeliers were purchased in the 1930s; replacements for the Victorian ones that had once adored the room. When turned on, the incandescent light they cast was shimmering and sparkling and equivalent to bright candle light.

The Victorian dining room table seated 22 guests, and was made of polished walnut. The entire table was usually covered by a white table cloth. The high backed Circassian walnut chairs were Art Nouveau, or Modern Style, as it was called in England. The chairs had been commissioned by the 10th Baron just before the outbreak of the Great War.

This evening would be an informal affair.

This evening, the dining room was crowded with three generations of the Barons Devereux. At the head of the table sat the 12th Baron, his white hair freshly cut like a British army officer's. The baron wore a white cotton button-down Oxford dress shirt, a pair of dark khaki trousers, and a dark blue wool blazer. The baron had had a difficult year, nearly losing his daughter Poppy. Now, Poppy and her infant twins were all healthy, happy, and safe in the family pile in the Lake District, faraway from any danger. The baron was happy to be surrounded by family and loved ones. The baroness, her long white hair up and held in place by silver hairpins, sat at the opposite end of the long table. The baron's son, James, and Mars, who was like a son, sat on either side of him. Brian sat next to James. Next to Mars, was Hugh ('Hughie' to his friends). Poppy sat on one side of the baroness, and opposite of her, where Gemma was usually seated, was Violet ('Vava' to the Inseparables of All Saints). James' wife, the blonde and slender Helen, sat next to Poppy. Next to Helen were her seven-year-old children, the always polite, well-behaved, blonde twins, Henry and Lucy. This evening, the guests were attired in a combination of country tweeds, Egyptian cotton, wool, and cashmere.

This evening, the Croatian house servants, Marija and Kata, on holiday in Croatia, had been temporarily replaced by two local girls from the village. The girls, clad in new black uniforms and wearing white cotton gloves, had helped seat the guests. Now they stood along the wall next to the entrance to the kitchen. Edward, the family chef, in a chef's white uniform, was busily preparing dinner with an assistant.

'The twins are sound asleep. Holly is with them now. She is an excellent nanny. You chose just the right girl, Mummy,' said Poppy.

'Yes, I've known Holly since she was tiny herself. She has always had a kind and gentle nature. I knew she would make a good nanny. When I heard she wanted to attend a nanny's college, we decided to help her. It's turned out well for everyone,' replied the baroness.

'Holly is well-mannered and kind hearted. She is a truly nice girl,' said Helen.

Dinner was served. The house maids, adeptly and smoothly, moved around the room serving the guests. Edward, as always, had prepared a sumptuous meal.

'It's good to have you back at the house, Mars,' said the baron.

'Thank you, sir. I am always happy to be back with the family, especially now that the house is filled with children,' replied Mars. 'The family has truly been blessed.'

'Yes. We are truly blessed, Mars.'

'I look forward to having Arthur and Waverly captain cricket matches in the castle,' said Brian and he smiled.

'Yes, I'm sure Henry and Lucy will be happy to don cricket whites and play cricket with them,' said James happily.

'Hughie, I've heard all about The Ptolemies from Poppy and Violet. How proud you must be to have Freya on stage as Cleopatra,' said the baron.

'Yes, Freya never ceases to amaze and surprise me. We had no indication that Freya was really interested in acting at all. And now this. I guess Freya is simply following in the footsteps of her Godmother. Gemma was instrumental in getting Jubal Wyatt to allow the play to be performed. Yes, I have always been extremely proud of Freya. I'm glad that Louise will be able to attend, but I am also concerned about her, said Hugh.

'Yes. Louise should be careful not to strain herself too much. Did you hear? Her novel is about to be published. She spoke with me about it last summer. I am, of course, curious to read it,' said James.

'Freya said it is quite good. Freya read parts of the novel last summer as it was being written,' said Hugh.

'I'm sure Louise will find success,' said James.

Another course was served under the incandescent light of the chandeliers.

'Violet, thank you for staying with us the last few weeks. You have been an enormous help to Poppy and the family. And we enjoy your company,' said the baroness.

'Thank you, ma'am. I have loved my time here with Poppy and the family. The twins are little angels. And it has given me a chance to bond with my goddaughter Waverly,' replied Violet.

'Waverly loves you, Vava,' said Poppy happily. 'And I will never forget that you were at my bedside in the clinic.'

The highly polished walnut walls glowed in the reflected light given off by the chandeliers. The housemaids replaced the white bone china plates with each course.

'Yes, sir. Louise will accompany us back to London on the train. She will be staying with us at the house in Mayfair. The hospital is nearby and my mother has hired a dietician to plan the meals. Louise will be in good hands,' said Hugh.

'I'm sure she will be,' replied the baron.

'Does anyone know what Gemma is planning to do for the holidays?' asked Mars.

'From what I understand, she will spend Christmas with Enoch Tara and his mother in Surrey. Afterwards, she will return to the Lake District and stay with us,' said James.

'I suppose Mr Tara will stay in the City,' said Mars.

'Yes. I'm sure of that. I was very lucky to escape for the holidays,' said Brian. 'I am happy to be back with the family.'

'And we are always happy to have you with us,' said the baron.

Gemma—An Invisible Fear—The Formal Hall

THE MIDLANDS

Freya stood in front of the mirror in her room in the residence hall. The Russell cord subfusc (of noble cut) fit her perfectly. Freya's long glossy blonde hair, in stark contrast to her black robes, practically glowed. Freya straightened the large collar of her white cotton blouse. She turned and walked over to her desk. She picked up the mortarboard and adjusted the gold silk tassel. Yes, of noble blood, Freya was entitled to a gold silk tassel.

There was a light knock and Jinx, in a black skirt, white cotton blouse, black silk ribbon, and black leather pumps, all under her black Russell cord subfusc and carrying her black mortarboard with a black silk tassel, entered the room.

'Ready to go?'

'I promised Wren and Wallis that I would meet them here.'

'Alright, said Jinx as she closed the glossy white door, 'I'll wait with you.'

THE DINING HALL

Wren, Wallis, Masako, Jinx, and Freya, in black academic dress, walked through the darkness, snow crunching underfoot, towards the dining hall. Wren was happy. Everything was coming together. She had made good friends, true friends; the manor house finally had a proper roof, and she was in the company of other glittering 'Hons' at a Formal Hall. The Formal Hall was a relatively small thing for Wren now; mostly, she finally had true friends.

The girls reached the large, weathered, wooden double doors of the dining hall and stopped.

'I'll get the door,' said Freya, her breath materializing around her in the cold air.

'Thank you, Freya,' said Wren.

Wren entered followed by Wallis, Jinx, Masako, and Freya. The honey blonde Wren was illuminated in candle light as she made her way through the (once ornate) dining hall. Yes, the gold tassels glinted in the candle light as the girls moved carefully down the aisle towards their table. Heads turned as they made their way through the male undergraduate section of the dining hall. (Yes, if one entered through the main entrance, one would have to walk through the male undergraduate section of the hall.) The girls walked past table after table of young undergraduates, all dressed in black subfusc, white dress shirts, and white bow ties. How handsome the boys all looked. How beautiful the girls looked. Yes, this was just as Wren had hoped it would be.

The girls reached their table and quietly took their places, all illuminated by the soft glow of the candle light.

Everything was perfect.

All was well.

Gemma—An Invisible Fear—Mr Percival

LONDON
Saturday. The East Anglian looked at the Omega watch strapped to his wrist: 7:40am. Harold Percival stood in the white walled hallway of the hospital. He had stopped just before the door of his daughter's hospital room. Harold had thought the daily visits to Louise would become easier; they hadn't. Each morning, he had awoken to regret and grief. He had neglected Louise horribly. Louise had been the victim of her father's weakness—cowardice, really. His wife's death in a car accident had crushed him completely. He didn't want any reminders of his late wife around him. Louise had been (and still was) the biggest reminder of them all.

Yes, the strawberry blonde Louise was now a carbon copy of her mother Edith Percival. The young brown eyes that gazed at Harold from the hospital bed were Edith's. And whenever Louise spoke, it was with her mother's voice. It was as if her mother was living through her. (Yes, but of course, she was.) What must Edith think of Harold's treatment of their only child? Harold knew. Edith must be heartbroken.

Harold wanted to make it up to Louise (and Edith)—desperately so. Harold despaired when he thought of what Louise must have gone through. And that he had done that to her.

Harold, in a black suit, white dress shirt, and silver tie, found himself trying to communicate with Edith on the other side. Yes. Edith was there. Harold could now feel her presence. She had always been there, only Harold had not noticed. Was Edith angry with him—or just deeply disappointed? Or both?

'I'm sorry, Edith. I have no excuse for what I did. I was weak. I was a coward. I couldn't face anything after you died. Louise suffered for it. I was wrong. I know that. I know that,' said Harold in voice that was barely above a whisper.

Harold was jolted back into the present by the sound of voices down the hall. Harold looked around. There was no one else in the hallway. He took a few more steps and then looked into the hospital room through the narrow window in the white door. Lying in bed was Louise in a white hospital gown. She was turning the pages of a notebook. Harold knocked gently and entered.

'Good morning, Louise. How do you feel?'

Louise looked up from her notebook. 'Better. How are you?' replied Louise.

Harold stepped into the hospital room and carefully closed the door. Louise was unused to seeing her father with white hair. For over a decade she had remembered him with dark brown. His hair was cut like a British army officer's. It had always been. Only now it was white. Harold, at only forty-nine, had a full head of white hair. Yes, his wife's death had turned his hair white.

Harold wondered what Louise now thought of him. Had she forgiven him? She had not said she had. And Harold didn't expect that she would. Harold really didn't want to be forgiven. What he had done to Louise was truly unforgivable. Louise had not shown her father any affection. Why would she? He was a stranger to her—a distant memory—and an unhappy and cruel one.

'I'm alright,' replied Harold. Only he wasn't.

Harold stood at the far end of Louise's hospital bed. Louise, in a white hospital gown and shrouded in white sheets, put down her note book.

'Please, have a seat.'

Harold sat down in one of the wooden chairs by the hospital bed.

'I'm studying for my exams. I'm going to take them in January. I'm transferring to another university. I've been accepted into Midlands-Hasegawa.'

Harold had never heard of the school. Why Louise wanted to transfer to an unknown university in the Midlands from a prestigious one in London was a mystery to him. Actually, everything Louise did was a mystery to Harold. Louise was practically a stranger to him too.

'You did very well academically at All Saints. I'm sure you will do well wherever you go. What are you studying?' asked her father.

Louise's father didn't even know what she was studying. He hadn't asked until this moment.

'Chemistry.'

'I studied Agriculture,' said Harold.

There was an awkward silence.

'Louise. After your mother passed away, I boxed up all of her things and took them to London. They have sat in a room in the house. Actually, your old bedroom, for the last ten years. Last night, I looked through the boxes of her clothes and found something I think your mother would like to you have.'

Louise felt a strange sadness welling up inside her while her father spoke. Yes, he had banished Louise along with all of her mother's possessions from the house in East Anglia.

Louise's father reached into his coat pocket and took out a slim, narrow leather case. What was it? A bracelet? A necklace? All that mattered to Louise was that it was something that had once belonged to his mother.

Harold held the small case out to her and Louise carefully grasped it. The narrow beige leather case was at once both cold and soft. Louise held it with both hands. This leather case had once been held by her mother. Louise opened the case; inside was a wrist watch. Louise placed the leather case on the white bedding and gently touched the silver cased watch. Louise felt an emotional spark when she touched the domed crystal. She carefully took the watch out of the case and held it up. The silver watch had a white dial, silver indices, and silver hands. The beige leather watch strap was somewhat worn. The watch was beautiful.

Louise tried to remember the watch on her mother's wrist. She couldn't. She had no memory of it. Louise turned the watch over and looked at the caseback. Engraved in the silver caseback was:

To Edith
Love, Harold.
1-10-1998

Louise carefully examined the watch. Yes. It had been her mother's. **It still was.** Louise carefully, gently, put the watch onto her wrist. She adjusted the leather strap. It fit perfectly. Louise caressed the leather watch strap. Yes, the watch fit her perfectly, almost spiritually. Yes, spiritually. Harold was right: Louise's mother would want her to have it. Louise looked up at her father. He was looking down at the floor.

'Thank you.'

Harold looked up. He nodded slightly. He didn't know what to say. What could he say?

'Louise…I found a photo of you and your mother in one of the boxes.'

Louise trembled at those words. All these years, and Louise had not had had a single photo of her mother. She had written and asked her father for a photo of her once while at All Saints; her father had completely ignored the request. The letter that followed was only a short note saying that he had paid school fees. How cruel. Yes, her father had been extremely cruel to her. Was that necessary? No. It wasn't. It was only cruel.

'I don't have any photos of my mother,' replied Louise quietly.

Harold took a small white envelope out of his coat pocket and handed it to Louise. Louise took it and opened the envelope carefully. She took out the precious photo. Trembling, she looked at the glossy image printed on the chemically sensitized paper. It was a picture of Louise and her mother taken just a month before her mother had passed away. How did Louise know that? Because it was Louise's eighth birthday party. Her mother had invited all of Louise's friends to the house in East Anglia. There had been cake, paper hats, decorations, and birthday cards and gifts. Louise's mother had given her a small teddy bear. Louise had taken it with her to her aunt's house when her father sent her away. Louise had loved that small bear because her mother had given it to her. One day, when Louise returned from boarding school, it was missing. Her aunt told her matter-of-factly that she had thrown it out. Louise was too old for toys. Louise had been devastated. How could her aunt do something like that? It was Louise's last physical connection to her mother. The teddy bear occupied a small place on a shelf in Louise's room. There was no need to throw it out. Louise cried for weeks afterwards. It was just one more act of cruelty directed at Louise, the unwanted little girl. Tears welled up in Louise's eyes as she studied the photo. Louise now looked just like her mother. Well, she had always looked just her mother. In the photo, Louise's mother held her smiling daughter's hand. Louise's other hand held the small teddy bear. Louise's mother, in a white blouse and navy blue cotton trousers, was beautiful, pure, and angelic. Louise felt a tightening in her throat. And there, on her mother's slender wrist, was the silver watch.

'That teddy bear. Mummy gave it to me for my birthday,' said Louise as she studied the photo.

'I'll look for it your room at home. I'll bring it to you the next time I visit you,' replied her father.

Aunt Eleanor—your sister—threw it out while I was away at boarding school. I was ten years old. It was all I had left of Mummy. And your sister threw it out,' said Louise quietly.

Harold felt a shock run through him. How could Eleanor—his own sister—be so cruel? But of course, she was. Harold had been cruel to Louise too. Louise had become an unwanted burden upon her mother's death. Harold's sister had never liked Edith; Eleanor had never approved of the marriage. Harold's sister had not wanted Louise either, and she had horribly mistreated the tiny, young, and fragile Louise. But so had he. Harold should have protected Louise, but he had not. Now it was Harold's turn to tremble.

Louise suddenly felt sorry for her father. Yes, **he had grievously wounded her**, but he was trying to make amends. Her father was trying. He was trying. There was a part of Louise that wanted to scream at her father for what he had done to her; what he had put her through, and the situations he had put her in, but, at that moment, she felt only pity for him. Louise realized at that moment, that her father would never be able to regain his place in her life as her father. Too much had happened. Louise had suffered too much. Yes, her father was filled with remorse and regret. But it wouldn't be enough to make up for what Louise had endured for most of her life. Louise's gaze met her father's, and at that moment, he knew that he had lost his place in Louise's heart forever.

Louise's father lowered his gaze back to the floor of the hospital room. The white vinyl floor tiles looked like part of a chess board. A chess board made up of only white squares. Yes, you have lost her, Harold. Deservedly so. But still, Louise was his daughter, and he loved her. It was too late now.

This feeling that was now washing over him was horrible. It was all his fault. Yes, accept what you have done, Harold. Accept that you have injured and damaged your daughter. Is it any wonder now that she looks at you in a cold and distant light?

Louise momentarily looked at her watch and noticed a small detail. The watch wasn't ticking.

'I'll buy a battery for it as soon as possible. I'm going to wear this watch for the rest of my life,' said Louise quietly.

Louise's father looked up, but without meeting Louise's gaze.

'I'll go across the street and get you a battery. There is a jewelry store. I'm sure they have some,' said Harold quietly.

'Thank you.'

'I'll go buy some right now. I want you to have it for the trip to Midlands-Hasegawa,' said Harold.

Harold stood up, adjusted his coat, and walked out the room. He closed the door behind him quietly as he left.

Gemma—An Invisible Fear—The Private Railway Carriage

LONDON
A gentle knock on the door of the hotel room alerted Jubal Wyatt that Gemma had arrived. Yes, she had telephoned him from downstairs a moment before. Now, after two decades, they would meet again.

Jubal stood up from the edge of the large bed in the large, rather posh, hotel room that Gemma had reserved (and paid for). He walked across the room and opened the door.

And there stood Gemma. As beautiful as he remembered her: glossy brown hair and bangs which sometimes partially concealed her blue eyes—only older. Gemma flashed her white smile; the same smile she had had at Oxford when he had met her at twenty (or was it nineteen?). Only now Gemma was forty-one.

Jubal Wyatt was boyishly handsome at forty-five. His brown hair glinted in the morning light with flashes of silver (like Gemma's). He was still slender and physically fit. And suddenly Gemma felt an emotion she had not expected: love. Yes, Gemma loved her friend Jubal. She loved him for his kindness, his patience, and his understanding. Gemma stepped forward, and in a highly unusual gesture that surprised Wyatt, she hugged him.

'It's good to see you, Gemma,' said Jubal in his Southern drawl.

'It's good to see you, too, Jubal. How was the flight?'

'Excellent. Really. I've never flown First Class before.'

'You can thank Enoch for that. He wanted you to be comfortable.'

'I'm sorry I couldn't bring Ian along, but he had to stay stateside with his family. His mother is rather frail.'

'I understand. Please tell him that I hope to see him at the wedding. Yes, you are both invited as soon as we finalize the date. The wedding will be in June.'

THE HOSPITAL

Louise, in a white waffle patterned bathrobe (a gift from Gemma), stood in the small white tiled bathroom adjoining to her hospital room. She was standing before the mirror above the sink. Louise studied the reflection that was illuminated by the florescent light of the small bathroom. Louise had taken a hot shower and shampooed her hair. Louise's damp hair reminded her of the day, three and half years earlier, when Freya had cut and styled her long strawberry blonde hair into a short chin length bob at All Saints. Louise, at nineteen, was poised to move on to a new phase of her life. Two weeks from now, she would sit for exams at her university in London. A week later, she would enter (the thankfully forgotten) Midlands-Hasegawa

University.

The image that stared back at Louise was diminutive, slender (alright, rather skinny), and cute. **Dangerously cute.** Louise turned her head to one side and then the other. Yes, she looked just like her mother.

'Mummy, I love you,' said Louise into the mirror. 'I miss you every day. I feel your presence sometimes, but even when I don't, I know you are here with me. I know you are here. I promise to be strong. I will never forget you. I love you, Mummy. When I visit your grave, I will bring you lavenders. I remember you liked them. Aunt Poppy likes them too. I will bring Freya with me the next time I visit. I would like you to meet her.'

MARBLE ARCH

'Yes, that's right. There will be seven of us…Yes, Mr Wyatt will have his own cabin…Yes. Have the girls prepare meals for the security team. Three will travel with us. Four more will meet at the station in the Midlands…Yes. It's a small town, a village really…I have never been there. The security team told me there is only one grocery store…Yes. That's right…Yes. The security team will ride up in the dining car…Yes, Alright…Thank you.'

Enoch tapped the luminescent screen of his smartphone. Everything was set for the railway journey to Midlands-Hasegawa. Enoch was excited about the visit to Muddy Hills. Yes, he was part of the group. He had been accepted into Gemma's close circle of friends. And he wanted to attend the play too.

Enoch was standing in the drawing room of his house in Marble Arch. The hardwood floor Enoch stood on was partially covered by a large Persian rug filled with intricate patterns of indigo blue, apricot orange, ivory white, madder red, and madder red edging (which was covered in elaborate ivory white Persian calligraphy). The high-ceilinged room around him was filled with white Mid-Century Modern furniture; all housed in a collection of white walls and under a white plaster Georgian ceiling. Enoch had selected some of the furniture himself. The rest was purchased by an interior decorator; one of London's most celebrated.

The 19th century oil painting of the ruins of Karnak was one that Enoch had purchased himself at auction. It hung over the mantel of the ornate white limestone fireplace.

The drawing room was filled with a silvery and wintery grey natural light.

Near the window was an extremely rare white plaster bust of Major General Lionel Charles 'Stalky' Dunsterville, CB, CSI on a small highly polish burl wood table.

In a book shelf that almost reached the ceiling of the drawing room stood several sterling silver (Asprey) framed photos: one of a teenage Enoch at Harrow; one of his late father in white tie and tails when Enoch's father had been only 23; a photo of his mother when she was sixteen, and one of Enoch in Cricket whites at Harrow. And there were books, an ocean of books, mostly history.

With the exception of the oil painting and the plaster bust, everything in the room was new, including the Persian rug.

In a few hours, they would arrive at Midlands-Hasegawa University. He wasn't sure exactly what would happen next. He knew that Freya would want to see Louise immediately. Enoch planned to walk around the small town and tour the university with Gemma and whoever else wanted to go with them.

He was looking forward to seeing The Ptolemies; this time as a member of the audience. Could the undergraduates of Midlands-Hasegawa recapture the energy of that night at Oxford? Enoch wondered a lot about that. That night with Gemma had changed everything. Enoch wondered who would be playing Cleopatra's brother Ptolemy.

Enoch was also looking forward to seeing Jubal Wyatt again. The Virginian was easily Enoch's favorite American. In 1998, a young Jubal Wyatt had directed them in a play that he had penned himself. And, as Jubal Wyatt had said in numerous interviews over the years, the performance of the two young actors in the final scene had been electric, bordering on the supernatural, and had made the play a critical success. The play had won Jubal a number of awards. It had, without a doubt, launched his career. And more than that, Jubal Wyatt was a true friend. The American, Jubal Wyatt, had encouraged Enoch in his acting. Why had Enoch allowed one English theatre director to derail him so completely?

'Are we ready?' asked Gemma happily.

Enoch, in a white dress shirt, blue blazer, and a pair of cotton khaki trousers (the same ones he had purchased that weekend with Gemma at Oxford University last summer), turned around. Gemma, in the same white cotton blouse and khaki trousers that she had purchased that same weekend, stood before him. She was also wearing her blue quilted Burberry jacket and her red, blue, and purple All Saints scarf. And yes, Gemma was beautiful.

Enoch smiled.

'Yes, I'm set. And the railway carriage is on schedule to be attached to the next train to the Midlands,' replied Enoch.

Gemma exhaled. 'Yes, this will be a fantastic weekend. I'm glad that Louise can attend the play. I worry about Louise, but this is important to her. And Freya has been so upset. Seeing Louise again will help calm her nerves. And, I am curious how they will perform The Ptolemies. I'm sure you are too.'

'Yes, I am very curious, Gemma. Oh, where will Jubal meet us?'

'At the station. He had to meet someone this morning. Something about the possibility of one of his plays being performed in the West End next summer. I hope it works out for him.'

'Yes, I would like to watch one of his plays in the West End. And I would like to meet Ian.'

'We'll meet him at the wedding.'

There was a knock on the large glossy white door of the drawing room in Mayfair.

'Yes, come in,' said Enoch.

''We're ready to take you to the train station, Mr Tara,' said a tall and athletic young man in a black suit, white dress shirt, and black necktie.

'Thank you. We'll be there in a minute.'

THE TRAIN STATION
The two glossy dark blue railway carriages were attached to the far end of the British Railways train heading north. Three members of the security detail, in black suits, white shirts, and black silk neck ties, stood on the train station platform, their breath materializing around them in the cold air. Yes, it was December, and it was freezing cold.

Onboard the second private railway carriage (the dining car), the two girls from Sussex, in black uniforms (with starched white collars and white cotton gloves), were busily making last minute cabin checks. A lone member of the security team looked around the dining car that was in front of the private railway carriage. Yes, the glossy burlwood interior of the dining car looked like a railway coach that would have been attached to a steam locomotive of the Orient Express in the 1920s, but with a few telltale modern touches. The tables had been set with white table clothes, but not silverware and bone china. That would happen after the train had departed. And the locomotive that pulled the railway coaches now was a dark blue Class 68 diesel-electric.

THE HOSPITAL
'Did you remember to pack my All Saints scarf?' asked Louise.

'Yes, it is in the top pouch of your suitcase,' replied Aurelia.

Louise looked in the cotton pouch which lined the top of her brown leather box suitcase. Ah, there it is! Louise carefully took out the blue, red, and purple All Saints scarf which Aurelia had thoughtfully wrapped in white tissue paper before placing in Louise's suitcase. Louise unwrapped it carefully and then wrapped it around her neck and shoulders. Louise, in a pair of faded blue jeans, a white cotton blouse (with a large collar), and a navy blue cashmere wool cape with a mink collar, carefully buttoned the tortoise shell buttons of the cape. Louise looked *quite smart*. Louise was now almost ready to leave the hospital for the train station.

But not quite.

'Louise, please put on the fur cap. It's freezing outside. And cold weather dangerous for someone who has had a stroke.'

Louise looked over at Aurelia. Yes, Aurelia cared about her. Louise smiled.

'Alright. Of course, you are right.'

Louise unwrapped the fur cap from the white tissue paper it was wrapped in in her suitcase. She held it aloft. It was mink. A bespoke gift from Violet, Freya's mother. It had been made by Vahtra, the outfitters owned by Külli Vathra. Yes, this beautifully made garment always made Louise feel loved by the Maud family. Yes, the Maud's were her family. Violet had telephoned and told her so a few days ago. Louise carefully put the fur cap on and adjusted it. She turned to face Aurelia.

'How do I look?'

'*Quite* posh, *yah*!' said Aurelia in her Singlish accented Sloaney intonation.

Louise smiled. 'Yes, you are a Sloane Ranger in the making, Aurelia.'

There was gentle knock at the door. The girls looked over and could see the diminutive Gemma standing outside the window.

'Come in, Gemma,' said Louise happily.

The door opened and Gemma and Enoch appeared in the large open doorway. Yes, Enoch was youthful and handsome. And Gemma, as beautiful as ever.

'We have a train to catch, girls. Are you ready?' asked Gemma.

'Yes!' said Louise excitedly. 'I have been extremely well taken care of here, but I am ready to go.'

'The world awaits you, Louise,' said Gemma happily.

'Have you had breakfast?' asked Enoch.

'I had some toast and a piece of bacon. I was too excited to have breakfast this morning,' chirped Louise.

'Well, not to worry. Lunch will be served on the train. I've ordered sandwiches with slices of turkey, avocado, and barbecue sauce, just for you, Louise,' said Enoch and he smiled.

'Oh, thank you, Enoch,' said Louise. 'You're really sweet.'

And Enoch smiled.

THE TRAIN PLATFORM

Louise looked at her watch. It had stopped at 3:32 a decade ago. No, Louise's father had gone out to buy batteries and not returned. Perhaps his feelings were too hurt to return to the hospital? Louise looked at her smartphone: 10:01am.

The train platform was crowded with passengers. But not at the far end where the small party had gathered for Muddy Hills. No, this end of the train platform was only for the passengers of the two private rail carriages.

'It's going to snow a little on the way up, but it should stop before we arrive,' said Gemma.

'That means Muddy Hills will be covered in a fresh layer of snow,' said

Aurelia and she flashed her white Californian-like smile. Aurelia, in a pair of faded denim jeans, a white cotton blouse, and a navy blue parka, boarded the train.

'The luggage is already in the cabins, Mr Tara,' said a young woman in a black wool top (over a white cotton blouse with a large white collar), a black wool skirt, and black patent leather flats. She also wore white cotton gloves.

'Thank you, Miss Smith,' replied Enoch politely.

The young housemaid nodded slightly and then turned and walked down the platform towards the dining car.

Gemma and Enoch stood on the platform next to Louise. Gemma was waiting for, oh, wait, there they are!

The dark haired Külli, at nearly six feet tall, physically fit, and strikingly beautiful, approached with Octavia; who could easily pass as Gemma's younger sister. (Hey, I'm not that much older! Okay. Sorry, Gemma. You're right.) …with Octavia who could easily pass as Gemma's twin sister. (Much better. Thank you.) Külli, clad in a pair of faded blue jeans, a white cotton blouse, and a heavy, cable knit beige sweater, walked towards the group waiting on the platform. Külli was also wearing her red, blue, and purple All Saints scarf.

'Gula, I was afraid you two would miss the train,' said Gemma.

'We did too, Gem. We got stuck in traffic. We paid the cab driver and walked the rest of the way to the station. It's a good thing we didn't bring much luggage,' said Külli while holding up a single leather box suitcase.

'It's only day trip, so we packed everything in one suitcase,' said Octavia. Octavia, beautiful, and still in her twenties, glowed with youth and vivacity. Her brown hair was worn in a large single braid down her back, her blue eyes partially hidden by her glossy brown bangs. Octavia, in a pair of faded denim jeans, a pale blue cotton blouse, and blue quilted jacket, smiled.

'Please, let me have your suitcase, ma'am,' said one of the members of Enoch's security detail.

Külli handed the leather box suitcase to the young man and said, 'Thank you.'

'It's alright. You arrived with ten minutes to spare,' said Enoch and he smiled. Külli and Octavia boarded the train. Gemma followed them up the metal steps.

And then Jubal Wyatt appeared carrying an aluminum suitcase and an orange leather gym bag. Jubal, in pair of blue jeans, white button-down dress shirt, and blue blazer, looked cold. Enoch was surprised by Jubal's youthful appearance. Jubal extended his hand when he reached Enoch.

'Good to see you, Enoch.'

'It's good to see you, too. You look great.'

'I was about to say the same of you,' replied Jubal with a handsome smile.

'You're freezing, Jubal. I'll talk with you on train. We're serving mushroom soup and sandwiches for lunch. I hope you like turkey and barbecue sauce.'

'My favorites,' replied Jubal happily.

One of the security men took Jubal's suitcase and gym bag and boarded the train. Jubal followed.

The platform was now practically empty, save for two uniformed British Railways conductors. Louise scanned the station for any sign of her father. There was no sign of him. Yes, wounded, he had retreated. Louise sighed.

Now it was only Enoch and Louise (plus two of the security detail) on the platform.

'Are you ready to board, Louise?' asked Enoch.

'Yes.'

Enoch took a few steps and then waited on the platform for Louise to board before him. Louise turned and then she heard a voice.

'Louise!' barked a masculine voice across the platform. Louise turned back and could see her tall, white-haired father, clad in a dark grey wool overcoat, black suit, white shirt, and a silver necktie, walking towards her down the platform. The leaden winter sky cast her father in a greyish light. Louise's father was handsome, in a soldierly way.

Enoch nodded to the two menacing looking security men flanking him. He boarded the glossy dark blue rail carriage car, the two other men turned and walked towards the dining car. Louise, in the blue cashmere wool cape and faded blue jeans, waited alone on the station platform alone.

I'm glad I caught you before you left,' said Louise's father. The store across the street was didn't have any watch batteries. Nor did the other store. I caught a black cab and went to a local supermarket. They didn't have any either. Well, eventually I found a store that did. When I returned to the hospital, you had already left. I was afraid I wouldn't reach you in time.'

Louise's father held out a pack of watch batteries encased in plastic and thin cardboard in his gloved hand. Louise reached out her soft hand and grasped the batteries.

Thank you.'

Harold nodded slightly. 'Well, I hope you have a nice time up north with your friends, Louise.'

'Thank you.'

A whistle blew. The train would leave in five minutes.

'You'd best board now. I'll see you at Christmas in Mayfair when you return,' said Louise's father.

Louise turned and started to walk towards the private rail carriage. Harold turned, and ramrod straight, walked back down the platform, completely defeated.

Louise stopped just before she boarded the train. And then she burst into a run. She ran after her father; within a few seconds she was upon him. She grabbed his hand.

'I know you are trying. I know that, Father. I know that. Thank you. I will see you in a couple of days. Alright?' said Louise, her voice breaking with emotion.

Harold could suddenly feel the cold air enveloping him. Harold was alive again. Louise, his only child, his horribly neglected child, still felt something for him. Something. Louise stretched out her arms and Harold bent down to receive her. She hugged him. Harold hugged her back. There was hope. Still hope. When they parted Louise was crying. Harold tried not to. He tried not to.

'I'm sorry, Louise. I'm sorry.'

'Father, please don't be upset. I don't want to hurt you. We have both been hurt. Please, just wait for me. Let's try together, alright?'

'Thank you, Louise.'

The whistle sounded.

'I have to go,' said Louise.

Louise then turned and sprinted down the platform. She boarded the train with a mere minute to spare.

THE PRIVATE RAIL CARRIAGE
As she made her way down the corridor of the private rail carriage, Louise, out of breath, suddenly felt like her mind was wobbling in her head—a side effect of the stroke. Louise placed one hand against the polished burl wood interior. Her mind felt rubbery. What a strange feeling. Okay. Take it easy, Louise. Give yourself a chance to heal. Just walk everywhere for the time being. Louise couldn't really say she felt dizzy; this was not dizziness. It was something else. Louise carefully slid open the door of her private cabin, she entered, and carefully closed the door behind her.

THE TRAIN STATION
Harold Algernon Percival waited on the platform of the train station and watched the train disappear into the wintery morning gloom.

THE LAKE DISTRICT
'Yes, well, I think we should go now. The railcar has already been attached. British Railways will not wait for us,' said Hugh as he looked at his platinum wristwatch while standing in the drawing room.

Violet, Poppy, Brian, the baron and baroness were all seated in the purple velvet Art Deco sofa and chairs in the drawing room. Hugh stood by the fireplace. Hugh, tall and powerfully built and wearing a pair of dark grey wool trousers, a white dress shirt (with a St James collar), a dark blue, grey, and red tartan necktie, a dark blue blazer, black leather belt, and a pair of black Chelsea boots, cut a dashing figure standing in the orange glow of the fireplace. The blond Hugh, though rather average in appearance, was physically fit, extremely intelligent, and kind. And Violet loved him.

'Yes', said the baron looking at his watch. I hope you enjoy the visit to Midlands-Hasegawa. Please tell Louise that the family wish her health and happiness. I hope she will feel well enough to visit us this Christmas holiday. But, only if she is well enough.'

'Yes, Father. I know Louise wants to visit. The doctors will have the final say. I worry about her too. We all do,' said Poppy.

'I will see you all later tonight night when you return,' said the 12th Baron happily.

THE PRIVATE RAILCAR

The cobalt blue railway car rumbled south. The glossy exterior of the family's private railway carriage reflected the varying hues of the grey and white natural light of winter and white snow which blanketed the landscape.

The trip to Midlands-Hasegawa would take just over an hour.

The four passengers all sat in the last train compartment, a standard railway cabin with single berths (upholstered in dove beige Conolly leather) and polished burl wood walls. One side of the compartment hosted a large window. This morning the passengers were content to lean back in the soft leather and watch the wintery scenery unfold outside as the train moved south. Violet and Hugh sat on one side of the compartment; Poppy and Brian the other.

'Where are we going to meet Gemma and the others?' asked Poppy.

'Gemma and the others are scheduled to arrive at the train station about twenty-five minutes before us. We are supposed to meet them at Midlands-Hasegawa—somewhere,' replied Violet happily.

'It will be good to see everyone again. I miss everyone,' said Poppy.

Gemma—An Invisible Fear—The New Ptolemies

MIDLANDS-HASEGAWA UNIVERSITY

An icy white ocean of snow had enveloped the entirety of 'Muddy Hills'. The overcast sky above, a mixture of dark and light grey clouds with wisps of white in between, was in stark contrast to the snow draped frozen earth below.

Freya and Jinx, both in knee length wool overcoats (Freya's was dark blue and had a light brown fur collar; Jinx wore an unadorned iron grey one), stood outside the front gate of the university. The ornate stone Edwardian gate of ~~Rhodes~~ Midlands-Hasegawa University was an impressive structure.

Years of neglect had made it appear medieval, even though it had only been constructed in 1903. The weathered wooden gates stood wide open.

Today, the end of the Michaelmas Term, meant the school play and an open house that allowed parents and other family and friends to visit the undergraduates and explore the university's stone cloisters, Victorian and Edwardian buildings, and (now the snow covered) grass quads. In winter, that usually meant only the family and friends of the two-hundred or so native British students who attended the overwhelmingly Asian university.

It was a cold and overcast day at the university. A dozen or so people passed through the gates, snow crunching underfoot, every few minutes while the two girls waited at the entrance to Muddy Hills.

Freya glanced over at the raven-haired Jinx. Her glossy black hair had been cut into a short, chin length bob. Yes, Jane's perfect profile silhouetted against the grey stone of the gate made her appear as a cameo portrait. Yes, Jinx was beautiful, a classic occidental beauty. Jinx (or Jane) was now viewed in a different light by almost everyone since her fashion show in Tokyo, the release of her first film, and her appearance in Japanese and Taiwanese magazines that many of the Asian undergraduates now read at the university. Jinx's celebrity, though minor, was rapidly growing. Freya wasn't jealous. She was happy for Jinx. She was also happy that Jinx had found Rex. Freya still viewed Jinx in the same light as before. Only now, Freya had become more protective of her.

'Look!' said Jinx. 'It must be them.'

Three glossy 2019 Range Rovers, two blue, one black, were slowly making their way down the narrow snowy street towards the front gate of the school. Yes, Louise would be inside one of the vehicles heading towards them. It had been two months since Louise and Aurelia had driven away from the Palladian country house in Northumberland.

Yes. Enoch Tara had arranged everything. A year ago, it would have been Gemma driving Louise to Muddy Hills in her white Peugeot hatchback; however, a year later, the situation had changed.

The three SUVs slowed as they approached the gate; the first Range Rover turned off and parked in front of the local cinema. The other two followed. The doors of the SUVs started opening. And from one of the blue SUVs appeared Louise—all 5'1" of her. Louise was wrapped in her navy blue cashmere wool cape, her strawberry blonde hair poking out from the edges of the mink hood. Louise smiled brightly. Freya felt her heart skip a beat. Freya looked both ways and then crossed the street; at first, she walked slowly, and then her pace picked up. Freya, at 5'9" inches was a giant compared to Louise. Louise, gentle, sweet, good hearted, kind, and fragile, opened her arms to receive Freya, her dearest friend in the world. Freya hugged Louise; the moment of contact was electric.

'I love you, Louise,' said Freya quietly into her ear.

'I love you, too, Freya.'

'Are you *really* alright?' asked Freya, her voice breaking with emotion.

The two friends hugged for a moment more and then Louise said, 'Yes. I'm alright, and I will be alright, Freya. We have our lives ahead of us. Do you really think I would abandon you now?'

'No. Never,' replied Freya quietly.

'It's good to see you, Louise,' said Jinx.

'Jinx. It's good to see you, too. I missed you. I want to hear about Japan,' said Louise happily.

Jinx then hugged Louise.

'Godmother, thank you so much for coming,' said Freya as she looked up and saw Gemma standing next to the glossy blue Range Rover. Gemma smiled; the bright and happy smile that Gemma had had at All Saints all those decades ago. 'I love you, Godmother. I have missed you too.'

'All is well, Freya. I am here. And I have brought a friend from America.'

Freya froze. Jubal Wyatt? ***The* Jubal Wyatt is actually here?** Of course, Freya knew he was coming, but the reality of it was nebulas at best until that very moment. Jubal Wyatt is here!

Jubal, in dark khaki trousers, a white button-down Oxford dress shirt, a dark grey silk necktie, and a blue blazer, stepped forward and flashed a handsome smile which seemingly melted all of the snow around them. Slim and fit, handsome in a very America way, subtly handsome in a uniquely Southern way, Jubal, a Virginian, looked like a film star. Jubal must have been in his mid-forties, at least, but looking at him one would never guess anything past thirty-five. Youthful and gentlemanly, Jubal bowed slightly.

'It's nice to meet you, Freya. I've heard a lot about you from Gemma. And I am looking forward to seeing you perform in my play.'

Freya smiled. And said nothing.

Gemma saved her (but Gemma always saved her) and said, 'Jubal, I'd like to introduce you to Jane Clarence. She's playing Arsinoë.'

Jubal smiled and said, 'Such a beautiful actress. I have always been blessed with beautiful actresses.'

Jinx blushed.

'Please, call me Jinx, Mr Wyatt.'

'Alright, well then, please call me Jubal,' he replied and Jubal Wyatt smiled.

'Alright, so who is playing Ptolemy?' asked Enoch who was clad in a blue blazer, dark khaki cotton trousers, and a red and blue tartan tie.

Freya and Jinx both looked in Enoch's direction. 'Yes, Jubal is right. He has always been blessed with beautiful actors,' said Freya happily.

Now it was Enoch's turn to blush.

'Ah, you're blushing!' said Louise happily.

And everybody laughed.

Aurelia, Külli, and Octavia had climbed out of the third SUV and now appeared on the pavement next to the blue Range Rover.

'I can't believe everyone is here. Thank you all for coming. Now I'm nervous,' said Freya and she smiled.

Külli, towering above everyone at nearly six feet in height, smiled and said, 'I wouldn't miss your theatrical debut for the world, girls.'

'Thank you for coming all this way,' said Freya.

'Yes, thank you for coming, Külli. It's nice to have you and Octavia here, with us, at Muddy Hills,' said Jinx happily.

The Singapore born Aurelia, blonde and blue-eyed, appeared, her form outlined in the greyness of a wintery day. She smiled.

'It's good to see you, Aurelia,' said Jinx. 'Finally, we get to show you around Muddy Hills.'

'You have no idea how much I am looking forward to moving into the alcove with you,' said Aurelia happily.

'Yes, and from our alcove, we shall absolutely rule Muddy Hills,' said Jinx and she smiled.

'As we did at All Saints from our alcove,' said Külli.

'Did we?' asked Gemma.

'Yes. *Rather.* Only you were so *terribly* popular and beautiful as not to notice,

Gem,' replied Külli in her Sloaney intonation.

'There will be five of us in the alcove, Louise,' said Freya. 'I'll explain everything later.'

'Octavia, thank you for coming,' said Jinx as a cold gust of wind chilled everyone to the bone.

'Thank you for inviting me,' replied Octavia.

Jinx could not help but notice how similar Gemma and Octavia were in appearance standing next to each other; only at 5'7", Octavia was much taller than Gemma who stood only 5'3" (at best).

'Let's get everyone out of the cold. Please, come with me. I'll take you to the dining hall. The school is serving refreshments,' said Freya.

'Let's take the cars, shall we?' said Enoch.

'Can we all fit?' asked Freya.

'Of course,' said Enoch.

THE DINING HALL

The large Portland stone dining hall was filled with the pale grey natural light of an overcast winter's day which poured in through the large pane glass windows. The giant, gilt framed portrait of the empire builder, Cecil Rhodes, loomed over the entire cavernous hall. Long wooden tables and chairs, relics of an imperial age, had been carefully lined up for the visiting guests. White table clothes covered every table. At both ends of the dining hall were wooden tables, each covered with a white table cloth and large silver Edwardian punch bowls. There was a silver ladle for each servant (in a black uniform with white collars and cuffs and white cotton gloves) who poured refreshments into a glass for every guest who approached. Hardly grand, but nice enough.

The large hall was half filled. Most of the people seated at the tables were native British students and their family and friends. A few Asian parents were also visiting, but not many. Yes, now that the morning chapel service and assembly were over, there was the option to leave the university for the holidays; attending the school plays was optional. Most of the undergraduates, however, usually did chose to attend the school play.

The twenty-nine-year-old Octavia, clad in a pair of dark blue wool trousers, a white cotton blouse (with open cuffs) and beige v-neck sweater, surveyed the aging dining hall around her. Yes, the hall was still impressive, if a bit neglected. A fresh coat of varnish, some silver polish, and a fresh coat (or two) of white paint would be enough to restore it. Octavia, her long glossy brown hair in a single braid down her back, smiled.

'Midlands-Hasegawa is a beautiful school,' said Octavia.

'Yes, I think so, too,' replied Jinx happily. 'This is not just a university; it is a fortress of free thought and tradition.'

Octavia, her smooth complexion illuminated in the wintery grey natural light, smiled. 'From what you have said, Muddy Hills is like the lost city of Atlantis. I'm happy that places like this still exist in England.'

'This is what Oxford was like when I was an undergraduate in the 90s,' said the dark haired Külli, who was wearing a pair of dark grey wool trousers, a white cotton blouse, and a thick beige cable knit sweater with raglan shoulders and dramatic sleeves full of thin knit cables. Külli's platinum wristwatch flashed every time she waved her hand or tapped on her smartphone.

Jubal, at the opposite end of the long table, smiled as he spoke with Gemma, Enoch, Louise, and Freya.

'I remember the first time I saw Gemma at Oxford. I couldn't believe my eyes. Gemma was easily the most beautiful girl I had ever seen.'

(Hearing this, Gemma blushed.)

'She was standing on stage at the Oxford playhouse. She was reading for a part in the play. Gemma was reading for one of the smaller parts. I realized after a few minutes that Gemma was a natural. So, I asked her to read from Scene I Act II. When Gemma turned to the page and realized it was Cleopatra's speech to the Macedonian nobles, she just looked up at me and froze.'

'I remember that. I was standing in the wings. That was the first time I had seen Gemma too,' said Enoch.

'You had no idea how shocked I was,' said Gemma. 'I had never acted in a play before. It was Violet that had encouraged me to try out for the role of Cleopatra. I never actually thought I would get it. I was hoping that I would be good enough to get a small part in the production.'

'It was obvious that Gemma had studied that speech because she lowered the script to her side and began to speak. Yes, it was Cleopatra speaking to me that afternoon. Such a crystal clear and beautiful voice, I had never heard. Regal and posh. Yes, I knew thirty seconds into that monologue that I had found my Cleopatra,' said Jubal in his Virginian drawl.

Gemma, shrouded in a white Egyptian cotton blouse (with a large collar), pressed her chin against her chest, and tilted her eyes upward. Gemma, as deliciously beautiful as ever, smiled.

Freya almost gasped. This was a revelation to her. So, this is what Gemma was like when she was younger? Shock and awe set in. Gemma was a natural beauty, but she had the easy ability to amplify it whenever she wanted. *Amazing.* Freya could not help but stare. **The look** had not been wasted on either man seated across from Gemma. Yes, she still had **it**. **It** was just under the surface, barely contained; waiting to be summoned.

Ping.

Freya's phone glowed momentarily. She picked up her smartphone and looked at it. 'It's Mummy. She's at the train station with Daddy. Poppy and Brian are with them.'

'I'll send the cars for them right now,' said Enoch.

'That's alright. Mummy said they are going to take the school shuttle from the station. But thank you, Enoch,' said Freya and she smiled.

'I wonder; could we visit the alcove today?' asked Aurelia.

'I don't know if visitors are allowed in the residence halls,' said Louise. Aurelia and Louise were seated in the middle of one of the long tables in the ornate dining hall. 'We can ask Freya and Jinx to show us the alcove room. Well, maybe not. They will be heading off to the theatre in a moment,' said Louise reflectively.

THE TRAIN STATION

Wallis, her eyes the same bluish grey of heron feathers, stood on the railway platform. The train from London had arrived. Her mother was somewhere on the platform. Wallis had tried calling her, but her mother had not answered. Oh, where could she be? Had she missed the train?

'Wallis. There you are,' said the 11th Baroness.

'Mummy. I was worried you had missed your train.'

The baroness, blonde, slender, and attractive, smiled. 'No, darling; I just forgot to bring my phone. I can't say that is such bad thing. It was nice to be free of distractions on the way up here.'

Wallis smiled and hugged her mother. 'I've missed you, Mummy. You have no idea. Four months has seemed like four years to me. Do I look different?'

The forty something, English baroness, in a knee length pike grey wool overcoat (with a black bear fur collar), and knee-high black leather boots, took one step back and studied her nineteen-year-old daughter's appearance. 'Yes, you look more beautiful than ever. I missed you, too, Wallis,' said the baroness in her posh and Sloaney intonation.

Mother and daughter hugged happily once more.

'Please, come with me, Mummy. I have some friends I would like you to meet. Oh, and I've invited Masako to spend the Christmas holidays with us.'

'How nice of you, Wallis. It will be *terribly* nice to have Masako spend Christmas with us,' said the baroness happily.

THE FRONT GATE

Wren, her honey blonde bangs partially obscuring her blue eyes, stood in front of the main gate of the university. She looked at her quartz wristwatch. Wren hoped they wouldn't be late. She wanted to watch the play with them. And as that thought crossed her mind, a glossy dark blue Riley automobile appeared off in the distance. The beautiful 1956 Riley Pathfinder looked brand new. The restored motorcar glided down the snowy cobblestone street. And behind the wheel was Wren's father, the 12th Baron and retired army major. And next to him was Wren's honey blonde Rhodesian mother. The car came to a complete stop at the gate; Wren opened one of the back doors of the Riley and climbed in.

'The car is beautiful,' said Wren as she settled into the new beige Connolly leather back seat.

'The garage does beautiful work,' said Wren's mother in a decidedly Rhodesian accent.

'Finally, everything is going well for us,' said Wren and she smiled.

THE DINING HALL

The Honourable Hugh Auden Maud, in a dark blue overcoat (with a light brown fur collar), and towering above the others, opened one of the double doors of the Portland stone dining hall, and a blast of cold air entered with Violet, Poppy, Hugh, and Brian.

Yes, the brand new white Toyota shuttle bus had taken them directly to the dining hall from the train station. It had only taken a few minutes. The town surrounding the university was quite small; more of a large village than a town really. The group made an impressive entrance, Poppy, Violet, Brian and Hugh in wool overcoats with fur collars, except for Brian, clad in a dark grey overcoat with a large thick black wool collar.

Freya stood up in the middle of the dining hall and smiled. The tall blonde Freya drew their attention immediately. The small party smiled. Yes, there she was. Louise also smiled as she stood to greet everyone. Louise was, once again, the center of attention.

'How are you, Louise?' asked Violet, her long, glossy, blonde hair shimmering in the silvery natural light of the dining hall.

'I'm doing well, Mrs Maud. And how are you?' asked Louise happily.

'I'm alright, if you are,' replied Violet.

'I'm quite alright, ma'am.'

Violet wanted to hug Louise right there, but decided against such a public display of affection.

'It's good to see you, Louise. Do you remember me? I haven't seen you in months,' said Poppy.

'Of course, I remember you,' replied Louise with a smile. 'It's good to see you, Poppy. You are more beautiful than ever. How are Arthur and Waverly?' asked Louise happily.

'Happy, healthy, and beautiful. I hope you will be able to meet them soon. I have brought some pictures of them with me.'

'I would love to see them,' said Louise and she smiled.

'We are looking forward to having you spend Christmas with us in Mayfair, Louise,' said Hugh, who towered over the tiny Louise. 'The chef is preparing thin crust pizza for you and Freya as we speak.'

Louise smiled and nodded slightly. 'Thank you, sir. I really appreciate you and the family inviting me and my father to spend Christmas with you.'

Hugh, deeply moved at Louise's sincere, gentle, and kind demeanor and words, smiled. Hugh wanted to hug little Louise, but he would wait until later.

'You're looking cuter than ever, Louise,' said Brian.

'**Dangerously cute**,' said Poppy impishly and Poppy smiled.

Louise blushed and smiled.

The new arrivals took their seats at the long table. Violet sat down opposite Freya; Hugh sat next to Enoch; Poppy next to Louise, and Brian next to Poppy. Freya and Jinx both excused themselves and went to get drinks for the new arrivals. It was while the girls were getting drinks that a nondescript man of medium build, age, and height approached the long table.

'Pardon me, but may I ask if you are Hugh Maud?'

Hugh, in suit and tie, looked up from the table and focused his gaze on the man standing before him in a grey suit, white dress shirt, and black silk necktie. Hugh slowly stood up. He nodded slightly in recognition.

'Howard? Is it you?' asked Hugh quietly.

'Yes. It's Howard. It's good to see you, Hughie.'

Hugh came around the end of the table and approached Howard, who spoke in a decidedly Rhodesian accent. Hugh, overcome by emotion, shook his hand strongly. 'Howard, I have thought of you often.'

'And I have thought of you, my dear friend.'

Hugh turned to the table and said, 'Everyone, this is Howard Jane. We attended boarding school together in Rhodesia. We grew up together. Howard is the best friend I've ever had.'

Howard, obviously moved, nodded slightly to everyone at the table.

The men all rose to greet Howard. After a round of introductions, Hugh invited Howard to sit with them at the table.

'I'm afraid I can't join you just yet. I have to meet my wife and daughter at the library in a few minutes. My daughter, Tasmin, is an undergraduate here. Please, my card. I live in Durham. We are going to watch The Ptolemies. We have to catch the train back to Durham immediately after the play,' said Howard.

Hugh took out his leather billfold and accepted Howard's card; Hugh then offered Howard one of his. Howard took it and said, 'Thank you, Hugh. It is fate that has reunited us.'

Hugh extended his hand and the two men shook hands once more.

'I pray fate will never separate us again, Howard. I live in London, when I am in England. My wife's family has a house in Northumberland. One way or the other, let us meet soon.'

'Yes. I would like to introduce you to my family. We have a lot of catching up to do.'

Howard nodded and departed, leaving through the main door and walking through the snow towards the large and imposing Rhodes Library.

Hugh, pale and visibly rattled, returned to his seat. It was at that moment that Freya and Jinx returned to the table with glasses of punch. Freya noticed the expression on her father's face and asked, 'Are you are right, Daddy? You look as if you've seen a ghost.'

Hugh looked at Freya and said quietly, 'I have.'

Freya arched an eyebrow; she then handed her father a glass of punch.

Freya then turned and handed her mother a glass. 'Here, Mummy. The punch is really *quite* good.'

'Thank you, Freya,' said Violet after Freya had handed her the glass.

The large double doors to the ornate dining hall opened and a cold gust of air entered with Wren and her parents. Yes, the 12th Baron and Baroness and the future 13th Baroness had arrived. Wren glowed with happiness. She had been reunited with her parents.

Freya turned toward her mother and said, 'That's Wren Talbot. The girl from Mercia that I told you about.'

Wren and her parents walked down the aisle between the long tables and stopped when they reached the party at long table in the center of the hall. A polite round of introductions followed. Wren's father, in coat and tie, handsome, well spoken, polite, and posh, cut an impressive figure. Wren's mother, beautiful, polite, and gloriously and unabashedly Rhodesian, charmed everyone. Freya's Rhodesian father, Hugh, (well, born of an English father and Rhodesian mother in Rhodesia), felt an immediate connection to Wren's mother. Yes, here, today, at the forgotten university, ~~Rhodes-~~Midlands-Hasegawa, being Rhodesian was a blessing, not a curse.

The Barons Talbot took their places at the table.

'I would like to introduce you to Louise Percival,' said Freya. Louise, this is Wren Talbot. She is going to be sharing the alcove with us next term.'

While everyone at the table continued to speak quietly with each other, Jinx looked at her smartphone.

Ping.

Finally, a text message from her mother.

We have just arrived, Jane. Sorry, we missed the connection. We are now waiting for the shuttle. I'm sorry we are late.

Jinx smiled and tapped out a response.

No worries, Mummy. I'm glad you are both here. I will be waiting for you in the dining hall. The shuttle will take you directly to it. I will introduce you to everyone when you arrive.

'My parents are here. I finally get to introduce you to them,' said Jinx happily to Freya, Louise, Aurelia, and Wren.

'It's always nice to meet other Rhodesians,' said Freya and she smiled.

'Would it be possible to visit the alcove room, Wren?' asked Aurelia.

'Yes, of course. The room is unoccupied. I'll take you over to the residence hall myself,' replied Wren happily. 'The room has a fireplace and four large windows. It also has a nice view of the entire school. The roof leaks—but only a little,' said Wren, and she smiled.

There was a burst of cold air and Jinx's parents entered the dining hall. Jinx looked in their direction. When she saw her parents, she smiled, stood up, and walked carefully behind the chairs and down the aisle to welcome her parents to Muddy Hills—the glorious Midlands-Hasegawa University.

'I would like to introduce you to my parents,' said Jinx happily. Jinx's father was around 5'10" and in his sixties. His brown hair was heavily flecked with the silver hair. He was rather plain looking, but had a nice smile. Jinx's slender mother, in her late fifties, was quite attractive. She had black hair and blue eyes. Yes, Jinx's had inherited her looks from her (Bulawayo born) mother. Jinx's parents smiled as they were introduced to everyone at the table.

And no, the Rhodesian accents did not go unnoticed.

Freya looked at her silver Cartier watch. 'I afraid we have to leave, Mummy. The play will start in ninety minutes.'

'Yes, Freya is right,' said Jinx to her mother. 'I will meet you in the lobby after the play.'

'Have you packed everything?' asked Jinx's father.

'Yes. My suitcases are in my room. We can come back and pick them up after the play,' replied Jinx.

Freya and Jinx both stood up—the men at the table all rose with them.

'Thank you, everyone, for coming to see us perform,' said Freya. 'This means a lot to us.'

'Yes, thank you,' said Jinx.

Freya and Jinx then both walked down the aisle between the long tables and exited the dining hall.

THE RHODES THEATRE

Freya and Jinx entered the front doors of the Portland stone theatre with a blast of cold air. Two members of the stage crew were walking through the lobby while Freya and Jinx stomped their Chelsea boots to shake off the snow. Freya checked her watch and then hurried into the main auditorium.

One of the doors to the theatre opened; another burst of cold air followed. 'Jinx, wait,' said a voice behind them. Jinx turned and saw Rex standing next to a tall, slender, and beautiful blonde woman that Rex bore much more than a passing resemblance to. 'I'd like to introduce you to my mother,' said Rex.

Jinx, caught completely off guard, stared blankly for a moment. Yes, Rex was making the effort to introduce his mother to her because Jinx meant something to him. Rex loved her. Jinx smiled.

'Hello, ma'am. It's nice to meet you. My name is Jane, but most people call me Jinx.'

Rex's mother smiled gently. 'It's nice to meet you, Jinx. Rex has told me a lot about you,' replied Rex's mother in a Rhodesian accent. Yes, Rhodesia was here again. And today, in a dilapidated theater at a forgotten university, in a forgotten town in England, Rhodesia shone once again. This nation of despised outcasts and refugees, now homeless and lost, had found a few small fragments of home. This was important. **This mattered**—at least to them.

Jinx stook a few steps forward, and then stopped in front of Rex and his mother. 'Thank you for making the effort to see me, ma'am. You have no idea how much this means to me.'

THE ALCOVE

Wren, her long glossy honey blonde entwined in her wool scarf and flowing down her back, led Louise and Aurelia to the girl's residence hall. The grey stone structure, shrouded in snow, glowed gently in the natural light of an overcast day.

The honey blonde Wren led them up the stone steps of the hall, snow crunching underfoot. The large double doors opened as they reached the top of the landing; two teenage Taiwanese undergraduates with long glossy black hair, in thin padded jackets and faded denim jeans, exited the hall. Both girls nodded and smiled in passing. The Inseparables returned the smiles and entered the Edwardian residence hall. White walls and hardwood floors gave way to a set of wooden stairs.

'Please, follow me,' said Wren as she walked up the stairs. Aurelia offered Louise her arm; Louise accepted, and the pair carefully climbed the worn wooden steps. The white walls of the hallway led to a single door at the end of a long hallway.

THE ALCOVE ROOM

The glossy white wooden door opened, and the girls entered the white walled room. The room was empty, save for four beds (with only blue and white striped mattresses on them), four wooden desks, four wooden chairs, and a stone fireplace. The large sash windows allowed natural light to fill the room. The hardwood floor creaked underfoot as they entered. The white walls reflected the natural light. The undecorated room looked rather spare and barren, but it held the promise of happy days with dear friends.

Louise smiled.

'Yes, this room is perfect. Could I have the bed near the window?' asked Louise.

'Of course,' said Aurelia and Wren simultaneously.

'I can't believe I am finally here,' said Louise. 'In a few weeks, the term will begin, and we will all be here together.'

'Yes. And having a fireplace means baked potatoes, baked beans, and warmth, even when the boilers are out,' said Wren happily.

'Do the undergraduates really cook in their fireplaces?' asked Aurelia.

'Well, we have since the boilers went out a few weeks ago. We baked potatoes in Suga's room. You'll meet her next term. She's really nice. My family cooks in fireplaces at our house in Mercia, but we always have. I don't know if undergraduates are allowed to cook in their fireplaces or not, but I don't think the occasional potato or a tin of baked beans will bother anyone. The boilers are working now, but if they go out again, we will have heat,' said Wren in her posh and Sloaney intonation, and she smiled.

Wren was an unknown quantity to Louise and Aurelia. Freya had said very little about her. That Freya had invited her to room with them in the alcove meant that Wren must be a good person. Wren, for all of her familiarity with Louise and Aurelia, was an absolute stranger. Wren didn't seem to know much about them either. Wren also seemed unaware that Louise had had a stroke just a week earlier. That wasn't Wren's fault. Freya must have decided to keep it between her and Jinx.

And the nineteen-year-old Wren was beautiful—*really beautiful.* Aurelia had noticed that immediately. Louise, overjoyed at the prospect of rooming with Freya again, had taken little notice of Wren. The posh honey blonde *Hon* from Mercia would be rooming with them. They would have plenty of time to get to know her. Aurelia, deeply worried about Louise, had little interest in asking Wren that many questions. To Aurelia, Wren was just one more Sloane Ranger she would have to adjust to; one more posh girl that Aurelia would marvel at; just one more girl that was beautiful when Aurelia was just plain.

'Does Muddy Hills have a kendo team?' asked Aurelia.

'I'm sure we do,' replied Wren.

'Thank you for showing us around, Wren,' said Louise politely.

'I hope we all become good friends. I really hope so,' said Wren quietly and sincerely.

Louise smiled. She could sense that Wren was sincere; that she wanted to be friends. Everyone needs a friend, and Wren was extending her hand in friendship. 'I'm sure we will be, Wren.'

And Wren smiled.

Gemma—An Invisible Fear—The Exiles

ACT IV
SCENE II
THE RHODES THEATRE
The large Portland stone Rhodes Theatre, with almost a thousand people in attendance, awaited the next scene of the play. Now, in Act IV, The Ptolemies was only one act from the end. The last ninety-minutes had been a triumph of youth and young voices. The cast of vivacious young undergraduates from ~~Rhodes~~ Midlands-Hasegawa had done very well. The performance, however, had not matched that night in Oxford in 1998. No, that spark had not yct appeared. It was about to.

The lights came up and there stood Arsinoë IV, the Macedonian former Queen and co-ruler of Ptolemaic Egypt with her brother Ptolemy XIII. The ill-fated Arsinoë IV was also the sister of Cleopatra VII. Having failed to secure her position on the throne and her brother, Pharoah Ptolemy XIII, having been killed in the Battle of the Nile, Arsinoë now found herself imprisoned in Alexandria.

Jinx—Jane Clarence—the young Rhodesian actress, her glossy jet-black hair shimmering in the bluish-white stage lights, was clad in a white linen skirt made up of elaborate folds and a white cotton top which clung to Jinx's every curve. Now striped of her pharaonic regalia and jewelry, Jinx appeared as a ghostly white figure shrouded in demi-darkness. Jinx also wore iron manacles around her slender wrists. Queen Arsinoë was now a prisoner of the Romans.

A Roman centurion, in full armor and with a helmet adorned with a crosswise comb horse's mantle, walked onto the stage. The young English actor playing the Roman officer was tall and muscular; he towered over Jinx.

ROMAN CENTURION: *I am here to take you to Rome. You will be paraded in a triumph.*

ARSINOE: *And after I have been completely humiliated, what will my fate be then?*

ROMAN CENTURION: *You will be exiled far away from Egypt. You will never see your homeland again.*

As the young English actor's words filled the theater, Jinx slowly bowed her head on stage. Tears filled her eyes. At that moment, a thousand memories flooded into Jinx's young mind: Rhodesia, the exile of her family, the brutal murder of her older brother in a farm invasion in Zimbabwe, and the unbelievable self-righteous scorn which awaited Rhodesian refugees across the world. Yes, here, in an audience with over a hundred Rhodesian exiles in attendance, emotions filled the young Rhodesian actress from Surrey. Jinx's demeanor suddenly changed. Jinx, tears streaking down her face, raised her head and looked out into the audience (who appeared only as an ocean of darkness) and spoke in a defiant, Rhodesian accented voice.

ARSINOE: *Never to see my homeland again? Never? How easy it is to say such words, when they do not apply to you, Centurion. Far away from Egypt. Never to see my homeland again. The humiliation of being dragged through the streets of Rome is but a trifle in comparison. Never to see my homeland again.* ***How cruel.***

ROMAN CENTURION: *Lord Antipater is dead. You will not share his fate. Your life has been spared by the Imperial Senate. That is a rare privilege for a defeated enemy of Rome.* ***I would not have been so kind.***

Jinx's voice trembled as she spoke. Her eyes remained fixed on the darkness which made up the audience just beyond the lights of the stage.

ARSINOE: *Lord Antipater is dead? Lord Antipater is dead. I would prefer that it was you who had decided my fate, Centurion. At least in death, I would be at peace. And in death, I could return to my homeland and be with my people—forever. Now, I have been condemned to exile. To be deprived of one's homeland is a far worse fate than death. One day, Roman, your nation will know the same fate, and the Romans, too, will be exiles; strangers in a strange land. Your nation will be ashes and memories.*

CENTURION: *You sound like a Carthaginian. They said such things, and yet, they are dust and Rome continues to grow stronger. Rome is of iron. Rome is eternal. Rome will never fall.*

ARISNOE: *One day, Rome too will fall. And you and your people will suffer my fate. Only then will you understand. Only then.*

Jinx then walked to the center of the stage; the lights dimmed, then a white spotlight tinged in blue illuminated her. Jinx, the Rhodesian exile, was starkly beautiful. The light cast long shadows behind her; the Roman centurion was left a shadowy form on the stage to her left. Jinx, tears filling her eyes, raised her manacled hands before and said in a clear and unshaking voice:

ARISNOE: *Only when you are an exile from your homeland, will you understand my fate.*

The audience sat spellbound by Jinx's words and movements. To the Rhodesians present, all was understood. Jinx was one of them. She spoke for all of them. Yes, they were exiles. None of them would ever see their homeland again. **The past is another country**, and Rhodesia now only existed in books and fading memories. Jinx's heartfelt words reverberated throughout the theater.

Lara Hasegawa, a Rhodesian from Bulawayo, shrouded in the darkness of the theater and seated next to her husband, Tōhaku Hasegawa, openly wept. And Tōhaku Hasegawa, for the first time in his life, had an idea of what his mother, Masako, the daughter of a kazoku baron, must have felt as an exile from Manchukuo.

The lights dimmed, then went dark. The audience, momentarily quiet, burst into wild applause.

Gemma—An Invisible Fear—The Rhodes Theatre

MIDLANDS-HASEGAWA UNIVERSITY
ACT V
SCENE III
'You would have done the same,' said Freya in a determined and haughty tone. The young and radiantly beautiful, blonde and blue-eyed Freya, resplendent in her Ptolemaic costume, pharaonic regalia, and red and white Pschent Crown, exited the stage. Yes, Queen Cleopatra VII, victorious over her royal siblings, had had the last word—even if they had only been uttered in a dream.

The stage lights dimmed and then faded to black as the curtain came down. A brief moment of silence followed, and then the audience burst into wild applause once more. The wave of emotion created by Jinx in the previous Act had carried into the final one. The last thirty minutes of The Ptolemies had been electrifying. Yes, the cast had done it; they had made The Ptolemies special again.

Jubal Wyatt smiled. 'You know…,' said Jubal while turning his head to speak to Gemma as they all applauded, 'My plays always seem to shine the brightest when they are performed here in England.'

The curtains slowly opened and the actors who had played Roman and Macedonian soldiers walked out from the wings of the stage and bowed. Kokoro, one of the Roman soldiers and one of Wallis' Japanese alcove roommates, bowed while maintaining the same serious expression she had kept throughout the entire play.

Over a dozen armor clad soldiers all formed a line on the left side of the stage and another cohort of actors, which included the diminutive Pasha and the much taller Nara, emerged from the right side of the stage. These were the Roman senators and the Macedonian nobles in their Roman togas and Macedonian robes. They all bowed together. The crowd continued to applaud. The actors formed a line on the right side of the stage.

Now the flaxen haired and curvaceous Suga, one of Cleopatra's scantily clad slaves, stepped onto the stage with another of Cleopatra's smolderingly beautiful slave girls, and the applause grew noticeably louder. Suga and dark-haired Alys, the other slave girl, both smiled as they bowed to the audience. The girls, both dressed in exotic costumes of white linen and cotton then moved to the left side of the stage. The applause continued.

The stage lights brightened, and Rex, who had played Lord Antipater, and Aubrey (the future 5th Baron) who had played Ptolemy, both entered stage left. Rex, an epicene beauty in Macedonian linothorax armor, and Aubrey, glittering in Pharaonic golden shirt of scale armor, a blue fabric pteruges skirt, and a blue Khepresh—the Blue Crown; otherwise known as a War Crown in Ancient Egypt—walked on to the stage, his blue eyes outlined in heavy kohl Egyptian makeup, and walked to the center of the stage and bowed as the applause intensified once more.

And then the entire cast turned stage right and bowed to the two actors who were stepping onto the stage: Freya and Jinx. Freya and Jinx, both in white linen and cotton costumes, and both now adorned in their Pharaonic crowns (Freya, a Pschent, the Egyptian red and white Double Crown; Jinx wore the gold Vulture Crown—a crown that depicted a vulture, with its two wings hanging from both sides of the head; a symbol of protection from the goddess Nekhbet) and pharaonic regalia, walked towards the center of the stage—the audience exploded in applause. The girls both faced the crowd and holding hands, bowed to the audience. Freya and Jinx shimmered under the lights. Yes, this brief moment of ethereal beauty would never be forgotten.

The entire cast then came together in a line, and holding hands, bowed together.

The curtain came down.

There were three curtain calls.

BACKSTAGE
'You were fantastic, Jinx!' said Freya excitedly. 'I felt like crying when I saw you on stage in Act Four.'

'Thank you, Freya. I couldn't help but thinking of Rhodesia,' replied Jinx.

'You were amazing, Jinx. Absolutely amazing,' said Suga in her gentle Scottish lilt.

The young actors, clad in their costumes and many with heavy Egyptian kohl eyeliner, moved about backstage happily and excitedly speaking with each other.

Jinx couldn't take a step without another actor stopping to congratulate her. It was almost overwhelming. Jinx, felt a little dizzy. Jinx, in a white dress of intricate folds and gold pharaonic Vulture Crown, walked through the crowd. She was looking for Rex. Where could he be?

'Jinx! You were electric!' said Rex happily. Rex had seemingly appeared out of nowhere. Jinx thought the nineteen-year-old Rex looked every inch the soldier he had portrayed on stage; the Macedonian linen linothorax armor fit him perfectly. The young, beautiful, blonde and blue-eyed Rex must have been what Alexander the Great had actually looked like, thought Jinx.

'Rex! Oh, thank you, Rex. Your final speech had me in tears!' said Jinx, her voice breaking with emotion. The innocent and pure teenage Rex, his epicene beauty, that very moment, at its captivating zenith, tilted his head to one side, and at that moment, cast his prepossessing Lysippean gaze in Jinx's direction. Jinx, carried away by emotion, leaned forward and gently kissed Rex.

Yes, remember this moment, Jinx. Youth, often wasted on the young; fleeting and unappreciated, was not unappreciated by either of the two young Rhodesians lost in an embrace that winter afternoon.

THE AUDIENCE

'I think the young actor who played Ptolemy did extremely well,' said Enoch. 'I think he captured the nuance of the role perfectly.'

'*Rather*,' said Gemma in her posh and Sloaney intonation. 'This play always manages to bring out the best in actors,' said Gemma as she brushed back her glossy brown hair with her soft manicured hand and tucked it behind one ear.

'Freya was so beautiful,' said Louise to Aurelia, who was seated next to her in the audience. 'I will view her in a Ptolemaic light for the rest of my life,' said Louise happily.

'Yes, she glided around the stage, didn't she?' replied Aurelia. 'And Jinx, what a transformation. I was left spellbound by her final speech. I could feel the sadness emanating from her,' said the slender and athletic nineteen-year-old Aurelia reflectively, her long blonde hair glowing in the dim light of the theatre.

'They recaptured the energy of the play in Oxford. The energy was different, but it was there,' said Violet.

'It certainly captured me,' said Hugh, who was seated next to the slender blonde Violet in a blue blazer, white dress shirt, and grey necktie.

Octavia leaned back in the chair in the third row of the theatre. 'I feel like I have just been through a hurricane. I have never seen a play performed like this.'

The dark-haired Külli, her eyes filled with tears and her voice breaking with emotion replied, 'Jinx expressed things that I couldn't. She made me understand how my parents must have felt all those decades in exile in England. How horrible. At least my parents lived long enough to be able to see their homeland free again. I was able to visit my ancestral homeland. Poor Jinx. She'll always be an exile. It's horrible.'

'Freya is a natural actress,' said a clearly astonished Brian. 'She could have quite the career on stage and in film if she chooses to. And Jinx? Well, I would never have guessed how fantastic an actress she is. Yes, I understand her in a way I never would have been able to without watching this play.'

'Yes, Freya was *absolutely* amazing,' said Poppy in her posh intonation. 'I think she would enjoy a career in theatre. She talked about just that last October at the house in Northumberland. And Jinx can summon emotions in a way that only an exile can. Yes, you are right, Brian. I have a much better understanding of Jinx now too, replied Poppy, her sterling silver Art Deco Egyptian bracelet glittering in the illumination of the theatre lamps.

'Freya performed the final scene the way it had been originally written,' said Poppy. 'I saw the play three times at Oxford, and the arrogant tone of the final scene is the way it was written. The closing night of the play in Oxford turned out quite differently.'

'How so?' asked Brian.

'Gemma performed the final scene in a deeply moving and melancholic way. It was mournful. I cried through the entire scene,' replied Poppy quietly. 'A lot had happened to Gemma, to all of us, during the first year at Oxford. It all culminated in the final scene on the final night of the play.'

Wren's mother, the baroness, her long, glossy, honey blonde hair over one shoulder, put on her tortoise shell reading glasses and looked carefully at the program. 'Jane Clarence. What a *marvellous* name. How did such a nice girl, such a beautiful and talented *Rhodesian girl* such as Jane end up being called "Jinx" I wonder?' said the baroness in her Sloaney and posh intonation.

'I have never asked, Mummy,' replied Wren. 'I will ask her next term. We are going to share one of the alcove rooms.'

'Jane, or Jinx, is a really good actress. Her last soliloquy was truly moving. Jinx is such a sweet girl. And her family is from Bulawayo. How nice,' said Jinx's mother is an unrestrained Rhodesian accent.

The audience started to disperse. Many of the audience members checked their wristwatches or smartphones as they made their way down one of the aisles of the large and ornate Rhodes Theatre. Those not driving home had reserved tickets on trains leaving in every direction. Now it was time to retrieve their (or their child's) luggage from their residence halls and make their way to the train station.

Jubal Wyatt, Gemma, and Enoch were walking up the aisle towards one of the exits when Elfie, the blonde Rhodesian stage director and undergraduate, in a dark grey pleated wool skirt, white cotton blouse, and a blue blazer, stopped them.

'Mr Wyatt. My name is Elfie Jolie. I'm the director. We have been exchanging emails.'

Jubal smiled. 'You're an exceptional director, Miss Jolie. I don't have the words to thank you enough for the performance of my play today.'

The attractive Elfie blushed. She hesitated for a moment and then asked, 'Mr Wyatt. Would it be possible for you, Mrs Ripley, and Mr Tara to meet the cast back stage? It would be a great honor for all of us to meet the playwright and some of the original cast members.'

'The honor would be ours,' replied Jubal in a southern drawl.

Gemma and Enoch both smiled and nodded.

BACKSTAGE

The entire cast, still in costume, and the stage crew, had assembled on the stage behind the curtain. Yes, hopefully, Jubal Wyatt and some of the original members of the cast would agree to meet them.

But, of course, they would.

Jubal, handsome and youthful, slender and gentlemanly, addressed the young undergraduates. 'The Ptolemies, today, was perfect. Just as I had written it, and just as I had hoped it would be performed. I am humbled by your performance.'

The cast and crew smiled. Yes, conformation from the highest source. They had breathed new life into The Ptolemies and now the man who had penned it was here to congratulate them on it in person.

'Today took me back to 1998. Youth is a good feeling,' said Jubal and he smiled.

The assembled undergraduates laughed happily.

Jubal then noticed the starkly beautiful Jinx (how could he not) and said, 'You provided quite the spark today, Jinx. It was a tsunami of energy after your final speech. How actors create such cosmic energy remains a mystery to me. And yes, you should definitely pursue acting.'

'Thank you, Mr Wyatt,' replied Jinx, the deeply moved and young Rhodesian exile.

There was the sound of footsteps as a couple made their way up the worn wood steps of the left side of the stage and walked onto the center stage of the Rhodes Theatre. The white-haired and diminutive Japanese billionaire Tōhaku Hasegawa, in a black suit, white dress shirt, and grey necktie, smiled as he stopped center stage with his wife Lara, who wore a white cotton blouse and a dark blue two-piece Chanel suit. Lara's long white and grey hair shimmered in the stage lights. Lara, through in her seventies, had retained much of her looks and was still attractive. Lara, the Rhodesian exile form Bulawayo, and Tōhaku, the only child of an exile from Manchukuo, made their way through the crowd of young actors, often stopping to exchange greetings with the undergraduates while looking for Jinx.

'Miss Clarence. Hello. My name is Lara Hasegawa. I wanted you to know how deeply moved I was by your performance,' said Lara in her posh intonation. And yes, Jinx could hear the Rhodesian lilt in Mrs Hasegawa's voice.

Jinx (or Jane), still in her white linen Ptolemaic costume, her golden Egyptian vulture crown glinting in the stage lights, smiled.

'Thank you Mrs Hasegawa. It is so nice of you to come back stage and speak with me.'

Lara smiled gently and said, 'I do hope you continue to act on stage and in films. I watched you on the silver screen last night with my husband, and you were fantastic.'

Jinx felt dizzy. Could it be that Mr and Mrs Hasegawa had seen her independent film? Mr and Mrs Hasegawa had both acted on stage. They were actors like Jinx.

Jinx blushed and replied, 'I'm happy that you liked the film. I had the nicest time working on it. The other actors and crew were all novices, but we all believed in the film we were making.'

Mr Hasegawa nodded and said, 'Miss Clarence, when you come to Tokyo, we would like to invite you to lunch.'

'And I will show you around Tokyo,' said Mrs Hasegawa happily.

Jinx smiled and almost in tears replied, 'Thank you, Mr and Mrs Hasegawa. You are both so kind.' Jinx paused, a bit flustered, and then said, 'I want you to know that my family is from Bulawayo. And please, call me Jane.'

Lara beamed with happiness. 'I knew there was another reason I liked you, Jane.' And then Lara reached out and grasped Jinx's soft hands and said, 'Thank you, Jane, for saying everything I have ever wanted to say.'

Enoch Tara, the mysterious billionaire and a former Ptolemy XIII, noticed the young actor who had portrayed the defeated Pharoah standing in the back of the group, still costumed in a glittering gold scale armor shirt, blue fabric pteruges skirt, and a blue Khepresh—the Blue Crown. The young actor made eye contact with Enoch and smiled nervously. Enoch nodded and smiled back. Enoch made his way through the crowd while the other actors were happily talking with Jubal and Gemma.

Enoch extended his hand; Aubrey grasped it.

'Hello. It's a nice to finally meet you, Aubrey. You act very well. You took a small part and made it into something great.'

Aubrey smiled. 'Thank you, Mr Tara,' said Aubrey (the future 5th Baron) in a slightly shaky voice. Your words mean a lot to me. I would like to become an actor one day. A stage actor.'

'You already are a great stage actor, Aubrey. Never let anyone tell you otherwise,' said Enoch.

'Oh, thank you, sir. I have always wanted to act, and this play, this small part in The Ptolemies, gave me that opportunity.'

'As it did me,' said Enoch. Enoch then reached into his blue blazer and took out a black leather billfold. He withdrew one of his business cards and handed it to Aubrey. 'Please, my card. If you ever need any assistance, or if you ever find yourself in London, please give me a ring. We could have lunch in the City.'

The svelte Aubrey smiled once more and took the white business card from Enoch carefully, gently. Yes, this card was now one of Aubrey's most prized possessions. Someone—a fellow stage actor—had recognized an ability in him that was worthy of assistance. This was just the confirmation that Aubrey had needed. Yes, one day, Aubrey would become a professional stage actor. He was now sure of it.

'What did you think, Godmother?' asked Freya, resplendent in white pharaonic costume, her blonde hair hidden under a Pschent, the Egyptian red and white Double Crown. Freya's pale complexion was flawless, beautiful, and smooth.

Gemma smiled—her All Saints smile; the smile she had had before being deeply wounded by George and Grey—and replied, 'I am proud of you, Freya. I have always been proud of you.'

Gemma—An Invisible Fear—The Texan

LONDON
The Texan studied the paper lists spread out before him on the wooden desk carefully. Yes, every soldier in the Core Army would be properly kitted out for the coming war. The weapons, which included a variety of (Russian and Yugoslav) small arms and light anti-tank weapons (Russian RPG-7s and Yugoslav M79 Osa) and anti-aircraft weapons (Russian 9K32 Strela-2s), were now secreted on a cargo ship which was—the Texan checked his wrist watch: 11:02am—at that very moment, steaming through the Dardanelles.

The Texan had rented a small, white walled, second floor flat in Covent Garden. The stay here had been an interesting one. The middle-aged Texan had enjoyed attending a play in the West End the night before. He had also had his meals in a different restaurant each time he went out. The Texan always made a splash upon appearing at the entrance of each dining establishment in cowboy boots and a worn cowboy hat, which he always removed as he entered to reveal a chiseled face. There were only two small restaurants (if you included the one at the truck stop) near his cattle ranch in Texas. Having this many options was a real treat. He had also ordered a Savile Row suit (charcoal grey) and a bespoke pair of black leather dress shoes. The Texan had enjoyed the first two fittings. The third and final fitting was scheduled for tomorrow. Yes, he would depart England with a fortune in gold bullion, a bespoke pair of leather shoes, and a Savile Row suit.

That is, if he survived the war.

The General had been quiet. No doubt he had read of the Brigada's murder in the Church. The Texan had no doubts at all that Carter Holland had ordered it, and the General had not. **How reckless.** The Texan had never met Carter Holland; he had never even heard of him before the General had recruited him for Carter Holland's impossible undertaking. Carter Holland seemed to be his own worst enemy—that is until he had his security team murder a member of Enoch Tara's Special Unit. With Tara's Special Unit now pursuing him, Carter could at least say with certainty that he was not his own worst enemy—the foreign mercenaries in the Special Unit were. Had the Brigada been left alone, the war ahead would be relatively smooth sailing. Carter Holland had made everything much more dangerous, much worse.

The small wooden desk was next to the white sash window of the bedroom. The Texan could see the snow clad Seven Dials from here. It was snowing lightly that afternoon. The sidewalks were crowded with people.

The Texan watched a young blonde mother in a dark blue parka and faded denim jeans pick her young (the Texan guessed kindergarten age) daughter up and hold her in her arms so that she could look into one of the shop windows at the Christmas decorations. A parallel universe existed just a block away from the middle-aged mercenary from Terrell. Yes, he had chosen the world he lived in; it was moments like this when he asked himself if it had all been worth it.

London had been beautiful when the Texan had visited it in 1992. Today, not so much. Yes, London, like the rest of the world, had changed a lot. The Texan doubted that things would change for the better. No, not for a while would that happen. No, the world was drowning in misery. The Texan could understand Carter's aspiration to create his own country, given the way things were going. What the Texan could not understand was Carter Holland's sudden recklessness.

Ping.

The Texan's encrypted smartphone glowed momentarily in the silvery grey natural light of the bedroom. He picked up the phone and looked at the screen.

Gemma—An Invisible Fear—The Dragon

THE PRIVATE RAIL CARRIAGE
After the play, the undergraduates of Midlands-Hasegawa—'Muddy Hills' to the undergraduates—scattered to the four winds. Aurelia boarded a train for the Cotswolds; Wallis, her mother—the 11th Baroness, and Masako, drove off in the silver 1966 Bristol motorcar for Surrey; Wren and her parents left for the family pile in Mercia in the glossy dark blue 1956 Riley, and Suga boarded the train for Scotland. Jinx and her parents, after meeting briefly with Rex and his Rhodesian mother, boarded the train for Surrey. Rex and his mother boarded the train for Rutland and their happy home, a mere hut hidden in a small grove of trees. Rex's roommate, Albert, boarded a train for London and a flight leaving Heathrow the next day for Taiwan. And the large party composing Freya's family and friends boarded separate trains bound in all directions. Poppy and Brian had already left for the Lake District on a regularly scheduled train almost immediately after the play after exchanging hugs and handshakes with everyone. Yes, they we all be seeing each other over the holidays.

THE TRAIN STATION
The regularly scheduled train (a four, now six railcar British Rail Class 755) to London, that night, had two private railcars attached to it: one cobalt blue, the other, dark blue. The railway platform, covered in a light layer of snow, was crowded with passengers (all of them undergraduates and the occasional family member) making their way to their respective rail carriages. It was only on the weekends and holidays that this small train station in the Midlands was crowded.

The diminutive, nineteen-year-old Louise, in a navy blue cashmere cape, mink hood, and a pair of dark khaki trousers, sat in her private berth on the

4th Baron's luxurious cobalt blue rail carriage. She had texted Gemma and asked to meet with her privately. She had something she needed to discuss with her. It was important.

Freya and her parents, Violet and Hugh, had already boarded the opulent private train carriage and were now having tea together in one of the cabins. Louise had politely declined the offer to join them and made her way down the glossy burl wood corridor to her private train cabin.

Gemma, in a dark blue Burberry coat (with silver buttons), walked down the railway platform, snow crunching underfoot. Gemma looked at her silver Cartier watch: 5:56pm. It was already dark. Gemma, illuminated in the light given off by the station lamps, glided down the platform towards the cobalt blue rail carriage.

Enoch had already boarded the dark blue rail carriage with Jubal Wyatt, Külli, Octavia, and a member of his security detail. Two other suited and booted security men stood on the railway platform. It was freezing cold. Beyond the lights of the railway station, there was only the twinkle of the electric lights of the small town that bordered Midlands-Hasegawa University.

Gemma reached the steps of the 4th Baron's private railcar, opened the glossy cobalt blue door, and stepped inside. Warmth immediately caressed her face as she closed the door behind her. The interior of the 4th Baron's private rail carriage was paneled in highly polished burl wood which gleamed in the electric light of the small disc lamps which lined the corridor of the private coach. Gemma made her way down the narrow corridor until she reached Louise's door. Gemma knocked gently on the door. It slid open slowly and carefully to reveal the strawberry blond Louise. The diminutive young woman from East Anglia smiled.

'Thank you for meeting with me, Gemma. Please come in.'

Gemma stepped into the cabin of glossy burl wood walls and supple Conolly leather berths. The sterling silver fixtures of the small cabin glinted in the electric light given off from the lamps on the train platform outside.

Gemma closed the door behind her.

'Please have a seat, Gemma,' said Louise.

Gemma, her blue eyes partially hidden behind the bangs of her glossy brown hair, unbuttoned her coat and hung it on one of the sterling silver coat hooks. Gemma, in a white Egyptian cotton blouse and dark khaki trousers, leaned back into the beige Connelly leather berth of the train cabin.

'Gemma, I don't know what to do about my father. He was out of my life for over a decade. He didn't want me in his life, and now he is here. My father abandoned me when I was eight years old. He is a stranger to me now. He was really horrible to me. After all of the cruelty, I don't know if I can ever forgive him.'

Gemma exhaled.

'My father abandoned me when I was eight years old too. After my mother passed away, when I was only twelve, my maternal grandparents took me in. I don't have any happy memories of my father. He refused to pay for any of my school fees—or any other expenses. It was my grandparents who paid my tuition at All Saints. My father never once contacted me while I was there. Not a single telephone call or even a brief note in the post. Nothing. I had almost forgotten him. When I was nineteen, during my first term at Oxford, I telephoned him. Not because I wanted to reconcile with him. I didn't. **I don't.** He had been so cruel and violent that I never wanted to see him again.'

Gemma paused. She looked out the large window of the private train cabin. Outside, it was starting to snow; more snow was now accumulating on the railway station platform. Gemma looked back at Louise. Louise, her blue cashmere cape now unbuttoned and opened to reveal a flash of the white cotton blouse she was wearing, met her gaze.

'I wanted to hear my father say that he was sorry for all that he had done. I wanted him to apologize to me for brutalizing my mother and my brother. I didn't even recognize his voice when I telephoned him. I had forgotten the sound of his voice. When I telephoned him, I simply told him who I was, and he started shouting at me. He asked why I was even calling him. And then he hung up.'

The train carriage jolted suddenly and then the train started to move forward. The British Railways train was getting underway. Gemma looked back at Louise. Her face was pale.

'How horrible,' said Louise quietly.

'At first, for a brief moment, I was sad. And then I was angry. My father had hurt me *again.* My father was not the aggrieved one. He was not the victim, yet I know that he thinks he is. He thinks that I owe him an apology. I know that's how he thinks. Arthur, my older brother, talked to me about our father and how terrible he really is. Arthur told me that our father would always think of himself as the victim. Worse yet, my father doesn't think he has done anything wrong. He really doesn't. My brother was so traumatized by my father that he left England and has never returned. Perhaps, after our father is dead, he will come back. I haven't seen Arthur since I was twelve. All these decades Arthur has been gone. I miss him. I would like to have had a brother all these years. But, I understand him.'

'That's terrible, Gemma,' said Louise.

'Louise, you have suffered a lot. I know that. It's up to you if you want to make amends with your father. It is entirely up to you. But, whatever you decide, I will support you. I am on your side, Louise. I am your friend,' said Gemma.

Tears started to well up in Louise's eyes.

'Thank you, Gemma. You are the only one I know who has been through what I have been through. I needed to talk with you. I don't know if I can ever forgive my father for all he has put me through. If it hadn't been for Freya, I would not have survived. I would have died from grief. I was alone for eight years. It was Freya who befriended me. It was Freya who saved me,' said Louise choking back tears.

Gemma leaned forward and grasped Louise's small soft hands in hers. Gemma caressed them gently.

'Louise, we are all here for you. You are surrounded by friends now. We will protect you. Nothing bad will ever happen to you again. I promise.'

Louise, her face wet with tears, looked up at Gemma. And at that moment, *Louise knew*. The dragon in her dream had been whispering to her about Gemma. Louise, startled, pulled her hands away from Gemma and fell back into the leather berth.

'What's wrong?' asked Gemma.

Louise suddenly felt an icy chill go up her spine. She gasped for air.

'Louise, are you alright. Are you having another stroke?' asked Gemma in an alarmed tone of voice. 'I'll call for a doctor. One will meet us at the next station.'

Louise shook her slowly. 'No. Gemma. I'm alright. It is you who is in danger.'

'What?'

'My dream. The dragon. I didn't understand what the dragon wanted. But now I do. Gemma. The dragon wanted me to warn you. Something bad is going to happen to you,' said Louise through tears. 'I wish it wasn't true. Please be careful, Gemma.'

Gemma, unnerved by Louise's sudden and completely unexpected declaration, could only ~~stare in disbelief.~~ No, **not disbelief**. Gemma knew the power of dreams and how some people could tap into that other world and be warned of things to come. Yes, what Louise was saying was true. Gemma felt a chill move through her entire being.

'Please, leave England. Just for a while, Gemma.'

'Louise, if I have learned anything in my life, is that it is not always possible, or even preferable, to run away from danger. Sometimes, you have to face it and hope you can defeat it, or at the very least, survive it.'

Louise shook her head, her strawberry blonde hair flashing in the electric illumination of the train cabin as the train rumbled down the tracks through the snow.

'Gemma, the dream is what caused my stroke. I'm sure of it. Please, listen to me,' said Louise.

'I believe you, Louise. I have always believed you. But, I know that I can't run away from this.'

'Please, tell Enoch. He can protect you. Promise me, you will tell Enoch. Alright?' said Louise while choking back tears.

It was disconcerting to see and hear Louise acting like this. Gemma, however, knew that Louise was telling the truth. Louise had been warned by the dragon in her dream. Outside, the train rumbled through the darkness and falling snow; the occasional electric light appearing only as a blip as the British Railway train passed quickly by.

'Alright. I will tell him. Please, don't worry, Louise. I don't want you to have another stroke. Please, calm down. I will be alright.'

Louise then leaned forward, wrapped her slender arms around Gemma, and started to cry.

5 ONLY THE WHISPER OF BLOOD IN MY EARS

Gemma—An Invisible Fear—The Warehouse

GREATER LONDON
Blurred forms moved through the darkness. The shadowy forms stopped at the edge of the snowy field. On the other side of the road was the large recycling plant. The industrial lights glowed just a short distance from their position next to the abandoned red brick structure—a former factory. The darkened structure looked like the carcass of a dead animal that had been partially eaten by jackals. Parts of the roof had collapsed, and through the large jagged holes, the star speckled night sky could be seen. The factory floor was littered with debris. The building had not been despoiled or stripped of any materials. No one bothered to come out to this area on the edge of London.

Harsh loud bangs and shrieks emanated from the recycling plant. The plant had once housed an engine factory. Part of the factory was an original red brick structure which had been built in the early 1940s. The factory had produced airplane engines, and after the war, engines for industrial trucks and tractors. The factory had gone bankrupt in the early 1970s, along with the rest of England. It wasn't until 2005 that new owners purchased the industrial site and transformed it into a recycling plant. Two more sections had been added; these were made of iron and steel. Giant machinery and conveyor belts had been installed, along with smelters. A new roof and additional soundproofing had also been necessary. Now, virtually the only traffic in the nearly abandoned industrial district, was the steady stream of heavy trucks which transported scrap metal.

The former industrial belt had only one other occupied structure: Colin Bailey's construction company. Colin's construction company did occasionally win contracts, but mostly the company was used to launder money. The warehouse was also a useful rally point for the gang. The police never came out to this area. It was pointless to patrol a nearly abandoned industrial district, especially when Scotland Yard's budget was under as much strain as it was. The workers who ran the recycling plant next door had never bothered Colin either. That side of the plant didn't even have windows facing the warehouse. The warehouse three blocks over, separated by derelict factories and poorly maintained and unlit streets, was of no concern to any of them.

Now, a thin layer of snow covered the fields, buildings, and streets. The structures were now dimly illuminated in moonlight, starshine, and the distant glow of industrial lamps.

Colin Bailey had led two separate groups of people here early that afternoon. A small group of white South Africans had arrived in four cars, now parked behind a derelict structure three hundred yards away. The South Africans had been observing the warehouse via a small drone and several pairs of state-of-the-art night vision goggles.

But, unknown to the South Africans, they were also being observed by a drone themselves. This one piloted by a young man with a Bristol accent who was stationed more than a mile away. A total of five vehicles had come with him. A dozen heavily armed people, eleven men and one woman, stood in the demi-darkness awaiting orders.

How strange it was that someone as minor a figure as Colin Bailey had attracted two high caliber groups of people. But modernity was a strange thing; it had turned everything upside down.

THE EDGE OF THE FIELD

The snowy white field glowed in the moonlight. Yes, the Moon would make it difficult for them. If there were any CCTV camera monitoring the area, the men would be spotted crossing the field. But, they had really had no choice, there would never be a better time and place to attack Colin's criminal gang.

The Comandante, now clad in a dark blue quilted jacket, a mock turtle neck jumper, and faded blue jeans, studied the drone footage carefully. Yes, there were lights in the warehouse, but the windows had all been painted over with an obscuring coat of white paint. There was only one large gate and a single door to the large structure. There were no vehicles parked outside. There also wasn't anyone standing watch. At least there didn't appear to be anyone.

The dozen men surrounding the former member of the Spanish Foreign Legión in the abandoned factory were all wearing body armor over thin layers of dark warm clothing and rubber soled leather combat boots. The Afrikaners, a collection of slender and athletic men with blond and light brown hair, all carried machine guns and pistols. All of them had black balaclavas topping their heads and ready to be pulled down across their face at a moment's notice. The balaclavas had microphones and tiny pods with earpieces sewn into them. These men stood motionlessly ensconced in silence and darkness, illuminated only by the bluish glow of the tablet computer screen which the drone pilot was using to monitor warehouse. The men had been there for over three hours. It was freezing cold in the abandoned factory; an icy wind blew through the structure at irregular intervals.

And then, movement.

The large gate to the warehouse opened and a white Citroën hatchback slowly emerged from the large structure; its headlights illuminating the area in front of it. Just as the hatchback cleared the gate, the door began to close. The gate closed and the car exited through the open gate of the warehouse complex and turned onto the road. It was impossible to see who was inside. The car slowly made its way up the darkened street, and turning left, it disappeared.

'Shall I follow it?' asked the drone pilot.

'No. There are still lights on in the warehouse. Someone is there. Now is the time to attack. If they felt comfortable enough to have someone leave in the car, they must be feeling pretty confident they were not followed,' said the Comandante. 'Get ready.' The men around him sprung to life. Weapons were checked one last time. The balaclavas were pulled down and adjusted. A few men put on night vision goggles.

Okay. Time to move.

First, one person sprinted across the snowy field, a dark and blurry figure illuminated in bluish moonlight. When he reached the other side, he peered into the abandoned factory through a pair of night vision goggles. No one was inside. The hooded figured turned and motioned for the next man to cross and then turned back to scan the interior of the abandoned building. When two other men had made it to the building, the first and second men, both wearing night vision goggles, entered the building pointing their machine guns. Soon all but the drone pilot and one other man had entered the building. It was time to move two hundred more yards ahead and then storm the warehouse. As the team approached the large brick structure, the confused clattering noise of the recycling plant grew louder.

THE WAREHOUSE

The gang of young hoodies in the warehouse had never really stood a chance. The first South African had entered through the unlocked door next to the gate. As he rushed inside, he was immediately spotted by a teenage gang member in a dark blue puffer coat and faded blue jeans. He had been standing next to a white Volkswagen hatchback and looking at his smartphone. The blast of cold air that entered the warehouse when the door was opened had alerted him. The last thing the teenager from Elephant and Castle saw was a balaclava hooded figure with a machine gun pointed at him. The next moment, he was dead. That had not been the intention of the South African, but bullets don't always do as they are expected to.

More South Africans flooded in behind him.

A half dozen other young men turned to face the Afrikaners. Gun fire erupted from both sides. The first South African was shot in the face; the bullet killing him instantly. The gang spread out, some hiding behind the bulldozer; others behind an old lorry. Bursts of machine gun fire and the sharp ring of pistol shots reverberated throughout the warehouse. Sparks exploded as armor piecing rounds punctured metal vehicles while other bullets ricocheted in different directions. The Comandante, now running through the icy darkness towards the warehouse, snow crunching underfoot, could hear the men shouting to each other in Afrikaans through small pod sewn into his black balaclava.

The fight was over before the Comandante burst through the door with his machine gun. The entire gun battle had lasted less than thirty seconds. Lying on the floor of the warehouse were eight young men. All wore blue jeans; a couple wore hoodies, one a parka, the rest wore puffer coats. All of the young gangsters had been badly bloodied. Only one of the criminals was still alive.

The Comandante knelt down next to the dead South African. Yes, it was too late to save him. He had died instantly. While three of the South Africans secured the warehouse and checked for survivors, another was helping to treat another Afrikaner who had been wounded in the thumb, arm, and shoulder.

One South African bound the teenage hoodie's wounds while another South African questioned him.

'Where's Colin Bailey?'

The young hoodie, his eyes partial covered by a mop of light brown hair and obviously in pain, moaned and gasped as he tried to speak.

'Where is he?' asked the young Afrikaner from Cape Town.

'You just missed…him. He left…with his girlfriend.'

'Where is he going?'

'To the clinic. To…check on his brother.'

'You mean Declan?'

'Yes.'

'Where is the clinic?'

'I don't know. Somewhere…in London,' the young hoodie replied in pain.

The Afrikaner studied the young teenager that lay on the ground before him. Yes, he was telling the truth.

'Alright. How badly wounded is Declan?' asked the South African.

'Bad. I don't know how bad. But…bad.'

Just beyond the wounded gangster stood the Comandante. His faced still covered by the black balaclava and holding a machine gun. He had been carefully listening in on the conversation.

'Why did you kill the Spaniard in the church last week?' asked the Afrikaner.

The young hoodie, his light grey hoodie splattered with blood and lying in a pool of his own blood, turned to look at the masked South African. He was fading away quickly.

'Am I dying?' asked the teenager.

'Yes,' replied the blond Afrikaner coolly.

The teenager's facial expression did not change upon hearing the news. He was bleeding out. He would die. A sudden burst of energy filled him; one last burst of energy before he perished.

'We wanted to kidnap him. That…was all. We didn't expect him to be armed.'

'Who is Declan working for?' asked the South African.

'I don't know. I…never ask questions,' replied the teenage gangster.

'Alright,' replied the South African.

And with a final gasp, the young man from Croydon closed his eyes for the last time.

THE ABANDONED GLASS FACTORY

The images on the tablet computer screen showed flashes of gunfire coming from the open door of the warehouse as men ran inside. A few minutes later three men, illuminated in the moonlight and in black balaclavas, wearing body armor, and carrying machine guns, emerged, one after the other. One had difficulty walking. The man ahead, aiming his machine in different directions as walked ahead. Then two men emerged carrying a dead body between them. A moment later, more shadowy figures emerged. The men moved rapidly in the direction that had come just ten minutes before.

'None of the gang has survived,' said the young man piloting the drone in a Bristol accent.

'Good. They've have done our job for us,' replied the young woman with light brown hair who shrouded in darkness.

'But we don't know who was in the car that left.'

'We'll find out soon enough. Let's get out of here before we are spotted by the Tara's Special Unit,' replied the young woman.

Gemma—An Invisible Fear—An Ocean of Books

CENTRAL LONDON
The used book shop at the end of a long narrow alleyway had been owned by the same English family for five generations. It had begun its life in 1903 as a used book store and it had remained a used book store ever since. It was not London's oldest family run business, but it had an interesting past.

The family had dwindled to a single surviving member by 1998. The elderly woman who owned it had inherited it from her aged father when he passed away. The woman, a retired civil servant, had found working in the book shop with a few young part-time assistants to be enjoyable.

The building, a former draper's shop, was two storeys; the top floor was a spacious apartment where she lived.

She had told her friends that she couldn't imagine ever selling the store; it had been in her family for so long. That is until the she had suffered not one, but three separate robberies; the last one had left her with a broken wrist and a badly bruised face. Each time the book store had been robbed, the criminal had escape with less than two hundred pounds.

London had changed. It was time to sell the book store and leave London. Forever.

The store had been sold to an anonymous buyer. The book store owner was relieved to have the store sold at her asking price. She hadn't even bothered to ask who had bought it. She really didn't care. She just wanted to escape.

Carter Holland had turned the keys of the store over to the Revenant for use as a safe house or meeting place. Carter had decided that a used book store, which was now always closed, would have its uses. He knew, after years of intrigue, that places like the book store were necessary.

The cobblestone alleyway was lined with two small dress shops, a florist, a coffee shop, a book store (that specialized in cook books), a watch store that specialized in repairing mechanical wristwatches and restoring grandfather clocks (which it also sold), and five private residences. All of the stores and residences had been robbed or burglarized at least once in the last year. Yes, London had changed. The situation had changed.

In the daytime, the alleyway bustled with people; after dark, it was practically deserted. The alleyway was well lit at the entrance and only partially lit at the end where the book store was located. The large, heavily weathered, wooden double doors of the book store appeared to be closed jaws ready to devour anyone who approached them.

It was late at night, when no one was around, that the Revenant would appear.

THE BOOK STORE

There was a loud knock on the front doors of the store. It was dark. The Revenant looked at his wrist watch: 11:45pm. Right on time. The Revenant walked through the dimly lit store, past aisle after aisle of old books, and stopped at the double door entrance. He looked at his smartphone. The CCTV above the door showed one man outlined in shadows. He tapped on the screen off his smartphone.

Ping.

The Texan's smartphone glowed momentarily. He looked at it and tapped out a reply.

A moment later, the Revenant opened the front door of the store.

'Come in.'

'Good evening, General,' said the Texan as he took off his weathered cowboy hat.

'Thank you for coming so quickly,' replied the Revenant in his indeterminable accent. 'There is a desk and chairs at the back of the store. We can talk there.'

The Texan entered the book store and after he had walked past the Revenant, the Revenant carefully closed and locked the wooden double doors of the store. The book store's interior was illuminated by a pair of lamps in the back of the shop. The book shop was a collection of shadows and silhouettes.

The two men, one of them in cowboy boots, made their way back down the aisle past wooden shelf after wooden shelf of old books, the hardwood floor creaking with each step. At the back, near the spiral iron staircase leading to the upstairs apartment, was an old wooden desk and three wooden chairs. There was also a white ceramic tea pot, a white ceramic sugar bowl, two white tea cups and saucers (each with a sterling silver spoon), and a small sterling silver container of cold milk.

'Please, have a seat,' said the Revenant.

'Thank you, sir.'

THE WARLORD

The Revenant, seated behind the desk, was illuminated by an old wall lamp. Dressed in a pale blue dress shirt, dark blue necktie, a dark grey wool suit, and a dark blue wool overcoat (with a light brown fur collar), the General looked like a City banker.

The Texan observed how plain, average, and nondescript in appearance the General really was. The Revenant's brown hair seemed to glint with silver in the lamp light. The General had perfect facial symmetry and good teeth. He looked to be in his fifties. Yes, the General was not the kind of man to get a second glance by most, unless they happened to notice his scarred left hand.

There was a story that the Texan had once heard, that said, if on a left finger there's a scar, it means that a person who loved you in a previous life could not forget you. And she (or he) will always be looking for you. The Texan knew that the Revenant had already gone through more in one lifetime than a hundred people would have been able to endure for even the briefest of moments. The Texan sometimes wondered what the Revenant had been like, in his previous life, before the General had taken to soldiering. Undoubtedly, thought the Texan, the Revenant's family missed him and was waiting for him on the other side.

The General was of average height, around 5'11". The Revenant rarely made eye contact with anyone. He tried to avoid it. He knew that only drew attention. He usually wore special transparent or black framed eyeglasses designed to foil facial recognition software when walking around London. But not always.

Yes, the General was a mystery to the Texan. However, three decades in the field—whatever one might choose to call this occupation—had taught the Texan not to ask too many questions. The General always operated under a different identity each time they had worked together. Alright, for whatever reason, the General wanted to protect (or hide) his true identity. That was fine with the American from Terrell. Everyone, but everyone, has secrets.

'Would you like a cup of tea?' asked the Revenant.

'Yes, thank you.'

'There is sugar and cold milk, if you like.'

'Thank you, sir.'

The Revenant poured the Texan a cup of tea and then one for himself. The Revenant waited for the Texan too add a dash of cold milk before he added a spoonful of sugar and a little milk to his tea. The Texan was a guest.

'I spoke with Carter Holland,' said the Revenant after he had placed the white tea cup back on the saucer. 'He has left it to me to eliminate Enoch Tara's Special Unit.'

'I'm not surprised, from what little you have told me of him,' said the Texan.

'You will not be part of that. I need you to focus on the Core Army. We remain on schedule. The war will begin in January,' said the Revenant quietly.

'So, it will you and Jem locking horns with Tara's men?' asked the Texan.

'No. Jem will continue to overseeing his part of the operation. I've given it to Attila.'

'Really? I thought he had retired,' said the Texan.

'He had. He has come out of retirement to help me. And, besides, I think he found retirement to be a bit too boring.'

'And you have an idea who the people in the Special Unit are?' asked the Texan.

'I have the identity of one of them. That person will lead us to the rest of the Special Unit. And then we will eliminate them all,' said the Revenant quietly. 'It's important that you stay on top of everything. I might not be around for a few days. You will have to see to all the final arrangements. It is as we have planned it from the beginning. There will be no changes. Just see things through. I am relaying on you to do that.'

'I will make sure of it, sir,' replied the Texan.

'Thank you.'

Gemma—An Invisible Fear—Obliteration

LONDON

Colin Bailey, behind the wheel of the white Citroën hatchback, slowed as he approached the intersection. Next to him was his girlfriend, Paige. Blonde and beautiful, Paige had found the money and the brutal glamour of consorting with a gangster to be as irresistible as it was exciting. Growing up with a single mother on a council estate had been a miserable experience. Paige's young life had been one of processed foods and tap water. Half the winter, the electricity had usually been off because her mother, though she worked two jobs, couldn't afford to pay the electricity bill that month. If he hadn't been for the school uniform, Paige would have been forced to wear her only pair of denim jeans or one of two pairs of cotton trousers that she owned to school every day. Life was drudgery, nothing more, until Paige turned fifteen, and turned into a swan.

The teenage Paige Wight was as truest a beauty as England had ever seen. The blonde and blue-eyed Paige, strikingly beautiful, walked the grey streets of London and soon drew the attention of Colin Bailey. It was Colin who bought her first pair of sunglasses at an upscale boutique. A closet full of designer clothes followed. And loads of cash. Paige happily paid all of her mother's bills. When her mother asked where the money was coming from, Paige told her that she had made it all at the salon. Paige loved her new life. Colin Bailey, while not handsome, not in a conventional way, was extremely attractive to her because he radiated power. Men feared him. And Paige grew to love him.

Yes, the slender Colin Bailey in a black suit, white shirt, black silk neck tie, and highly polished black Chelsea boots, was a real gangster. Paige found the parties, the money, and gangland exploits to all be very, very exciting.

Until it wasn't.

And now, it wasn't exciting anymore. It was terrifying.

Paige, exhausted from days of sleepless nights and draining days of silence, had fallen asleep in the front passenger seat of the hatchback. The Christmas lights and decorations reflected off of Paige's smooth pale face as the car moved slowly down the snow-covered streets.

Inhale.

Exhale.

Occasionally, Colin would glance over at the sleeping Paige. Yes, Paige was beautiful. Declan, his older brother, had had a lot of girls just like Paige, but Declan had always been handsome, unlike Colin. Colin had finally found a girl like Paige. Now, if he could survive what was coming, Colin told himself he would cash out and move to Spain. They would buy a house, start a family, and live happily ever after. Gangland would only be a memory (albeit a mostly happy and exciting one).

If he could somehow manage to survive.

Somehow.

There was a safe house in London; one that Declan had set up just in case of a situation like this. Declan was clever. Yes, Declan had been a career soldier in the Parachute Regiment, and he understood the world in a way that Colin never would. It was Declan that had saved Colin's life.

After Gareth's murder, Colin watched his mother's rapid decline. Gareth had been her baby. And her baby had been murdered. 'He killed my baby,' Colin's mother had said over and over again as she wondered around their council flat house night after night. Colin didn't want to live anymore. Gareth was dead and their mother was dying. Declan had been crushed by his youngest brother's death too. Their mother's anguished cries rang in their ears as they broke down the front door of the house belonging to the family of the Jamaican Yardie who had murdered Gareth out of sheer boredom. Colin had watched as Declan slashed the middle-aged Jamaican woman's throat with a straight razor. Colin had slipped in blood as he ran up the stairs of the house to the second floor where the two younger brothers of the yardie were cowering in their bedroom. Declan and Colin brutally beat and slashed both of the teenage boys to death. It had been cathartic for both of them. Emerging from the bedroom, both covered in blood, they felt lighter. The final burden would be lifted when the yardie who had murdered their younger brother had breathed his last blood choked breath. For Colin it had been a form of liberation. It had, however, not been enough to save his mother; she drank herself to death a few months later.

This episode had taught Colin a few things: That **might** is all that matters. The ability to generate **fear** in others is the greatest ability a man can possess. And that **violence** is the greatest expedient.

THE SAFE HOUSE

The small terraced house on a tree lined side street rarely had visitors. It was in an expensive neighborhood; at least it had been expensive since the late 90s. The neighborhood, once the domain of the working classes, was now a Bohemian address peopled by the talentless children of millionaires, wealthy foreign university students, unknown artists (who displayed their art at sparsely attended exhibitions in art galleries owned by friends or relatives), young divorcées (or never marrieds) of wealthy men with young children and nannies (who tooled around London in silver Volvos or gold BMW Minis), and a few gangland types—like Declan and Colin Bailey. Yes, the formerly working class neighbor was now a posh one.

And a good place to hide out for a gangster.

Colin had parked the car at the end of the street and the two of them had walked down the pavement through the demi-darkness of a partially lit street, snow crunching underfoot. Now, in the safehouse, they could relax, just a little.

The house security system was disarmed and then rearmed quickly as they entered the house and they locked the door behind them. The drawn curtains remained drawn. Upstairs, in one of the bedrooms, Paige had crawled into bed and gone to sleep. In the room across the hall, Colin had tried calling his mates in the warehouse. No one answered.

At 2am, his phone rang. Colin looked at the Caller ID. It was Mason. Colin answered.

'For fuck's sake! Where have you been?! I've calling you for the last three hours!'

The voice that answered was not Mason's.

'We need to meet.'

Colin froze. It didn't take a moment to figure that Mason was most likely dead. Colin listened carefully. He could hear the person on the phone breathing. Colin didn't answer.

'Who are you working for? Tell us that much, Colin, and we will never bother you again.'

Colin listened, but said nothing.

'I am not a kind man, Mr Bailey, but I am a reasonable one. Tell us who ordered the attack on the Brigada, and we will let you go.'

Colin Bailey did not answer.

'Colin. I am going to give you one last chance. Please, take it. Tell me who you and your brother Declan are working for.'

Colin, his heart pounding in his chest, did not answer.

The line went dead. Colin stood in the center of the bedroom; a room bereft of furniture, and looked across the hall through the open door and focused on the dark shape of Paige sleeping in the bed. They had to leave the house immediately. Colin looked at the phone; the small blue light blinking on the side of the plastic casing. He dropped it to the floor and then stomped on it. The smartphone broke into pieces.

'Paige! Wake up! We're leaving!'

Gemma—An Invisible Fear—The Hussars

GREATER LONDON

'Attila', physically fit and of average height, and in a pair of charcoal grey trousers, a white dress shirt, a black leather belt, and a pair of black Chelsea boots, checked his watch: 1:33pm. The Hungarian sifted through the photos and maps on the wooden table.

Attila studied the photo of a relatively young woman. She had brown hair and blue eyes. She had a pale complexion. Attila had three photos of the woman. She wasn't smiling in any of them. The athletic young woman wore a pair of clear plastic framed eye glasses in all three photos. In the first photo she wore a pair of dark grey wool trousers, a dark blue v-neck sweater over a white cotton t-shirt. She wore a wristwatch of some kind. It looked like a dive watch. In the first photo she was leaving a post office in North London. The young woman was not attractive. She had a rather plain appearance. In the second photo she was behind the wheel of a white 2018 Volkswagen Polo. The hatchback was stopped at a red light. The young woman had the same unsmiling expression as the first photo, but she was wearing a navy blue parka. The third photo showed her sitting in a café near St Pancras Train Station in Central London. This photo was different: the young woman, clad in faded blue jeans and a beige wool sweater, was speaking with someone at the table. The Magyar studied the photo. The person she was speaking to was partially hidden behind an ornate white wooden pillar. According to the hand written note on the back of the photo, the unseen person was the Brigada—now dead. This photo had been taken a few days before the Spaniard's death in the Medieval church.

The Revenant's strenuous efforts had led him to the young woman. Attila had no idea how the Revenant had found out about her, but he had, and he had had her followed. And this morning, the white envelope that had been hand delivered to the Hungarian hussar from the Revenant not only included photos of the young woman, but also something even more important: her name.

Ingrid Mavis Steyr—South African born, she hád two passports: South African and British. Her documents stated that she was thirty-three years old. She was an only child. Her listed residence was a small flat in North London that she had not visited since the Revenant had discovered her existence. Yes, she was living somewhere else. She had graduated from the University of Natal. Her father, now dead, was South African. Her mother, a landscape architect, was English. Ingrid had enlisted in the British Army and entered the Royal Corps of Signals (The 11th Regiment). She had served in the army for twelve years. She had an eDV security clearance. Ingrid Steyr had left the British army as a warrant officer. Her (official) resume since she had left the army was unimpressive: a series of part-time jobs at cafés and restaurants. She now worked in a plant nursery in Crews Hill that was owned by her mother. This was quite a fall for someone who had once helped run the British army's communications networks. Former WO2 Ingrid Mavis Steyr seemed to be stuck in a series of low paid jobs. Undoubtably this was untrue. It was merely part of her cover. The young Afrikaner was part of Enoch Tara's Special Unit. What the former warrant officer's role in the unit was remained unknown. The Revenant's men had first observed the former Signal Corps soldier entering a small church in Northumberland a few weeks ago.

The Hungarian lifted up another photo. It was of the Brigada. The Spaniard was walking out of the café a few minutes after Ingrid had. He had left the building and walked in a different direction. The Magyar studied the Spaniard in the photo. The Brigada looked brutal.

There was more.

Ingrid's license plate number. Yes, that had made life easier. The car was registered to an M.E. Steyr who lived in a modest small end of terrace house in Chipping Barnet. There were several photos of the terraced house. Parked nearby was Ingrid's white Volkswagen hatchback.

There were several pages of typed notes that the Revenant had included in the large sealed envelope.

The blue-eyed Hungarian had been carefully reading through and studying the papers, maps, and photographs all morning. Yes, this young woman would lead them to the Special Unit. And then the Hungarian and his men would kill them all.

And her, too—if necessary.

Whenever a woman picks up a sword, she surrenders her womanly protections. Chivalry does not make allowances for a female combatant. The former warrant officer had placed herself in harm's way. The Hungarian would treat her no differently than any of the men in Tara's Special Unit.

THE SAFE HOUSE

The twenty men that sat on folding metal chairs in the drawing room of the terraced house were a brutal lot. These men had all been handpicked by the Revenant for their ruthlessness. Of the twenty men who surrounded the Hungarian Hussar, eight had served in the French Foreign Legion. The oldest of the group had fought in some or all of the Yugoslav civil wars—Croatia, Bosnia, and Kosova. One had fought in the 2008 war in Georgia against the Russians. A few, including a Crimean Tatar, had fought in the ongoing war against Russia in Ukraine which had started in 2014. All of the men had served in armies in their native homelands. The Hungarian, in his mid-fifties, was the oldest of the group. The other men present were all in their late twenties to their late-forties. Attila, standing before them in front of a white board, felt old.

'We don't have that much information of the Enoch Tara's Special Unit yet. However, more information is coming in every day. The General sent over a dossier this morning,' said the Hungarian authoritatively. He then started taping photos to the white board. 'Her name is Ingrid Steyr. She is a former warrant officer in the British army. Signal Corps. She is part of the Special Unit. I'm going to have some of you follow her. A couple of you in cars and another with a drone. She will lead us to the rest of the Special Unit,' said Attila in mildly accented English.

'And what will we do once we find them?' asked a Lithuanian (former) hussar officer.

'We will kill them,' replied Attila.

The men in room did not react. Attila continued. 'It is imperative that the Special Unit be totally destroyed within the next seven days. We do not have time to waste.'

Attila cut his brown hair like a City banker; the better to hide the scars on his head. Attila, slender and physically fit, stood 5'10". Attila was not attractive. Attila had never been what most would consider even remotely attractive. He had looked rather plain while growing up in Debrecen, Hungary. The war in Croatia had changed that. While fighting against the

Serbs and Montenegrins in Osijek in 1991, shrapnel from an exploding chetnik artillery shell had left him badly wounded and near death. It had also left him disfigured. A team of highly specialized plastic surgeons in Zagreb (which including two Croat surgeons who had returned temporarily from Austria and Germany) had managed to reconstruct his jaw and repair his chin, but the right side of his head was left a long scar. After recovering from surgery, he returned to the Croatian army and continued to fight, even participating in Operation Storm in 1995.

Attila had never married. He was childless and alone. When not on assignment, he lived alone in a small stone house on an acre of land in central Hungary. The house, built in 1912, was shaded by large maple trees. The large trees also shielded the house from the dirt road in front of his house. They also protected Attila. He liked the house. He felt safe there. The white walls of the main room were lined with books. Attila enjoyed reading. And yes, Attila hated his reflection.

It was the Revenant that found him and gave him purpose again. Few would consider employing such a human wreck like the Hungarian that now stood before the white board. Attila had worked on various assignments with or for the Revenant for almost two decades. Attila was grateful. Attila's loyalty to the Revenant was absolute. It was the money Attila had made working for the revenant that had allowed him to buy the house and survive financially. Knowing that the Revenant prized his abilities had also repaired Attila's psyche. One last assignment and Attila would have enough money to retire from the world for the rest of his life.

'We start immediately. Albin. You, Ante, and Michal will drive out to Crews Hill. If you see Miss Steyr, contact me immediately. Do you understand?'

'Yes.'

Attila looked to his right. An Estonian mercenary met his gaze.

'Ardo, you will go with them and operate the drone. Take Amet with you in a separate car.'

'Yes, sir.'

The rest of you will break up into your assigned teams. You will wait for my signal. Does everyone understand their orders?' asked Attila.

'Yes,' the men said in near unison in a myriad of different accents and even different languages.

6 THE LONDON LANDROMAT

Gemma—An Invisible Fear—Londongrad

THE CITY

The three large digital screens flickered with numbers, letters, and symbols. Carter Holland, in a pale blue dress shirt, a dark blue neck tie, a pair of dark grey trousers, and a black leather belt with a silver belt buckle, studied the screens carefully. The svelte and handsome Carter Holland, not a blond hair out of place, tapped on the white keyboard in front of him.

Yes, everything was going to plan.

QUADRIGA INVESTMENTS

A small team City bankers and IT engineers, a collection of pale blue and white dress shirts, English cut neckties, and dark blue and charcoal grey Saville Row suits, tapped on white computer keyboards while carefully studying computer screens. The two dozen men gathered in this room were part of Carter Holland's unbelievably daring and dangerous enterprise. They were risking all to be part of Carter's seemingly impossible endeavor. They would assist Carter Holland in changing the course of history. Yes, they would all make history together. There were no doubts—none at all—in the large white walled room on the third floor of the Edwardian era colonial merchant bank building in the City.

Natural light flooded into the cavernous minimalist office space from the large white Edwardian sash windows on either side of the long white walled room—which took up the entire floor of the Grade II listed building. The London that appeared beyond the windows was grey and overcast. From one of the windows, there was a clear view of the glittering seventy-two-storey Shard; from another, the glassy and luminescent Gherkin could be seen, shrouded in the wintery gloom.

LOOT THE LOOTERS
Millions of dollars were streaming through the offices of Quadriga Investments every minute of the day and night. The men who labored here knew exactly what they were doing. Modern finance was far more brutal than anyone could imagine. Algorithms and Artificial Intelligence had changed the financial landscape beyond recognition. Now capital moved across the globe in a mere fraction of a second. No mortal man could keep up with it. No mere mortal could defeat or even hope to compete with an AI system. Artificial Intelligence was unstoppable and invincible. Well, not quite. There was one mortal that had been blessed with a level of **Jupiterian discernment** that not even an AI program could ascertain. Was that possible? Yes. One man had been blessed with this extraordinarily phenomenal gift—albeit, an unwanted one.

Enoch Tara.

Enoch Tara operated in obscurity. Power was best exercised when cloaked behind an impenetrable cloud of mystery. And that dark veil which the mysterious Mr Tara had hidden behind had never been pierced—ever. It was maddening for Carter Holland. How was it possible that Enoch Tara had kept everything about his operations absolutely secret? Enoch Tara sailed the dark and icy waters of secrecy effortlessly. Carter Holland had utilized resources that only a multibillionaire could have at their disposal, and still, nothing had been uncovered that was not already in the public domain.

Carter Holland had long suspected Enoch Tara's true abilities. Having been unable to discover any of Tara's weaknesses, Carter had long accepted that going head-to-head with Enoch Tara in the financial realm was impossible. Carter Holland would be routed quickly. Carter's defeat was certain. No, there had to be way to defeat Enoch Tara. And Carter had found it. It was implementing the plan that would be the main challenge now. Carter needed the right people to carry out his plans. Once carried out, Tara would fall.

Carter Ajax Holland, an aloof and distant figure, did not say much, and when he did speak, he said little. No dissent was tolerated. Carter gave orders and his minions executed them without question. Carter Holland's demeanor, a clenched jaw, an unsmiling face, a ramrod straight posture, and enigmatic gaze often lost in distant mediation, had not gone unnoticed by his underlings, followers, and rivals. Carter Holland, ever cold and ever distant, ruled his financial empire through signs, gestures, cryptic pronouncements, and symbols.

Carter swiveled around in his minimalist black leather chair. He looked out on the City below. **It was time to separate the wheat from the chaff.** Yes. The plan would work because it had to work. Nothing could or would stop Carter Holland. Not Tara's Special Unit nor Enoch Tara himself. Carter Holland would travel to the east, create a new country, create a new Byzantium, and crown himself emperor. Carter would bring the last splinters of Western Civilization with him.

All was in order.

Now.

Onward.

Gemma—An Invisible Fear—Elephant and Castle

SOUTH LONDON

The pizza shop stood on a side street. The once dilapidated two-storey structure had been purchased and renovated by Colin Bailey almost a decade ago. The modernist structure had been built in 1961, part of the reconstruction of the area after the Second World War. The building had housed several different businesses: a florist, a pharmacy, a record store, and a cell phone retailer. None of the previous owners had properly maintained the building. When Colin Bailey purchased it, the building had stood empty for almost a decade. Colin had invested a small fortune renovating the structure.

THE PIZZA SHOP

Colin had always liked pizza. The idea of opening a pizza shop had actually been his brother Declan's idea. An idea made in jest, but, nonetheless, a good idea. Colin had hired one of his mates from school to run it. Jamie, a self-taught pizza chef, was efficient and hard working. And an excellent chef. The pizzeria was an instant and enormous success. Colin was happy. Not only was this shop a cash cow, he liked eating pizza. Colin didn't need the extra cash stream, but he was happy to take the money. Colin was not greedy; he split the profits with Jamie. Jamie and Colin were mates. And mates look out for each other—especially in Elephant and Castle.

The first floor was a large open area that had had a dozen high back wooden booths installed throughout. Customers could sit with their friends and family (or a date) and enjoy a modicum of privacy.

There was a large plate glass window on the opposite wall where customers could watch the chef make pizza. Jamie enjoyed twirling the pizzas in the air as he made them. Put on a good show for the audience. Jamie, always a bit of a showman, enjoyed it. The pizza shop was usually crowded with customers, especially on the weekends. Colin Bailey was proud of the restaurant. It showed everyone that he had true business acumen.

The second floor of the building was a series of offices and store rooms, most of them unfurnished. There was an office upstairs were Colin often met members of his gang. They would sit around the large desk, eat pizza, and talk business.

Jamie, while fully aware of Colin's true occupation, was not a member of the gang.

ELEPHANT AND THE CASTLE

Colin and Paige had left the safehouse early that morning and spent the day hiding out in a public library that was housed in a brutalist concrete structure. They didn't venture out of the library until nightfall. Both of them were exhausted.

Half of Colin's gang was now dead. And Colin was on the run. He was afraid to return home. People would be waiting for him there. He was being hunted by a myriad of enemies. He knew that Tara's Special unit was after him. What he did not know was that two other separate groups were also pursuing him.

Stay calm.

Colin had parked the white Citroën three blocks away from the pizza shop. Colin parked on a side street. He didn't know if he had been followed. He assumed that the men hunting him were aware of the houses he owned. He could only hope that they were not aware of the pizza shop.

Colin wanted to take the A1 out of London and drive all the way to Scotland. He had friends there who would help him, protect him. But he couldn't do that, not with his brother lying badly wounded in a clinic in London. Declan had to be protected. Colin knew that the men looking for him were also looking for his older brother. Colin had to stay in London.

'Come on, Paige. It will be alright. We will be safe here,' said Colin quietly as he unbuckled his shoulder belt.

'Are you sure? Let's just drive to Scotland right now. Your brother will be alright. They won't be able to find him. Please, Colin, let's just go,' said Paige, who did nothing to hide the fear in her voice.

'Paige, nothing will happen to you. I promise.'

The young and beautiful Paige shook her head and said, 'Please, Colin. Let's get out of here. I'm scared.'

'No.'

The couple, both clad in faded blue jeans, got out the white hatchback, and walked quietly through the darkened streets, being careful to stay within the shadows and avoid standing directly under the street lamps. It was freezing cold. A light layer of snow covered the pavement. Paige adjusted her dark blue wool scarf and beige sweater.

The young couple walked past stores and shops that twinkled with Christmas lights. Normally, Paige would stop and admire Christmas decorations. Paige loved Christmas. At that moment Paige wondered if she would live to see Christmas, just two days away. Her mother would be worried about her. She wanted to call her and speak with her—even if it was just to wish her Merry Christmas one last time. But she couldn't; Colin had smashed her phone to pieces before they had left the house. Paige, her long glossy blonde hair worn in two large braids, like the tails of horses, could hear her heart beating as she walked down the street towards the pizzeria. Paige, at that moment, wished she had never met Colin. He was endangering her life. All Paige had ever wanted was to be married and have a baby, preferably a little girl with blonde hair the same as hers. What kind of life could she have ever hoped to have with Colin? The money and the parties had been fantastic. Paige had really enjoyed it all. But now, all she wanted to do was go home and return to her little life; work at the salon, and have Christmas dinner with her mum.

'I'm sorry, Mummy,' said Paige under her breath as she walked along the street, snow crunching underfoot. Paige felt sick to her stomach. She had never been so scared.

They reached the edge of the building and then Colin took her small soft manicured hand and led her down the dark alley to the side door. Colin took out a key, opened the door, and stepped into the darkened interior.

Paige, for a moment, had thought of making a break for the street. The subway station was close. She could board a train and escape. Paige imagined her mother's smile as she answered the front door. 'Yes, Mummy, I'm home. I'll never leave you again. I'll just work at the salon and we can save our money and one day buy a small terraced house in the Midlands, in a small village, just liked you talked about, Mummy.' Paige then imagined herself in her mother's embrace.

The slam of the door behind her jolted her back into reality.

Colin quickly locked the door. He turned on the lights. He reached up and bolted the door.

'Let's go upstairs,' said Colin.

Paige could hear noisy customers in the dining area of the pizza shop. She could smell pizza. She could hear people cheering. There was a game on the giant plasma screen television in the dining area. Paige could hear loud and excited voices talking about football. She could hear someone shout something about Blackburn and Wigan.

It was warm in the back room. She wanted to open the door and enter the dining area, find a booth, sit down, and order a pizza. She would be safe in a crowded restaurant. Wouldn't she? Then she could borrow someone's cell phone and call her mum. She would tell her how much she loved her and then walk with some of the customers to the Underground station and take the subway home.

Only she didn't do that.

The slender and athletic Colin walked to the narrow wooden steps leading to the second floor of the building. Colin, unbuttoned his dark blue parka to reveal the light grey jumper underneath.

'Come on, Paige. We'll be safe upstairs.'

Colin walked up the wooden steps.

Paige followed.

THE SECOND FLOOR

Paige sat in the beige leather armchair in the corner of the white walled office. The armchair, a rather expensive one, had been a gift from Declan. Paige, numbed by the events of the last few days, sank into the chair.

CCTV

Attached to one of the white walls of the office was a plasma screen. It glowed with CCTV images of the main dining area, the staff room, the kitchen, the alleyway, and the five rooms on the second floor. Colin studied the screen for a moment. The restaurant was crowded. Jamie and two assistants were moving around in the stainless steel kitchen. Jamie and the two assistants wore white tunics—just like chefs. Jamie had never attended a culinary school, but, nonetheless, he considered himself a professional chef. Colin watched the flickering image of Jamie on the screen for a moment.

There was a large wooden desk in the middle of the office surrounded by five folding metal chairs. A silver laptop computer had been left in the center of the desk. Colin unlocked one of the desk drawers. He took a German pistol out of the top drawer and placed it on the desk. He then took a smartphone out of the drawer and turned it on. He placed it on the desk top and unlocked another drawer as the phone slowly sprang to life. Colin sifted through the files in the side drawer. He found a small black notebook, took it out, and locked the drawer.

Ping. Ping. Ping.

The phone was now awake and receiving incoming text messages. Colin picked up the smartphone, tapped on the screen, and started to read through the messages.

'I'm hungry,' said Paige quietly.

Colin looked up from the phone. 'Would you like a pizza from downstairs?'

'Yes.'

'I'll call down and order one. What would you like?' asked Colin.

'I'll go down and order it,' said Paige quietly.

Colin arched an eyebrow wearily. He shook his head. 'Paige. You wouldn't make it home alive.'

Paige inhaled deeply and then exhaled. Tears filled her eyes. Was this the end?

'I'm only twenty, Colin. Please, let me go,' said Paige choking back tears. 'Please, I just want to go home and see my mum.'

'No.'

Colin looked at his phone. He tapped on the screen. A minute later, the smartphone glowed momentarily. Colin tapped on the screen. He read the text message. He exhaled. He tapped out another message. He waited. And waited.

Paige, slumped in the leather chair, had her wool scarf wrapped around the lower half of her face. Paige, now more exhausted than scared, stared off into space.

Ping.

Colin's smartphone glowed with a white light for moment. Colin tapped on the phone. He read the text message. He exhaled and began to type out a response. He sent it.

After a few minutes, the smartphone glowed in Colin's right hand. Colin tapped on the screen and read the text message. He typed out another response and sent it. He exhaled.

Colin Bailey had never met Carter Holland. Declan had told his younger brother that he was never to mention Carter's name to anyone. And Colin was only to contact Carter Holland in absolute emergencies. As far as Colin was concerned, this was an absolute emergency. What Colin Bailey did not know and would have never even guessed was that Carter Holland was the last person in the world that he should have contacted. Carter Holland was seeking to eliminate him and his brother Declan in order to protect himself from Tara's Special Unit.

Declan had always emphasized loyalty. And Declan and Colin had always been loyal to each other and their mates. Loyalty had held the gang together and allowed it to weather the worst that gangland could throw at it. Not in his wildest dreams did Declan ever think that Carter Holland would turn on him. Declan Bailey, formerly of the Parachute Regiment, now lay in a private clinic in London fighting for his life. Colin had expected Carter Holland to help him and his brother escape Tara's Special Unit and the fanatical and merciless Spaniard who led it. All Colin's text message to Carter Holland had done was lead the Evil Spirit to both of them.

The gangster from Elephant and Castle was now waiting in the upstairs office calmly, if somewhat impatiently, for help to arrive. Colin looked at his wrist watch: 8:13pm. Colin wondered if was doing the right thing. Perhaps they should have just driven to Scotland?

'I'm sorry, Paige. I'm sorry I got you into to this.'

Paige did not answer. She simply stared off into space.

BLOOMSBURY

The wrinkled visage looked at the text message that glowed on screen of the encrypted smartphone. Carter Holland had forwarded the text messages from Colin, which including the address of the pizza shop and the clinic where Declan was now being stitched back together, to the man from East Anglia.

The Evil Spirit, in a charcoal grey suit, white dress shirt (with a Windsor collar), and black silk necktie, stood in the white walled entry hall of an empty house in West London. He was alone. He leaned up against the ornate balustrade at the base of the stairs. The balustrade had been carved out of Indian teak. The previous owner, a former officer in the British Indian Army, had left India in 1947, but had taken the balustrade from his house in Jeypore (now Jaipur) with him. He had had this small reminder of the British Raj installed in the house in London; a reminder of the place he had been born, raised, served in, and then been expelled from. The balustrade, a carved wooden pillar, was Victorian—its ornate design was a combination of both English and Indian elements. The wooden steps had once been covered with a sumptuous Persian stair carpet runner; however, the current owner had had it removed. The Evil Spirit wanted to be able to hear people ascending or descending the stairs.

The Evil Spirit had purchased the house in the late 1980s from a distant cousin of the previous owner. The empty house had needed extensive repairs. The Evil Spirit, in a former life, had been a normal person with common aspirations. That had all ended with the brutal and horrific murder of his twenty-one-year-old pregnant wife by a foreigner who should have never been allowed into England. The man, shattered by the shocking loss of both his wife and unborn daughter, had been transformed into an Evil Spirit—neither really living, nor really dead—a walking corpse, a shell. The Evil Spirit rarely thought of his former life. And when he did, it was as if he were reminiscing about the life of an entirely different person. The naive and short-sighted policies of Modernity had destroyed the Evil Spirit's family and robbed him of life and hope.

The house, a relatively modest Edwardian semi-detached, was where the Evil Spirit resided when not in East Anglia. The Evil Spirit hated London. London had become an alien city in the Evil Spirit's ancestral homeland. The white walls were undecorated. The polished hardwood floors reflected the light from the overhead lamp in the entry hall.

The drawing room had a modern sofa upholstered in light grey fabric. There was an inexpensive (mass produced) coffee table and a heavily worn leather single armchair (which had belonged to the British cavalry officer). There was Victorian grandfather clock (constructed of Indian teak) in one corner. It had not been wound since the British colonist had left Calcutta. Upon arriving in England, the retired army major had decided to keep it at the time it had run out in India. It had been left behind when the house was sold. The Evil Spirit had never bothered to either restore it or remove it..

The three white walled upstairs bedrooms were completely empty, save the one the Evil Spirit stayed in when in London. It had a simple modern wooden bed frame, box mattress set, and white bedding. There was a modern wooden night stand next to the bed. The Evil Spirit would place one (or two) smartphones, a sterling silver keyring, a cut throat razor, and a pistol on the night stand when he was ready for bed. Two business suits hung in the wardrobe along with a dozen white dress shirts.

The murder of the Englishman's wife and daughter had prematurely aged him. The wrinkled visage that appeared to the world was the same age as the youthful and attractive Carter Holland. The failed policies of Modernity had left their mark on the former human.

The Evil Spirit walked into the drawing room. He didn't bother to turn on the lights. He sat down in the leather armchair; his twisted face illuminated by the bluish light emanating from the screen of the smartphone.

Ping.

Another message from Carter Holland. Carter couldn't believe it; Colin was walking directly into the trap. The Evil Spirit tapped out a reply. And then another to the young woman from East Anglia.

Ping.

The smartphone glowed momentarily with each incoming text. The Evil Spirit unbuttoned his dark grey coat. He leaned forward and tapped on the screen of the smartphone.

Outside the house, it was freezing cold. An icy wind had carried the cold all the way from Northumbria. Sometimes a cold gust of wind would rattle the windows of the drawing room. Occasionally the drawing room would be illuminated by the lights of a passing car.

A dark blue Audi A6 was now making its way to a popular pizza restaurant in Elephant and Castle.

The Evil Spirit tapped out one final message. He then leaned back into the leather chair. He stared at the broken grandfather that stood in the shadows of the room. It had stopped working at a minute after midnight. The Evil Sprit often imagined that he could turn the hands back on the clock and go back in time and save the lives of his wife and unborn child. Time was so unforgiving. One could not reverse tragedy. No one could. One could only move forward. But what does someone with no future do with the time left to him?

England had died with a young pregnant wife on a cold night in 1998.

Now the only way forward was to create a new homeland. And the only one who on the Earth who was capable of carrying out such an enormous undertaking was Carter Holland.

THE RESTAURANT

The three men and one woman, all wearing eyeglasses that interfered with facial recognition, denim blue jeans and parkas, had been seated in a booth in the back of the crowded restaurant. The waitress gave them each a menu. As soon as she had departed, the young woman with light brown hair stood up and left the booth. The athletic young woman from East Anglia had made her way down a narrow hallway in the restaurant, past the restrooms, and found the door to the back room unlocked. She opened it and entered the room quickly, closing the door behind her. Within in three minutes the other three men had joined her.

THE BACK ROOM

The back room was empty. There was a dead bolt on the inside of the door. The young woman turned the lock after the last man had entered the room.

'Alright,' said the young woman quietly as she pulled a black balaclava from the inside pocket of her grey parka. The others took black balaclavas out of their coats and put them on. The young woman pulled down her balaclava and took out a straight razor. 'Let's make this quick.'

The other three men drew pistols: one a Yugoslavian M57, the other two Russian 9mm Makarovs. One man with a Makarov made his way up the stairs. The young woman went next. The other two followed.

THE OFFICE

Colin, exhausted, had fallen asleep on the sofa. He had taken off his dark blue parka and was now using it as a blanket. Carter Holland had told him that it would take at least two hours for his security team to arrive at the restaurant. Carter had instructed him to stay out of sight until then. Colin's safety was paramount. Colin had also texted Carter the address of the clinic where his brother was recovering. Carter had assured him that Declan would be moved to a secure private clinic in West London. Declan would receive top notch medical care. 'Do not worry,' Carter had texted him. Colin had breathed a sigh of relief.

The security team from East Anglia had arrived in thirty-nine minutes, not two hours.

It was Paige, not Colin, that had been awakened by the creaking of the hardwood floor as the four people slowly made their way through the upstairs rooms. She looked over at the sofa and saw Colin fast asleep under a blue dark blue parka. She shifted her gaze towards the plasma screen—her eyes suddenly widened.

'Colin. Wake up,' said Paige quietly as she jumped up from the leather chair. The four images onscreen wore balaclavas and carried guns. She shook him and Colin's eyes opened. 'Trouble,' said Paige in a quiet but panicked tone of voice.

Colin jumped up from the sofa and looked at the screen. They were now only a few feet away on the other side of the door. Colin picked up the German pistol and pointed it at the door. He looked in Paige's direction and was about to say something when the door burst open and a hooded figure with a cut throat razor bounded into the room and attacked Colin like a blood starved spider. There was a split-second flash of metal as the razor sliced into Colin's face—blood spurted out and a second later there was another flash of metal and Colin's throat was cut. Colin dropped the pistol and fell backwards onto the hardwood floor. Three men brandishing pistols stormed into the office. They surrounded Colin and began to kick and stomp on him with heavy leather boots.

Paige did not scream. She stood rooted to the floor like an obelisk and watched in horror as Colin was slashed and kicked and stomped to death under heavy boots.

The hooded young woman turned to face the trembling twenty-year-old from a council estate in London. The plain looking young woman from East Anglia could not fail to notice how starkly beautiful Paige really was—before moving forward and slashing her throat.

Gemma—An Invisible Fear—The Black Sea

MAYFAIR

Carter Holland, in a pair of pale blue pyjama trousers, a white t-shirt, a white cotton honeycomb bathrobe, and white cotton slippers, examined that large map that lay on a large wooden table before him. Carter Holland's well defined abdominal muscles could be clearly made out through his cotton t-shirt. The blond and blue-eyed Carter appeared to be sculpted out of living marble.

It was late. Outside, on the street below, a lone automobile made its way down the snow-covered street; its bright headlights cutting through the demi-darkness. Carter, unable to sleep, had gotten up and walked down the long bluish-light grey walled hallway to the white walled library on the top floor of the Grade II listed Georgian house in Mayfair.

The large paper map of Europe on top of the large modern table was both political and topographical. The political borders printed on the map were the current ones. Carter had outlined his new country in yellow highlighter. Yes, in a few months, the map of Europe would change.

And a cataclysm would follow.

The old order would end. A necessary end executed with maximum chaos.

Simply declaring a breakaway region in an irrelevant country in an irrelevant Eastern Europe after a short pantomime war would not assure the new country of survival. No, just the opposite. Global entities would embargo and blockade the new Byzantium that Carter Holland had created. Carter's country would be ground into powder. That is, unless, global entities found themselves overwhelmed with other far more pressing issues—like the survival of the global financial system. Carter had mined all the roads and bridges of the global economy. The West—the only place on the face of the Earth that truly mattered—would be too busy trying to right their own ship by the time Carter Holland had emerged from the shadows and crowned himself emperor of the new state. Carter Holland, secure in the new country on the Black Sea behind a wall of revolutionary technology, would be invincible. The West would have no choice but to accept the fait accompli that would soon appear on European soil.

And that would only be the beginning.

Undoubtably, millions would flock to the new country, the new Byzantium. Carter would be inundated with the talent and wasted potential of the West. And the West, bereft of its greatest resource—its most intelligent people—would slowly collapse. New countries would appear in Europe. Carter Holland would be the herald of a new Golden Age. The new Europe that would emerge would be made up of countries that were either dynamic utopias or dystopian failed states. There would be nothing in the middle. The failed states would starve; the dystopian badlands acting as de facto walls that shielded the new utopias from the unwanted foreign hordes. And what of Carter Holland's new country? It would expand as the countries around it imploded. Carter Holland did not want to save the world. He wanted to destroy it. Yes, this would truly be a new world order.

Outside, it had begun to snow. Carter walked to the large white pane glass window. Four stories below, the thin layer of snow on the pavement reflected and amplified the illumination given off by the ornate iron street lamps. The snow-covered cobblestone street below was now like an icy white river flowing gently and silently through Mayfair.

Carter looked up and in the direction of the City. In the distance, he could see the glassy, elongated, and curved Gherkin at 30 St Mary Axe. The red aviation lights glowed on either side of the shimmering tower. Carter's blue eyes focused. The Gherkin had represented so many things to him over the last year: a laughing opponent, a fragile pillar that could be shattered with a single hard blow, and now what did the ghostly white hexagonal structure represent?

The light at the end of the pier.

Carter Holland now had everything had had worked for his entire life within his grasp. He was so close. So close.

Gemma—An Invisible Fear—The Studio Flat

LONDON
It was dark. Gemma slowly opened her eyes. The white ceiling above her was dimly illuminated by the street lamp below her second floor window. It was warm inside the small studio flat just two subway stops from London's financial district, the City. Gemma, underneath a large white duvet and soft, white Egyptian cotton sheets; her head resting on a large white pillow, stretched. What time was it? Gemma glance over at the lucent blue glow of the aluminum LED clock: 8:01am. It was still a few minutes until sunrise. Night came early and the morning light late in the winter in England.

It was December 24, 2019.

CHRIST THE REDEEMER
Gemma climbed out bed. Gemma, in a pair of dark blue tartan pyjama bottoms and a white t-shirt, walked around the low white bookcase that separated her bed from the rest of the small apartment and plugged in the green ceramic Christmas tree on top of the bookcase. The small ceramic tree illuminated the room with rays of blue, white, and red light. Taped to the bookcase were a dozen Christmas cards from Gemma's closet friends—most of them from the ranks of The Inseparables. Gemma prized cards more than any expensive boxed gift.

Christmas was not about exchanging gifts. It was about remembering the sacrifices of a man who had been sent into the world to forgive mankind for their sins—it was up to the individual to decide whether or not they chose to accept His absolution. It was also a time to gather with loved ones and spend the precious and limited time one has on this Earth with them. God had guided Gemma through the storm of the previous year. Without a doubt, God had saved Gemma.

And now, another storm was gathering.

Gemma opened one of the cards and read it. It was from Freya, her Goddaughter. Freya always wrote the most beautiful things in the cards she mailed Gemma. Gemma held the Christmas card to her chest. She said a prayer for Freya. Gemma then taped the card back on to the bookcase.

Today Gemma would stop by the offices of Millennium Investments and make sure everything was in order. The staff in Singapore was now running the day-to-day operations. Gemma was scheduled to meet with Helen, the receptionist, Tarquin, a financial analyst, and Isolde, recently promoted to assistant office manager. Alexa was now in the Cotswolds with Aurelia and the rest her family.

Isolde had proven herself to be indispensable to Gemma. It was Gemma that had recommended her for promotion. Alexa had agreed. It was at that moment both women realized that Gemma would leave Millennium Investments after marrying Enoch. Yes, The Honourable Gemma Ophelia Ripley would soon become Mrs Gemma Ophelia Tara. It was not until that very moment Alexa had agreed to promote Isolde that Gemma had realized she was leaving the company. Yes, it had remained unspoken, but it might as well been cast in iron. Gemma was about to begin a new phase of her life. It was important that a competent and energetic person replace her.

Gemma undressed. Naked, she stretched. She opened the door to the small white tiled bathroom, entered, and closed the door behind her.

Gemma—An Invisible Fear—Mayfair

THE FOYER

The flaxen haired Freya, in a pair of faded blue jeans, a white cotton blouse (with a large collar and open cuffs), made her way down the stairs like a panther on the prowl. She reached the bottom of the stairs and then stepped onto the white and black checkerboard marble floor. Standing in front of the double doors of the entry hall was a uniformed courier, the yellow reflective strips down the sleeves of his dark blue parka reflecting the incandescent light of the crystal chandelier which hovered above the large cavernous Georgian room. A housemaid, in a black wool uniform (with a white collar and white cotton gloves) was standing next to the courier. She nodded slightly to Freya as she approached.

'Miss Maud, a parcel has arrived requiring your signature,' said the young housemaid.

'Thank you, Alice,' replied Freya politely.

Two cardboard courier boxes wrapped in brown paper and tied with white string sat on the entry hall table. Each parcel had a plastic pouch stuck to it with a hand written address on it as well as a couple of courier stamps. Freya recognized Gemma's florid handwriting on the labels. She smiled slightly as she accepted the clipboard and pen from the courier.

'Thank you, ma'am,' said the courier after Freya had signed the form and returned the clipboard to him. The uniformed servant, with a flash of white gloves, opened the large gorgeous black door—which allowed in a blast of icy wintery air into the foyer—and the courier turned and left.

Freya picked up one of the boxes. It wasn't very heavy. Freya could hear the subtle shifting of…biscuits inside the box. Gemma had not forgotten. But, of course, she hadn't. Undoubtably, a box of freshly baked raspberry chocolate biscuits—make that two boxes—of freshly baked raspberry chocolate biscuits had been sent over to the house in Mayfair for Freya and Louise. Freya held the box to her chest. Yes, Gemma, her Godmother, loved her. And Freya loved her Godmother Gemma.

Freya placed one box on top of the other, picked them both up, and carried them both up the stairs.

THE BEDROOM

Louise, clad in a pair of red and purple tartan pyjamas and beige cable knit sweater, lay on her stomach on top of the large white duvet on top of the queen sized Edwardian bed in Freya's white walled bedroom. Louise had practically sunk into the white duvet. A pile of notebooks lay on the nightstand. Louise was studying one of two open notebooks and an open textbook on the bed.

Louise would sit for exams after returning from the Christmas holiday and then, three days later, move into the alcove room in Midlands-Hasegawa. In spite of the stroke, Louise, intended to take her exams in London before transferring to Muddy Hills in the Midlands. The instructors at her university in London had told her that they would tabulate her final grade without her taking the end of term exam, but Louise had refused.

Louise, still recovering from the stroke, was taking it easy. Freya's parents and paternal grandparents had welcomed her into the large Grade II listed Georgian house in Mayfair. The 4th Baron (Lord Maud) had been especially happy to welcome Louise. The baron had taken an instant liking to the tiny girl from East Anglia the year before. The 4th Baron had also helped navigate the return of Louise's father. With Louise's permission, he had invited Harold Percival to spend Christmas Day with the family. The baron and his wife had also been consulting with a nutritionist from the hospital about what Louise could and could not eat. They also made sure Louise remembered to take her medication. The entire family was deeply concerned about Louise; concerned for her health and hopeful that she would be able to reconcile with her father—if that's what she wanted.

Louise looked up from her notes when Freya opened the glossy white door to the bedroom. The bedroom was filled with natural light; the light of an overcast wintery day.

'Gemma sent us a couple of parcels,' said Freya happily. And Freya smiled as she placed the boxes on the maple desk near the large sash window.

Louise smiled. 'Could it be, really, my dear Freya, a box of our favorite biscuits?'

'Why don't we open one and find out?' said Freya in her posh and Sloaney intonation.

Louise carefully climbed out of bed. She put on the pair of white cotton slippers and crossed the hardwood floor. Freya handed Louise a pair of scissors. Louise cut the string and then tore off the brown paper. Freya then took a sterling silver letter opener from the desk drawer and cut the tape sealing the box. Freya shifted the box in Louise's direction. Freya smiled gently. Louise carefully opened the cardboard box and the girls looked inside. The two teenage undergraduates could smell the chocolate and raspberries of the freshly baked biscuits. Yes, even in the midst of the chaotic whirlwind return from the day spent in Muddy Hills, Gemma had found time to bake the girls' favorites.

'You first, Louise,' said Freya happily.

'Thank you, Freya.'

Louise bit into one of the biscuits and chewed it very slowly. It was heavenly.

'I haven't had raspberry chocolate biscuits in *yonks*,' said Louise in her Sloaney and posh intonation happily.

'Gemma is as thoughtful as ever,' said Freya.

'Yes, she is. We are blessed to have Gemma in our lives,' said Louise.

THE GHERKIN

Gemma had stomped the snow off of her tall black leather boots before entering the vast minimalist foyer of white walls and glass windows of the Gherkin through the large glass revolving doors. A light snow was falling outside. The beautiful, slender, and glossy Gemma, warm underneath her blue wool Burberry coat (with silver buttons), a light grey pleated knee length wool skirt, and a white Egyptian cotton blouse (with a large collar), and carrying a black leather Montblanc briefcase, took out her smartphone as she walked past the giant Christmas tree (which was decorated with white, red, and silver bulbs, plastic icicle ornaments, and twinkling white and pale blue Christmas lights) towards the elevators. Gemma walked along side dozens of other suited and booted City workers as she took out her digital access card and scanned the glowing screen of the digital reader as she passed through the security barriers. The elevator was crowded with young men wearing wool overcoats and English cut neckties and women wearing wool flat front trousers and pencil skirts under wool overcoats. The ride up in the crowded lift was silent. No one spoke.

The day before Christmas, and the Gherkin at 30 St Mary Axe was swirling with activity. Yes, not even the Christmas holidays would slow the shadowy assault on the global financial markets. Gemma stepped off the elevator and made her way down the white walled hallway to Millennium Investments.

The young, attractive, blonde and blue-eyed receptionist, Helen, smiled.

'Merry Christmas, Mrs Ripley.'

'Thank you, Helen. Merry Christmas. What are you plans for the holidays?'

'I'm going to spend them with my family in Cotswolds.'

THE CONFERENCE ROOM

Tarquin, in a charcoal grey wool suit, a white dress shirt (with a St James collar), and a red, grey, and blue tartan tie, sat across the glass conference table from Isolde and Gemma. Isolde, young, blonde, and beautiful, looked through the documents before her. Gemma marvelled at the young Isolde's professionalism, efficiency and resourcefulness. Yes, Isolde would soon replace her at the company. Gemma was relieved that her replacement at Millennium Investments would be someone as competent and reliable as Isolde. Gemma, at forty-one, albeit, a youthful forty-one, suddenly felt her age seated at the table with the young staffers.

'Mr Lee emailed me this morning. We will forward all of the email traffic from our office to Singapore for the next few days. Also, I have rescheduled the meeting with the CEO of IDK Chemicals for January 5th,' said Tarquin.

'Thank you, Tarquin.'

'Yes, ma'am. As requested, all of the quarterly reports will be emailed to the investors on the third of January. And, I will be on call at home, if you need anything,' said Isolde in her posh intonation.

Gemma smiled.

'Thank you, Isolde.'

THE ELEVATOR

Gemma, waiting patiently for the lift, looked at her silver Cartier wrist watch: 5:03pm. Yes, Enoch would pick her up at home at 5:45pm and they would head off to Marble Arch. She would have enough time to make it home on the subway. The Tube station was only a short walk from her apartment. Gemma had already packed her purple leather Asprey box suitcase. They would stay the night at Enoch's house, attend the Anglican Nine Lessons and Carols service on Christmas Eve at Westminster Abbey, and spend Christmas with Enoch's mother at the house in Marble Arch. Gemma liked Enoch's mother. She was intelligent and kind, and most importantly, she was accepting. Mrs Tara had welcomed Gemma into her life the moment Enoch had introduced her. In spite of the scandals and Gemma's ruined reputation, Mrs Tara could see that Gemma was a good person. The silver haired Mrs Tara truly cared about her.

'Gemma,' said Isolde as she walked towards her. 'You forgot your phone.'

Gemma reached for the pocket of her coat. Yes, the smartphone was not there. Gemma, in the rush to leave, had forgotten it. 'Thank you, Isolde.

'You left it on your desk. I thought you might be needing it,' said Isolde with a smile.

'Thank you, Isolde.

Isolde handed Gemma the black plastic smartphone. Gemma quickly placed it in her coat pocket. The elevator doors suddenly opened. Gemma stepped into the elevator, turned around, and just before the doors closed, she smiled and said, 'Merry Christmas, Isolde.'

And just as the doors closed, Isolde flashed a smile as white as a Siberian winter.

Gemma—An Invisible Fear—A Necessary End

NORTH LONDON
Declan Bailey had been drifting in and out of consciousness for a week. The doctor had been forced to perform surgery in the small clinic in London in a makeshift operating room with the assistance of a Romanian nurse that he had worked with on several clandestine operations. The nurse, in her late fifties, had been brought over from Bucharest by the surgeon. He had helped her get employment with the NHS. When the doctor called her in the middle of the night and told her he needed her assistance, the woman had driven to the private clinic immediately. The doctor had performed not one, but three separate surgical procedures on Declan Bailey that week. The former British Para was in a lot of pain. When not on the operating table in the clinic, he was in a bed in one of the small white walled rooms of the clinic.

The last week had been phantasmagorical for Declan. Several times he had awoken to flashes of sharp pain and the florescent lighting of the clinic. Images blurred, eddied, and swirled around in his mind. Sometimes he could hear the doctor and nurse speaking in Romanian. Other times he would see the young faces of Aiden or Johnny, two members of Colin's criminal gang, hovering over him. Other times, either going into surgery or coming out of it, Declan would stir awake momentarily and see the medical staff in blue surgical scrubs and wearing white surgical masks.

THE CLINIC
Aiden and Johnny had spent the week texting back and forth with Colin on Declan's status. The two young gangsters, in faded blue jeans, white t-shirts, and parkas, had survived on pizza and Chinese take away for the last week. They both slept in one of the clinic's four hospital rooms. Colin had transferred a thousand pounds into each of their accounts to cover expenses. The boredom was only broken by watching television in their hospital room, or when putting on blue surgical scrubs to help wheel

Declan in and out of surgery, and the occasional text from Colin.

And then one night, a text arrived from Colin Bailey. Some people would soon arrive at the clinic and Aiden and Johnny could go home. The two young men were relieved. Also, they feared that the police would soon raid the clinic and arrest them all.

Johnny told himself that he would cash out and move up north and start some kind of business, maybe a landscaping company. Anything to get away from the life of crime he was involved in. Neither Johnny nor Aiden knew about the massacre at the warehouse two days before. The bloodied corpses of the gang left in the warehouse had not yet been discovered. Johnny had been instructed not to text anyone but Colin. And Colin had said nothing about the fate of the others. He had only told them that they would be on their way home in an hour.

Aiden walked into the doctor's white walled office. The unattractive and chubby middle-aged nurse was seated next to the craggy faced doctor in a worn wooden chair. Both were in blue surgical scrubs. Both were smoking cigarettes.

'Good evening, Doctor. Colin just text me. He said that some people were on their way over to the clinic. They are going to take Declan to another clinic in London. Colin said that I was to tell you that you will be paid for services rendered No worries, mate.'

The fat and craggy faced doctor took a drag off of his cigarette, the end of it glowed a brilliant bright orange. The doctor exhaled and smoke filled the small office. The craggy faced doctor did not show any emotion. The doctor leaned back in the chair. 'Good, Aiden. I am tired. Tell Colin that Declan will be alright. All three surgeries went smoothly. The damage will not be permanent. Declan will recover…in time. Ask Colin to text me. I have some things to discuss with him.'

'Sure enough,' said Aiden wearily. Exhausted, the twenty-year-old from Elephant and Castle turned and walked out of the office.

The doctor looked over at the nurse, and in Romanian said, 'Don't worry, Nadia. Declan and Colin have always paid well.'

THE FRONT DOOR

A young woman with light brown hair, in faded blue jeans, a dark blue parka, wearing a pair of transparent framed eyeglasses and with a grey wool scarf wrapped around the lower half of her face, walked to the front door of the clinic that stood on a side street in North London, snow crunching underfoot.

It was late at night, and an icy cold northern wind had brought lower temperatures with it. The white blinds of the clinic were drawn and the clinic appeared to be closed. Of course, the team assembled outside knew that was not case.

Three more men, all clad in faded blue jeans and wearing puffer coats (one dark blue, the other two dark grey), all three with their hoods up and wearing black framed glasses that foiled CCTV recognition software followed her.

A car door could be heard closing further down the cobblestone street. Within a minute, the Evil Spirit, in a charcoal grey suit, white dress shirt (with a forward point collar), and a black necktie, appeared. Their breath materialized around them in the freezing cold wintery weather.

'Alright. After this, you are all to return to East Anglia. Take separate trains. Do you understand?' said the Evil Spirit.

The group nodded in near unison.

The young woman knocked on the front door. No answer.

The Evil Spirit took out his smartphone and tapped on the screen. A moment later the smartphone's screen glowed in the darkness. A lock clicked and the door opened. A skinny young man in a red parka answered.

'We've been expecting you. Please, come in.'

The group walked into the clinic and the young man from Bristol closed the door behind them.

'Where is Declan?' asked the young woman with chin length bobbed hair.

'He's in the last room down the corridor. He's asleep. I think,' said the young hoodie in a grating working class accent.

'Where is the doctor?' asked the young woman.

'He's in the office,' replied the young hoodie.

''How many people are in the clinic?' asked the young woman.

'What does that matter?' asked Aiden nonchalantly.

'We need to know. It's a security issue,' said the young woman nonchalantly.

'Five, including me.'

'I'll go down and check on Declan,' said the Evil Spirit. 'I'm a doctor.'

'Alright,' said Aiden.

Aiden walked down the hall leading to the doctor's office. The young woman and the three young men followed.

THE HOSPITAL ROOM

It was the blast of bright florescent light that awoke the heavily bandaged Declan from a troubled sleep. He opened his eyes slowly and focused. A white haired and wrinkled visage, in a dark wool suit, hovered over Declan. The man's appearance was sinister. The unsmiling man shook his head slightly.

'Carter Holland sent me here. Your brother, Colin, is dead.'

Declan's eyes widened; he felt his chest tighten; he had trouble breathing, trouble taking it all in. Tears welled up in Declan's eyes. Colin had not only been Declan's brother, but his best friend. Tears started to run down Declan's face. The physical pain vanished as the emotional pain of losing his younger brother swept through him.

'What happened?' said Declan in a gasping whisper.

'Your brother paid the price for failure; as will you,' said the Evil Spirit.

Declan needed no further explanation. There was shock at Carter Holland's betrayal, but now, in his present semi-drugged state and badly wounded condition, there was nothing Declan could do. He tried to move his muscular arms. He wanted to fend off the attacker, but the muscular and powerfully built retired army sergeant could not move. It was over. Despair competed with grief. Declan did not bother trying to negotiate with the withered visage that seemed to float above him in the hospital room. Declan knew that was pointless.

The Evil Spirit drew a cut throat razor from his coat pocket. He opened it to reveal the sharp straight razor inside. The razor glinted and gleamed in the florescent lighting.

Resigned to his fate, Declan closed his eyes.

'I'll see you in a minute, Colin. I love you. It will good to see you again, Gareth. I've really missed you. See you soon, Mummy. I'm sorry I couldn't save you,' said Declan in barely a whisper.

7 A NOSTALGIA BORNE OUT OF DESPAIR

Gemma—An Invisible Fear—Westminster Abbey

LONDON
Gemma, Enoch, and the silver haired Eloise Tara, had, at Gemma's request, sat in the last row of chairs in the back of the Grade I listed 11th century Medieval church in London. Above them hovered the beautiful, carved, fan-vaulted, stone ceiling. They were shrouded in a pale darkness broken only by the candle light of the Nine Lessons and Carols and surrounded by the pomp and majesty that one would expect of the Anglican Church.

Gemma had stopped attending church regularly several years ago. Gemma, after being dragged through the mud in the press by her ex-husband, former mother-in-law, and an eager Fleet Street during her egregious ex-husband's criminal trial, had found many of her fellow Anglicans to be unwelcoming (to put it mildly). She had spent years praying alone in the small forgotten church of St Albans in central London. Gemma had only felt comfortable attending church services in the small village church near Poppy's country house in the Lake District. Gemma had always found solace in God. Being a social pariah had taught Gemma many things; one of them being that it wasn't necessary for her to attend church with others. God was always with her.

Enoch had drifted away from regular church attendance as well, but for different reasons. Enoch had felt he had been forsaken by God for the last two decades. Enoch could not understand why everything in his life had gone so wrong. It was Gemma that had saved him. And now, on Christmas Eve, less than a year after reuniting with Gemma, Enoch had found himself wanting to return.

Enoch, in a dark blue wool suit, pale blue dress shirt, and a dark blue silk neck tie, prayed for his mother, his departed father, Gemma, Louise, and the peace of the world.

Enoch's mother, Eloise May Tara, had been invited to attend with them. Eloise, though in her mid-seventies, was quite outgoing, active, and rather independent. Enoch loved his mother and made an effort to spend as much time as possible with her.

Enoch, struggling to comprehend the ongoing financial turmoil, would not be able to get away from the office in time to attend church in Surrey, so Gemma and Enoch had decided to attend Anglican services in London and spend Christmas Day at Enoch's house in Marble Arch. Eloise, always understanding, told him not worry. She was happy to spend time with her son and future daughter-in-law anywhere.

NINE LESSONS AND CAROLS

Gemma, in a dark blue dress and black patent leather pumps, had a lot on her mind. Gemma could neither forget nor ignore Louise's warning on the train the night before. Gemma crossed her arms and exhaled, her platinum and diamond engagement ring sparkling in the candle light which illuminated the nave where they were seated.

Yes, Louise had had a dream so powerful that she had had a stroke. Yes, this had been no ordinary dream. The dragon, was, undoubtably, real. And for some reason, it had warned Louise. But what did it all mean? How was Gemma involved in all of this? Why would she be in danger?

Enoch Tara now faced not only financial ruin, but the very real possibility of a violent death. One of his security team, the Brigada, had already been murdered, and now his Special Unit was engaged in a secret war in London. Enoch had signed off on the death of others. He had unleashed his Special Unit on a group of unknown enemies. It had not been an easy decision. But, considering the situation he now faced, it seemed the only thing he could do. Enoch, seated between his mother and Gemma, the soft voices of the choir drifting by him and a myriad of troubles swirling around him, slowly closed his eyes and prayed.

COVENT GARDEN

The svelte and middle-aged Comandante, formerly of the Spanish Foreign Legión, leaned back in the wooden chair. The Spaniard's smooth face was illuminated in the bluish light of the computer screen that glowed before him. The Comandante, in a pair of blue tartan pyjama trousers and a white cotton t-shirt, was about to go to bed when a news report caught his eye.

Click.

Colin Bailey was dead. Colin and his girlfriend had both been murdered in London. The police were describing it as a brutal gangland killing. The police were investigating. The police, however, had quickly concluded that Colin and his girlfriend had been the victims of a rival criminal gang. There was no mention in the news report of the pile of corpses in Colin's warehouse in Greater London. Obviously, the police had not searched it. Not yet.

There was no mention of Declan Bailey either. What did that mean? Was Declan still alive, or had he also been killed? And, most importantly, at least to the Comandante, who had killed Colin and his girlfriend? Was it really a rival criminal gang? No. That would be too easy. Far too easy. No, there was another group on the prowl in London. But who was backing it and for what reason?

Ping.

The Spaniard's encrypted smartphone glowed momentarily. The Comandante tapped on the screen. It was Ingrid. She had some information. She had intercepted something in the digital ether. It was important. They had to meet as soon as possible. Yes, Ingrid Steyr, the former warrant officer, had used the state-of-the-art technology Mr Tara had supplied her and the training that the Her Majesty's Armed Forces had imparted to her, to uncover something important. Had Ingrid discovered the identity of Colin Bailey's employer?

Ping.

Yes, I know tomorrow is Christmas, but this will not wait. Meet me in the garden at 6pm. Bring the entire team.

Gemma—An Invisible Fear—Christmas in Mayfair

MAYFAIR
Major Harold Algernon Percival (Ret'd) climbed out of the backseat of the glossy black cab and stood on the snowy pavement along a street lined with some of the most expensive terraced houses in the entire world. The retired army major, in a charcoal grey wool suit, white dress shirt (with a Windsor collar), and regimental tie, carefully buttoned the dark blue cashmere wool overcoat while holding a dark green paper shopping bag which contained Louise's Christmas present.

OMNIA OMNIBUS UBIQUE
The day before had been spent shopping in one of London's most luxurious department stores, which was housed in a Grade II listed building in central London. Harold hadn't visited the store in almost a decade. He had quickly become lost amidst the gilded interiors of the famed British department store. The interior was just as one would expect: glossy marble floors one could see their reflection in, ornate and iconic pillars, an Egyptian themed escalator, and a bespoke contemporary glass chandelier which hovered over the base of the escalators through the revamped entrance.

What would Harold buy his daughter Louise? He had no idea what she liked. Louise was now a stranger to him. And it was all his fault. Harold had chosen to abandon his daughter after the death of his wife when Louise was so tiny and fragile. Should he buy her something expensive? No, that would be vulgar. He wanted to find something that would have special meaning to Louise. But what? The retired Major Harold Percival, formerly of the Coldstream Guards, was at a loss. And then, an idea.

THE GEORGIAN TOWNHOUSE

The Grade I listed Portland stone Palladian house loomed up before Harold. Its large glossy black door (adorned with a berried eucalyptus Christmas Wreath) seemed to stare back at him through the grey and cold wintery afternoon. Harold breathed hard; his breath materializing around him in the cold air. Harold could sense that today would be his last chance to reconnect with his only child—a daughter he had chosen to throw away when she was eight years old.

Harold walked up the steps and knocked on the door. The door opened and a young housemaid in a plain black wool uniform and white cotton gloves greeted him.

'Merry Christmas, sir. Please, come in.'

THE DRAWING ROOM

The highly ornate plaster ceiling of the drawing room was gloriously Jacobean—unexpected in a Georgian house. The original ceiling had been damaged in 1941 during the Blitz. After the war, the owner had taken the opportunity to have a copy of the Jacobean ceiling of his country house recreated in the drawing room in London. The 4th Baron, Lord Maud, had liked the ceiling so much that, on the merits of the Jacobean ceiling alone, he purchased the house in 1967.

The baron and his Rhodesian wife, had filled the room with an eclectic mix of furniture and paintings. The drawing room, however, was quintessentially English. Both sofas had Victorian square sides, had been constructed of maple, and had been upholstered in an expensive bespoke brocade fabric. There was a large decorative Bath stone Georgian fireplace, several high back chairs that had been upholstered in refined and elegant jacquard woven silk damasks and brocades, stunning embroideries on silk satin grounds and sumptuous pure silk jacquard velvet weaves.

The richly textured oak floor boards were partially covered by an Isfahan Persian rug on a silk foundation. The knotted Persian rug was mostly madder crimson red with touches of a shimmering gold. The intricate white patterns and beige Persian motifs, which glowed with an aura of blissful purity, framed a scene of wild pantherine Persian lions, peacocks, gazelles, and even elephants wandering among a forest of willow trees and exotic flowers. The opulent rug had been purchased by the 4th Baron on a trip to Iran in the late 1970s, just before the Persian Shah had been toppled from power.

Yes, the entire room was quite sumptuous.

In one corner of the drawing room stood a large Christmas tree—a Nordmann Fir—beautifully decorated with Christmas bulbs and other ornaments, twinkled with tiny white electric lights.

The aged baron, in a dark blue blazer, grey wool trousers, a white dress shirt (with a Windsor collar), and a striped necktie, had met and welcomed Harold to the house in the foyer. The white-haired and elderly 4th Baron, a kind and understanding man, could see that Harold was rather nervous. Yes, this would be a pivotal holiday for both Harold and Louise.

THE BEDROOM

Outside the white sash windows of the bedroom on the third floor of the house in Mayfair, a cold and overcast day had filled the room with a silvery natural light. The nineteen-year-old Louise, in a dark blue velvet skirt and white cotton blouse, sat on the edge of the bed. Louise's glossy strawberry blonde hair, cut into a chin length bob, framed her smooth pale face.

Louise was holding the tiny silver wrist watch that had once belonged to her mother in her small soft hands. Louise carefully examined the worn beige leather strap. Yes, Louise's mother had once worn this. This watch strap had touched her mother's wrist.

Louise had thought about her mother, Edith, every day. Her father's unexpected appearance in her hospital room had unleased a tsunami of emotions in Louise. The deep emotional wounds that Freya had been able to partially heal over the past four years had been ripped open again. Louise had envied her classmates at boarding school for having parents that truly loved them. Louise just wished that she could have her mother back. That her father had sent her away at the worst moment of her life had made the unbearable even worse. The coldness and cruelty of it had left Louise horribly traumatized. How could her father have done that to her? And now her father wanted to be back in her life. Was that possible? Did Louise want him back? Was this change of heart only temporary? Was all of this real? Could a leopard really change its spots? Louise really didn't know. If Louise took her father back and he betrayed her again, Louise wouldn't be able to bear it. It would sink her. The burden would have to be on her father, not her. Louise was under no obligation to take her father back. And then anger started to well up in Louise again. Her father had hurt her, and he had allowed others to injury her through neglect. All the years of suffering she had endured, and for what? Had casting Louise aside benefited her father? Had her father found solace in abandoning Louise to boarding schools? Had ignoring Louise's letters helped him overcome his grief? Had punishing his daughter for surviving her mother been therapeutic for him?

Louise looked at her mother's watch: 12:53pm. Her father would be arriving any minute. Louise carefully, gently, being careful not to damage the leather strap, put the watch on her slender wrist. She carefully adjusted the leather watch strap. There. It fit perfectly.

Louise looked outside the window; the sky was a stagnant mass of grey and white clouds. Snow covered the roofs of the terraced houses along the street. Louise wondered if the people in any of the houses were truly happy. Undoubtably, they were wealthy, but, as Louise, Freya, and Gemma had all learned, money is no assurance of happiness.

Louise searched the cosmos for some sign of her mother. What did Edith think of Major Percival's sudden return? If only Edith would contact her. Louise needed her mother's guidance. Was this what Edith wanted? Did Edith really want Harold to return? If only, if only, her mother would give her a sign.

Louise could hear someone walking down the hallway—the hardwood floor creaking underfoot. There was a light knock, and the wide white door opened. Freya, her long glossy blonde hair practically glowing in the wintery natural light, stood in the open doorway.

'Your father is here. He's in the drawing room. My grandfather and father are talking with him. Mummy and grandmother are in the kitchen. My uncle and his family have just arrived at the airport. Their plane was delayed in Ottawa by heavy snow. I haven't seen any of them in almost two years. They always seem to visit when I am away at school. My cousin Morton is with them. I haven't seen him in *yonks*. Morton's a year older than me, but the way he talks, he must think he is a good two generations ahead of me. He attended Eton. He didn't have any of the troubles in school that I had. Morton is studying agriculture in Cirencester. He'll take over the family's agribusiness one day,' said Freya in posh and Sloaney intonation.

Freya then went silent. She sighed. Freya, in a dark grey wool skirt, a white cotton blouse, and a pale blue v-neck cashmere sweater, stepped into the room and closed the door quietly behind her. Freya leaned up against the white glossy door.

'I can imagine this must all be rather difficult,' said Freya quietly.

Louise nodded her head.

'I remember how wounded you were when I met you at All Saints. I was wounded too. But I had Gemma and Karmen. You didn't have anyone. I know how terrible it was for you. You are my best friend. You are my sister, Louise. I love you. Whatever happens, you will never be alone again. I want, what you want, Louise.'

'Thank you, Freya.'

It was unnecessary for Louise to say anything else. Freya knew Louise's heart. Louise was grateful for everything thing that the family had done and was doing for her. The extraordinary effort Freya's grandfather had made to reach out to Louise's long estranged father after her stroke. Yes, the baron was so kind and thoughtful. Louise wanted to cry when she thought about all he had done for her. Sincere kindness, in whatever form, small or great, should be appreciated.

Louise touched the face of her mother's silver wrist watch. Yes, her mother was here with her. She always was, but at this moment she was silent. Was it because this decision was so important that it had to be left up entirely to Louise?

Louise stood up from the bed. She adjusted her velvet skirt and said, 'I am curious to meet Morton and your uncle,' said Louise.

'Yes, Uncle Edmund is kind hearted, like my father. He's very tall like most of the Maud's. Except for Morton—who is only 5'8"—at best,' said Freya with slight smile. 'And before the day is out, Louise, The Honourable Morton Lloyd Maud will remind you that he is the future Baron Maud,' said Freya laughingly.

And both of the girls laughed.

THE DINING ROOM

The long highly polished Circassian walnut dining table was covered in a white table cloth and set with sterling silver utensils and white bone china Wedgewood plates. The guests were seated around the table on sumptuously upholstered George III mahogany chairs. Above the guests hovered a beautiful early 20th century crystal chandelier. Standing along the walls, two on either side of the limestone fireplace, were four housemaids clad in black wool uniforms with starched white collars and white cotton gloves. A butler and two underbutlers in black coats, black ties, and white cotton gloves, helped seat the guests as they arrived at the double doors of the opulent white walled dining room.

Christmas dinner would be served at 2:30pm.

The guest list was made up almost entirely of the noble Maud family (that were currently in England). Seated around the dining table were the 4th Baron, the Baroness (Lady Maud), Hugh and Violet, Edmund and Stella,

Harold Percival, and the Bright Young Things: Freya, Louise, and Morton.

This year, the 4th Baron's only daughter, Vivienne, was spending Christmas with her family in Scotland. The baron's English son-in-law, a warfare officer on a nuclear submarine, lived in a relatively small Edwardian country house in Scotland that had been a wedding gift from the 4th Baron and Baroness. Vivienne's aged and frail mother-in-law now lived with the family. The naval commander, his wife, and two young blonde daughters, and mother had found happiness in the frozen north. Karmen, Freya's former nanny, now worked for the family. Karmen, at that moment, was spending Christmas with her family in Zagreb.

Louise had been seated across from her father. Yes, that was better. Louise would talk with her father after dinner—alone. Freya was seated next to Louise. Morton was seated next to Louise's father, which turned out to be fortuitous. Both men were involved in farming and would have a lot to talk about. And that would help break the tension between Louise and her father.

Louise, through treated like family, still felt much the outsider. Louise surreptitiously observed the other guests during dinner. The Honourable Edmund Maud, the future baron, was tall (6'4") like his father. He was rather average looking, like Freya's father Hugh. He was also rather posh, unlike Hugh, who, though well spoken, came across as a no-nonsense corporate CEO (that he was). 'Hughie' had been left in charge of the family's global mining operations, and had spent most of his life outside of England. Yes, Edmund was an English lord, and Hughie was a corporate CEO—and both were English gentlemen.

Stella, Edmund's wife, was from an upper-middle class family. Her father, a commoner, had been a career Royal Air Force officer, piloting Avro Vulcan bombers. Stella's Welsh mother had been a ballerina who had performed with the Royal Ballet. Stella, her long blonde hair held up with silver hairpins, was kind and outgoing. She was not posh, not really. Stella had never been a Sloane Ranger like Violet. She was without any pretentions. Stella, in her early 50s, was quite attractive. Stella was also poised, polite, and well spoken. She had met Edmund at Oxford University in the late

1980s. Childless throughout most of the 90s, her pregnancy had been a happy surprise.

Violet, Freya's mother, was blonde and attractive. Violet spoke in a posh and Sloaney intonation and was as posh as one could ever aspire to be. She was slender and elegant. She had a beautiful and glowing complexion and though almost 42, she looked to be in her early thirties. And she was a nice person. Violet had always been nice to Louise, even when she had not been to Freya (in the past). Violet was now a completely changed and far better person.

Hughie, tall and powerfully built, had the build of a rugby player. He was blond, like his Rhodesian mother. There was also the slight hint of a Rhodesian accent sometimes when he spoke. Hugh had a special place in Louise's heart. She knew that Freya's father had gone out of his way to be nice to her. Years of compensating for Violet's lack of maternal instincts had left him capable of much more affection than he had been before Freya was born. Louise knew that Hugh looked upon her as a daughter—Freya's sister. That knowledge filled Louise with a happiness she had not felt since her mother had passed away.

The 4th Baron, Lord Maud, was good hearted and intelligent. More than any other quality, Lord Maud was kind. And Louise loved him for it. Louise also knew that Lord Maud had protected Gemma from the other Mayfair oligarchs who had sided with Gemma's ex-husband George Howard and George's well-connected and poisonous mother (herself a baroness). Gemma had few friends left among the nobility in England, but the ones she did have were all lions like the 4th Baron.

The Baroness, Freya's Rhodesian grandmother, was lively and good hearted. She had a keen intellect that Freya had inherited from her. Lady Maud had always been very sweet to Louise. What Louise did not know, was that the Baroness had pulled every single string available to her to get Louise admitted to Midlands-Hasegawa after nervous administrators tried to delay her entrance to the school after Louise's stroke. Louise and Freya needed each other. And Louise needed Freya now more than ever. The Baroness had personally telephoned the president of the university (a

Rhodesian) and asked him to make an exception for Louise. He had agreed.

The young Morton had glossy blond hair, which was cut like a City banker's. He was slim, and through almost twenty-one, looked to be about sixteen. He was not handsome. He was rather plain looking, but quite posh. Morton, an Old Etonian, was as posh a person as Louise had ever met. Louise liked how Morton spoke and the way his clothes fit him. Yes, Morton was elegant. The light grey suit, pale blue dress shirt (with a Windsor collar), and dark blue tartan tie suited him perfectly. Yes, all of the Maud men were always sharply attired. Morton seemed really nice. Whenever their eyes met, Morton would smile slightly. Morton and Harold happily chatted about agriculture and the new innovations in farming over dinner.

Major Harold Percival, Louise's father, cut a sharp and dashing figure. Harold, though only in his late-forties, had snow white hair. Harold was extremely handsome; his full head of white hair had enhanced his appearance. Louise had no doubts that the grief and shock that Harold felt at his wife's unexpected death had turned her father's hair white. Her father was every inch the Coldstream Guard officer he had once been. And more, Harold spoke freely and openly with Morton and the other guests. Louise had never seen her father speak so freely. He always said very little to her. The recent situation had not altered that. Harold was uncomfortable with her—he had always been uncomfortable around Louise since Edith had passed away. Louise also looked nothing like her father. Harold had attempted to smile when he met Louise in the drawing room before dinner. Louise did not smile. Harold only managed to say, 'Merry Christmas, Louise' before lowering his gaze.

'Merry Christmas,' Louise had replied quietly. There was no reference to Harold being her father. Harold thought it best to wait and try to speak with Louise after dinner alone. He placed the dark green paper shopping bag on a side table in the drawing room before walking down the white walled hallway to the dining room for Christmas dinner.

THE DRAWING ROOM

After dinner, the party had moved to the drawing room. Outside, a light snow was blanketing London. It being winter, nightfall would come early.

Gifts had been exchanged after breakfast that morning. Surprisingly, the family did not spend that much on gifts, unless it was for the children.

Books—real paper books—seemed the most popular of gifts.

There was also a pair of military grade German binoculars given to her brother-in-law Edmund by Violet, who called them '*bins*' in a way that only a Sloane Ranger could. 'The *bins* might be of some help when you when are out in the field, Edmund,' said Violet.

'Thank you, Violet. They're just what I needed.'

Natural rubber wellies were also popular Christmas presents.

Freya received a bespoke dark blue British cavalry twill wool hunt coat from Vahtra—'Gula designed this coat for you herself, Freya,' said Violet. And for the young Morton, a pair of bespoke leather riding boots (from Vahtra). Remembering how much her mother had liked Gemma's gift from the year before, Freya had given her mother a coffee table book on Fabergé.

'Thank you, Freya. I shall spend the Christmas holidays reading this book from cover to cover.'

The flaxen-haired Freya, admiring the workmanship of the leather shotgun bandoleer (also from Vahtra) that Violet had given her replied, 'I'm glad you like it. And I think I will look quite dashing in this, Mummy.'

Louise had received a beautiful dark blue British cavalry twill wool frock style hunt coat from Violet and Hugh for Christmas (also from Vahtra), a pair of bespoke leather riding boots from Vahtra (a gift from Külli Vahtra herself), and a bespoke English willow cricket bat from the Baron and Baroness. And from Freya, a silver bracelet from Asprey. This would be Louise's first piece of jewellry.

THE MUGHAL GOTHIC BALLROOM

The Palladian house in Mayfair had once had a Georgian ballroom. It had been converted by a past owner (an English baron) in 1901 into a Mughal Gothic one. The baron, having served with his regiment in India for several years, had returned to England with a profound interest in Indian architecture and culture. He employed an Indian underbutler and a young Indian Ayah from Calcutta (now Kolkata) to teach his three children one of the myriad of languages of the Indian subcontinent—the children spoke Bengali like natives and usually had to be reminded to speak English with visiting house guests. Yes, the British Raj, still in its ascendency, was having (and still had) an enormous impact on British society. The baron was in the process of redesigning other rooms in the house in the same Mughal Gothic style when he was recalled to India with his regiment. He would return intermittently to England, but not for long enough to redecorate the library or the drawing room. He would be killed in France in 1915. The baron's youngest (and only surviving) daughter inherited the house in 1928, and laden with large debts, sold it to an affluent Mancunian industrialist.

The large white walled ballroom, extravagant and eccentric, had been completely restored almost a year earlier. No expense had been spared; no corners had been cut. The Mughal Gothic ballroom had been fully restored to its Anglo-Indian glory. The principal English touches to the décor being the two large crystal chandeliers which had both been manufactured in 1913.

Louise had quietly asked Freya if they could speak in private. Freya had nodded in agreement and led Louise to the ballroom down the hall from the drawing room. The tall and wide Georgian windows of the room allowed what remained of the grey natural light of the overcast day to dimly illuminate the large room. In a few minutes, it would be dark.

The two Inseparables walked to the center of the ballroom.

'I wanted to give you your Christmas present privately, Freya,' said Louise. Louise handed Freya a slim box wrapped in shiny red and white Christmas wrapping paper. 'I hope you like it.'

Freya smiled and said, 'I'm sure I will.'

Freya tore the wrapping paper off to reveal a plain brown cardboard box. What could it be? Freya placed the small box on one of the side tables in the ballroom. She lifted the lid. There was something under layers of white tissue paper; she unwrapped it. Freya gasped.

It was a brand new copy of Louise's novel—**The Undaunted.**

'That is the first copy that was printed. The editor sent it to me just before I left the hospital. The novel will be published in January. I want you to have the first copy, Freya. It's a special edition hardback the publisher's made just for me. You inspired me to write this story, Freya. Your kindness that turned into love is what saved me, Freya. Thank you,' said Louise, her voice breaking with emotion.

Freya took the book out of the box, looked briefly at the glossy hardcover, and then held it to her chest.

'Thank you, Louise.'

'Please, open the book,' said Louise quietly.

Freya opened the book and printed on the first page was: To Freya. I would be lost without you.

Louise had dedicated the book to Freya.

'I have always felt the same, Louise,' said Freya quietly. Freya held the book to her chest, and the two Inseparables hugged each other in the large Mughal Gothic ballroom.

THE HALLWAY

Freya, carrying the book, empty carboard box, and torn red and white wrapping paper, was walking down the hallway from the ballroom when she encountered Harold Percival.

'Hello, Freya. You wouldn't happen to know where Louise is, would you?'

'Yes, Mr Percival. Louise is in the ballroom, right through doors behind me.'

'Thank you.'

THE MUGHAL GOTHIC BALLROOM
Harold stopped in the front of the large glossy white double doors. In his left hand he held a dark green paper shopping bag from Harrod's. He hesitated for a moment. He still was unsure what he would say to his daughter. Harold slowly opened one the doors to the large ballroom. He walked into the large partially illuminated white walled room.

Outside the tall pane glass windows of the room, the twilight was quickly giving way to night. Louise, diminutive, strawberry blonde, and gentle, stood in the gloaming in the center of the room. She was looking out the windows at the final moments of twilight. The chandeliers had been turned on by Freya just before she had left the ballroom. Louise, her strawberry blonde hair cut into a chin length bob, stood under the incandescent glow of one of the crystal chandeliers. She turned to see who had entered the long, wide, and cavernous white walled room. It was her father. Louise's indifferent facial expression did not change as she noticed her father entering the room.

Yes, Louise was a carbon copy of her mother Edith. The resemblance was uncanny. However, while Edith had always been outgoing and lively, Louise was more reserved with her father. No, not reserved, Harold—damaged. Louise had been left badly damaged by years of neglect and mistreatment. A situation that had only come about because you had allowed it.

Harold paused for a moment before he spoke.

'This is an interesting room. I recognize the Indo-Gothic architecture. The orangery on the edge of the estate was built in a similar style by your great grandfather, Colonel Algernon Percival, in 1920. We used to have a rubber plantation in India, during the Raj. The orangery is rather rundown now.

Do you remember it, Louise?' asked Louise's father in his posh intonation.

'No.'

Harold took a few more steps and stopped under the other crystal chandelier. He placed the paper shopping bag he was holding on the hardwood floor of the ballroom. Harold, in a charcoal grey Savile Row suit, white dress shirt, and blue and red striped regimental tie, shimmered in incandescent light. This was as hard as he feared it would be.

'Louise. I have wronged you. I have damaged you. And I allowed others to harm you. I am sorry for all that I have done to you. I will never ask you to forgive me. I don't deserve forgiveness. I know that. I know that I can never repair the damage that has been done to you. I can never give you back those lost years. I can never take away the trauma that you suffered. There is no excuse for my behavior. I was cowardly, weak, and selfish. I love Edith as much as I ever have. When your mother passed away, it broke me, Louise. You didn't deserve what happened to you. You did nothing wrong.'

Harold paused. Louise was staring directly into his eyes; she was searching for something. Harold fought not to break away from Louise's forensic gaze.

'I would like to be back in your life again, Louise. In whatever capacity you choose. I am unworthy to be your father again, but if you could find it in your heart to allow some small role for me in your life, I would be grateful.'

Harold paused once more. The words he spoke next would be dangerous to him, but they had to be said.

'If you don't want me back in your life, I will understand. And you would be right not to want me back.'

Louise simply stared at her father for a long moment. And then stared at him for a moment longer.

Louise finally spoke, and whenever Louise spoke, she always spoke with her mother's voice. 'I'm afraid I can't forgive you. The damage is too great. A few words from you will not wash away what I have been through. No, if I were to pretend otherwise, I would be hurting myself even more; and I have suffered too much already. I have to think of myself because you never did. I had to survive all on my own, for years, until I met Freya. If it had not been for Freya, I would have died. You have no idea how bad things were for me. You didn't care. I needed love and kindness and protection after Mummy passed away. All I received was cruelty from you and your sister. No. I can't forgive you. No, I don't want you back in my life. I tried, but I can't bring myself to forgive you. I can't. I can't. Please, go away. Don't bother me anymore. I have a new family now; one that loves me. One that protects me. I don't think someone can change so easily. You are what you are. And I am what I am because of how you treated me.'

Louise composure suddenly collapsed and she started to cry. Now, tears were streaking down her face.

'You can't imagine how horrible it was for me,' said Louise through tears. 'I have had to completely rebuild my life, and now, you reappear. It's too late.' Louise started to gasp for air.

'Please, Louise. Alright. I'll leave,' said her father. At that moment, major Percival was afraid Louise would have another stroke. Harold, distraught and completely defeated, turned and started walking back towards the double doors of the ballroom, all the while he kept looking back to check on Louise's condition. He opened the double doors of the ballroom, stepped into the hallway, and closed the doors quietly behind him.

THE HALLWAY

Harold, pale and ashen, walked down the hall towards the drawing room. The 4th Baron met him walking the other direction.

'Ah, there you are, Mr Percival,' said the baron in his clipped Mayfair accent, and then he noticed the look on Harold's face. 'Is everything alright?'

Harold, trying to maintain his composure, replied, 'Thank you for your kindness, Lord Maud. But, I have to leave. Please, see to Louise in the ballroom. I'm afraid I have upset her.'

The baron could only guess what had happened between Mr Percival and Louise; however, he could clearly see how upset Harold was. 'I'll show you out, Mr Percival.'

When Freya saw her grandfather walking towards the foyer with Louise's father, she knew things had gone badly. Freya, now terribly worried about Louise, walked quickly down the other hallway towards the ballroom. When she arrived at the white glossy double doors, she opened one and walked inside.

Louise was standing in the middle of the ballroom sobbing.

'Louise, please don't cry,' said Freya as she walked towards the whippet-thin and diminutive young Louise. When she reached her, Louise turned and hugged Freya, crying uncontrollably. 'Please, Louise, calm down. I am here.'

Louise continued to cry. Freya had never seen Louise cry so hard. It scared her. She was afraid Louise would have another stroke. Freya gently caressed Louise's shoulder.

'Let's go upstairs, alright?' asked Freya gently.

Louise nodded slightly while trying to regain her composure.

'Today has been a long day for you,' said Freya gently.

Louise nodded. She was still crying. Freya led Louise out of the ballroom and through the double doors.

The dark green, glossy, paper Harrod's shopping bag with Louise's Christmas gift had been left sitting in the incandescent light of one of the large shimmering crystal chandeliers.

Gemma—An Invisible Fear—Christmas in Marble Arch

MARBLE ARCH

Gemma stared at the white plaster ceiling above her. The dappled natural grey light of a cold, wintery, and snowing day filled the bedroom. Gemma, shrouded in layers of white Egyptian cotton sheets and a large white duvet, stretched. The scent of Gemma's Korean cold cream permeated the soft white pillows. Gemma brushed away her glossy brown bangs with her soft and manicured right hand and looked outside. A snowy London stretched out before her.

It was Christmas.

Outside, in the hallway, Gemma could hear two of the housemaid's talking quietly as they walked down the hall.

Enoch had decided to stay in London for Christmas. Enoch, weighed down by work, now rarely went anywhere but his office in the City. He had had his mother Eloise driven to London from Surrey the day before by members of his security team. She was staying in a bedroom down the hall from Gemma. Enoch was blessed; he still had his mother.

Gemma's mother was with her too; only Gemma's mother was on the other side. Yes, sometimes Gemma would wake up in the middle of the night and she could smell her mother's cold cream. Sometimes she would dream about her. Sometimes Gemma could physically feel her mother's gentle presence next to her. It was on Christmas Day that her mother's death affected her the most. Gemma could remember the little things that her mother had done for her on Christmas in the past: baking biscuits, singing Christmas carols with her, and most of all, hugging her and telling Gemma how much she loved her. The most precious things in life cannot be bought. Love is all that matters and all that remains. One day, Gemma would be reunited with her mother in Heaven. And with her maternal grandparents who had taken care of her when Gemma's mother no longer could. 'Yes, I'll see you all in Heaven one day,' thought Gemma. Gemma had often dreamed of touching her mother's hand once again; embracing her once more—in Heaven. Yes, Gemma would her see her mother and grandparents again. The first thing she would do would be to apologize to them for not truly appreciating them as much as she should have while they were alive.

Gemma reached over to the night stand and grabbed her silver Cartier watch (that the bailiffs had missed) and looked at the time: 8:11am. It was time to take a long hot bath. Breakfast would be served downstairs in the dining room at 9:30am.

THE DRAWING ROOM

The large Christmas tree (a Norway Spruce) had been decorated by Gemma and Enoch three weeks earlier. Yes, Gemma loved Christmas. Gemma had purchased the Christmas lights and decorations at a small shop in Covent Garden near Poppy's semi-detached. Gemma had lived there with Poppy for three years and knew the area well. The salesgirls were all really nice and very helpful. Gemma enjoyed shopping, though she rarely bought anything.

Gemma's childhood had been a frugal one, so frugality came easy to her. Gemma was able to enjoy simply spending time with loved ones. Talking over a cup of tea made Gemma as happy as anything else. Decorating the tree had been really fun. Gemma could put her artistic and creative talents to work. And Enoch had decorated the tree with her.

Yes, she had also chosen a Christmas wreath of blue pine, white oak, pine cones, red ilex berries, silver baubles, eucalyptus and a large white ribbon at the florists for the front door of the house in Marble Arch. Yes, the wreath was beautiful. Both Enoch and his mother liked it and had thanked Gemma for selecting one that was so beautiful.

Eloise, dressed in dark blue cotton trousers, a pale blue blouse (that matched her blue eyes), and white cotton slippers, had chatted happily with Enoch and Gemma over a breakfast of pancakes, bacon, sausages, and toast. She was happy to see her son happy. She was happy that Enoch had found someone who loved him as much as he loved her. And Eloise had grown to love Gemma.

Enoch, though under a tremendous amount of pressure because of recent and ongoing events, was happy to lose himself on Christmas Day with his beloved mother and Gemma. Enoch was blessed, and he knew it. And he thanked God for it every day. And then Enoch would think of the murdered Spaniard's family in Ceuta, alone and without him this Christmas, and a stinging pain would fill Enoch's heart. Yes, the people responsible for his murder would be hunted down and killed. That thought—the very idea of revenge—did not trouble Enoch in the slightest. The world was degrading more and more every day. England, now burdened with a shockingly dysfunctional legal system and a badly hobbled police force, this would be the only way to get any kind of justice at all. This course of action was, unfortunately, all that was left to him and the others. Yes, vigilantism would be the only true justice left in England going forward.

Eloise, her silver and grey hair held in place with silver hair pins, grasped Gemma's soft hands in hers after breakfast and told Gemma how much she appreciated and loved her. She told Gemma how happy she was to have her as a future daughter-in-law, and how much she had truly helped Enoch heal from past wounds. Gemma, deeply moved, could only say how much Enoch had also helped her heal from her past wounds as well.

'I never thought I would find anyone who loved me so truly as Enoch. I only wish I that I had realized that at Oxford,' said Gemma.

'The important thing is that you have finally found each other, Gemma. That's what matters most. Most people go through life without ever finding anyone.'

'Yes, you are right,' replied Gemma. 'I have the rest of my life with Enoch ahead of me now. I am blessed. Truly.'

Gemma gave Eloise a white Egyptian cotton blouse (with a large collar) and an Icelandic wool sweater (or lopapeysa as the Icelandics called them) for Christmas. Eloise happily tried the wool sweater on over her pale blue cotton blouse. The dark grey, light grey, and white sweater was beautiful.

'Thank you, Gemma. This is such a beautiful gift. Every time I wear it, I will think of you,' said Eloise with a smile.

Gemma gave Enoch a special edition of The Meditations of Marcus Aurelius. The book had been quarter-bound in full-grain leather blocked in gold foil with paper sides that had been hand marbled. The words of the ancient emperor had been printed in both English and Latin and set in Albertina and printed on Artic Volume Ivory paper. When Enoch unwrapped the book, he smiled gently. He understood Gemma's intentions. She was completely unaware of how bad a turn things had really taken, but none the less, Gemma wanted to help him. This book was one way for her to do it.

'Thank you, Gemma. This really means a lot to me. I shall bring it with me to the office and read a few pages every day. I believe it will help me a lot.'

Enoch, his brown hair freshly cut like a City banker's and clad in the dark khaki pants and white cotton button-down Oxford dress shirt he had purchased in Oxford last summer, opened the book and carefully looked through the smooth white pages. Yes, it was a beautifully bound book. A paper book. The way books should be read.

Gemma also gave Enoch an Icelandic wool sweater. Enoch tried on the dark blue, white, and beige sweater. It fit perfectly. And yes, it was beautiful.

Gemma also gave Enoch and Eloise each a tin of Toffolossus biscuits from Fortnum and Mason. Eloise was the first to try one. Yes, the plump dates covered in some of England's finest chocolate were wonderful.

Eloise gave Enoch and Gemma boxes of Godiva white chocolate starfish filled with Raspberry jam. That had been a long-held tradition between Eloise and her son. Now, Gemma would be part of that tradition too.

Eloise also gave Gemma a deliciously soft pale blue cashmere v-neck sweater made by a small English company in Mercia. It fit Gemma perfectly.

Enoch, still wearing the Icelandic sweater, waded through the torn Christmas wrapping paper, ribbons, and bows that covered the floor of drawing room and gave Gemma a beautiful art book on Sir Lawrence

Alma-Tadema, OM, RA, one of Gemma's favorite painters. The limited edition book was filled with gorgeous prints of the Dutch (and British denizen) artist's most popular and alluring paintings. The book was quarter-bound in buckram with vegetable parchment. The sides had been blocked in gold and colored foils and with edge-gilding on all the sides. Gemma loved the book. It was quite thoughtful of him to give her this particular (limited edition) book.

Gemma loved classical art, unlike Violet who mostly collected the works of Vorticist painters. Yes, The Honourable Violet Valkyrie Maud owned one of world's premier Vorticist collections and was considered an expert on Vorticism in international art circles. Violet had written several articles on Vorticism for English newspapers, art magazines, an art catalogue and several exhibition catalogues. That Christmas, Gemma had given Violet a book on Vorticist art which had been published only a week earlier. Vava loved the book.

Violet had given Gemma a Lake Blue tweed (with a light blue contrast overcheck and dark blue velvet facings) hunting jacket (from Vahtra) and a pair of rum colored, narrow leg, cavalry twill trousers (that were tough enough to climb over barbed-wire fences in). The outfit had been a bespoke order from Vahtra and made to the highest standards.

Külli and Octavia had given Gemma a pair of bespoke leather gaiters and a pair rugged brown leather walking shoes from Vahtra. Gula had made them herself. They had been made to fit perfectly with the brown leather shoes that Külli had also made. Gemma rather liked the thick leather soles of the shoes. Gemma had enjoyed trying on the shoes and gaiters on that morning in the drawing room. Yes, this outfit would see a lot of use on the Scottish Borders—and in Surrey too.

Gemma had sent all of her friends beautiful Christmas cards (which she had made herself). Gemma usually gave her friends books for Christmas, usually limited editions if Gemma could find the titles and topics her friends liked. This year had been no exception. However, she had sent plush toys to Henry and Lucy: a soft white dragon for Henry and a silky white horse for

Lucy. And Gemma had mailed tiny navy blue quilted jackets (from Vahtra) for the Poppy and Brian's twins to wear when they turned three. (It's always good to think ahead.)

Enoch also gave Gemma a pair of black Dior sunglasses. Gemma tried them on. She walked over to the Venetian mirror in the drawing room and looked at her reflection. She smiled, turned around, and asked, 'How do I look?'

'Like a movie star on the French Rivera in the 1950s,' said Eloise happily.

'Really?' asked Gemma,

'*Rather*,' replied Eloise in her posh intonation.

'Thank you, Enoch. I shall wear them on our trips to the South of France. Yes, we will be visiting the French Riviera often,' said Gemma as she tilted them back on her head of glossy brown hair and smiled happily. Gemma then started laughing.

Enoch smiled, and for a tiny moment, he forgot about his troubles and was lost in Gemma's smile and laughter. 'What would I do without you, Gem?' asked Enoch happily.

'You will never have to find out. You are stuck with me,' replied Gemma and she smiled once more; a smile that illuminated the entire drawing room. Gemma, now standing in the middle of the large red Persian rug and in front of the Christmas tree amidst torn Christmas wrapping paper and ribbons, looked about the room. 'Well, not a bad haul this year.'

'Oh, there is one more gift that you missed, Gemma,' said Enoch.

'Yes, really?' asked Gemma.

Enoch walked out of the room and closed the wide white glossy door behind him.

Eloise glanced over at Gemma and said, 'I am as curious as you are.'

After a few minutes, the glossy white door to the drawing room opened and Enoch entered carrying a small cardboard box. He handled it very carefully. It was unwrapped. What could it be?

'Please have a seat, Gemma,' said Enoch.

Gemma, the black Dior sunglasses still resting on her head, sat down in one of the high back armchairs. She was curious. Enoch carefully handed her the box. She held it in her lap and then she heard the faint cries of a baby kitten. Gemma looked astonished. She opened the box and inside was a small black short haired kitten—a baby.

'Oh, Enoch. He's so cute. Thank you,' said Gemma softly as she carefully lifted the small cat out of the box. He was adorable.

'He's about six weeks old. I think. He came running up to me when I stopped at a petrol station in Surrey a few days ago. The station manager said the kitten had been wandering around the station for a few days. I asked if I could keep the kitten, and he let me have him. I know you're a cat person, Gem, so I thought, why not? Do you like him?'

'I love him already. Thank you, Enoch,' replied Gemma, who was now holding the small kitten in her arms and gently petting him. He was purring loudly. He had found a mother after a long search.

'He's been at my office with me for the last couple of days. The staff has been spoiling him rotten.'

'What are going to name him?' asked Eloise happily.

The black kitten climbed up and rested his tiny head on Gemma's shoulder and continued to purr loudly. Gemma gently caressed his soft glossy back. Enoch's gaze drifted from the kitten to Gemma. Yes, Gemma, glossy, strikingly beautiful, intelligent, and kind, was now at the center of Enoch's life, as he had wanted since that night on stage in Oxford over two decades ago. Was all this really happening, or would Enoch wake up from this happiest of dreams a moment from now?

Gemma considered what to name him for a moment, looked at Eloise and Enoch, and then Gemma said, 'Soot'.

'Soot. Yes, I like that name too,' said Enoch and he smiled.

'Enoch, I have some bad news,' said Gemma.

'Oh?' asked Enoch.

'Yes. You now have some very real competition for my attention. Baby Soot.'

And Gemma smiled.

And everyone laughed.

Gemma—An Invisible Fear—The White Dragon

THE COUNTRY HOUSE
The stone country house, built in 1897, was draped in a white layer of snow. The trees which surrounded the two-storey Victorian structure in the Lake District were bereft of leaves and their long branches sagged under the weight of the snow. The ponds around the country house and the castle ruins were frozen and a thin layer of transparent ice covered the streams that flowed across the snowy ancestral lands of the Barons Devereux.

THE DRAWING ROOM
Poppy adjusted the sterling silver Egyptian Art Deco bracelet on her slender wrist. Poppy, her glossy blonde hair tied back with a white ribbon, leaned back into the soft velvet high back chair. The floor of the drawing room was covered in discarded Christmas wrapping paper and ribbons. There was a red velvet stocking with a white bow laying on the coffee table; the contents, an array of chocolate and hard candy, had been spilled across the glossy wooden table top.

Poppy, wearing a new set of warm flannel red, blue, and purple tartan pyjamas (a Christmas gift from Gemma), surveyed the room. In one corner was a large decorated Christmas tree—a Norway Spruce. Some of the Christmas ornaments on the tree were Victorian, others Edwardian, still others had been purchased in the 1920s and 30s. The tree was topped with an Edwardian glass star. Only the white Christmas lights had been purchased recently.

The angelic and good-hearted twins, Henry and Lucy, also in flannel pyjamas and slippers (Henry's were blue velvet; Lucy's were purple velvet) were playing together in front of the tree. The flaxen haired Henry with a white dragon plush toy and Lucy with the silky white toy horse they had unwrapped excitedly that morning.

'I'll save you, Lucy!' said Henry courageously.

'Oh, thank you, Henry. You're a good brother. Please, save my horse too. She is afraid of the dragon. You will save her too, won't you?' asked Lucy.

'Of course. I will save both of you from the dragon. You are my sister, and I love you.'

The eight-year-old Lucy, her long glossy blonde hair framing her smooth pale face and blue eyes, hugged her twin brother and said, 'Thank you, Henry. You saved us. I love you, Henry.'

Henry then crumpled down and lay on the floor melodramatically and said, 'The dragon hurt me and I am dying, Lucy.'

Lucy, carrying her toy horse plush toy, knelt down beside Henry and said, 'Please don't die. You are so brave and you defeated the dragon. You can't die. I love you, and my horse loves you.'

Henry touched one hand to his heart and said, 'I die so that you could both live. I would die a thousand times for you, Lucy. I am your brother. I have to protect you. Good bye, Lucy.' And then Henry closed his eyes.

Lucy looked sad.

'Don't worry, Lucy,' said James. 'I know how you can save Henry.'

The tiny and whippet-thin Lucy looked up. 'Please tell me, Daddy. I want to save Henry.'

'If you hug him, he will come back. He sacrificed himself for you. Your love will bring him back.'

Lucy knelt down and hugged Henry, who was now lying on the floor. Henry slowly opened his eyes.

'Lucy. You saved me. Thank you.' Henry then stood up and the twins hugged each other once more.

The Honourable James, in a pair of dark khaki wool trousers, a white dress shirt (with a St James collar), and a pair of blue velvet slippers, knelt down and said, 'I want to a hug too.' Father, son, and daughter then all hugged each other.

The slender and beautiful Helen, her long blonde hair tied back with a white ribbon, and wearing a set of navy blue flannel pyjamas (with white piping) and a pair of white cotton slippers, smiled and said, 'You're not leaving me out.' Helen then took a few steps forward and hugged her husband and children.

Seated across from Poppy, in one of the purple velvet (with white piping) Art Deco chairs, was Mars. Lord Noel, the 13th Baron Noel, as much a son to the 12th Baron as James (the future 13th Baron Devereux), was carefully reading the book that Gemma had given to him for Christmas. The beautifully wrapped present had arrived in one of three boxes from Gemma two days before. Gemma had wrapped all of the gifts for the family herself. Gemma enjoyed wrapping presents. The cards she made for people were beautiful in both appearance and thought.

The good-hearted Gemma had suffered so much, and yet, she had survived. A year ago, in this very house, Gemma had revealed her most terrible of secrets to Poppy. Gemma, so fragile, had been broken. Poppy had been afraid that Gemma would destroy herself out of despair. Gemma, with Poppy's help, had physically survived Grey. And Gemma's ex-husband George Howard. And so many others. Bad people, like sharks, could smell blood in the water. And sensing weakness, attacked. The friends that Gemma had now were like a phalanx surrounding her. No one would ever harm Gemma again. And just after Gemma had finally escaped from Grey's grasp, Enoch Tara had appeared. Gemma had found love. Gemma had made it. She was safe.

Poppy closed her eyes and prayed. She prayed for herself, her entire family (which included Mars), and her friends. Poppy said an extra prayer for Gemma. She didn't know why, but a cosmic tug on the line told her to do so.

'Those look really nice on you, Poppy,' said Brian.

The diminutive, blonde Poppy opened her eyes. It was Brian. Brian, in a pair of dark khaki cotton trousers, a pale blue, white, and light grey Tattersall dress shirt (with a Clifford collar), and the pair of purple velvet slippers that Poppy had given him two years earlier, smiled. Brian, his hair cut just the day before like a British army officer's and freshly shaved, was handsome. And Brian was good and kind and considerate and thoughtful. And Poppy loved him.

'Gemma designed the tartan pattern herself. An artisanal weaver created the material for her. It's based on the All Saints school colors. She had the seamstress in London that made my maternity clothes make the pyjamas for me. Gemma did all of this for me.'

'You are true friends. You are blessed to have each other,' said Brian. 'And I am blessed to have you and the twins. God has truly blessed us all.'

Poppy reached up from the chair and held Brian's hand. 'I love you, Brian.'

'And I love you, Poppy.'

'How are our twins?' asked Poppy.

'They are sleeping soundly. Your parents are in the bedroom with them now. Your father thinks that Arthur has your blue eyes, but my nose,' said Brian and he smiled.

'Yes, I can see that. Arthur will grow up to be as handsome as you.'

Brian smiled.

'Yes, Poppy, I am glad that I attended your presentation on gold ETFs in the City that day.'

THE COTSWOLDS
The village green, now covered in a thin layer of snow, crunched under the boots of the Külli and Octavia as they made their way to the center of the field. The sky above was overcast and it was freezing cold. Külli, at nearly six feet tall and clad in a pair of faded blue jeans, a navy blue wool peacoat, and her red, blue, and purple All Saints scarf, stopped and turned to face Octavia.

'The turkey was good,' said Külli.

Octavia, in a pair of dark khaki wool trousers, a white cotton blouse, a navy blue quilted jacket (from Vahtra) and a beige scarf that she had wrapped around her head and shoulders, arched an eyebrow.

'*Rather*. Mummy has always been a good cook,' said Octavia in her posh and Sloaney intonation.

'I love the gloves your father gave me,' said Külli, holding up hands now under a warm pair of light grey knit gloves.

'Father loved the wool overcoat you gave him. The detachable fur collar was especially appreciated,' said Octavia.

White flakes of snow were now falling gently and some of it was falling onto Octavia's soft brown hair. Yes, Octavia, nubile and alluring, did have more than a passing resemblance to Gemma. However, Külli had always, from the first instant they had met, separated the two in her mind. Octavia had never been a substitute for Gemma. Külli had always loved Octavia for Octavia. Gemma had freed Külli and she had been blessed with Octavia at the precise moment when Külli was ready to accept her. After two decades of heartbreak, Külli's mended heart had found love.

'Thank you for inviting me to spend Christmas with you.'

'We are happy to have you. I can't imagine spending another Christmas without you,' said Octavia happily. You are part of the family now. I have a few cousins I would like you to meet. You will like them. Most of them live in Canada or Australia.'

'Octavia.'

'Yes.'

'Is this all a dream?' asked Külli.

Octavia smiled. 'I know it feels like a dream. I ask myself this question every day…Before I met you, I had started to think that I would never meet anyone special and that I would be alone for the rest of my life. And now, I have you, Miss Vahtra. I'm glad you're a Tory. I'm glad you like going on hunts. I'm also glad that you are so tall, so beautiful, and so intelligent. I guess… what I am trying to say… is that all I really know for sure is that I love you. And I need you.'

Tears started to fill Külli's eyes. She tried to speak, but she couldn't find the right words. Okay. Give me a minute. Külli, lost in thought, then reached out and held Octavia's hands in hers and said, 'And I need you.'

Gemma—An Invisible Fear—The Honourable Morton

MAYFAIR

Louise, her blue velvet skirt and white cotton blouse now heavily wrinkled, lay on her back in the middle of the white duvet. Louise's eyes were red from crying. Emotionally drained and physically exhausted, Louise sank into despair.

No—she could not bring herself to forgive her father. She had suffered far too much damage. Had her father really changed? Was his remorse real—or just a temporary retreat? Louise, staring at the invisible landscape of the past, could only conjure up cruel and traumatic memories of her father. It was easy to ask for forgiveness when you were not the wounded party. Yes, perhaps her father's remorse was real, but was it enough to make up for what Louise had suffered for years? When would her father and aunt suffer for what they had done to her? When would they feel the despair that they had inflicted upon her? A part—a very small part—of Louise felt guilty for driving her father out of the house and her life just an hour before. But why should she feel any guilt at all? What had Louise ever done to her father? Why did some people believe that it is necessary to forgive those who ask forgiveness? The people who said things like that had not really suffered at all. No, it was up to the individual to decide whether or not to forgive someone or not. At the very least, grant the victim that choice.

Louise felt dizzy.

She turned her head and looked out the window, only darkness and the lights from the sash windows of houses across the street. Were the people over there having a nice Christmas? Louise suddenly wished her father had never reappeared. She had come to terms with never hearing from him again. His sudden reappearance had left her traumatized.

And then she thought about the Mauds. Had she ruined their Christmas? She hoped not. Lord Maud had only wanted to help. No, Louise was not angry with him. The baron's heart was true.

Louise climbed out of bed. She felt another spell of dizziness as she walked towards the entrance to the bathroom. She grasped the doorframe. She steadied herself. Had she had another stroke? Louise stepped into the bathroom and leaned up against the white marble sink. She stared into the mirror; the reflection of Louise's smooth pale complexion in the florescent light of the lamps of the white tiled bathroom was hauntingly beautiful. Louise had grown into a beautiful young woman. She turned on the tap and gently splashed cold water on her face. The water still running, she looked at her reflection once more. The redness in her eyes had largely disappeared. Louise turned off the tap. She took one of the white soft cotton hand towels and gently dabbed her face dry. She adjusted her white cotton blouse and blue velvet skirt and stepped out of the bathroom.

There was a gentle knock.

'Who is it,' asked Louise quietly.

'It's Morton. Freya, are you there?'

Louise walked over to the glossy white door and opened it. Yes, it was Morton in a light grey wool suit, pale blue dress shirt (with a Windsor collar), and dark blue tartan necktie. The posh and slender Morton nodded slightly and smiled.

'Sorry to bother you, Louise. I was looking for Freya.'

Louise looked at her silver wrist watch. Two hours had passed since her father had left the house.

Freya and her mother, Violet, had helped her up the stairs and hovered over her while she lay in bed. Yes, they were worried about Louise. Violet had gone downstairs and returned with a glass of cold milk for Louise. Violet had done that herself; she had not asked one of the servants to do it. It was something that Louise had found rather touching. Yes, Violet truly cared about her. Freya had sat on the edge of the bed and watched over Louise. Freya had said very little beyond urging Louise to go to sleep. Louise had spent the last two hours drifting in and out of sleep.

'Freya and Violet stepped out a few minutes ago. I was half asleep. I'm not sure where they went.

'Well, I'm sure Freya will turn up sooner or later. Louise, it's nice to have finally met you. I have heard so much about you from everyone. My parents were happy to finally meet you too.'

Morton suddenly seemed to remember something.

'One day we will both be running farms.'

'I am studying Chemistry. What does that have to with farming?' asked Louise.

'Plenty. I have a book downstairs, a Christmas present from my father, on agricultural innovations and fertilizers. Please allow me to show it to you.'

The nineteen-year-old Louise arched an eyebrow. Here, at a traumatic moment in her life, was Morton, and he wanted to show her a book on agriculture. Apparently, Morton was unaware of what had transpired in the ballroom just two hours before. Louise, desperate to distract herself from the current turmoil, nodded. 'Yes, I'd like to hear about your book.'

THE DRAWING ROOM

The opulent drawing room was empty. The discarded Christmas wrapping paper and ribbons had been cleared away by the household staff and the room appeared to have been freshly vacuumed. The white Christmas tree lights had been left on. The fresh and clean scent of the Nordmann Fir was very light and only barely noticeable when standing next to the tree. The fire in the Bath stone fireplace had been put out and only ashes and darkness remained. The room was now lit by several hand painted blue and white English floral porcelain table lamps with white satin lamp shades. A series of translucent points of light filled the room with a soft but surprisingly bright glow. Louise had always liked the white walled drawing room in the house. Louise could easily picture Jane Austen wandering around the room. Yes, the white walled purity of this English space was deeply comforting to Louise.

Morton, at around 5'8', was unlike Freya in almost every way. He was not really attractive. Like the other Maud men, he was rather plain looking.

However, unlike the others, he was not a towering and powerfully built giant. And where Freya was warm and outgoing, Morton seemed to be quite reserved, especially for such a young person. Louise did, however, like how Morton carried himself. He was posh and had the same military bearing as Freya. He also had the family's glossy blond hair.

'Yes, the family always gives me such useful presents. Mummy gave me a nice set of natural black rubber wellies. I shall use them on the farm. And my grandparents gave me a beautiful beige sweater. Yes, it will come in useful this winter. And my father gave me this,' said Moton as he picked up a beautifully bound book off of a highly polished burl wood side table.

'Father had this edition printed just for me,' said Morton as he opened the book filled with gilt edged pages. Morton smiled—an innocent and beautiful smile. Yes, Morton appreciated the important things in life. Louise could tell that Morton loved his father. He appreciated the book he held in his soft manicured hands. Morton's long tapered fingers gently turned each page of the bespoke book carefully, almost reverently.

'The book is a collection of articles that my father put together. It is quite a useful reference. I shall take it with me wherever I go. The family has land all over England, Scotland and Wales. Father spends so much time away from us. We have land in Canada and Australia too. One day, I will inherit the title and the responsibility for the family's agricultural holdings. It's important that I am prepared for it.' Morton carefully looked through the book. 'Ah, here it is. Fertilizers. You see, Louise. Fertilizers are as essential as water to growing modern crops. You could use your chemistry studies to create new and more effective fertilizers.'

'I've never even thought about that. I was thinking of improving soft ice cream,' said Louise and she smiled.

The reference to Baroness of Kesteven was not lost of Morton. He smiled. 'Yes, I'm sure you will. Your father told me he expects you will invent new types of fertilizer. He told me how proud of he was of you while I was showing him my new book. He told me that your mother loved the white wood anemones that grew all over your farm in East Anglia.'

There. The mere mention of Louise's mother hit her hard in the heart. Louise had almost forgotten the small five-petaled white flowers that covered the green landscape which surrounded the house in East Anglia. Yes, Louise now remembered. Louise turned inward for a moment while Morton continued to speak of all things agricultural. Edith, Louise's mother, always kind, patient, and understanding, had never left Louise's thoughts. Yes, Louise's mother had told her every day how much she loved her. No, Louise's mother had not abandoned her—not even in death. Her mother was with her, even if it were difficult for Louise to sense her presence sometimes. Yes, Edith loved her and Louise loved her mother every bit as much. Louise looked at the silver watch on her slender wrist. This tiny object was so important to Louise. It was a small portal to her mother.

'Of course, the rose remains my favorite,' said Morton.

Louise smiled. 'Yes, I like roses too. And I like your new book, Morton. It was very thoughtful of your father.'

'Yes, I'm blessed to have such a family. And the family is blessed to have met you, Louise. The family loves you. But I think you know that.'

Louise turned inward and after a moment of reflection, nodded slightly.

'One of the housemaids found this in the ballroom,' said Morton while motioning to a dark green paper shopping bag on the coffee table. The present has your name on it.'

Louise looked at the Harrod's shopping bag. Yes, her father had left it in the ballroom when he had retreated from the room.

'Thank you, Morton,' said Louise somewhat sleepily.

'It's been a long day. Everyone else has already gone upstairs,' said Morton.

'Yes, I think I should too. Thank you, Morton. It was nice talking with you.'

'Good night, Louise.'

'Good night, Morton.'

FREYA'S GEORGIAN BEDROOM
Louise placed the paper shopping bag on the nightstand next to the bed and sat down on the white duvet which covered the Edwardian bed.

Yes, her mother had guided Morton to her that evening. She wanted Louise to remember the white wood anemones. Had her mother also wanted her to retrieve the Christmas present left behind in the ballroom?

Louise took the paper bag off of the nightstand and held it in her lap. She studied the paper shopping bag for a moment. Inside was a professionally wrapped Christmas present from her father. Louise pulled the slender box out from the paper shopping bag. The glossy red wrapping paper had a white silk ribbon and a white envelope under the white silk bow. Louise pulled the envelope from under the ribbon and held it in her hands. It was sealed. Louise used one of her finger nails to open it. She pulled out a plain white card. She opened it and began to read.

Dear Louise,

Christmas was the second happiest time of the year for your mother, your birthday being the happiest. Not a day goes by that I do not think of you and your mother. In spite of all you have had to endure, you have turned out to be a kind, intelligent, and beautiful young woman. I am proud of you, Louise, as I am sure your mother is too. Yes, I now realize that she is with us. I can sense her presence now, thanks to you. And I am filled with bitter regret that I abandoned you. I know that you have suffered terribly because of my actions, and it hurts me. I also know that whatever I have suffered, you have suffered much worse. I will never forgive myself for what I have done to you. I am deeply sorry for everything. I know your mother is upset with me. She loved you more than anyone in the world. I want you to know, Louise, that I love you and I have always loved you. I was absolutely wrong to shut you out of my life. You were just a little girl. I should have been there for you. I was not. I should have protected you. I did not. I know I can't make up for any of it, but I wish I could. I know that things will remain difficult between us, but I would be grateful if I could be even a small part of your life in the future.

Love,

Your father

Louise stared at the card for a minute. She then closed the card and set it on the white duvet. She slowly started to unwrapped the present her father had given her. Louise let the shiny red wrapping paper and white ribbon fall to the floor. Now she held a carboard box in her small hands. Louise carefully lifted the lid. Inside was a beige v-neck sweater. It was beautiful in its simplicity. Louise lifted it out of the box. She stood up and walked over to the tall gilt framed mirror in the corner of the bedroom. She put on the sweater and adjusted it after pulling it over her head. Louise also adjusted the large collar of her white cotton blouse. She looked at her reflection in the mirror. Yes, the sweater looked nice on her. And then Louise remembered something.

Louise walked over to her leather box suitcase. She found the white envelope with the photo of her mother that her father had given her in the hospital. She held the photo out and looked at it carefully. There was Louise at eight years of age. The tiny Louise was wearing a beige v-neck sweater over a white t-shirt. The sweater had been a gift from her father. Yes, now she remembered. And so had her father.

Louise walked over to the mirror. She looked at her reflection and then looked back at the photo. Yes, she looked exactly like her mother; only her mother had always kept her strawberry blonde hair long. And then Louise felt something: her mother's embrace. Yes, it was unmistakable. Tears filled Louise's eyes. Louise did not move. She didn't want this feeling to disappear.

'I love you, Mummy. I miss you. Thank you for visiting me. Please visit me often,' said Louise softly as she looked into the mirror. Louise felt the embrace tighten and then fade away.

Louise stared at her reflection for a few minutes. Louise turned around and walked back to the bed. She took off the sweater, folded it, and placed it back in the box. She placed the torn wrapping paper in the green paper shopping bag.

Louise undressed and changed into a pair of red and blue tartan pyjamas. Louise carefully hung her blue velvet skirt and white cotton blouse up in the closet. She then climbed into bed and quickly fell asleep.

Gemma—An Invisible Fear—The Nursery Centre

CREWS HILL
Down the M25, in the middle of a greenbelt, was Crews Hill. A lush and green place in the summer, but in the winter, empty and cold. The barren branches of tall trees swayed in the freezing wintery blasts. More than a few people were about in the summer. And there were few to none in the area in the winter. Crews Hill boasted one of the least utilized train stations in London. The perfect place to meet in secret.

The white Volkswagen hatchback's headlights could be seen in the distance as they illuminated the road ahead. Ingrid slowed her car as it approached the intersection in the sparsely populated, but heavily forested, borough in North London. She stopped at the red light. It was only 5:23pm, and it was already dark. The car idled at the intersection, illuminated in the reddish light of the traffic signal.

Ingrid checked her smartphone: no messages. Her mother's nursery centre, closed for the holidays, was just up ahead. The light changed, Ingrid shifted into drive, and the car moved forward.

It was a clear night. Snow had fallen earlier in the day, but the skies had cleared an hour before twilight. The sky above was an ocean of stars, inky blackness, a barely visible New Moon, and a small mechanical device which moved silently through the darkness—a military grade drone. The pilot, seated in a moving car three kilometers away, looked at the glowing screen of his tablet computer. He tapped the screen and the white image moving under the street lamps became clearer.

'Turn left at the intersection,' said the drone pilot to the dark-haired Crimean Tatar behind the wheel of the Audi A6.

Within a five-kilometer radius of the dark blue Audi were five other cars approaching the garden centre from different directions. Yes, Ingrid had been spotted leaving her mother's terraced house in Chipping Barnet after nightfall and been followed through North London. It was Christmas Day. If Ingrid were driving out to Crews Hill, it was to meet with the Legión Comandante. Yes, this was the moment the Hussars had been waiting for.

Everyone had been alerted half an hour before. Attila was the first one out the door of the safe house in London. Twenty men, all heavily armed and wearing body armor under their winter coats, and travelling in groups of three or four men per vehicle, were now moving through the wintry frozen night. Attila, seated in the front seat of a silver Volvo S60, watched the white hatchback move down the road in Crews Hill on a tablet computer; the Hungarian's heavily scarred face illuminated in the bluish light of the screen.

The Hussars operated under radio silence. Attila knew that Ingrid would be monitoring radio and cellphone traffic from inside her car. Ingrid's telecommunication abilities made her a dangerous opponent. Attila would communicate via encrypted text messages in a variety of languages, but not English. Ingrid was not a linguist. Attila tapped out instructions in Croatian, Hungarian, German, and French. Yes, everyone understood what was about to happen.

The drone hovered high above Crews Hill; its electronic eyes searching the roads below. Where were the others?

There!

Two cars had just exited the M25 and were now heading down the empty road through the forest and moving towards the garden centre. Was it really them? Could the Estonian drone operator be sure? Of course, it was them. Who else could it be? Alright. The Estonian tapped out a message on his encrypted smartphone in German and sent it to Attila.

THE GARDEN CENTRE

The garden centre was a rather large, sprawling complex of wooden sheds, polycarbonate paneled greenhouses, and London stock brick offices partially hidden behind large English oak and Field maple trees. Ingrid's mother had bought the garden centre in 1992, just as the real estate market collapsed. She had worked hard throughout the 1990s to make it a success. Ingrid had worked on and off at the center throughout her life. One day, Mrs Steyr would pass the centre on to Ingrid. It was a solid business, regardless of the economy. In December, the garden centre sold Christmas trees: Norway Spruce, Nordmann fir, Blue spruce, Fraser Fir, Douglas fir, Lodgepole pine, Noble fir, and Scots fir. This Christmas had been better than most. A few unsold Christmas tress still lined the foyer of the garden centre and one of the large green houses.

The garden centre also allowed Ingrid to meet with Enoch Tara when necessary. Enoch always ordered plants from the nursery in Crews Hill, and it was Ingrid who would always deliver them to one of his offices or private residences herself. The last face-to-face meeting she had had with Enoch Tara had been when she had followed the lorry that delivered a Norway Spruce to his house in Marble Arch. She had spoken with Mr Tara while two men from the garden centre had carried the tree into the drawing room. Mr Tara was always nice and very polite—a true English gentleman. He had served Ingrid and the two nursery employees tea in the drawing room after they had set up the tree for him. Well, actually, a young servant from Northern England had served everyone tea. The house maid was very nice, but the South African born Ingrid could barely understand anything the young woman said—such was the Berwick dialect.

The white hatchback rolled to a stop on the side of the main building that lacked outdoor lighting. Ingrid knew where all of the unlit areas of the complex where located.

Ingrid had also turned off the CCTV system at the centre the day before. Ingrid always did that before she met with anyone from the Special Unit at the garden centre. No one on the staff ever checked the CCTV footage. No one had ever noticed the gaps in the digital surveillance tapes.

Ingrid turned off the headlights and got out of the car. She zipped up the front of her navy blue puffer coat, wrapped a dark grey scarf around her neck and lower half of her face, stuck a Walther PPK into the IWB holster in the denim waistband of her faded blue jeans, and walked towards the front doors of the centre, all the while being illuminated in the light given off by the lamps in front of the main entrance. Ingrid noticed the shadow she cast as she made her way to the front doors. She stopped at the front doors of the main building, looked around, and then turned back and unlocked the front doors. Ingrid stepped inside, and then without turning on the lights, closed the doors and stood waiting in the darkness.

THE COMMANDANTE

The physically fit and middle-aged Spaniard sat in the front passenger seat of the dark blue Audi A7. The driver, a twenty-eight-year-old blond Afrikaner, scanned the road the ahead. Nothing could be seen within the beams of the headlights but a well-maintained rural road lined by snow clad barren trees. In the back seat of the Audi, buckled into the black leather seat, was a young twenty-something Rhodesian exile.

A few hundred yards behind the dark blue Audi was a metallic silver 2019 BMW 5-Series carrying four South Africans mercenaries.

Not one of the men said a word the entire time. All were focused on the tasks ahead. They would find out who was behind the murder of the Brigada and the murder of Colin Bailey two days before. They would have to move rapidly to destroy their invisible enemy before their hidden enemy destroyed them. Yes, the situation had changed; it had become far more dangerous.

The dark blue Audi pulled into the small parking area of the garden centre and came to a stop under a large barren English oak tree, its branches covered in a thin layer of snow. The three men got out and walked to the front doors of the garden centre. Just as Ingrid opened the front doors of the main building, the men were momentarily illuminated in automobile headlights. The silver BWM drove past them and into the tree lined parking lot. The driver switched off the headlights. Doors could be heard opening and closing. Four more figures moved through the shadowy demi-darkness of the narrow parking lot, snow crunching under foot.

THE MAIN BUILDING

Ingrid, in a pair of faded blue jeans, brown Chelsea boots, and a navy blue puffer coat, closed and locked the double doors to the main building after the last man had entered. Two of the men stayed in the foyer; the rest of the group walked down the corridor.

'There is a small office in the east wing where we can talk,' said Ingrid, her breathe materializing in the cold air.

The five men and one woman made their way through the long and dimly lit greenhouse which was paneled in polycarbonate sheets. It was freezing cold inside the clear paneled structure. The green house, which was about ninety-five feet long and twenty feet wide, was lined with dozens of unsold Christmas trees, mostly Blue spruce and the odd Scots fir. Several florescent lamps hung from the ceiling of the green house. Only two had been left on. Walking through the forest of unsold trees, which cast chaotic and disconcerting shadows in every direction, in the ashen lighting of the long and narrow greenhouse at night, was an almost surreal experience. Ingrid led the way. At the end of the greenhouse was a bright glossy blue door in a plywood wall that made up the end of the polycarbonate structure.

Ingrid unlocked the door and turned on the lights. Ingrid and the Comandante entered the office; the rest of the men in winter parkas and denim blue jeans, waited outside, spread out through the large structure.

The interior of the small spartan office consisted of plywood walls and an overhead fluorescent lamp. There was a small wooden desk, three folding metal chairs, and a large clock hanging on the wall that ticked loudly. The Comandante, in faded blue jeans, a white button-down Oxford dress shirt, and a blue knit half zip pullover, stood in front of the desk.

'Please, have a seat,' said Ingrid.

The Spaniard, his light brown hair cut like a British army officer's, sat down in one of the folding chairs.

Ingrid sat down in one of the empty metal chairs and turned on her tablet computer. It quickly came to life.

'I managed to trace some of the text messages that Colin Bailey made from a phone in the pizza shop an hour before he was killed. He contacted two different people. One number I could not trace, but the other, I could. I cracked the encryption codes of Colin Bailey's phone.'

Ingrid then took a folded collection of white paper documents out of an inside pocket of her puffer coat.

'Here, I traced seven text messages to a house in the Mayfair. The house is owned by Carter Holland. Do you know who he is?' asked Ingrid.

'No.'

'Carter Holland is the CEO of Quadriga Investments.'

The Comandante gave Ingrid a stony look.

'Carter Ajax Holland is a billionaire—a multibillionaire. And he has quite the reputation.'

The Comandante crossed his arms at stared at Ingrid.

'Ingrid, I don't have all night. Please get to the point,' said the Comandante in his mildly accented English.

'Carter Holland is a borderline gangster. People say that he is a money launderer and that he has laundered tens of billions, if not hundreds of billions of dollars through the City,' replied Ingrid.

'That's half the banks in London, Ingrid.'

'Carter Holland is somehow connected to Declan and Colin Bailey. Colin contacted someone in the house in Mayfair. It's Carter Holland. He is behind the murders,' said Ingrid.

The Comandante picked up the documents and looked through the codes, charts, and numbers printed out on the documents. He flipped through the pages slowly, often flipping back to look at an earlier page. Ingrid was amazing. How she managed to do all of this, the Spaniard really didn't know. The technology was far beyond him. Ingrid had done it. Without her, this mystery might have remained unsolved. And Enoch Tara might easily have wound up dead.

'Yes, I think you're right. You have found our invisible enemy,' said the Spaniard as he studied one of the pages.

'Why do you think Carter Holland ordered the murder of Colin Bailey?' asked Ingrid.

'I think that Carter Holland is trying to cover his tracks. He has had some of his own men murdered to cover up his involvement in the Brigada's death. **That's something I would never do**,' said the Spaniard. The Comandante shifted in the chair. The Comandante was aware of some of the goings-on in the City, but he had never heard of Carter Holland. There were a lot of billionaires in London these days.

'Why do you think Carter Holland is interested in Enoch Tara? If he just wanted him dead, it would not be that difficult. Enoch Tara moves about unguarded sometimes. Why even bother with Mr Tara at all?' asked the Comandante.

'That's a good question. It's a mystery to me. Both of them are multibillionaires. How much more money could someone need? They have never had any business dealings—which is unusual considering how active both of them are in the markets. I think you will have to ask Mr Tara about that,' said Ingrid.

'I will ask Mr Tara tomorrow,' replied the Comandante.

'And what happens after that?' asked Ingrid.

'Simple. We kill Carter Holland and put an end to all of this immediately;' said the Comandante matter-of-factly. The Comandante looked at his IWC wristwatch (which was on a natural rubber strap). 'Where is Carter Holland now?'

'I don't know. That particular phone has not been used since the night of the murders. Carter Holland might have already destroyed it. He owns a dozen homes in London alone. There is also a large country house in East Anglia which is surrounded by thousands of acres of ancient woodland. Carter Holland has *a lot of heavily armed security* around him—practically a private army,' said Ingrid.

The Spaniard leaned back in the folding metal chair and looked directly at Ingrid and said, 'Good work, Ingrid. I will make sure you receive a large bonus from Mr Tara. One that will allow you to finally buy a home of your own in London, or wherever you choose to live. Please stay with the Special Unit. You are invaluable. If we were in the Spanish Foreign Legión right now, I would have you promoted and decorate you myself.'

Ingrid knew that the Comandante was a man of few words, and that when he did speak, he meant every word he said. The retired Spanish army major had paid Ingrid a great compliment. Yes, the Comandante would make sure she received a million pounds from Mr Tara, at the very least. And more than the money, the notion that the comandante valued her and had openly expressed it, meant more to Ingrid than any amount of money.

'Thank you, sir.'

'The rest of the unit will be here in half an hour. I would like you to brief everyone on what you just told me. After that, we will leave, and you will go home and stay home until after the New Year. I will contact you in a few weeks. Alright?' said the Comandante.

'Alright,' replied Ingrid.

THE MAIN BUILDING

A shadow cast by someone unseen in the parking lot alerted one of the blond Afrikaners who was guarding the entrance. He pulled out his 9mm pistol and shouted, 'Visitors!' in Afrikaans.

The other Afrikaner pointed his Czech Škorpion vz. 61 machine pistol at the white pane glass double door entrance.

A few seconds later, the sound of machine gunfire and shattering glass filled the foyer. The Afrikaner near the entrance went down in a hail of bullets; blood splattered on the white walls of the foyer as he crumpled to the floor. Suddenly there was a loud explosion and a blinding flash of light filled the entire foyer. The other South African, temporarily blinded and with one of his ear drums most likely blown by the flashbang grenade, pointed his Czech machine pistol in the direction of movement and fired it on full auto. The blinded and disoriented Afrikaner had killed one and wounded another with the single burst, but he would never know it—he would be dead within seconds, shot through the throat and face by another attacker.

THE GREENHOUSE

'Ambush!' shouted one of the Afrikaners in the demi-darkness of the greenhouse. The men all drew their pistols and started moving through the Christmas trees towards the exit which opened into the main building. The Comandante and Ingrid drew their pistols in the office. Suddenly glowing tracer rounds and an array of invisible bullets punched through the polycarbonate panels of the greenhouse. Being plastic, and not glass, the panels did not shatter, they splintered with strange popping noises and loud cracking sounds. The tree branches of the unsold Christmas trees splintered and snapped and fell to the floor of the greenhouse as a wave of undulating, deafening, and discordant machine gun fire smashed through the polycarbonate and steel framed structure.

'I've been hit!' shouted one man in Afrikaans; the shadowy figure then leaned up against the steel frame and fired his 9mm pistol at the attackers hidden in the darkness outside. Another Afrikaner, a blond thirtysomething from Cape Town, was hit in the chest by an exploding bullet. He died instantly, knocking down two Scots pine as he collapsed to the floor. A moment later, the wounded Afrikaner was hit by several more bullets and slumped down to the floor, polycarbonate shards falling with him.

Outside, half a dozen slender and athletic men in a variety of black and dark grey tactical pullovers, bullet proof vests, black balaclavas, military grade night vision goggles, and carrying machine guns, fired on full auto into the large paneled structure, occasionally stopping to reload.

Inside the dimly and partially lit polycarbonate and steel greenhouse, the surviving members of the Special Unit maneuvered through the splintered trees, unseen flying bullets, glowing tracer rounds, and shattered plastic panels trying to escape into the main building. The Comandante and Ingrid were half way through the paneled structure and firing their pistols when Ingrid was hit in the stomach by a bullet (or two). She gasped loudly and then went down on one knee while pressing one hand to her wounded abdomen. The Comandante spotted two of the attackers outside through a broken polycarbonate panel, briefly illuminated by burst of gunfire from their machine guns. Bang! Bang! –both attackers, shot through their heads, collapsed dead in the snowy field. The remaining four Hussars stopped shooting and retreated back into the darkness.

The two Afrikaners at the exit of the greenhouse were reloading their pistols after killing five heavily armed and hooded attackers in the foyer. The foyer's white walls were splattered with blood, and the lobby was covered in broken glass, bullet casings, and eight bullet riddled corpses.

'Come on, Ingrid. I'm taking you out of here,' said the Comandante, his Spanish accent suddenly more noticeable, as he knelt down in the swirling demi-darkness of the greenhouse and picked up the diminutive and slender South African woman while putting one of her arms around his shoulder. Ingrid gasped as she choked on her own blood; sharp pains raced through her body.

'Are you still with me?' asked the Comandante as they started to walk through the broken shards of polycarbonate, tree branches, and past the bloody corpses of their fallen comrades.

'Yes…Yes,' gasped Ingrid as she coughed up blood. Her strength quickly ebbing away, Ingrid dropped her pistol to the floor. Blood poured from her wounds; her faded blue jeans were soaked in blood as was her torn puffer coat. Her brown hair caked with blood, Ingrid's head fell to one side and she was now cheek to cheek with the Comandante as he carried her through the wrecked greenhouse. A few steps later, Ingrid's legs stopped working and the Comandante was dragging her, a thick trail of blood behind her.

'Ingrid, we are going to make for the car, alright?' said the Comandante.

Ingrid was silent.

'Ingrid? Are you still with me?' The Comandante turned his head and Ingrid's lifeless head fell forward, blood pouring from her mouth. The Comandante breathed hard. He gently lowered Ingrid's lifeless body to the floor which was covered in jagged pieces of polycarbonate and broken tree branches.

'Comandante. We have to make a run for it. They are regrouping—somewhere—out there,' said the twentysomething Rhodesian exile calmly while holding a Czech machine pistol and pointing out into the darkness with his other hand.

The surviving Afrikaner dialed his smartphone—someone answered—and he started speaking urgently in Afrikaans. A voice on the line responded in near shouts. 'They'll be here in about twenty minutes,' said the Afrikaner holding the smartphone in one hand and a German 9mm pistol in the other.

'Take their machine guns and whatever ammunition they have and let's go,' said the Comandante in heavily accented English.

The Comandante moved hurriedly into the darkened foyer with the other two surviving members of the Special Unit and grabbed a Yugoslav AK-47 machine gun and then unbuckled the leather belt and canvas ammunition pouch from a dead man who wore a black balaclava. The Spaniard grabbed a second Kalashnikov and handed it to the Afrikaner in the foyer. The Rhodesian picked up an AK-47 as he walked through the wrecked foyer. He stopped momentarily to look at the dead bodies of his comrades. No, there was nothing that anyone could do for them now. 'Go with God,' said the young Rhodesian as he approached the blasted entrance of the main building.

The three surviving members of the Special Unit peered out into the darkness. Footprints and tire tracks crisscrossed the partially illuminated snowy parking area. Just twenty yards away, parked under a large tree, was the dark blue Audi A7.

'Let's just make a run for it, Comandante,' said the young Rhodesian calmly and quietly.

'Alright,' said the Comandante, 'On the count of three, we run for the car. Don't worry, I have the keys.' The Comandante peered once more into the darkness. Yes, **they** were out there—waiting for them. The Comandante was calm. He now fell back on his training and experience. His training would take him and the others to the car and they would escape. The Comandante inhaled and then slowly exhaled.

'One. Two. Three.'

The three men sprinted out of the main building, through the darkness, across the narrow parking lot, the snow crunching under their boots. As they reached the dark blue sedan, machine gun fire erupted from the far end of the complex. Bullets whizzed by their heads. A couple of high velocity bullets struck and sliced though the car with bright flashes and sparks in their wake. The three soldiers did not panic; the Rhodesian fired his Kalashnikov on full auto in the direction of the attackers. The Comandante opened the door to the car and climbed in; having activated the ignition via remote as he ran, the engine was already running by the time his closed the driver side door. The Afrikaner fired a burst of machine gun fire into the darkness before opening the front seat passenger side door of the Audi and getting in. The Rhodesian opened the back passenger door as bullets struck and shattered the rear window of the sedan. He climbed in.

The Audi's engine revved as the gauges on the dashboard brightened; the Comandante slammed down on the accelerator, and the Audi 7 bolted forward in a burst of bright white headlights.

The German car accelerated violently as it disappeared into the darkness leaving maelstrom of snow, shards of broken glass, glowing tracer rounds, and red tail lights in its wake. The air was filled with lead and there were bright sparks from impacting rounds as the car sped away. The Audi's headlights cut through the darkness as the car moved rapidly down road, barely making its turns because of gravity and the occasional patches of snow and ice. After a few minutes, the car suddenly started to slow and then drifted off onto the shoulder of the road before coming to a complete stop.

'Why are we stopping?' asked the young Rhodesian exile in the backseat.

'Comandante?' asked the blond Afrikaner seated next to him in the front passenger seat. The Afrikaner reached through the dimly illuminated interior of the car and grasped the Comandante's shoulder. The Spaniard slumped forward, his head hitting the steering wheel. The Afrikaner pulled him back. That's when he noticed the blood. The Comandante had been shot in the side, but he had said nothing.

'The Comandante. He's dead,' said the Afrikaner quietly.

THE M25

The white sedan, its bright headlights illuminating the road ahead, glided off the exit ramp and made its way onto the tree lined thoroughfare and moved quickly through the Moonless night towards the garden centre.

And then the white BWM decelerated suddenly.

Up ahead was an ocean of flashing blue lights and intense burning white phosphoric light. Heavily armed members of the Metropolitan Police had blocked the road. The German sedan came to a stop behind a dozen other cars and trucks.

Two policemen, in yellow reflective jackets and carrying large flashlights, stood on the snow-covered shoulder of the road. They were partially illuminated in the incandescent white phosphoric glow of the road flares which had been staggered across the roadway.

Three police cars, their blue lights flashing and their bright headlights lighting up the check point, were blocking the road ahead.

The driver behind the wheel of the white automobile could make out five authorized firearms officers, in black tactical vests, body armor, and carrying Heckler & KochG36C carbines, spread out across the tree lined thoroughfare ahead.

Further down the country road, the driver could see three more police cars, their blue lights flashing in the darkness, speeding towards the garden centre.

'Turn the car around,' said the middle-aged man in the front passenger seat in Afrikaans.

The driver nodded and the white BWM turned slowly, maneuvered carefully, turned around, and drove away.

8 THE VORTEX

Gemma—An Invisible Fear—Boxing Day

MARBLE ARCH

Steam rose from the translucent water in the large white modern bathtub. Gemma, her head resting against a folded, wet white cotton hand towel, closed her eyes. A hot bath was easily one of Gemma's favorite activities. Here, safe from the world in the water's embrace, Gemma could release every bit of tension in her body and truly relax. The white tiled walls of the bathroom dripped with moisture; the mirror was obscured by condensation. With the exception of the water in the bathtub, not a sound could be heard. Gemma floated away.

THE DRAWING ROOM

Enoch, freshly shaved and wearing the red and blue tartan flannel pyjamas, white waffle pattern robe, and white cotton slippers that Gemma had given him for Christmas, inhaled the steam which gently rose from the white bone china cup. Yes, the scent of honey filled his lungs. It was Boxing Day. Enoch had slept well for the first time in weeks. After a restful sleep, Enoch had taken a hot bath that morning.

Enoch, his mother Eloise, and fiancée Gemma, had spent the evening before happily playing with Gemma's kitten. Soot, the tiny stray black cat from Surrey, had completely captured Gemma's heart.

'I love you, Soot,' Gemma had said repeatedly the night before. Sometimes she had said it softly, gently, quietly to Soot when he was sitting in her lap or resting on her shoulder. Sometimes Gemma had said it happily when Soot had played wildly in the empty cardboard boxes, wrapping paper, and ribbons that dotted the drawing room floor that evening. Yes, baby Soot was Gemma's little boy. Gemma had taken Soot with her to bed that night. Soot had spent the evening nursing Gemma's head of glossy brown hair before going to sleep and purring next to her. That Gemma was happy was all that mattered. Yes, Gemma's unbridled happiness had been the perfect distraction for Enoch Tara that Christmas.

There was a knock on the door of the drawing room. The glossy white door opened and a young housemaid in a black wool uniform and white cotton gloves nodded slightly.

'Good morning, sir,' said the housemaid in a Northumbrian accent. The young brunette, her hair held up with silver hair pins, stepped into the white walled drawing room. 'There is a man outside that I have never seen before. He would like to speak with you. Two of the security team are outside talking with him now.'

'Did he say who he was, Miss Smith?'

'No, sir. He said that he had a to speak with you privately. He said that the Spaniard had sent him.'

Enoch arched an eyebrow. The Comandante would never send anyone to the house. That would be breaking the security protocol. Something had happened. Enoch leaned back into the high back armchair.

'Where is Edward?' asked Enoch, referring to the head of his security detail.

'He's outside, talking with the man on the front step. Should I ask Edward to come inside and speak with you, Mr Tara?' asked the young woman in a Berwick accent (which meant a distinct pronunciation of the letter R and elongation of vowels).

'Yes, please.'

The young Northumbrian housemaid departed and a few minutes later, Edward, a well-spoken former British Para from Boars Hill, knocked on the door to the drawing room. Enoch rose from the chair and said, 'Come in.'

Edward, 6' 1" and with a slender but athletic build, entered the room. He was wearing a black suit, white dress shirt (with an English spread collar), and black silk necktie. His dark brown hair was cut like a City Banker. He was extremely handsome. Edward, at 39, was considered relatively young to hold the position he did.

'Good morning, sir. A man has arrived that I have never met. He is an Afrikaner. He gave me this to give to you,' said Edward as he held up a white paper envelope. 'I think it best if I open the envelope, Mr Tara,' said Edward.

'Alright,' said Enoch.

The security chief opened the envelope. Inside was a white slip of paper with the Comandante's full name typed out on it. Edward read the name aloud. So, the man outside knew the true identity of the leader of the Special Unit. Edward then walked over and gave Enoch the slip of paper.

'What is going on, Edward?'

'I don't know, sir. The man outside says that it is urgent. He refuses to show me any ID. He's polite. And he has the bearing of a professional soldier.'

Enoch looked at the white slip of paper for a moment. Yes, all of this was unorthodox, but whatever was going on needed to be ascertained.

'Please, let him in. I'd like you and another member of the security team to be with me when he enters.'

'I recommend you not meet with him, Mr Tara.'

Enoch looked out the window of the house. It was an overcast wintery day in London. The calm Enoch had felt just a few minutes before suddenly vanished. Something was wrong.

'Send him in.'

THE SOUTH AFRICAN

The svelte, middle-aged, and handsome (in a soldierly way) Afrikaner that appeared in the doorway of the Georgian drawing room had dark brown hair which had been cut like a British army officer's. He wore a pair of black frame glasses (which foiled facial recognition software), a charcoal grey suit, a white dress shirt, and a dark grey silk necktie (which had been tied in a Windsor knot). When he had arrived at the front door, he had been wearing a black Homburg hat and a dark grey wool overcoat with a black bear fur collar that had been flipped up to obscure his face (or perhaps to protect him from the cold). The wool overcoat and Homburg had been left in the foyer. He had the bearing of a Prussian Junker. The older man nodded slightly. Enoch rose from the chair to greet him.

Edward and another former British Para stood behind the South African; their dark wool suits contrasted sharply with the white walls and Georgian crown molding of the drawing room.

'Good morning, Mister…may I know your name, sir?' asked Enoch politely.

'Mr Tara, could I speak with you alone?'

'No,' said Edward sharply.

Enoch looked at his security chief and then he looked back at the South African who stood before him.

'Please, tell me what this all about,' asked Enoch.

The man hesitated for a moment.

'The man whose name is on that slip of paper is dead,' said the Afrikaner quietly.

Enoch went pale. He felt a shock run through him. Was this true? How could this be?

'What happened to him? Why did they send you?' asked a clearly shaken Enoch.

'Mr Tara, could we speak privately?' asked the South African.

'Alright.'

'Mr Tara, I think we should stay,' said Edward.

Enoch exhaled and looked up at the ornate white plaster ceiling above him.

'Please, leave us.'

'We'll be right outside, if you need us, sir,' said Edward. The former British Para nodded, turned, and left the room with the other former Para.

'Where is Ingrid? She usually liaisons for the Special Unit.'

'Mr Tara, Ingrid Steyr was killed last night. I was never supposed to meet you. However, the chain of command has been broken. The Special Unit has been decapitated. The Comandante was killed along with Miss Steyr and several others. The Comandante appointed me to be one of the team leaders. As the other two team leaders were killed last night, I am now the most senior member of the Special Unit. I would like only you to know my real name.'

Enoch's head was spinning.

'How can this be happening? What happened exactly?'

'Mr Tara, in order to ensure **plausible deniability**, I can't tell you that.'

'May I ask you your name?' asked Enoch.

'My name is Blair Hertzog. I am South African, but I am now a naturalized British citizen. I was officer in the South African SAS in the late 1980s and early 90s. The Comandante told me that I would be in charge of the Special Unit in the event of his death. I don't have your phone number, Mr Tara; otherwise, I would have telephoned you and arranged to meet you at the safe house in Surrey.'

'Plausible deniability…Am I never to learn the fates of my fallen soldiers?' asked Enoch quietly.

'It's for your own good, sir. There are legal implications.'

'So, the people who murdered the Brigada have struck again?' asked Enoch rhetorically.

'No, Mr Tara. This was a different group.'

'What?'

'There is more than one group operating against us in England. Miss Steyr, apparently, had learned the identity of the man behind the murder of the Brigada. She spoke with the Comandante privately, but from what the Comandante had told me before he left for Crews Hill, Ingrid had cracked it.'

'How many of my men were killed last night?' asked Enoch quietly.

'Five, not including Ingrid.'

'Have their families been notified?'

'No. Not yet. The BBC ran a report on the incident this morning. A total of fifteen dead at a garden centre in Crews Hill. It's been described as the beginning of a full-fledged gangland war. The press has been speculating that the murder of a gangster in Elephant and Castle is somehow connected to what happened last night in Crews Hill. The police have only been able to identify the body of Ingrid so far. Everyone else either had a fake ID or no identification on them at all. They say the entire gun battle was over in ten minutes. The CCTV at the garden centre had been turned off for the meeting. That was Standard Operating Procedure for the Unit. Ingrid's mother owns it. Ingrid Steyr was careful to compartmentalize the Unit. There is no discernable connection between the Special Unit and you, Mr Tara.'

'How will we give any of them a proper burial? The police won't be able to identify them. These people have families,' said Enoch.

'Mr Tara, these men accepted that this could be their fate. The Comandante did not have any immediate family. The others were unmarried. I know their families. I will inform them privately, not mentioning you, of course. Money will be transferred to their accounts, and that is how it will end, unfortunately. The families will understand the situation, Mr Tara.'

Enoch looked out the window. He would never speak to the Comandante or Ingrid again.

'Thank you for coming in person, Mr Hertzog. I will give you an encrypted smartphone before you leave. And my private number. If the Comandante wanted you to lead the Special Unit, then I will confirm your position right now. How many men are left in the Unit?'

'Twenty-three, including myself, Mr Tara. We are ready to undertake any assignment you give us, sir.'

'What happens next?' asked Enoch.

'I recommend that you stay at your offices in the City. The merchant bank building is a much more secure location. Members of the Special Unit will be stationed in the area—and they will be armed. It's necessary, sir.'

'And what about the people responsible for the murder of my soldiers?' asked Enoch in a quiet and disconnected tone of voice.

'We will pursue them. Eventually. Right now, we have no idea who these people are. We must recruit a new communications officer to replace Miss Steyr. That won't be easy. She was an extraordinarily talented person,' said the South African.

'Yes, she was.'

'Mr Tara, these soldiers were my comrades. It is important to me that we avenge them. However, it is paramount that you are protected. That has always been the Special Unit's priority.'

'I will pack my bags now and go to my office in the City. I am the target. I have known that from the beginning. It's best I be a lone target,' said Enoch.

THE BEDROOM
'Soot, where are you?' said Gemma happily as she entered the bedroom.

The rock salt grey walled room (with ivory white Georgian crown molding) was filled with natural light. The large bed of white bedding was unmade and looked like a snowy mountain range. There were four white pillows piled high against the glossy birch Mid-Century Modern headboard.

The tiny black kitten was nowhere to be seen. Gemma, in a white waffle patterned bathrobe and with her wet hair wrapped up in a white towel, sat down carefully on the edge of the bed being careful not to sit on a sleeping kitten. Gemma looked around. There was no sign of Soot. Where could he be?

'Ouch!' said Gemma as she felt sharp tiny claws attacking her feet.

'Ah, so the panther attacks!' said Gemma happily. Soot, now standing next to Gemma's feet, looked up at her.

'You are so cute, Soot.'

Gemma knelt down and tried to pick Soot up, but, alas, Soot patted her hand and ran back under the bed.

'Baby, where are you?'

Gemma noticed Soot darting across the hardwood floor towards the upholstered George III armchair near the white sash window. Soot stopped and then ran back towards Gemma and clawed his way of the white duvet and onto the bed. He stopped at the edge of the bed and looked at her. Soot was so tiny, fragile, and cute. And, to Soot, Gemma was now his mother.

'Are you hungry, baby?'

Gemma reached out and picked up Soot. She carried him in her arms and walked over to the Mid-Century Modern black walnut desk near the large sash window. There was a sterling silver tray with a white porcelain tea cup and saucer, a sterling silver bowl of sugar, and a Britannia silver container of cold milk.

Gemma placed Soot on top of the desk. She then placed the tea cup on the tray and lifted the white saucer up and placed it next to Soot. She carefully poured some cold milk into the porcelain saucer. She gently picked up Soot and placed him next to the saucer. Soot began to purr loudly as he drank the cold milk.

Gemma gently petted the tiny black kitten as he drank. Gemma smiled.

And then Gemma suddenly remembered the dragon in Louise's dream. She had promised Louise that she would tell Enoch about it. Yes, the dream was important. Gemma was aware things were not going well, but she had no idea there was violence involved. She believed that Enoch, like the rest of the financial world, was fending off attacks from an unknown enemy. Yes, she would tell Enoch today. Gemma was worried. She had been worried about the dream since Louise first told her. Yes, it would be best if Enoch knew about it.

Gemma gently petted the baby cat as he drank the cold milk. Soot purred happily as she did so. He was now loved.

Gemma—An Invisible Fear—Plutonian Winter

MAYFAIR

Carter Ajax Holland watched the flickering images on the digital screen. He listened carefully to every single word the reporters were saying. Images of a wrecked nursery, ambulances, and police cars flashed across the plasma screen. Police crime scene investigators in white smocks were shown walking through the ruins of the garden centre in Crews Hill.

Incredible. Tara's Special Unit had been decimated—several mercenaries were now bullet riddled corpses on cold steel slabs in the morgue. The Revenant had done it. **What agency.** The 11th Baron had been right all along. The Revenant, a man without a country, without a biography, a foreigner, a war refugee, was the only man in England capable of seeing the enterprise through to the end—and much more. Much, much more. Yes, the foreign warlord had proven himself. He had not failed Carter where others had failed him. No, the enigmatic and inscrutable foreign warlord was truly cut from a different cloth.

Carter, in pale blue cotton pyjama trousers, a white t-shirt, and a pair of white cotton slippers, smiled. Yes, it was all going to plan.

Wintery grey London was covered in an artic white layer of fresh snow. The cadaverous sky was a gossamer veil of nebulous greys and strangely luminous strands of white. There was something about snow—alluring and deceptive at the same time. A fresh blanket of snow could make any place look beautiful—even a rotting corpse like England. A man lost in a blizzard knew he was in danger when he started to feel warm in the cutting cold. When a snow drift started to look balmy and inviting, a man knew he was near death. That morning, the London that appeared before Carter looked like a collection of ornate tombs; London seemed to speak to Carter in sepulchral voices and half-strangled screams.

Ping.

Carter's encrypted smartphone glowed momentarily. He picked it up, tapped the screen, and smiled. He quickly tapped out a response. Carter Holland put smartphone down on the nightstand.

The white walls of Carter's Georgian bedroom reflected the silvery natural morning light.

Carter Holland had spent the day before, Christmas, brooding. Carter, alone on the upper floors of his Grade II listed Georgian house in Mayfair, had had a lot on his mind. He had spent the day wandering the hallways and rooms of the top two floors of the house. He looked at maps in the library; he went over lists of military equipment, and most importantly to Carter, exercised in the gym on one of the upper floors of the terraced house.

Hard exercise helped Carter focus. Carter would stretch, do at least a hundred pushups and sit-ups before moving on to lift weights, run on the tread mill, train on the Ellipticals, utilize the rowing machine, and end most of his workouts on the stationary bicycle. He would always drink a lot of bottled water during the workout. Yes, water was essential. After finishing his ninety-minute daily exercise regimen, he would usually cool down for around twenty minutes—drinking ice water while standing at one of the large white sash windows of the gym on the fourth floor of the house and surveying London's constantly changing skyline. The last few months had seen Carter staring at the helix-like glassy Gherkin, just three miles away from the house in Mayfair. It was amazing how close he lived and worked to his rivals in London. He would then take a lukewarm shower for about fifteen minutes. He would emerge from the shower naked and walk back into the gym and stand in front of one of the mirrors. Yes, at fifty-two, the blond Carter Holland still had the body of an Adonis. Yes, the svelte Carter was beautiful—Carter had always been beautiful. Carter would admire his muscular chest and abdominal muscles. He would twist his slender hips and pose naked before the large mirror—yes, Carter was both a physical and intellectual colossus. Carter Holland was driven by an inner vision which would alter the age that he and everyone else on this planet lived. Carter would change the world. Forever.

The highly professional and uniformed household staff downstairs had prepared a large and sumptuous Christmas dinner for Carter and dozen guests. Carter wasn't hungry. And Carter hadn't invited anyone to spend Christmas with him this year. Carter had spent most of 2019 alone. He had much to attend too. He had told the staff, a wave of black wool uniforms and white cotton gloves, to avail themselves of the feast they had so adeptly and artfully prepared. A dozen vicious and brutal members of Carter Holland's suited and booted security team had spent the day patrolling the area around the house and having Christmas dinner with the dozen or so members of the household staff who had crowded into the large modern kitchen on the first floor of the house to watch Christmas specials on a flat screen television while partaking of a heavenly Christmas dinner.

Carter was generous with the household staff. Carter expected two things of his servants: that they keep the house hygienically clean and orderly and that they were as quiet as possible while carrying out their daily tasks. Beyond that, Carter Holland was rarely seen and almost never spoken to by the housemaids, footmen, or underbutlers. The Majordomo of the house would usually be contacted by the head of security whenever Carter wanted something. Carter hired staff that were expected to keep secrets and not engage in idle gossip—especially about him. In exchange for all of this, Carter paid double the average wage.

With Declan and Colin Bailey dead, a cordon sanitaire had been created around Carter Holland. No one would be able to connect him to the murder of the Brigada. And, more importantly, Enoch Tara's Special Unit had been effectively destroyed. It would take, at the very least, several weeks, most likely several months, to rebuild it. Carter was about to put all of his plans into motion. And Tara was, for the most part, now defenseless. Enoch Tara had lost his eyes, ears, and fists with the annihilation of the Special Unit.

Carter was becoming more and more impatient with each passing day. He wanted to get the war in the East underway. He just wanted to leave

England and never return, never look back, and escape the intellectual vacuity and hopeless morass that was now England.

The London Stock Exchange was closed on Christmas and Boxing Day. Alright then, tomorrow the last phase would begin. In a few days, Carter Holland would be the richest man in the world. He would board a private plane and depart this blessed plot, this earth, this realm, this England. Forever.

Gemma—An Invisible Fear—The Special Unit

MARBLE ARCH

Enoch Tara stopped at the base of the stairs. He grasped the white banister with a trembling hand. The Comandante and Ingrid were dead. Ingrid's family would be able to hold a funeral for her. Ingrid had died so young. It was horrible; however, the church service and a proper burial could, perhaps, offer Ingrid's family some kind of closure. The Comandante, however, would lay in the morgue unclaimed. Or would his comrades from the Spanish Foreign Legión come for him? Yes, the Legión would claim him and take him back to Spain. At least, Enoch hoped so.

Enoch had spent a little time with Ingrid over the last couple of years. He had liked Ingrid from their first meeting. Her briefings were always clear and concise. She had a high level of technical prowess that had impressed Enoch. She was also friendly and a dash of humor usually accompanied her informal presentations in the drawing room over tea. Enoch had always offered a wide selection of biscuits and he had noticed immediately how much Ingrid had liked Rose biscuits from Fortnum & Mason. Ingrid had found the very idea that crystallised *French* rose petals had been added to them to be amazing. Enoch had had the kitchen staff stock up on them, just for Ingrid's visits. He had also given her a rose colored tin of them as a small Christmas present a few days before her violent death. Another death had been added to Enoch's conscience. Another death along with several others in last three weeks.

The Comandante had worked for Enoch for several years, and yet Enoch knew almost nothing about him. The Spanish Legionnaire had always maintained a professional distance from his employer. It was better that way, Enoch supposed. The Comandante had always been polite and respectful. Enoch had been impressed with not only his physical appearance but the man's undoubted courage and loyalty. He could also sense an underlying sense of common decency in the Comandante.

Blair Hertzog, the new South African commander of the Special Unit, had informed him, at Enoch's request, of what had actually happened in the garden centre in Crews Hill, as reported to him by the two surviving members of gun battle. Yes, the Comandante had tried to save Ingrid's life. Mr Hertzog told Enoch that Ingrid had died in the arms of the Comandante. She had not been abandoned. The Afrikaner had felt that was important for Enoch to know. Enoch had found the new commander's explanation of events to be deeply moving.

No. The Special Unit did not know the identity of the people behind the attacks. That information had died with Ingrid and the Comandante.

The deaths of the members of the Special Unit weighed heavily on Enoch. He wanted to do more for them. The South African commander had assured him that he would do all that he could.

Enoch slowly ascended the stairs of the house in Marble Arch. Each step felt heavier than the last. The departed would never see any of their loved ones again. And they had all been killed on Christmas Day. And now Christmas would be a horrible memory for their families.

Enoch really liked Mr Hertzog. The South African soldier was an absolute gentleman. He wasn't very old, his mid-fifties at best, and yet he came across like an aged Emperor. Yes, Enoch could detect an underlying kindness in his nature. Yes, Blair Herzog was a worthy successor to the Comandante. No wonder the Comandante had selected him. Enoch would be safe. The Special Unit was still largely intact. And its members were brave and loyal. Yes, whatever lay ahead, Enoch need not fear for his security. Undoubtably, the people behind this were the ones behind the upheaval in the global markets. And they would be making their final push soon enough.

And Enoch Tara would be ready for them.

THE GEORGIAN BEDROOM

Gemma, in a pair of navy blue tartan pyjama bottoms, a white t-shirt, white cotton slippers, and the heavy beige sweater she had purchased on the trip to Scotland with Enoch earlier that year, was holding a long white ribbon. Soot, the tiny black kitten, was chasing the ribbon around the base of the bed. Gemma, sitting on the edge of the large bed, smiled.

'You're so cute, Soot! Are you hungry? Would you like Mummy to give you something? A small treat perhaps?'

There was a light knock.

'Come in,' said Gemma happily.

The door opened and Enoch entered. Enoch, in his red and blue tartan pyjamas, white waffle bathroom, and white cotton slippers, looked disoriented. Gemma stopped playing with Soot and asked, 'What's wrong, Enoch? Please, tell me.' Soot clawed his way to the top of the bed and sat down next to Gemma.

'Gemma, I need to leave for my office in the City. I'll be there for the next week or so. Please, stay here. My mother is going to stay here at the house for a while. I would feel better if you stayed here with her.'

Gemma exhaled. 'Enoch, what has happened?'

Enoch walked over to the bed and sat down next to Soot. The small kitten was playing with the white ribbon on top of the white bedding. Enoch watched the kitten for a minute. How he wished he could be as carefree as baby Soot. Enoch hesitated. He wanted to tell Gemma everything. He wanted to. He couldn't. It would only upset her. And to what end?

Enoch reached out and gently grasped Gemma's small soft manicured hand. Gemma's small hand was warm and that warmth now started to move through Enoch. Gemma smiled gently. Gemma was a true patrician beauty. A true English beauty—a beautiful, ethereal, elegantly anxious English beauty. And Gemma was good hearted and kind. Gemma was intelligent, understanding and patient. And he loved her. And she loved him. And Gemma was fragile—like Enoch. (Or were they both much stronger than even Enoch realized?)

'I am blessed to have you, Gemma.'

It was obvious to Gemma that something had happened that morning. More bad news had been delivered. Yes, the pressure had really gotten to him.

'Enoch, no matter what, we have each other. And baby Soot. And in the spring, we will plant all kinds of vegetables in the garden next my house in the Lake District. And we will be happy there till the end of our days,' said Gemma quietly, softly, and gently.

Gemma was the gentlest creature Enoch had ever known. And now, besieged on every side by unknown and terrifying enemies, Enoch just wanted to run away from it all. But he knew could not do that. He had to stand and fight. Enoch knew the next few days would be pivotal—they would be make or break days.

'Gemma, after all of this…has passed. I…want to escape London with you. All that I want to do now is spend the rest of my life with you, my mother, our friends…and Soot. In a month all of this will be in the past...and we can be together. I can't explain what is happening to you now, Gem, but I promise I will. I wish we could run away to **another country**. One that was **safe** and **calm**. But, for now, **none exists**. Our lives are here, and we have to do our best to make our lives worth living…I might be out of contact for a few days.'

Enoch then went ghostly pale. Yes, something terrible had happened. And Gemma now correctly surmised that it was more than just the financial machinations of unknown enemies. There was danger. It was real. And there had been victims.

'Gemma, you wanted to tell me something yesterday, what is it?' asked Enoch quietly.

Gemma had wanted to tell Enoch about the dragon in Louise's dream. She had told Louise that she would. But now, seeing Enoch in the state he was, Gemma did not want to add to his burden. Enoch needed her to be brave. Gemma was brave and **she was strong**. She would tell him about Louise's dream after he returned to the house in Marble Arch.

'I'll tell you later. How about I stay with you at the office? I could make you lunch and dinner and tea. And Soot could play with you,' said Gemma.

Enoch shook his head gently. He would not endanger Gemma. She would be safe at the house in Marble Arch. 'Please, stay here, Gemma. I would feel better knowing you were here.'

Gemma rested her head on Enoch's shoulder. Gemma's long glossy brown hair covered his shoulder. The scent of Gemma's hair, the light scent of vanilla on a gentle spring breeze, surrounded them.

'I love you, Enoch.

Enoch gently caressed Gemma's small soft hand and said quietly, 'I love you, too, Gemma.'

Gemma—An Invisible Fear—The Beige Sweater

MAYFAIR

Freya, her long glossy blonde hair partially covering her face, slowing opened her eyes. The white walled room was filled with natural light. Freya stretched, looked around, and noticed that Louise was not there. She could hear someone splashing around in the bath tub. It must be Louise.

Freya wondered how Louise was doing. When she returned from speaking with her parents and grandparents last night, Louise was already fast asleep. Freya was deeply worried about her. Last night she was afraid Louise would have another stroke. Yes, it had been less than a month since Louise had had her stroke and Freya was worried that she would have another one. She had stayed with Louise in the bedroom until Louise, still fully clothed, had fallen asleep.

Yesterday had been a disaster. Everyone had hoped that Louise could reconcile with her father, but everyone who knew Louise knew that that would not be easy. Louise had had an extremely traumatizing life because of her father. Violet had been upset by the turn of events. Violet, who had had a rough start with her own daughter Freya, had hoped that things would work out. Violet had a lot of sympathy for Harold Percival, much more than Freya had. Freya knew that her father, Hugh, was on Louise's side and always would be. He had witnessed the damage to Louise first hand. Violet had been indifferent to Freya during her childhood; Major Percival had been far worse than Violet. The 4th Baron, Freya's paternal grandfather, was upset about it. He felt personally responsible for what had happened. He had brought Louise's father back into her life, and it had seemingly gone all wrong.

BOXING DAY

Freya sat up on the edge of the large Edwardian bed. She wrapped the large, white duvet around her. There was a morning chill. Freya liked the cold, so she usually turned the heat down in the bedroom before she went to sleep. She looked out one of the large white sash Georgian windows. It was another cold grey wintery day in London.

The sound of a lock turning drew Freya's attention to the bathroom door. The wide glossy white bathroom door opened and Louise, in a white cotton bathrobe and her wet hair wrapped up in a white cotton towel, stepped into the bedroom.

'Good morning, Freya,' said Louise.

'Good morning, Louise. How are you feeling this morning?'

'Much better…Freya…I would like to speak with your grandfather and tell him that I am glad he telephoned my father. He did the right thing. I don't want him to be upset. I know he is good hearted.'

Louise was very thoughtful and considerate, perhaps because so many had not been so with her.

'You always think of others, Louise. Yes, the family is concerned about you and my grandfather was worried that he had made a big mistake contacting your father,' replied Freya.

'No, I know your grandfather's heart. I would like to tell him myself not to be upset,' said Louise quietly.

'He will be having breakfast with us this morning. I'm sure he would like to speak with you. He really cares about, Louise. We all do.'

'And I care about all of you,' said Louise quietly.

THE HALLWAY

Louise, clad in a pair of dark blue cotton trousers, a white cotton blouse, and the beige v-neck sweater her father had given her for Christmas, was walking down the hall when she spotted the elderly white-haired 4th Baron about to enter the dining room. The baron, at 6'4", towered over the 5'1" Louise.

'Good morning, sir,' said Louise.

The baron turned and saw Louise walking down the white walled hallway.

'May I speak with you for a moment before breakfast?' asked Louise.

'Good morning, Louise. How about we talk in the drawing room?' replied the baron in his clipped Mayfair accent. The baron, unbeknownst to Louise, was nervous about what she would say to him. He didn't want to have disappointed her with a misguided decision.

THE DRAWING ROOM

Lord Maud asked Louise to be seated on the sofa. Lord Maud, in blue blazer, white dress shirt, and a pair of Charcoal grey wool trousers, sat down opposite her in one of the upholstered armchairs.

'I wanted to thank you for telephoning my father when I was in the hospital, sir. You were right to contact him. And, I think, very brave. Most people would not have done it. I'm glad you did. Things have not gone very well with my father, but I am grateful to you for bringing him back into my life,' said Louise quietly.

The baron, deeply moved by Louise's kind words, could not speak. Not at that moment. Lord Maud, a stiff upper lip Englishman, was not one for public displays of emotions; however, at that moment, he wished he were.

'I don't know what will happen with my father,' said Louise. The baron could see Louise starting to physically tremble as she continued to speak. It worried him. He didn't want Louise to become upset again. Lord Maud was worried it could lead to another stroke. And that could spell Louise's end. The baron did not what anything else to happen to her.

'Louise, thank you for speaking with me this morning. I am concerned about your well-being. We all love you and consider you to be part of our family. Whatever you decided, we are with you, Louise. The choice you face is a very personal one. I just want you to find peace and happiness.'

Louise tried to smile, but she couldn't. 'I apologize for my behavior yesterday, sir. I hope I didn't ruin Christmas for everyone. I don't know what came over me. I'm sorry.'

'You didn't ruin Christmas, Louise. We just want you to recover and be healthy again. In a week, you will have to take your exams in London. And three days after that, you will enter Midlands-Hasegawa. It's an excellent university, Louise. You will receive a sterling education there. And Freya needs you. Please focus on that,' said the baron.

'Thank you, sir. You are very kind.'

The baron smiled. 'And besides, Freya needs a chemistry tutor.'

And Louise smiled.

THE BOOK SHOP
A large map lay across the old wooden desk at the back of the shop. Behind old wooden shelves of old books, low voices could be heard. Had anyone else been in the book shop that morning, they would have seen two middle aged men in wool overcoats, one with a scarred face, seated on either side of the desk.

'We had to leave quickly. The police arrived at the garden centre a few minutes after we escaped. Unfortunately, we were forced to leave the men where they fell,' said the heavily scarred Hungarian in near perfect English.

'I understand,' replied the Revenant. The Revenant studied the list of names that Attila had handed him a minute before. Yes, he recognized three of the names. He had known them for a long time. Their deaths hurt him. One never does get used to losing friends—not even someone like the Revenant.

'I will have money transferred to their accounts. Secrecy and operational security force me to rely on you to handle all of this. How long will it take to get their affairs in order?'

'One day,' replied Attila quietly. Yes, Attila had lost not only soldiers, but friends. His physical scars did much to hide his reactions.

'Thank you, Attila. In a few days, I will contact you. And we will go east.'

'And we will be ready, sir.'

THE DINING ROOM IN MAYFAIR
The day after Christmas found the Maud family enjoying breakfast in the large white walled dining room in the 4th Baron's house in Mayfair. The smile on the faces of the baron and Louise as they entered the dining room together came as a relief to those in the family aware of what had transpired the day before. Yes, some sort of peace had been restored. The mood that morning was a mixture of relief and happiness.

'What will you do today, Freya?' asked Violet, who was dressed in a pair of charcoal grey wool trousers, a white Egyptian cotton blouse (with a large collar), and a pale blue cashmere sweater.

'I don't know. Louise has to study for her exams, and I am happy to lay in bed and read one of the books that I was given for Christmas. I think I'll start with the book you gave me, Mummy,' said Freya happily.

Violet smiled; she beamed with happiness. Yes, Freya loved her. She had forgiven her. Freya was truly Violet's daughter.

'I hope you like the book on Venice, Freya. I stayed at our house in Venice with Gemma, Poppy, and Akiko during Christmas break while at Oxford. It was the winter of 1997. It was absolutely freezing. It snowed the week we were there. We hired a gondola and while going down the Grand Canal, the gondolier started to sing. He had a beautiful voice and afterwards Gemma asked him if it would be alright if she sang aloud. Well, Gemma, *ravishingly* beautiful at twenty, charmed him with a smile. Gemma stood up and started to sing in French. French! In the middle of Venice. Well, the other gondoliers piloting the canal loved it. When Gemma stopped singing, the gondoliers all started clapping. It was such a *hoot*,' said Violet happily in her posh and Sloaney intonation.

'The family had a house in Venice? It's too bad the family doesn't own it anymore. I would have liked to have stayed there,' said Freya, whose deep disappointment was apparent.

'*Rather*. We still own it. I haven't been there in *yonks*, but Septimus stays in it all the time. The stone house is *terribly* small, but it is at the end of *marvellously* long and twisting alley. The door to the crumbling house is gloriously glossy black, like the door to our house in Marylebone,' said Violet in her posh and Sloaney intonation. Yes, the Sloane Ranger had never and would never disappear from The Honourable Violet Valkyrie Artemis Maud (née Airey).

'We still own it? Septimus has never mentioned the house in Venice to me. Well, then again, we don't really see each other that often,' replied Freya.

'Demetria stayed there with her friends last May. If you want, I can arrange for you to stay there,' said Violet.

'Yes, I would love that, Mummy.' Freya, her long glossy blond hair framing her smooth face, looked at Louise and said, 'Louise, how about we spend a week in Venice next spring after the Hilary Term?'

Louise smiled. 'Yes, I have never been to Venice, and I would love to go.'

'The house only has two bedrooms, a small drawing room, and a tiny tiny kitchen and bathroom. There is a balcony on the second floor and a rooftop with nice views. Gemma liked to sit up there and watch the sunsets,' said Violet.

'It sounds beautiful,' said Louise.

'I went to Venice once,' said the flaxen-haired Morton happily. 'It was winter when I was there. It was *terribly* cold—*positively* freezing. I was there with a friend from Eton. We nearly froze to death taking public transportation. They have boats there, like London has buses. Only they are open to the weather. It was late at night; I was only wearing a water proof parka and a pair of cotton trousers, and I thought I would freeze to death before I made it back to the hotel. I did like Doge's Palace though.'

'A water proof parka? In winter? In Venice? Next time, Morton, wear furs,' said Freya and she smiled.

Morton smiled. 'Venice isn't Helsinki, Freya. I think a wool great coat with a fur collar will more than adequate.'

'What type of fur?' asked Louise.

'Buffalo,' replied Morton. 'When I return to Canada after Christmas, I shall hunt buffalo.'

'Please bring me back a buffalo hide, too, Morton,' said Louise. 'I will make a coat of my own for the winters in East Anglia.'

Freya arched an eyebrow. Was Louise talking about her father's farm in East Anglia or perhaps a small cottage of her own?

'Alright. I will. As matter of fact, I shall bring back an entire pallet of buffalo hides and leather for everyone,' said Morton. 'I shall have to dust off the rifle when I get home.'

'That's very thoughtful of you, Morton,' said the 4th Baron. 'I shall need a winter coat for my trips to see Vivienne and the grandchildren in Scotland.'

'Yes, I would like to go with you to see the family and spend some time with Karmen,' said Freya happily.

'Yes, the grandchildren love Karmen every bit as much as you do, Freya. She has taught the girls to speak Croatian. They speak it when they don't want their parents to know what they are saying,' said the baron.

'Imagine that,' said Freya, and she laughed.

Gemma—An Invisible Fear—The Terraced House

CENTRAL LONDON

The glossy blue Range Rover slowed to a complete stop in front of the modest two-storey terraced house. The driver, in black suit, white dress shirt, and red and blue tartan necktie, put the SUV in park and turned off the engine. The young and athletic man in the front passenger seat, in a dark blue suit, pale blue dress shirt, and a dark blue necktie, looked back at the lithe figure in the back seat of the Range Rover.

'We'll wait in the car for you, Miss Percival.'

'Thank you,' replied Louise politely.

Louise looked out of the passenger side window. She had only vague memories of the Edwardian house. The terraced house seemed dead, like a spell had been cast on it. Louise remembered spending a few days at a time in it with her parents. She remembered her father polishing his black leather shoes. Louise also remembered the closet full of beautiful military uniforms. Her father was the one who had cleaned the house. Everything was in military order. Edith, Louise's mother, did all of the cooking. Louise remembered her mother making chocolate frosting and giving her some of it in a metal spoon. Louise would eat some and then ask for a little more, which her mother always gave her.

Louise had not been in the house since her mother had passed away.

The young man then climbed out of the SUV and opened the passenger door for Louise. 'Thank you,' said Louise politely as she climbed out of the Range Rover. The cold snapped at her as soon as stepped onto the pavement.

It was a gloomy and overcast wintery day in London. Upstairs, a light was on. Louise was unsure if her father was here or if he had returned to the farm in East Anglia. She hoped he was here. She had to speak with him today, **or she never would**.

Louise buttoned up her petrol blue wool coat and looked at her silver wrist watch: 11:12am. Louise walked towards the front door of the terraced house, the snow crunching underfoot. She knocked on the weathered wooden door.

There was no answer.

Louise knocked again.

Still, no answer.

Louise took a few steps back and looked up at the second floor pane glass windows. There was no detectable movement. Louise took a few steps forward and knocked on the front door again. Suddenly, inside the house, she could hear someone moving around. Her heart began to beat faster. And then the front door opened.

Harold Percival, in a pair of charcoal grey wool trousers, a crisp white dress shirt (with a Windsor collar), and black leather belt (with a silver buckle), and pair of black Chelsea boots, answered. Her svelte father looked freshly shaven and there was not a white hair out of place. Yes, her father was the consummate professional army officer.

And then Louise noticed how sad and lost her father looked. It hurt her.

'May I come in?' asked Louise quietly.

'Of course.'

THE FRONT ROOM

Harold walked into the front room and offered Louise a seat in the old worn leather armchair in the corner. She remembered the chair, just a little. The white walled Edwardian room was immaculate. Louise's father cleaned compulsively. It calmed his nerves. The house looked vaguely the same. At least, as far as Louise could remember, the house had remained unchanged. The hardwood floor creaked slightly underfoot. There was a large modern cornflower-blue velvet sofa that Edith and Louise had bought from a furniture store on their last trip to London over a decade ago. It looked brand new. The white plaster crown molding seemed to almost glow in the electric light given off by the table lamps.

Louise's father waited until Louise had taken a seat before sitting down on the sofa. Louise observed her father in the electric illumination of the white ceramic table lamp on the table stand. Her father was handsome. Louise could see why her mother would have been attracted to him. Today, however, Harold looked defeated.

'This chair is the kind one would expect to find a Parisian club in the 1920s,' said Louise.

'It is from Paris. Your great grandfather bought in in the 1920s. It has been in the house ever since. This house has been in the family since 1901, the year it was built,' said Louise's father quietly.

Yes, Harold had been deeply wounded.

Louise, still buttoned up in her wool coat, inhaled and then slowly exhaled.

'I don't like to see you like this,' said Louise quietly. 'In the past, I wanted revenge. I wanted you to suffer for what you did to me. But seeing you like this, hurts me. I know you are trying, Father. Promise me...promise me that you will not change back to what you were before. Is this change of heart real? I have to know...If you go back to your old ways, I won't survive it. Tell me, is this really you?'

Harold breathed hard. He stared at the floor for a moment.

Louise started to tremble.

Harold looked up at Louise and wiped tears from his eyes. This was the first time she had ever seen her father cry. It was almost unnerving. Yes, her father was suffering terribly. He had suffered terribly ever since Edith had died in a traffic accident. Shutting everyone out of his life was how he had chosen to survive it. It had been a horrible mistake, and Louise had suffered the most for it.

'Yes, Louise. This is really me. I will never go back to the person I was before. I can't explain my actions. How could I have been so cruel to you? I have spent the last eleven years out of my mind. I want you to live and have a happy life, Louise. I am so scared you will have another stroke. I don't want to lose you again. I love you, Louise.'

And with those words, Harold put his head in his hands and started to cry.

Louise, her face wet with tears, stood and walked over to her father. She gently placed her soft tiny hand on her father's broad shoulder. Harold looked up; tears filled his eyes; his whole body was trembling.

'It's terrible for me to see you like this. I believe you, Father. I do. And I love you...Father...I forgive you. I forgive you.'

Gemma—An Invisible Fear—The Final Phase

THE TOMB

The Revenant, in a dark blue wool overcoat with a light brown fur collar, walked slowly down the stone corridor, a single beam of light from his smartphone lighting the way through inky black darkness of the tomb in Highgate Cemetery. It was icy cold. The stone floor clicked under the heels of his black leather Chelsea boots. When he reached the iron door, he turned off the lamp and stepped into the stone room. The Revenant looked at his wrist watch: 5:03am.

It was December 27th, 2019.

The stone room was illuminated in the ghostly white electric luminescence of a lamp that had been placed on the floor of the tomb. Standing next to the large stone sarcophagus was Carter Holland. Carter, in a black wool overcoat (with a coyote fur collar) which had been unbuttoned to reveal a bespoke charcoal wool Savile Row suit, a crisp white dress shirt, and a slate silk grenadine tie, looked at his platinum wrist watch.

'Good morning, General,' said Carter in an authoritative and commanding voice.

The Revenant observed his client carefully. Yes, Carter Holland was handsome and physically fit. He looked like an American movie star. Carter's glossy blond hair, freshly cut like a City banker, shimmered in the lamp light. His complexion was smooth, flawless, and youthful. Carter stood ramrod straight and moved with the bearing of a professional soldier. Only he wasn't one. Carter Holland had not suffered the traumas of trench warfare—Carter had never fought on the losing side of a war—or any war. Carter had all the arrogance and confidence of the untried and the uninitiated.

'Good morning, Mr Holland.'

'You have not failed me, like so many others have failed me,' said Carter.

'Your orders, Mr Holland,' said the Revenant in his indeterminable accent.

The reluctant warlord was uninterested in listening to another one of Carter Holland's monologues. Carter Holland had never been completely forthcoming with him, the Revenant doubted that he ever would be.

'This morning, I will begin the final phase of my operation in England. I am going to loot Enoch Tara's financial empire and then leave this godforsaken country. I have a bolt hole. I will stay there until the war in the east is over.'

Carter smiled slightly in pale light of the tomb.

'Tara's Special Unit has been knocked out,' said Carter.

'For a while,' replied the Revenant.

'For longer than we need,' said Carter. 'Is the Core Army ready to move?'

'Yes. Everything is in order.'

'Alright. Well, you have only one final task to complete before you leave England,' said Carter.

The Revenant, his face like an alabaster mask, stood motionless in the tomb. This inscrutability had bothered Carter in the past, but no more. The Revenant was now a known quantity. He would complete whatever mission was assigned to him. The Revenant's loyalty was unquestioning and absolute. Yes, the foreigner was a military robot.

Carter took a smartphone out of his pocket and held it out to the Revenant who simply stared at it.

'This is for you,' said Carter.

The Revenant grasp the cellphone and took it from Carter.

'Today, you will track your target via this phone. One of my operatives has placed a hidden app on the target's smartphone that will allow you to trace the target and, at the right moment, jam their phone.'

'And what am supposed to do then?' asked the Revenant, his breath materializes in the cold air around him.

'The target will be driving towards Surrey this morning. You will follow the target's car and when you are in an isolated area, you will run the target's car off the road. You will kill the target. Afterwards, you will notify me by texting me the number 'three'. When I get that text, I will know that the mission is complete. After eliminating the target, you will then make your way to the airport—anyway that you think is best—and fly to Istanbul. I will see you in a few weeks, after you have secured victory.'

'Who is the target?' asked the foreign warlord.

'What does it really matter?' replied Carter

'I do not enjoy the challenge of uncertainty,' said the Revenant.

'Operational security is paramount. You will find out once you have been contacted by my operative. She will guide you to the target. There is a white Audi A7 waiting for you in front of the book store. Here are the keys. You can park this car anywhere you like after you have completed the mission,' said Carter.

'Why is killing this person so important to you?' asked the Revenant.

'This target has always been the most important part of the entire operation. Eliminating the target will upset the entire order of things. It will throw everything out of balance. Eliminating this person will allow me to loot the City,' said Carter matter-of-factly.

No, when Carter Holland spoke, there was no theatrical language or pretention. Carter spoke in a cold and analytical voice. Carter simply issued orders and they were obeyed. Carter was methodical and merciless. The Revenant supposed that a person had to be merciless if they wanted to succeed at such a wildly impossible enterprise such as Carter Holland had put in motion. Whoever this person was, this target, had to be eliminated.

The operation—this enterprise—**had to succeed** if the Revenant was to return to his homeland and free it. If the Revenant was to avenge his family and people, then Carter's new country, this new Byzantium, must be created.

'Alright.,' said the Revenant.

Carter reached into his coat pocket and took out a set of car keys and placed them on the stone sarcophagus. He reached into an inside coat pocket and took out a white envelope. 'Here are the flight confirmation codes and itineraries you will need to collect your plane tickets. There are several transfers and you will fly on different airlines each time. Oh, and I have transferred an additional ten million dollars to your bank account. That's for destroying Tara's Special Unit.'

The Revenant picked up the keys and white envelope off of the large, grey stone sarcophagus. He placed them in the inside coat pocket of the dark blue overcoat. The Revenant nodded slightly and turned to leave. He took a few steps and then stopped. The Revenant turned around and looked at Carter Holland, who was buttoning up his wool overcoat.

'Mr Holland. I read about Colin Bailey in the newspapers. You wouldn't happen to know anything about that, would you?' asked the Revenant in his indeterminable accent.

Carter stopped buttoning his overcoat and looked up at the Revenant. Carter's smooth beautiful face was like a piece of cold iron shrouded in the coyote fur collar of his black wool overcoat and illuminated in the ghostly white light of the tomb.

'A man must never recoil from doing what is necessary.'

The Revenant felt a shock go through him. Yes, Carter Holland had had one of his own men murdered. Declan Bailey, the Revenant assumed, had also been murdered—on Carter Holland's orders.

'I don't tolerate failure,' said Carter nonchalantly as he adjusted his overcoat.

Gemma—An Invisible Fear—The White Peugeot

MARBLE ARCH

The old television—a black plastic box from the late 1990s—sat on top of a table in the unused white walled room on the third floor of the house. It was here that Enoch stored things from his previous life, the life of a stage actor. There were over a dozen cardboard boxes and several plastic storage bins stacked in the room. Gemma opened the white curtains and natural light flooded into the room through the white sash Georgian windows.

Gemma was looking for an old record player that Enoch had told her about. It was portable. Enoch had given it to her the night before when she mentioned that she was going to buy one online. She was going to take it to her flat next week. She had purchased several old vinyl records at a record store in Covent Garden the day after attending the concert in central London. She had found a vinyl record in the store that had been pressed in 1967 that her mother had once owned. She wanted to play it in her small studio flat. Soot and Gemma would continue to reside in the studio flat until Gemma and Enoch married in June.

Soot appeared in the open doorway. The tiny black kitten jumped up onto a cardboard box, and a moment later jumped up on top of the wooden table. Soot then jumped up and stood on top of the television. The short-haired Soot watched Gemma as she looked around the room.

After a minute, Gemma noticed him.

'Soot. You look just like an Egyptian god.'

Soot reached out and touched the sleeve of Gemma's white cotton blouse. That was Gemma's cue to pet Soot. Gemma petted him gently on the head and Soot responded by leaning into her soft manicured hand and purring loudly.

'Soot, next week you will come and stay with me at my flat in central London. Don't worry, you will like it. It's tiny, but it is mine.'

Soot purred happily as Gemma spoke.

'Ah, here it is,' said Gemma as she spotted the inexpensive wooden box record player. Gemma picked it up by its plastic handle. She picked up Soot in her free hand and carried them both out of the room.

THE GHERKIN

'Millennium Investments,' said Isolde after picking up the receiver. 'Yes, Tarquin is here. He is the conference room. He is in a video conference with the office in Tokyo…Alright. I'll tell him, sir. Yes…Thank you. Good bye.' Isolde returned the receiver to the phone.

The blonde Isolde, in a white cotton blouse (with open cuffs and a large collar), a dark grey wool pencil skirt, and a platinum wrist watch, surveyed London through the curved glass wall of the Gherkin. The sky was slate grey. It looked like it could snow at any moment. Today would be a pivotal day in her life—and the lives of so many others. Isolde would soon leave England and never return. She would not miss England. Isolde had no idea where Carter would take her. She really didn't care. She just wanted to stay at Carter Holland's side. Isolde was not privy to much of the ongoing machinations, but she had always been aware of the most important aspect of it. And it really didn't bother her.

'Good morning, Helen,' said Gemma happily as she walked through the glassy entrance of Millennium Investments.

'Good morning, Mrs Ripley. Did you have a nice Christmas?' replied the young blonde receptionist.

'*Marvellous*,' replied Gemma in her posh and Sloaney intonation. 'How was Christmas in the Cotswolds?'

'Wonderful and snowy,' replied Helen.

The slender and shapely Gemma, in a dark blue wool pencil skirt, a white cotton blouse (with a large collar), a dark blue wool coat (with silver buttons), a pair of knee-high black leather boots, and carrying a black Montblanc soft briefcase, smiled as she entered the glassy round office.

'Good morning, Isolde. How was your Christmas?'

'Very nice, Mrs Ripley' said the flaxen haired Isolde and she smiled. Yes, Isolde was young and beautiful. She had a brilliant career ahead of her in the City.

Soon Isolde would replace the beautiful and glossy Gemma Ripley. Gemma would marry Enoch Tara and they would start a new life together in the Lake District. Enoch would convert one of the former Royal Airforce annex buildings into an office and he would work from there. Gemma would tend to the garden and they would raise baby Soot together. Gemma would also help Poppy raise her twins. She would also play cricket with Henry and Lucy in the castle ruins with Enoch and the rest of the family. They would live a quiet and happy life in the English countryside—away from England's blighted and scarred cities.

Gemma placed her black suitcase on her desk and began to unbutton her wool coat. Today the office would operate with a skeleton crew. Most of the employees would not return until after the New Year. The office in Singapore was now overseeing the day-to-day operations of both offices.

'Oh, Gemma. A package was delivered to a post office in Surrey this morning. It's important. It came from a client in Tokyo. He telephoned me about it this morning. When I told him it hadn't arrived, he tracked it to a small post office in a village in Surrey.'

'How did it end up in Surrey? We don't have a post office box there.'

'I don't know. I telephoned the post master in the village and he said it was registered in your name. You have to sign for it.'

'Well, this is inconvenient. Who sent it?'

'A Mr Eichi Mikitiani,' replied Isolde.

'I've never heard of him. Is he a new client?' asked Gemma.

'I don't know. Alexa is still in the Cotswolds. Should I telephone her and ask?' replied Isolde.

'No. Let's not bother her. It's the holidays. I'll drive out and pick the package up right now,' said Gemma and she started to button up her coat.

Isolde stood up and handed Gemma a white slip of paper. 'Here is the address. I made a map for you. I highlighted the short cut you can take. It's about 40 minutes away.'

Thank you, Isolde.'

'You're welcome, Gemma,' said Isolde.

And Isolde smiled.

Gemma—An Invisible Fear—The Long Road

SURREY
The traffic in London was heavier than Gemma had expected; however, with a small Peugeot hatchback, it was easier to maneuver her way through it. After Gemma had motored into the suburbs, she slowed down. The countryside was under a light layer of snow and there were, undoubtably, patches of ice on the road.

Gemma took out the hand drawn map that Isolde had given her. Yes, the turn off was just up ahead. Gemma would take the short cut through the forest. The traffic would be lighter and she could drive slower. The snowy countryside was beautiful. Gemma loved snow and cold weather. The winter was Gemma's favorite time of the year.

THE CITY
Enoch Tara stood in front of the mirror in the white tile bathroom which was on the top floor of the Grade II listed merchant bank building. He had spent the night on a camp bed in an empty office. He had not slept well. Shrouded in white cotton sheets and white duvet with his head resting on a

large white -pillow, Enoch had spent most of the previous night trying to figure out who was behind the shadowy raids on global finance. Enoch no longer doubted that the people who had murdered members of the Special Unit were also the same ones looting the global financial system.

'It is not death that a man should fear, but he should fear never beginning to live.'

—Marcus Aurelius

That morning had found the pyjama clad Enoch sitting on the edge of the camp bed in the empty office in the merchant bank building reading the edition of the Mediations of Marcus Aurelius that Gemma had given him for Christmas. Yes, the book was comforting and timely—or perhaps it would be better to say, it was timeless. Yes, now at this moment of crisis, Enoch needed this book. He found its words reassuring.

Enoch had taken a long shower that morning. Now, in the white waffle pattern bathrobe that Gemma had given him for Christmas, and with his hair still wet, Enoch studied his reflection in the mirror. Yes, next week he would leave London. He would keep this office in the City open and conduct meetings with his staff via encrypted video conferences and email. At least once a week, a couple members of the staff would take the train to the Lake District for face-to-face meetings with him. Yes, it would all work out. Occasionally they would visit London—Gemma, was, after all, a London girl.

Enoch applied warm shaving cream to his smooth face. He took out a safety razor (Enoch's skin was far too sensitive for a straight razor) and he began to carefully shave his face.

THE OFFICE

Enoch, in a pair of charcoal wool trousers, a pale blue dress shirt (with a Windsor collar), and a dark blue silk necktie, sat at the large wooden desk in the top floor office. The white walled office (with ornate white plaster Edwardian crown molding) was cavernous and took up half of the top floor of the building. Through the bullet and bomb proof double doors at the opposite end of the open floor plan office space, was another large office space with two secretaries. Each young woman sat at a wooden desk behind a computer and there were two different phones on each desk. A large Japanese photo copier had been installed near one of the large white sash windows.

A folding table had been set up in on one side of the room in front of the windows. Four suited and booted hard men were now seated around the table. Whenever the elevator activated, the four men would stand up and two of them would stand near the elevator doors. None of these men were armed. One floor below and out of sight, there were heavily armed security men. They could access the top floor by using two different sets of stairs, or if possible, the elevator.

Before Enoch were three different computer screens, all of which monitored the markets. On the desk were three different laptop computers, all encrypted. There was a small side table with a printer and a fax machine on it. There were several folders, documents, and bound reports on the large wooden desk. Behind Enoch were three metal filing cabinets—yes, they still used them. Enoch adjusted the natural black rubber strap of his silver Omega dive watch as he leaned back in the beige leather chair and studied the fluctuations in the markets.

And then, like a white squall, the markets were suddenly being torn apart in a violent and totally unexpected financial storm.

EAST ANGLIA

Carter Holland had flown in his private helicopter to East Anglia immediately after meeting with the Revenant that morning. His final assault on the global financial markets was to be conducted from a set of rooms in his Grade II listed Georgian country house. Here he would be surrounded by thousands of acres of land and ringed by heavily armed security teams. The bankers and IT engineers had all relocated to the large stone country house the day before. A large white walled room on the ground floor of the house was filled with modern desks, minimalist leather arm chairs, computers, and large computer screens. The men in the room all wore white or pale blue dress shirts, English cut ties, and dark wool suits. Carter

Holland did not believe in casual dress at the office. The team was now heavily engaged in the final assault. The men moved with celerity. Celerity of action is vital war, whether on the battlefield or in the financial markets. A svelte investment banker in his early thirties, wearing a platinum IWC Portuguese Grande Complication wrist watch, was looking through a file of documents. Another man, in a pale blue dress shirt, dark blue suit, and beige knit necktie, leaned forward and typed out something on his white keyboard and after a moment watching the lucent computer screen, smiled. Occasionally one of the two dozen men in the room would consult with one of his co-workers. The other would nod slightly and often laugh.

Yes, it was all so easy and it was all going to plan.

THE FEAST OF PIRATES

Carter Holland had set up his own desk in a white walled room adjacent to the 'war room' on the first floor of his country house. Carter Holland's office was located behind two large highly polished maple double doors. The plaster crown molding that adorned Carter's office was Jacobean—its design was beautiful and quintessentially English. It was the interior decorator from London that had saved it from being torn out and destroyed during the restoration of the house. An English country house does not only belong to the owner of the house, but to the English people. One day, though the decorator, the house would be sold to a new owner. Hopefully one that would appreciate this small historical detail. Carter Ajax Holland had taken no notice of it.

Carter Holland's platinum wrist watch glinted and flashed in the silvery natural light of a winter's day. On the desk before him was a single silver laptop computer. Three different screens had been set up in front of his desk at different angles. Two of them monitored the financial markets. The remaining monitor was a television with the volume muted.

Carter, in a bespoke charcoal grey Savile Row suit, a white dress shirt, and a slate silk grenadine necktie, studied the screens before him. The markets suddenly registered massive disruptions. It had begun. Finally. Decades of struggle, sacrifice, and planning were now playing out across the globe. Yes, panic was started to spread across the world. It was too late to sell. The die had been cast.

Carter looked at his encrypted smartphone. No messages. Carter placed the phone back on his desk and leaned back in the minimalist black leather chair.

It was all going to plan.

THE LAKE DISTRICT
Brian Atherton, in a pair of dark khaki wool trousers, a white dress shirt (with a St James collar), and wearing a pair of purple velvet slippers, had been having coffee in the drawing room with the pyjama clad Poppy and her elderly parents, the 12th Baron and Baroness, when his smartphone started to ring. He looked at Caller ID. It was the bank president. He answered it immediately.

'Yes, sir? Is something…'

'Brian, the markets are melting down. I need your assistance. You did bring the encrypted laptop with you, didn't you?'

'Yes, sir.'

'Please go online immediately. Call me back when you are ready. I am at the office in London. I have summoned everyone. This is going to be a long day.'

THE BALLROOM
Mars, reclining in a wooden deck chair in front of the large stone Victorian fireplace in the ballroom, had been reading the history book Gemma had given him for Christmas when Poppy entered the room through the large double doors.

'Mars. The global markets are under some kind of attack. It's huge. Brian is upstairs on his computer. He is talking with the bank in London,' said the flaxen haired Poppy as she walked across the ballroom in her red, blue, and purple pyjamas and a pair of white cotton slippers.

'Well, I have been waiting for this. Launching it now, during the Christmas holidays, is excellent timing for a group pirates,' said Mars as he placed the book on a narrow arm the wooden deck chair. Mars, in a pair of dark khaki trousers and a white cotton dress shirt, stepped into a pair of black velvet slippers, stood up, and looked at his silver Omega watch. 'Yes, the markets opened only 33 minutes ago.'

The double doors on the opposite wall of the ballroom opened and James, his glossy blond hair still somewhat damp, stood in the doorway of the Victorian ballroom. James was in a set of dark blue paisley cotton pyjamas, a white cotton Turkish bathrobe, and carrying a worn and battered leather laptop bag over one shoulder. The freshly shaven James still had some shaving cream on his neck and face.

'I suppose you've heard? I came downstairs to get my laptop. The markets are under attack. The bank called me a few minutes ago. Mars, if you have any ideas, please let me know. I'll be upstairs in my room,' said James in a sangfroid manner that would have surprised most. James then smiled and closed the doors.

'I suppose I should open my laptop too,' said Mars as he crossed his arms.

Poppy looked at him, but before she could speak, Mars answered her anticipated question.

'No, I'm completely out of the markets. I knew this was coming. However, I would like to help whomever asks for advice. Please, let Brian know that.'

'Thank you, Mars. Do you have any idea who is behind all of this?' asked Poppy.

'No, but the list has narrowed considerably.'

Poppy looked at the door of the temporary bedroom. 'I'm going to spend the day with Arthur and Waverly. I'll send someone around to find you when lunch is served.'

Mars smiled. 'Yes, a little English calm is needed in moments like this. And thank you, Poppy. I'll be upstairs in my room. You wouldn't happen to know what is for lunch, would you?'

'I was thinking of requesting Edward make steak and salad,' replied Poppy.

'Sounds good.'

'How do you like your steak, Mars?' asked Poppy and she smiled.

SURREY

Gemma's white hatchback slowed as it neared the village. Yes, the post office should be just up ahead. A stone church steeple appeared above the snow draped treetops at the edge of the snowy village; the red tail lights of Gemma's Peugeot glowed a little brighter momentarily as she braked slightly. Yes, past the Anglican church and the village graveyard. Gemma's hatchback signaled and the car took a slow right turn.

Parked near the church, under a large English oak, was a white Audi A7. The driver's smartphone had been tracking the approaching vehicle for the last fifteen minutes. The driver had watched in silence as the white hatchback had slowly passed. Yes, he knew immediately who the driver of the compact Peugeot was.

The Revenant leaned back into the beige leather car seat. He took out a pair of German binoculars and trained them on the post office. Gemma got out of her car, closed the door, and walked into the post office, leaving a trail of footprints in the snow behind her.

The Revenant picked up the paper map in the front passenger seat. The possible routes between here and London had been highlighted in yellow marker. He looked up from the map. Gemma, in a dark blue wool coat, a pair of black leather knee-high boots, and carrying a colorful cardboard box with airfreight stickers and a plastic envelope with documents inside, walked out of the small post office. She opened the driver's side door and placed the package in the front passenger seat. Gemma then climbed into the car. She closed the door.

There was a sharp and unusual sounding ping. The smartphone glowed for a moment. The phone indicated the Gemma was calling someone at Millennium Investments. Gemma talked on the phone for twenty-eight seconds and then hung up.

The Revenant buckled his shoulder strap and started the car. The Audi purred like a tiger. The sedan idled next to the church. Gemma was too far away to notice. The Revenant watched as Gemma started the small white hatchback, backed out of the parking spot, turned, and drove away through the snowy morning weather.

The Audi rolled forward, turned onto the road, and picked up speed as it followed the small hatchback out of the village. The Revenant looked at the digital map on the smartphone: Gemma was driving back to London. And she was taking the short cut through the forest, just as Carter Holland had predicted she would.

THE CITY

Enoch, his dark blue tie loosened enough to reveal a white undershirt under his pale blue dress shirt, watched as financial disaster unfurled before him. Billions of dollars were disappearing from banks, mega-corporations, financial institutions, the bank accounts of private citizens, and the central banks of dozens of nations. Panic was spreading. Several governments had already moved to close their stock markets and shutdown their banking systems in a vain attempt to stave off financial collapse. The world shuddered and gasped as the enormity of what was happening had become apparent. Yes, they were all staring into the abyss.

How was it possible that one entity be behind all of this?

The glossy burl wood double doors at the end of the long cavernous office opened and two brutal looking members of Enoch's security team, both former Royal Marines, entered the room. One man wheeled in a large white cardboard box on a hand truck and the other carried a burl wood television stand. Behind the men, just beyond the entrance to the office, Enoch could see several of his employees in coat and tie exiting the elevator and two other members of his security team standing next to one of the wooden desks which flanked the entrance to the office. Yes, the entire building was now churning in a manic tumult.

And at center of this storm was the mysterious Enoch Tara. Yes, study the patterns and the modes of attack. You will uncover the identities of the invisible enemy by studying the wake they leave behind them. These nearly invisible slipstreams were imperceptible to most, but not to Enoch Tara. These subtle and translucent sequences were becoming more and more visible to him with each transaction.

While the two men set up the plasma screen television just to the side of the large Mid-Century Modern desk, Enoch tapped on the keyboards of a white laptop. The markets surged forward; he typed on his keyboard for a few minutes, and the stock market rallied. Enoch was battling with the invisible entity that was attempting the audacious looting of the industrialized world.

The flat screen television came on and a flurry of reports on the international chaos in the markets blared from the undulating digital screen. Obviously panicked central bankers, in coat and tie, spoke to crowded press rooms full of jostling journalists who shouted questions while the flashes from cameras practically blinded the government officials who were attempting to calm the shattered nerves of the financial markets. Enoch continued to tap on the screen of an encrypted tablet computer while half listening to a nearly hysterical report coming out of Wall Street. There was a breaking news report: The President of the United States was about to address the nation. Reporters speculated about what the President would say to the American people. Enoch listened as a panel of former British cabinet ministers spoke on television. Wild speculation followed—none of it helpful. The reality was quite simple: no one had any idea what was really happening or who was behind it.

Enoch looked at one of the computers screens on his highly polished black walnut desk and noticed another wave of attack forming on the international banking system. And a moment later, central banks in India,

Holland, and Luxemburg found themselves being looted. International conglomerates teetered on the brink of collapse.

There!

Enoch noticed another swirling pattern of attack forming in Asia. Enoch's mind—as infinite as the universe—suddenly expanded. Yes. There **they** are. Now. Track them. Following them back to their lair. Enoch's blue eyes followed the invisible wake across the capital markets.

SURREY
The white and frozen landscape that unfolded before Gemma was starkly beautiful and strangely calming. Both sides of the country road, parts of it paved in Roman stones, were white and icy walls of snow-clad English oaks, London plane trees, and English elms. There didn't appear to be anyone else on the road. The road ahead was covered in a thin layer of snow. There were no discernable tire tracks ahead of her. Gemma appeared to be the only one on this snowy throughfare this morning. Gemma slowed as she approached a gentle curve in the cobblestone road. Now a light snow began to fall. Gemma looked at her phone. No messages.

THE ROMAN ROAD
The white Audi moved adeptly through the forest and down the section of the Roman road. It was unnecessary for the Revenant to use the tracking app on the encrypted smartphone that Carter Holland had given him earlier that morning; he need only follow the lone set of tire tracks through the snow ahead. Yes, Gemma was only a mile ahead of him. Now he would have to approach her quickly, slam into her small white hatchback, and run her the road. That would be easy enough.

The Revenant picked up the phone, and with a single tap, jammed Gemma's smartphone. If she attempted to use her cell phone now, it would appear to her that she was out of signal range. Not unexpected in such an isolated area. It would also make it impossible for anyone else—like Scotland Yard—to track her whereabouts. Gemma will have simply disappeared on an isolated stretch of road without a trace.

The Revenant slowed at the curve in the road and as the white sedan cleared the corner, Gemma Ripley's white Peugeot hatchback came into view, just a hundred or so yards down the road. The Peugeot's red tail lights glowed brightly for an instant as she gently braked the car.

The gauges and dials of leather dashboard glowed in the silvery grey natural light of the Audi A7s interior. The Revenant shifted and the car decelerated.

No, Gemma had not spotted him. Not yet.

The Revenant watched as the small white hatchback made its way down the isolated country road. In a few minutes, Gemma would reach the intersection and the opportunity to attack her alone on the road would be lost—forever.

It was now or never.

The Revenant shifted and the white Audi bolted forward.

THE HUSSAR ROOM

Mars Rupert Arthur Noel, seated at the Indian teak Victorian writing desk in front of the white sash window, studied the shimmering computer screen in front of him. Yes, only catastrophe appeared before him. Yes, the international financial system—and the global political order—stumbled and staggard under the weight of the attack. There was much more to this than mere money. Unfathomable wealth was not the true intent of this unprecedented and invisible blitzkrieg of unimaginable ferocity. This distress of nations, where would it end? A new global order was in the offing.

Lord Noel, the 13th Baron, leaned back in the upholstered Edwardian armchair. He looked out the sash window. It was snowing. Outside was an ocean of white under a leaden overcast sky. A short distance away were the castle ruins. Yes, the Barons Devereux had owned the castle for over nine hundred years. The castle had been besieged many times. Its garrison had been starved, savaged by enemies, and the castle badly damaged, but it had never fallen. It was the indomitability of the Barons Devereux who had stood shoulder to shoulder with the other defenders who had staved off defeat.

Could defeat be averted today?

Would men's hearts shall fail them for fear and for looking after those things which shall be coming on the Earth? Were the Heavens shaking now?

Mars, his face illuminated in the lucent glow of the computer screen, looked at the Omega wrist watch that he had purchased in the IFC Center in Hong Kong twenty-five years before. Its silver seconds hand glided over the indices. Was time working for or against them now?

THE ART DECO EGYPTIAN BEDOOM
The white walled room, the enormous bed downstairs in the temporary bedroom, was now a large nearly empty space. The room was edged in a wide plaster crown molding depicting Egyptian hieroglyphics. The ceiling was more of the same.

Brian had relocated to this quiet and empty room on the second floor of the family pile. He now sat at a wooden Bauhaus style desk of highly polished burl wood in an uncomfortable Bauhaus style wooden chair. Outside, it was snowing and occasionally a gust of wind would rattle the white sash windows. The room was drafty and cold. Whenever Brian walked across the room, the wooden floorboards creaked underfoot.

The bedroom had been made to resemble the interior of an ancient Egyptian temple in the 1920s. The lighting was set along the edge of the walls, hidden behind the plaster crown molding. It flooded out and across the ceiling when the lights were turned on. The glow those few bulbs emitted cast long shadows from between the hieroglyphs carved into the crown moldings. This morning, however, Brian did not work under the hypnotic effects of the shadows cast be the electric light. No, now the room was filled with the grey natural light of a cold snowy day.

Brian’s smartphone lay on top of one of wooden desk. The phone had been plugged into an electric outlet and was recharging. Occasionally it would glow with a bluish light. Brian would tap on the screen and check the incoming messages. Sometimes the phone would ring and he would answer. He spoke to either the bank president or one of the senior bankers.

Yes, the situation was bad. Perhaps, when this was over, Brian would pick up the pieces of his shattered life and retreat to the country house in Lake District and grow vegetables.

Or maybe not.

No, the battle had been joined and Brian and the bank would fight to the bitter end. The bank's clientele had entrusted him with their money. This was no mere job to Brian; it was a sacred trust. Brian was calm. The staff at the bank was calm. Yes, the situation was bad, but not all was lost. Not yet.

Stay calm and carry on.

EAST ANGLIA
The encrypted smartphone glowed monetarily—a blue light emanated from it. And like a tiger, Carter pounced on it. He picked up the cell phone, tapped the small shimmering screen, and exhaled heavily while at the same time shouting exultantly, 'Yes!'

THE CITY
Enoch studied the chart on the lucent computer screen.

There.

He had correctly predicted the unseen enemy's next move. Now he had to walk it all the way back to the source. Yes, **they** were good at this—very good. However, the enemy was human, and humans make mistakes. Algorithms had their limits. As the hours passed, the invisible enemy started to leave larger ripples in their wake. They had become overconfident. And overconfidence was more dangerous to an assailant than their opponent.

Click.

Enoch searched through the various charts, graphs, and numbers that appeared on the screen with each click of the mouse. Yes, **they** were there, somewhere out there. Somewhere.

Enoch looked over at the television. More scenes of market pandemonium. A moment later and a blonde woman MP stood in the House of Commons and spoke gravely of what was to come. There was talk of the possibility of foreign countries being behind the mayhem. A minister in a dark blue suit stood up and announced that the Her Majesty's Armed Forces had mobilized.

Yes, it was all unraveling.

Click.

Enoch noticed a small detail—reminiscent of the nail of shoe belonging to a horse that belonged to a rider that belonged to an invisible empire.

Enoch printed out what had appeared on the luminescent screen. The printer on the table behind him sprang to life and documents began to appear in the tray beside it. He stood up and walked over to the printer. He picked up the documents. They were warm to the touch.

Enoch walked back and sat down at the large wooden desk. He took out a yellow marker and highlighted certain sections of the documents. He took a sip of ice water from a tall transparent plastic tumbler on the wooden desk.

Enoch stood up and walked over to the white wall behind the desk. He taped the document to the wall next to several other documents that had been marked in yellow highlighter and had had some sections underlined in blue and black ink. Yes, a pattern, a sequence, a framework, had emerged.

Enoch crossed his arms and studied the documents on the wall carefully. He looked at his dive watch. Four hours had passed since the markets had opened. It had felt like a thousand years.

Enoch looked out one of the large white sash windows of the office. It was snowing. In the distance, Enoch could see the glassy and hexagonal Gherkin; the oval Post Modern structure's red aviation lights glowing brightly in the winter gloom. Gemma was undoubtably over there on the 12th floor of the building at her desk or perhaps in the glass walled conference room talking with the Singapore or Tokyo office. The very thought of Gemma made him smile. Yes, to love and be loved was life's truest happiness.

Enoch walked back to the white wall and studied the documents taped to the white plaster wall once more.

Yes. He had almost unmasked them.

Ping.

The encrypted smartphone was used strictly to communicate with the Special Unit glowed momentarily, and then the pale blue light faded away.

Enoch walked over to the desk, picked up the cell phone, and tapped on the screen. A photo appeared. It was of a white hatchback driving down a narrow snowy country road (only the road itself was not visible). Snow draped trees lined either side of the image and the sky above was a mixture of light grey and white clouds, falling snow, and the white hatchback. The entire screen appeared to be a blank white slate with the exception of the yellow number plate affixed the back of the car. Enoch recognized both the number plate and the white Peugeot: it was Gemma's hatchback.

The sender was unknown. Why was the Special Unit following Gemma?

Enoch put the smartphone down and picked up his regular cell phone, but before he could dial Gemma's number, Enoch's encrypted smartphone **rang**. The electric ringing of the smartphone echoed across the largely empty office space.

Enoch arched an eyebrow. This phone had been reserved for the Special Unit. Was Enoch about to be attacked by the invisible enemy? Had heavily armed men surrounded the merchant bank building in the center of London? Would the invisible enemy be that brazen?

Enoch picked up the phone. There was no Caller ID.

Who could this be? What was going on?

The smartphone continued to ring.

Enoch tapped on the screen.

'Hello?'

'Don't hang up,' said an unknown voice. The voice was icy and inhuman. Enoch felt a chill go down his spine. Enoch listened carefully. He couldn't hear anything, not even the man on the other end of the digital line breathing. Was this the voice of a computer? No. The voice was definitely human, or it had once been human, but now belonged to one of the undead.

'I'm listening,' said Enoch.

'Mr Tara. The photo we sent you was taken ten minutes ago.'

There was a momentary pause, and then the otherworldly voice continued.

What do you care most about, Mr Tara? Or, perhaps I should say, who do you care most about?'

Enoch froze. He stopped breathing. His heart skipped a beat—or perhaps it had stopped beating altogether.

'Who is this?' asked Enoch.

'Only an evil spirit,' hissed the man on the end of the line.

'What do you want?' asked Enoch. His heart was now pumping again;

Enoch could hear it pounding in his ears.

'Mr Tara. I once lost the most important people in my life to violence, so I know how you will feel after this phone call.'

There was a momentary silence at both ends of the line.

Enoch's hands were trembling. Blood was rushing into his head. The room started to spin. He felt tears welling up in his eyes and a burning sensation filled his entire being. No. This can't be happening. I was the target, not her. No. No. No. It wasn't supposed to end like this. Please, God. Please.

Enoch, one smart phone held in place next to his ear by his cheek and shoulder, picked up a different smartphone from the desk and dialed Gemma's number. The phone rang and rang and rang. Enoch, tears running down his face, could feel something break inside of him as the phone continued to ring. There was no answer and suddenly Enoch realized, there never would be.

'Mr Tara. A few minutes ago, Gemma Ripley was torn to pieces. She cried out your name as she was killed. We wanted you to know that. You will find Gemma next to her white Peugeot hatchback on the side of a country road in Surrey. Good bye, Mr Tara.'

The line went dead.

And Enoch Tara wished he had died with the signal.

Gemma—An Invisible Fear—A Wisdom Born of Regret

THE CITY
'Mr Tara?' asked the young banker for the third time. 'Mr Tara, what would you like us to do?'

The slender, raven-haired, thirty-year-old woman from North London, in a grey pencil skirt, white blouse, and grey jacket, was standing in front of Enoch's desk. Three large flat screens were staggered around the large wooden desk; they all flashed and pulsated with digital images. The plasma screen television that had been set up off to the far side of the desk flooded the room with panicked voices from across the globe.

THE OFFICE

Enoch had telephoned Millennium Investments immediately after the phone call from the Evil Spirit. Isolde had answered. Yes, Gemma had spoken often and highly of Isolde. She would know where Gemma was. For sure. For sure.

'Millennium Investments,' answered a young woman in a posh intonation.

'Yes, is Gemma Ripley there?'

'May I ask who's calling?

'Yes, this is Enoch Tara, Gemma's fiancé.'

'Yes, Mr Tara. Mrs Ripley left the office a couple of hours ago. She had to pick up a package at a post office in Surrey. She should have returned by now. I tried calling her, but she doesn't answer. Can I take a message?'

'Do you know which post office she picked up the package from?' asked Enoch. Enoch was trying to stay calm, but it was a losing battle.

'No. Mrs Ripley didn't say. Can I take a message?' asked Isolde.

'No.'

Enoch had hung up and immediately dialed Gemma's cell phone number again.

Come on…Come on…Answer…Please, answer…

That had been ten minutes ago.

The slender Enoch, visibly shaken, stared out one of the large Edwardian sash windows.

'Mr Tara? We are doing are best to stem the damage, but we need further instructions.'

Enoch, his hands shaking and white as ghost, turned to the young woman and said, 'Please leave me.'

The woman could see that Enoch was deeply distressed—she assumed the financial shocks had left him numb. She hesitated for a moment. What should she do? She decided to go back downstairs and ask the bank director. She nodded slightly, walked out of the office, and quietly closed the double doors behind her.

Enoch pushed a button on the large wooden desk, and the double doors locked remotely. Everyone in the outer room of the main office noticed when the titanium locks of the heavy doors bolted shut with an audible set of clicks. Enoch's secretaries and security detail had all turned to look at the imposing and now secured glossy burl wood double doors.

THE OUTER OFFICE

Ten minutes later, when several members of the staff had come upstairs to inform Enoch Tara of the continuing and increasingly brazen attacks on his international conglomerate and financial holdings, he had not responded to their knock on the door. And, deeply concerning to the senior members of the staff, the doors to the office had been locked, something Mr Tara had never done before.

The double doors had remained locked. Enoch Tara had never behaved in such a manner. One of the bank directors had informed the leader of the security detail and now a former Royal Marine and a British Para were both attempting to break down the doors to Enoch's office.

'Mr Tara! Are you alright?!' said a loud voice from behind the heavy double doors of the office. Several heavy fists could be heard pounding on the doors. 'Mr Tara! Are you alright?! If you don't open the door, sir, we are going to break them down! Mr Tara!'

Enoch Tara could have heard the voices and loud banging—had he not been a million miles away from the City in his own shattered mind. Enoch Tara, completely broken and inconsolable, sat slumped in the beige leather chair behind his desk.

THE OFFICE

The three white laptop computer screens shimmered in the grey natural light of a wintery day in London. Two of the large screens that stood in front of his desk flashed with information from the global markets. The large television screen showed scenes of desperation and despair from the trading floors of Wall Street and The City. Enoch held one of his smartphones in his hand; it continued to ring Gemma's number. There was no answer. Two of Enoch's encrypted smartphones were ringing and glowed continuously with incoming messages. One of the cell phones rang steadily with frantic calls from the Special Unit. The other smartphone was being flooded with telephone calls and text messages from Enoch Tara's underlings—Tara's financial empire was crumbling under a barrage of merciless and relentless attacks from invisible and unknown enemies. Millions were being stolen every minute by a pack of invisible jackals. The attacks were moving forward with increasing violence, speed, and momentum. A couple more hours of this, and Enoch Tara's international conglomerate would be ashes and dust.

Enoch, in a state of shock, was oblivious to the sounds of the ringing smartphones, loud banging, and shouts from behind the double doors of the office. He was completely lost. Nothing mattered. Gemma had been murdered. Gemma had cried out his name as they killed her. The mere thought of it stunned and horrified him. He had been left breathless.

Why had he not realized that Gemma had been the target all along? Why had God granted him the gift of financial prescience and Jupiterian discernment, but not the ability to save the ones he loved? Why had God brought Gemma back into his life, just to take her away so cruelly? Gemma had suffered a horrible death. She had cried out his name as they killed her. Yes, it was true. Gemma had been murdered because she was important to him.

Enoch suddenly imagined that he could go back in time and take Gemma with him to his offices in the City the night before. She would be safe here. Gemma would play with Soot in the office while Enoch worked at his desk. Yes, Gemma would be safe. Gemma should have quit her job at Millennium Investments immediately after their engagement. She should have never gone back to the Gherkin. Or he should have given her own security detail. Gemma would have been uncomfortable with one, but she would have accepted it—had he offered one to her.

But her hadn't. And now he would never see Gemma alive again.

'I'm sorry, Gemma. I'm sorry. I'm sorry…I'm sorry,' said Enoch aloud as he choked back tears. Enoch raised himself up and leaned back into the chair. The lucent digital screens in front of him showed his empire under attack—and Enoch really didn't care. What was money without Gemma? Enoch, through tears, watched passively as his holdings withered away. The total loss of everything he had worked for meant absolutely nothing to him now. Enoch, numb and emotionally and physically drained, slumped down into the beige leather chair. The room was filled with eddies of grey light.

This can't be happening. This is a nightmare and I will wake up and everything will be alright. Please, wake up. Please, wake up. Gemma, I need you. I need you.

The loud banging outside the double doors suddenly stopped.

'Alright. We're going to have break the doors down, Mr Tara!'

EAST ANGLIA

Carter Ajax Holland, alone in his office, watched the computer monitor in front of him in an awed silence. Could this be true? Was all of this really happening? Tara's empire was disintegrating before Carter's very eyes. And Tara wasn't even putting up a fight. Why would he? As Carter had predicted; as Carter had planned from the very beginning; Enoch Tara had been broken by the murder of Gemma Ripley. It had been a necessary evil among so many other necessary evils Carter had committed in order to secure victory. Yes, history would record all of it—and future societies would understand and forgive him for all of it. Every bit of it. Yes, the ends justify the means. Without darkness, there could be no light.

There was knock at the one of the wooden double doors of the white walled office. Outside, through the large Georgian sash windows, it was snowing.

'Come in,' said Carter.

One of the polished maple doors opened, and a tall and athletic young man from Yorkshire, in black suit, white dress shirt, and a black silk tie, entered.

'Mr Holland. The jet has completed a service check and is fueled and ready to take off.'

'Thank you. Tell the crew to stand by,' replied Carter.

The young man backed out of the office and carefully closed the door.

Carter stood up and walked over to one of the windows. Carter could feel the very Cosmos surging through his veins. This was the moment he had spent his entire life ~~waiting for~~ **working towards**. Carter Holland did not thank God for anything. Why should he? Carter had created himself. Carter was a self-made man. Carter's impossible plan had worked. Carter had made the impossible possible. Carter Holland had done it all by himself.

All by himself.

THE GHERKIN

Isolde, young, glossy, beautiful, and serene, sat at her desk in the main office of Millennium Investments. Inside the glass walled conference room stood the dark-haired and thirtysomething Tarquin (or was Tarquin a twentysomething?) in front of a giant video conference screen. Isolde could see two people in coat and tie gesturing and talking frantically with Tarquin through the plasma screen.

The shapely young woman, from one of London's most notorious sink estates, had done it. Carter had never doubted her. Carter had told her she could do it, and Carter was, as always, right. Gemma Ripley was dead. And her death had made Enoch Tara's holdings easy prey. Isolde had to suppress laughter as she watched the economic disaster unfolding on the screen of her laptop computer. Isolde had only one question: What was Carter's end game? What would he do after all of this? Eventually the bone heads in MI5 and MI6 would figure out who had been behind all of it. Or would they? The British government was not what it had once been. No, Carter was right. England had died with the empire. There was nothing left. Isolde was about to leave nothing for something. Whatever that something was didn't really matter. Isolde would escape and she would never look back.

Isolde looked at her watch. Isolde's platinum wrist watch glinted and flashed in the silvery natural light. The watch was beautiful. It had been a gift from Carter Holland the night before. It was worth the price of a cottage in Sussex—or perhaps a large house on the Scottish Borders. Yes, Carter rewarded loyalty.

'I didn't expect it would take so long to get back. I tried calling, but I couldn't get a signal. Not even in London.'

Isolde froze and looked up at the sound of the frighteningly familiar voice. **It was Gemma.** Gemma Ripley, her long glossy brown hair framing her pale and smooth face, was holding a Japanese airfreight package under one arm and her black Montblanc soft briefcase in her free hand.

Isolde felt a shock go through her that she never felt in her entire life. The color drained completely out of her face. How can this be? Gemma was dead. The murderer had confirmed it. Carter had only launched the attack on Tara's holdings only after confirming Gemma's death. How was this possible?

Gemma noticed the deathly paleness of Isolde's face and became worried about her.

'Are you alright? What's wrong?' asked Gemma as she placed the airfreight package and her Montblanc briefcase on top of her modern desk. 'I'll get you a cup of water,' said Gemma as turned and walked over to the water cooler. Isolde watched as Gemma walked through the ghostly silvery grey natural light that poured in through the curved glass walls of the building.

Isolde was trying to take it all in. No. This was impossible. How could Gemma not be dead? What should she do? Should she kill Gemma herself? Yes, **she would kill Gemma herself** and then flee the building.

Isolde opened the desk drawer and grabbed a pair of stainless steel scissors. She stood up. Gemma, in the process of filing a paper cup with cold water for Isolde, was completely unaware of what was about to happen to her.

'Gemma. Where have you been? Alexa is in a conference call with the Tokyo office right now. Alexa is still in the Cotswolds, but she will be here later today. Allegra and Rupert are on their way to the office now. I have been calling you for over an hour,' said Tarquin, as he emerged from the glass walled conference room. Isolde, startled by Tarquin's voice, turned around to face him. She was holding the gleaming pair of scissors in her hand.

'I'm sorry, Tarquin. My phone isn't working. The traffic was heavier in London than I expected. The roads in Surrey were practically empty, but I got stuck in traffic on the way back into London. What's going on?'

Tarquin, in a dark blue suit, pale blue dress shirt, and a dark grey tartan tie, shook his head. 'The global economy is collapsing. Alexa has been trying to call you too. I think you should try calling her from the office phone.'

Isolde turned back around to face Gemma. And before Isolde could stab both Gemma and Tarquin to death, Rupert, the twenty-three-year-old new hire from Norton South (of all the places in the world), entered the office. The tall and gangly Rupert, in a dark grey wool suit, pale blue dress shirt, and the London School of Economics three-fold silk reppe school tie (which included purple stripes), was rather plain looking. The working class Rupert was extremely intelligent and had graduated at the top of his class from the London School of Economics. Alexa had hired Rupert over more experienced applicants simply because he was polite and truly good hearted. There was a certain air of innocence about him that both Alexa and Gemma had liked.

Gemma began to unbutton her wool coat.

Isolde was panicking under her icy mask. Despair now filled her. No, she had not failed. The man that Carter had sent after Gemma Ripley had. Carter had to know that Gemma was still alive.

'Thank you, Isolde, but I can do it myself,' said Gemma as she held out her hand. Isolde, now standing in a crowded office, unthinkingly, like an automaton, handed the scissors to Gemma. Gemma picked up the slender cardboard airfreight box and cut the white packing tape that sealed one end of the package.

Isolde, without saying a word, walked out of the office.

Isolde stumbled as she walked past the front desk. Helen, the blonde receptionist, noticed, but decided to say nothing. Isolde made her way down the hallway and past the elevators. She walked down another hallway and stood at the end of the hall next to a vacant office on the 12th floor. Behind her, the curved glass walls offered a sweeping view of wintery London. Outside, it was snowing and millions—perhaps billions—of snowflakes swirled around the Gherkin.

Isolde dialed a number. And after a few rings, Carter Holland answered.

Gemma—An Invisible Fear—Jupiter Awakens

THE CITY

Enoch placed his smartphone down on the desk. Its battery had nearly been depleted. It was pointless to keep telephoning Gemma. The two other smartphones had stopped ringing a minute before. Enoch picked up a remote control from the desktop and turned off the television. He picked up another remote control and turned off the two market tickers. The office suddenly became quiet. There was no banging on the double doors at the end of the cavernous office. No more text messages arrived on any of his smartphones. Now, only the digital images on the computer screens on his large desk flashed before him.

Enoch stood up and walked over to one the large white sash windows of the top floor office. In the distance, shrouded in the silvery natural light of a wintery day, stood the Gherkin. Enoch, his pale blue dress shirt glowing in the wintery gloom, noticed his reflection in the window glass. His brown hair, freshly cut like a City banker, was tousled. It had been an eternity since the phone call which had destroyed his life. (In reality, it had only been half an hour.) Enoch had fallen. Enoch wondered how much longer he would have to wait before the enormity of what had happened truly hit him. Now he was floating—in the state of shock—all of this was surreal. Enoch kept wondering if this was a just bad dream. He kept hoping that it was. There was a small part of his being that told him it was and that everything would be alright. Only Enoch knew it wouldn't be.

Enoch's smartphone—the one he used for personal calls—began to ring softly. Enoch imagined that he could see inside the small plastic phone and watch the semiconductors inside operate. He could see flashes of electricity and light pulse through the circuit board. Enoch did not wonder who was calling him. He didn't care.

THE ELEVATOR

Stuart, the head of Enoch's personal security detail, and two other former British Paras, all in coat and tie, stood quietly in the elevator as it ascended from the underground parking deck. Yes, there was one way around the bomb proof wall and double doors to Mr Tara's office—the private elevator. Stuart had worked for Enoch Tara for almost two years. Mr Tara had always been kind and thoughtful. Mr Tara's safety and well-being were of both personal and professional concern to him.

THE OFFICE

The ringing stopped and after a couple of minutes, it began again. Tara noticed the snow falling outside of his window. He touched the cold glass with his warm hand. He inhaled and then exhaled slowly. The phone was still ringing. It was probably the bank director. He should answer it.

Enoch turned away from the window and walked back to the desk. He looked at the ringing smartphone. He noticed the caller ID. The caller was unknown. Enoch picked up the cell phone and tapped on the screen.

'Hello?' said a familiar voice. 'Enoch? I've been trying call you. I saw the news. Perhaps I shouldn't bother you at a moment like this, but I am worried about you,' said Gemma.

Enoch felt a bolt of electricity smash into him. His entire being trembled. Tears well up in his eyes. He struggled to speak.

'Are you there?' asked Gemma.

'Gemma? Is it really you?' asked Enoch through tears, his voice shaking with emotion.

'Yes. It's me. Are you alright?' asked Gemma gently and softly.

'Gemma. Where are you?' asked Enoch while the room began to spin once more.

'I'm at Millennium Investments. The news reports are terrible. The entire building is in an uproar. My smartphone is malfunctioning. Everyone has been trying to telephone me all morning.' asked Gemma.

Enoch steadied himself against the wooden desk. He breathed heavily. He felt dizzy. What had happened today? The voice on the encrypted smartphone had been sincere. Somehow their plans had gone awry. Thank God.

Enoch closed his eyes and thanked God for saving Gemma's life. Enoch thanked God for everything. **Enoch was now a man reborn.** He gasped for air. He looked out the window and saw the large glassy Gherkin in the distance. Yes, Gemma was there, working at her desk, on the 12th floor.

'Gemma…I thought I had lost you,' said Enoch choking back tears. Enoch had been caught up in a massive emotional tsunami of happiness and disbelief at the same moment. Enoch struggled to find the right words. Enoch, emotionally overwhelmed, quickly gathered the words. 'Gemma, I love you. I love you so much. And I will always love you. Always.'

'I love you, too, Enoch. What's wrong? Please tell me what is wrong. If you have lost your fortune, don't worry. We can live in my country house in the Lake District and grow sweet potatoes,' said Gemma quietly and gently. 'Enoch, we have each other. That's what really matters.'

Yes, it appeared to Gemma that Enoch had been financially ruined. Yes, the mysterious Mr Tara had been financially ruined by the day's cataclysmic events—like so many others.

'Enoch, I have never cared about money. I love you and I will always be with you. Alright?' Gemma, the rush of events overwhelming her, started to cry.

'Gemma. Please, don't cry. I'm alright. If you're alright, then so am I. Gemma. Stay right where you are. I'm sending my security team over to the Gherkin right now. Don't move. Something is happening, and I need you to stay there. Do you understand?'

'Yes. I understand. Are you sure you are alright?' Gemma had no idea what had transpired a half an hour before. The conversation had been confusing and unsettling.

'Gemma, I will explain everything later today. Soon. And I will never let you out of my sight again. I'm sorry that I didn't protect you the way I should have,' said Enoch.

'Enoch, I'm alright. Please, stop this.'

Gemma's voice—her gentle and kind voice—had been a balm—a cure all for Enoch. God had answered. Enoch prayed silently and asked God to forgive him for doubting Him.

THE PRIVATE BATHROOM

The three former Paras exited the elevator. Stuart stopped the elevator on the top floor with a digital card and a code number. One of the Paras stayed by the open elevator. Stuart and the other Para opened the door to the hallway and then walked down the wood panelled corridor and opened the door to the large, white tiled bathroom. Stuart could hear Enoch Tara speaking on the phone through the door of the bathroom. He stopped at the door and knocked.

'Mr Tara. It's Stuart. Are you alright?'

Enoch, startled by the knock turned around. 'Just a minute, Gemma. Stuart is knocking on the door to the bathroom.'

'What?' What's going on, Enoch?' asked Gemma.

'Yes, come in, Stuart,' said Enoch.

Stuart opened the door and stepped into the office. Enoch, his dark blue necktie loosened, his hair tousled, and his clothes looking rumpled, smiled.

'Stuart! It's good to see you!' said Enoch like he was greeting a long-lost friend.

'Mr Tara, we have all been very concerned about you,' said Stuart.

Enoch, still holding the smartphone up to his ear, turned slightly and said, 'Gemma, I'm sending Stuart over right now. Okay?'

'Okay. Enoch, please tell me what is going on,' said Gemma.

'Gemma, I love you, and I will be over there soon. I have a long afternoon ahead of me. I'm going to stay on the line with you until Stuart reaches you, okay?'

'Okay.'

Do you mind if I get back to work, Gem?'

'No…Sure…Are you alright?' asked a bewildered Gemma in her posh intonation.

Enoch turned back to Stuart, covered the receiver, and said, 'Gemma is in danger. Please get to the Gherkin with all of the men you have with you. How many men are here with you?'

'Three, sir,' replied a very confused Stuart.

'Go immediately. Take the Volvo downstairs. Gemma is in her office at Millennium Investments. And don't let Gemma out of your sights. Alright?' said Enoch.

'Alright, sir.'

Stuart, still confused, but now deeply worried about the strange turn of events, walked back into the large private bathroom and made his way to the elevator.

Enoch, still holding the cell phone to his ear, walked over to the look at the wall covered with documents. He tore off one of the documents that he had taped to the wall and studied it carefully for a moment.

Yes, he was onto them. And he would find them and destroy them. All of them.

Jupiter had never known a rage such as this.

THE WAR ROOM

It began with a minor disruption. A thirtysomething banker, who wore a platinum Vacheron Constantin wrist watch, was the first person in the 'war room' to notice it. The disruption became of a ripple, that became a wave, that became a tsunami.

'My god,' said the piratical banker. The pirate's eyes widened as one by one market gains were reversed and secret bank accounts were instantly drained of their stolen monies. Alibaba's cave had been discovered and it was the looters that were now being looted. The banker became pale. He gasped for air.

Yes. Truly. It was over.

And one by one—or rather by twos and threes—the other pirates in the war room became aware of what was happening. The markets surged, swayed to the left and then back to the right. Suddenly, someone having ripped open one of the digital fortress walls, information started to pour out. Government agencies, once blinded by the attack, could now see. Central bankers leaned into to their computer screens. Yes, they could now see the sources of the attacks on them. They immediately set about recovering stolen funds. (And more than a few central banks and hedge funds helped themselves to a little more than they were entitled too.) Yes, the entire edifice was collapsing.

The end was a rather curious one. It began when one pirate stood up. He looked around at the others at working at their keyboards. What was he doing here? It was time to go. He buttoned his jacket, adjusted his silk necktie, and walked out of the room. In less than a minute, half the room had followed him out. The remaining pirates continued to battle with the invisible enemy.

It was hopeless.

Within ten minutes of the counter attack, the entire war room had emptied.

There is no honor among thieves.

Or loyalty.

THE GEORGIAN OFFICE

Carter's smartphone rang. Carter looked at the glowing digital screen. It was Isolde. Carter arched an eyebrow. What had compelled Isolde to telephone him at this moment?

'Hello?'

'Gemma's alive,' Isolde whispered into the phone.

'What?' asked Carter in shocked disbelief.

'Gemma is not dead. She's sitting in Millennium Investments right now. She walked in ten minutes ago.'

'That's impossible,' replied Carter Holland in a stunned tone of voice.

'Gemma is here. What should I do now?' asked Isolde.

The line went dead.

'Hello? Carter? Are you there?' Carter?'

THE WAR ROOM

Carter stood in the entrance to the now deserted and freezing cold war room. The white walled Georgian room was now a sea of computers, minimalist desks and leather chairs, and large computer screens emanating a bluish digital light. Carter walked over to one of the computers and looked at the screen. Yes, it had all gone sideways. And Carter had been abandoned by the men he had trusted the most. The same men that he had enriched beyond their wildest dreams had abandoned him. Documents were scattered across the hardwood floor. Computer screens flashed. The polished Georgian double doors to the entry hall stood open. The vaulted entry hall beyond was filled with a silvery grey natural light and flakes of snow were drifting in. The glossy black doors to the country house had been left open as his minions had scattered to the four winds.

Carter could hear people approaching down one of the long hallways. A dozen men from his security unit, in black and charcoal grey wool suits, white dress shirts, and black silk neckties stood before him.

'We are still loyal, Mr Holland. What are your orders, sir?'

Carter could not feel the cold wind that swirled around him in the white plaster foyer of the country house. The world had collapsed, yet he was still alive. How could that be? How cruel.

Carter Holland looked at the dozen men standing in front of him in the entry hall. They were all young and strong.

'Death would have been easier,' said Carter quietly as he stared into the Cosmos.

'Mr Holland. What are your orders?' asked the young man from Yorkshire.

'Bring the car around,' said Carter quietly.

MILLENNIUM INVESTMENTS

Gemma held a phone receiver against her ear as she typed out something on the keyboard in front her. Three suited and booted of members of Enoch's personal security team stood at the entrance leading into the lobby of the office.

The thirtysomething Stuart, the head of the security team, tall and extraordinarily handsome in a dark blue suit, pale blue dress shirt, and dark blue necktie, stood near the curved glass wall of the office drinking cold water from a paper cup. He hovered over Gemma like a hawk. He was still in the dark as to what had happened earlier, but he knew that this was a very dangerous situation. Nothing would be allowed to harm Gemma Ripley. Nothing.

The staff at Millennium Investments had shrugged off the appearance of Tara's security team. They had other things to worry about. Allegra was now in the conference room. A large digital image of Alexa appeared on the scintillating screen. Tarquin sat at his desk. He was printing something out while looking at his wrist watch. Rupert was typing away at a keyboard. And Helen was standing at a side table. She had just brought up warm drinks and sandwiches from a coffee shop a block from 30 Mary St Axe. Yes, she had purchased drinks and sandwiches for the security team as well.

The situation in the global markets had done a 180° and then a 360° and then another 180°. And then the global markets had righted themselves. Well, not exactly by themselves. The mysterious Mr Tara had helped—quite a bit.

Gemma really didn't understand what had gone on in the markets that day. She didn't really understand financial instruments or economic indicators. What she did know was that Millennium Investments had not only survived the day's tumultuous events, but had somehow managed to make a profit. Even Alexa was left wondering how that had happened. Nonetheless, everyone in the office—in the entire financial world—breathed a sigh of relief.

OZYMANDIAS

Titanium, carbon fiber, steel, and aluminum. The driver shifted and the titanium engine block roared like a dragon. The car exploded forward. The digital speedometer, a black disc filled with streaks and lines of white, red, and blue, glowed intensely. The sports car had been designed and built to the driver's exact specifications. The gear shift was unusual: it was stainless steel and the gears were exposed, not concealed under leather, carbon fiber, or a titanium shell. The exposed gears seemed almost raw. The driver shifted once more, and the titanium engine block, its twelve pistons sheathed in silver, shrieked like a banshee keening. The mid-sized vehicle surged forward effortlessly. The driver, secured in the titanium, carbon fiber, and black leather car seat, scanned the road ahead. The car was moving through a vortex of sound and air. The driver sat alone in the car. The dark blue car appeared as a blur as it moved down the long narrow snow-covered country road. In in few minutes, it would be dark. Yes, in winter, in England, the days are very short. The car accelerated as it approached the village.

All had been lost. All lost because of treachery. The treachery of one man. A man without a country. A man without a biography. A man without so much as a name.

Carter Holland, incandescent with rage, had already dispatched a team to hunt him down and kill the reluctant warlord. The men had several ways to track him: his encrypted smartphone (which had been given to him by Carter Holland—which the Revenant had already and unsurprisingly smashed and disposed of) and the white Audi A7 that the Revenant had driven out to Surrey that morning. Carter's men had already ransacked the Revenant's apartment in Mayfair (that Carter had rented for him), disabled the dark blue Peugeot sedan that the 11th Baron had purchased for him years before, and searched the rented office in central London. The staff at the Revenant's London office had already shredded all of the documents in the files and fled.

Carter could not fathom why the Revenant had turned against him. Carter really didn't understand how this military robot could go against his orders and derail everything. Had not Carter rewarded him richly? The warlord had already killed so many people in the course of this enterprise, how would one more make any difference? The Revenant had never even met Gemma Ripley. Why did he spare her life? Why this woman? Carter no longer cared. He wanted revenge. If Carter Holland had no future, then neither would the nameless man without a country.

The Revenant had seemingly disappeared.

But not quite.

The Revenant had already been tracked to a small stone house in the Midlands.

The ornate, stone, Georgian pillars that stood on either side of the cobblestone road appeared in the distance. The stone obelisks looked like the skeletal ribs of a giant; the grey stone pillars stood in stark contrast to the white snow that surrounded and capped them both. Carter, despair now overwhelming rage, shifted once more and the titanium engine shrieked. The blue blur bolted forward. Carter steered the carbon fiber and titanium supercar a little to the left—the stone pillar swiftly grew larger—and the blue blur shrieked forward.

JUPITER

There was not a soul in the financial world (well, for those who in the world of finance who still had a soul) that was as happy as Enoch Tara that cold winter night. Enoch's empire had been left badly mauled, but not so much that he could not recover from it. Yes, in time, he would recover and become even wealthier and stronger than before. Perhaps.

THE OFFICES OF MILLENNIUM INVESTMENTS

Gemma, wearing a pair of tortoise shell reading glasses, looked at her silver Cartier watch (that the bailiffs had missed): 7:02pm. It was dark. Everyone in the office had gone home half an hour before. Except for Gemma, Stuart, and the other three security men who now stood outside the entrance of the Millennium Investments.

Gemma had told everyone that she would stay and lock up. Which is what Gemma had always done. It was part of her job as office manager. And Gemma liked her job. She would miss it.

Enoch had telephoned Gemma just after 5pm and asked her to wait for him in the office. Would that be alright?

Sure. Besides, Gemma had another problem to deal with: Isolde had disappeared without a trace. And Gemma had no idea why. She had called her phone throughout the day (via the office phone) and Isolde had never answered. Gemma was worried about her. Perhaps the pressure of events had proven too much for her?

The airfreight parcel turned out to be a Japanese technical manual for jet engines. Why had the client sent them that? Alexa had never heard of Mr Mikitiani. Gemma had left the box on Alexa's desk in her office.

It was a cold wintery night. Outside, through the curved glass walls of the Gherkin, the glorious lights of London twinkled like brilliant stars in the heavens. The snow had stopped and the Shard, translucent and beautiful, shown brightly in the darkness.

'Gemma?' said a quiet, trembling voice behind her.

Gemma spun around in her minimalist black leather chair. It was Enoch. He was standing in the entrance of the office buttoned up in a dark blue wool overcoat (with a light brown fur collar) and a pair of charcoal grey wool trousers. He was trembling and tears were in his eyes. His normally neatly kept brown hair was tousled and he looked quite pale. Behind him stood three brutal looking men in wool overcoats. The security men all towered over the 5'9" Enoch.

Yes, it had been a very long day for everyone.

Gemma smiled. 'There you are, Enoch. I've been *terribly* worried about you,' said Gemma in her posh and Sloaney intonation as she rose from the chair. Gemma tilted her reading glasses back on her head of glossy brown hair as she walked towards him.

Yes, this fragile and gentlest of souls loved him. Gemma, a gentle and beautiful soul, loved him. And he loved her. And today, he thought he had lost her—forever. However, God had saved Gemma's life. What had actually transpired on that road remained a mystery to Enoch. But, at this moment, all that mattered to Enoch was that Gemma was alive and safe. He had another chance with her. They had another chance.

Enoch tried to speak, but the words could not come out.

Gemma, still confused about what had gone that day, walked over to Enoch. She smiled and all of Enoch's wounds were instantly healed. Gemma, hauntingly and starkly beautiful, touched Enoch's soft brown hair. She tried to straighten it. There, that's a little better.

'I love you, Gemma. I will explain everything to you later. This day—today—has been the hardest day of my life. I need you, Gemma.'

Gemma, still in the dark about what had really been going on, was happy that whatever had had happened was over because of the terrible effect that it had had on Enoch.

Enoch, in a burst of emotion, embraced Gemma. And Gemma embraced him. The moment Enoch had felt Gemma's gentle embrace, he quietly began to cry.

The suited and booted members of the security unit looked out the windows or up at the ceiling. Except for Stuart, who never took his eyes off of his charge—Gemma.

9 THE MAN WITHOUT A COUNTRY

Gemma—An Invisible Fear—The Man Without a Country

THE MIDLANDS

The small detached stone house stood a short distance from a small village in the Midlands. The house, built in 1923, had been purchased by the Revenant with the money he had earned working for the 11th Baron. The Revenant had hoped that the house would offer him a respite from the world whenever he entered it. He had been disappointed. No, the Revenant took all of his regrets and memories with him wherever he went.

The small house was sparsely furnished and undecorated. The white walls had been left unadorned. There were no area rugs, only cold hardwood floors. The Revenant had no photos of his mother, daughter or wife to display. They had perished along with everything else in the war. The Revenant, like any traumatized war refugee, was grateful to once again have a place that he could call his own. However, the memories of his past failures would never leave him. He had known no peace since escaping from his defeated homeland. And now, he had given up his one true chance to liberate it.

The Revenant would never murder Gemma Ripley. No, the mere thought had never even crossed his heavily scarred mind. He had simply followed her—as per Carter Holland's orders—and taken a photo of the white hatchback as it returned to London and the City. Yes, he had sent the photo to some unknown person in London and they had forwarded it to Enoch Tara. The Revenant had sent a text to Carter Holland informing him that Gemma was dead. Of course, it was untrue.

The Revenant had followed the white Peugeot through Surrey and stopped behind Gemma at the intersection. When the light changed, he had simply accelerated and passed her in the right lane. He had driven directly from there to his house in the Midlands without stopping. He had parked the white Audi next to his house. He had exchanged the number plates, burying the stolen ones next to a tree that stood a short distance from the house. He had entered the small detached stone house, sat down in the light grey upholstered high back armchair and waited.

Yes, they would be here soon.

The Revenant had watched the financial news on a small television set that he had bought on sale at a store in Manchester in 2003. The plastic box still worked. The Revenant made a cup of tea the way his mother had made it for him—two decades ago. He had loved his family more than anything in the world. The Revenant's mother had been his guide. Yes, 'Always choose to be good' she had told him. He had failed in that regard many times. And he knew it.

The last twenty years had meant unceasing agony for the Revenant. He often wished that he had been killed in the fighting. That would have been better. He could have been at peace with an honorable death. And he would have been reunited with his family in Heaven. Yes, it would have been better if he had died in the war and had had never set foot in England.

No, it **would not** have been better if you had died in the war. If you had, you would not have been able to save the life of a defenseless innocent. Your mother, wife, and daughter, were defenseless women. Do you want someone to do to Gemma Ripley what evil men did to your family? **Of course not.** The strong should defend the weak. Have you thrown away your chance to avenge your family and people? Or have you passed the final test? Is this the price of absolution? Have faith in God to avenge past wrongs. These evil creatures will not escape final judgement. **They will not.** Is it really God's Will that you murder an innocent person to avenge your family? **Of course not.**

The Revenant had watched the news unfold throughout the day. And yes, once Mr Tara had gone on the offensive, Carter Holland's attack and been foiled. The Prime Minister had come on television and stated that the government was conducting a wide-ranging investigation and promised that those responsible for the events of the day would be apprehended and brought to justice. Which meant that the British government (and all of the other governments) really had no idea who was behind it all. They would find out. Enoch Tara would want to find the people behind all of it in order to protect Gemma Ripley.

And, of course, Carter Holland would have his revenge.

Where was Carter Holland now? Had he already fled into exile? The Revenant assumed that he would. Carter Ajax Holland didn't seem like the kind of person to just give up.

The Revenant looked at his watch. He had considered telephoning Jem and the others, but had decided against it. He would have liked to have said good bye to Jem, the Texan, and Attila. He wanted to thank them for their loyalty and, above all, their true friendship. In the end, he had decided it was better to just leave things as they were. They all knew the warlord's heart.

The Sun would go down very soon. It was time to step outside and walk to the car. The Revenant stood up. He walked across the nearly empty room and took his blue wool overcoat (with a light brown fur collar) off of the coat rack. He put it on and buttoned it up.

He walked over and looked in the small mirror over the fireplace. He was only in his early fifties and completely worn out by life—if you could call what he had been living life. Yes, this plain and forgettable face was his. He looked at his reflection in the mirror. Yes, he could see traces of his beautiful mother in his reflection. He was grateful to God for that. He no longer had any photos of her, but she had lived on through him. He had only one physical reminder left of his departed mother: a small card she had sent him. Where was it? Oh, yes. It was in the drawer next to his bed.

He walked into the white walled bedroom. Next to the unmade bed, which was covered in white cotton sheets, a dark blue wool blanket, and several white cotton pillows, was a small night stand. He opened the drawer and took out the card that had been carefully, gently, and lovingly wrapped in wax paper. He removed the card from the wax paper and opened it. Inside, in his mother's beautiful hand writing, was his name and three sentences. **She loved him.** The Revenant read the words written in the card out loud. He could feel his mother's love through this simple card. He touched the hand written words on the white card with his fingertips. Oh, how he wished he could go back. He would make everything right. But, of course, he could not go back. His life had come to its end. Soon he would be reunited with his mother, daughter, and wife in Heaven. He closed the card and pressed it against his chest. He closed his eyes.

God help me. Please. God forgive for all of my sins, my failures. And I ask everyone I have failed to forgive me—if they choose to.

They Revenant opened his eyes. Yes, the room had grown darker. The Sun was going down—somewhere behind the leaden sky, the glorious Sun—the blazing, burning orb of blinding light—was slowly disappearing.

The Revenant unbuttoned his blue wool overcoat. He then unbuttoned his wool blazer and placed the small white card in an inside pocket. He would take this with him. He buttoned up his wool blazer and the wool coat. He walked back out of the bedroom and back into the main room. He adjusted the light brown fur collar of his overcoat. He took the car keys from his coat pocket and walked across the room, the worn floorboards creaking underfoot. He unlocked the front door. He inhaled deeply and then exhaled slowly.

This was difficult, so much more difficult than he imagined it would be. The Revenant didn't want to die, but he didn't want to live either. A now he remembered something that a long dead comrade had told him some twenty years ago: Dying was not hard; it was just what came before it that was. Yes, the explanation seemed so obvious, but now that the Revenant was facing his own brutal end, he understood how profound those thoughts and words had really been.

The Revenant reached for the door latch. It clicked as he turned it. He stopped. It would be good to see his family again. Please, God, let me see my family in Heaven. Please. The Revenant opened the door and a blast of cold air hit him. The shock of cold fresh air was refreshing. He could see his breath materializing around him in the cold. A white blanket of snow surrounded the house. A few yards away was the white Audi A7.

Okay.

You are going to walk out to your car, unlock the door, and…we will see what happens, alright?

The Revenant stepped outside, turned around, and locked the door behind him—for the last time. And he knew that it would be the last time. He turned back around. He looked skyward. Yes, the overcast sky had stared to break up and the last gentle rays of the Sun were breaking through the clouds. The last rays of sunlight caressed his face.

He walked towards the white motorcar, the snow crunching underfoot.

Yes, the house was partially surrounded by tall trees, but only partially. Over his shoulder he could see the lights of the village.

He walked to the driver's side car door and unlocked it.

He opened the car door.

Gemma—An Invisible Fear—The Golem

EAST ANGLIA

The blue supercar had been accelerating towards the single stone Georgian pillar when Carter Holland slammed on the brakes. The gauges and speedometer glowed brightly; the smell of rubber and carbon filled the air, red lights flashed on the dash board, the engine shrieked and the brakes grinded heavily, sharply, loudly and, with the assistance of onboard microcomputers and titanium, the car had come to a complete stop just three inches from the grey stone 18th century pillar.

What a machine.

The shoulder strap had tightened instantly and had held Carter in place as a heavy shockwave of gravity slammed into him. Carter, the wind knocked out of him, gasped for air and coughed for a few minutes.

The blue bespoke supercar, illuminated in wintery, slatey gloaming, now idled in the snow before the stone pillar. Carter leaned back into the black leather seat. He was barely able to shift the car into park. He gasped for air. Okay. Breathe. Alright. You are alright. Carter looked around the interior of the supercar. He was encased in black leather, titanium, and carbon fiber. He caught a glimpse of himself in the rearview mirror. His smooth face looked as if it had been chiseled out of marble. Carter was handsome. And he was intelligent. And Carter Ajax Holland was strong—physically, mentally, and spiritually.

The twelve-cylinder titanium engine purred like a tiger. The red lights on the dashboard slowly disappeared. The car had restored itself via onboard microcomputers. Amazing.

Carter leaned back in the black leather seat. He had to collect his thoughts. Carter Holland was still a multi-billionaire. Yes, he had suffered a major setback, but he was far from ruined. He would escape, rebuild, and eventually triumph. No, the Cosmos had not placed Carter Holland on this Earth to fail. He would, one day, create his own country. Nothing would stop him. Especially not a nothing of a being like the Revenant. Yes, it was time to regroup. Carter looked at his platinum wrist watch in the dying twilight. He took out his encrypted smartphone and tapped on the screen.

'What is your status?' asked Carter.

'Fueled and ready to take off, Mr Holland,' said a young confident voice.

Carter Holland, illuminated the in red, blue, and white lights of the speedometer and other gauges, adjusted the shoulder strap carefully.

'I'll be there in ten minutes.'

Carter tapped the screen and put the smartphone back in his coat pocket. He shifted, and the blue supercar backed up. He turned onto the darkened cobblestone road, shifted once more, and the car started to slowly move forward. Once Carter had cleared the stone gates, he began to accelerate; the supercar's headlights cutting through the Cimmerian darkness.

Carter would make it. He would escape. He would create a new country. He would not fail.

Ready.

Set.

Go.

And Carter smiled.

Gemma—An Invisible Fear—Muddy Hills Forever

HALCYON DAYS

The first week of January found the strawberry blonde Louise and flaxen haired Aurelia taking their exams at their (soon to be former) university in London. Aurelia had studied very hard and done moderately well (kind of). Louise had studied quite a bit over the holidays; however, with her peace of mind restored, she had sailed through her exams and done extremely well.

Aurelia had decided to stay with her parents and younger sister in London for the last few days of the Christmas holiday before boarding the train to Midlands-Hasegawa. Aurelia's father had returned to England for Christmas, and she wanted to spend as much time as possible with him before he flew back to Singapore. Aurelia was happy to hear that Louise had resolved her differences with her father. Aurelia had happily hugged Louise and Freya at the house in Mayfair on December 31st and told them she would see them next week at Muddy Hills.

Violet, Hughie, Lord Maud and his Rhodesian wife, the baroness (Lady Maud), had all been overjoyed and relieved to hear of Louise's reconciliation with her father. The 4th Baron, still worried about Louise's health, continued to consult with specialist physicians and dietitians.

Louise had made a new friend in The Honourable Morton Lloyd Maud, the future baron. Morton was kind, and it was Morton that kismet had sent to Louise to urge her to give her father one more chance. Louise was glad that she had met Morton; glad that Freya had been out of the room when he had come by; glad that she had agreed to look at the book Morton's father had given him for Christmas. One day, Morton and Louise would share agricultural ideas and innovations. And they would become lifelong friends.

And an entirely unexpected thing happened: Tatler contacted Louise the day she completed her exams and asked to photograph her for the February cover of the magazine. Her novel had received glowing reviews from a literary critic at the Daily Telegraph (who had received an advance copy of the book) and he had declared Louise the next literary 'It Girl'. Louise was thrilled. Freya had gone with her to the photo shoot which had taken place in a studio in Covent Garden. Louise had worn a shimmering white beaded dress and diamond tiara from Cartier. Freya had been amazed by how beautiful Louise looked in the photos. Louise had grown into a beautiful young English woman.

Poppy and her family (which, of course, included Mars) had had a delicious dinner after the long day of financial and political upheaval had subsided that afternoon.

Poppy had taken Brian up to the roof (via the ladder) that evening and looked at the stars above. Yes, mankind would never create anything as beautiful as what God had created in the heavens. Poppy could not help but think of the night, a year before, when she had gone up to the roof with Gemma and they had both made a wish upon a falling star. Poppy, under a beige sweater, a dark purple cashmere wool cape (with a mink collar) and a fur hood, had gently kissed Brian and told her how blessed she was to have found him. Brian, overcome with emotion, had told Poppy how blessed he was to have met her and how grateful to God he was that he had spared her life. Poppy and Brian had held hands that night on the flat roof of the country house and Brian had listened carefully while Poppy pointed out the Constellations to him. And then, just before they decided to go back downstairs, Poppy shouted, 'Look!' as a shooting star fell to the Earth. They had both wished for the same thing.

Külli and Octavia had had a happy Christmas holiday with Octavia's family in the Cotswolds. They had attended Christmas services at the small Anglican church and gone caroling in the village. Octavia's grandfather, a retired army major, had asked Külli when she would marry Octavia. Külli had been happily surprised by the question and had answered, 'Soon.'

Vahtra had had its most profitable Christmas yet. The outfitters had sold out of nearly everything and bespoke orders were now piling up in the workshop.

Külli Vahtra had found true love. Külli (or Gula, to the girls in the alcove) still loved Gemma as much as she ever had. And she was happy that Gemma had also found true love. Külli was at peace with the world.

And what of The Honourable Gemma Ophelia Ripley?

Gemma had been shocked and deeply distressed at what Enoch had gone through. Enoch had broken down and cried when he had spoken of the events of that afternoon. Gemma had gently embraced him and told him not to worry. That she planned to stay with him for a long time. Forever actually.

Gemma had also been deeply shocked when she realized that Isolde had been part of it all. Why had a young woman as intelligent and talented as Isolde conspired to murder someone? Isolde had disappeared without a trace. Scotland Yard had informed Gemma that 'Isolde' had used a stolen identity. An infant girl, born in Norwich some twenty years earlier, had died ten weeks after she was born, and Isolde had assumed her identity. Gemma sometimes wondered what had become of her. Gemma had truly liked Isolde. Gemma had considered her a friend and loyal co-worker. Gemma actually felt sorry for the twenty-year-old (or so) young woman. What would become of her? A life on the run from conspiracy to murder charges—what kind of life would that be? And if Isolde (or whatever her real name was) were captured, she would rot in prison for decades. Her life had ended, really. She would spend the rest of her life looking over her shoulder.

THAMES HOUSE

Investigations conducted by Scotland Yard and MI5 had been unable to piece together exactly what had transpired that day in Surrey. Apparently, a trap had been set for Gemma, and Isolde had joined Millennium Investments solely to spy on Gemma and eventually lure her into it. However, there had been an unexpected turn of events for those behind it. The person tasked with murdering Gemma had, for reasons unknown, failed to follow through.

MI5

This was the second interview that the Security Service had conducted with Gemma in the white walled office in the Portland stone HQ of MI5 in London in the last four days.

Enoch Tara had also been interviewed, but was careful to keep the Special Unit out of it. MI5 had never asked him about the gun battle in the Garden Centre in Crews Hill. They had probably not connected the events. Enoch had to use every bit of his acting talents to protect the highly secretive and shadowy Special Unit (and keep himself out of trouble). Yes, Enoch Tara was a very good actor.

And so was Gemma.

'It's a bit of speculation on our part, Mrs Ripley, but the person in the white car that followed you through the forest did take a photo of your hatchback and send it to Mr Tara. Yes, it is this person who was supposed to murder you. And, for whatever reason, he did not. He drove past you and let you live,' said the middle-aged intelligence officer in a light grey suit. 'I would like to think that whatever humanity this person had, stopped him from following through.'

'Do you have any idea who this person is?' asked Gemma.

'No. None,' replied the man in the light grey suit. 'The surveillance cameras in the village failed to capture the car on film. You still don't remember what the make and model of the car was?'

'No. It was just a white sedan. I didn't take much notice of it. The car appeared and disappeared in less than twenty seconds. When I stopped at the traffic light, I was trying to use my cell phone. When the light changed, I put the phone down and drove through the intersection. The white motorcar passed me in the right lane a few seconds later. It was snowing. I was more focused on the road.'

Gemma started to become emotional. One of the men, in a dark blue suit, said, 'We understand how upsetting this be for you, Mrs Ripley. However, we have to conduct a thorough investigation.'

'We will continue to look for the driver, Mrs Ripley,' said a young man in the charcoal grey suit from MI5.

That MI5 would continue to hunt for driver of the white sedan almost caused Gemma physical pain. Gemma secretly hoped—and later that afternoon prayed—that the man in the white sedan would escape. He had spared her life. The man in the white sedan had saved her life. She could feel that in her heart. Gemma didn't know what kind of person this man was, but she could sense that he was not truly bad. Gemma's heart could feel it.

As the young intelligence officer in the charcoal grey suit opened a file and started placing dozens of photographs on the white laminate table top, Gemma suddenly realized that the man who had spared her life must have paid a very high price for it. Undoubtably, the others involved in the murder plot would be angry with the driver. Gemma became pale and she looked out the white sash window of the second floor office while trying to regain her composure. Yes, the man who had saved her life had most likely sacrificed his life for hers. Gemma felt a wave of sadness move through her. Gemma hoped, and later prayed, that the man who had saved her life had somehow managed to save himself.

'Mrs Ripley?' asked the man in the dark blue suit. 'I know you must be rather tired, but please bear with us for a little while longer.'

'Yes. Please continue,' said Gemma quietly as she adjusted the large collar of her white cotton blouse. Gemma seated in front of a large modern table, which was in the center of the room, shifted uncomfortably in the wooden chair.

'Do you know Carter Holland?' asked the man in the light grey suit.

'No.'

'As I am sure you have read in the papers, it was Carter Holland behind all of it. You have never met him?'

'I had never even heard of him until last summer. He outbid Enoch on a Byzantine codex at an auction in London. Enoch told me his name, but said nothing else about him. Do you have any idea where Carter Holland is now?'

'I'm afraid we are not allowed to talk about that with you, Mrs Ripley. The investigation is only in its early stages,' said the man in the light grey suit.

Gemma, took her tortoise shell reading glasses out of her beige leather clutch and looked at the photos on the table. There were several of Isolde—images taken from CCTV in the Gherkin and one from her fake identification card. Isolde was beautiful—starkly beautiful. There were also a few of Carter Holland, taken from CCTV images and magazine articles. Gemma motioned towards the photos and asked, 'May I look at them more closely?'

'Of course, Mrs Ripley,' said the man in the dark blue suit.

Gemma picked up a photo of Carter Holland. Yes, the blond and blue-eyed Carter was truly handsome. He didn't look sinister at all. His appearance in the photos fluctuated between the benevolent and the benign. He looked like a movie star. He could have been one, had he chosen to, but he had not.

There were several other photos on the table of different men, but none that she recognized. Wait, there was one face that she did. Yes, **the man in the dark blue wool overcoat with a light brown fur collar**. He was walking out of the Bond Street Station several feet behind another man whose face had been circled in the photo. The man in the crowd looked like the man behind the wheel of the white motorcar. She studied the photo for a moment longer. This was the man that had saved Gemma's life. Gemma was sure of it. **How she wished she could have a copy of this photo**. Gemma put the photo down and then picked up another one of a man in a dark grey suit that she had never seen before. It was important that she protect the man in the dark blue overcoat. Yes, how unremarkable the man in the dark blue wool overcoat looked. How unassuming his appearance was. Yes, Gemma was sure the man in the previous photo was him. Gemma put down the photo she was looking at and picked up another. She studied the image. The photograph was a high-resolution image of an athletic young man in a blue blazer and beige knit tie. No, she had never seen him before either. Gemma did not want to risk drawing attention to the man in the crowd, so she studied the image of the completely unknown man in the blue blazer for over two minutes. She wanted to throw the men in MI5 off of the nondescript man's trail. Gemma could sense that the extremely intelligent and highly cunning men in the office were studying her reactions.

Gemma picked up a photo of the blonde and blue-eyed Isolde. Gemma sighed. How could Isolde, of all people, have betrayed her so horribly? How had Gemma not suspected her? Isolde was an extremely talented actress. She could have been a successful film actress or a supermodel, had she wanted. But she hadn't. Isolde's choices in life had been difficult to fathom for Gemma. But Gemma had learned through her own experiences that difficult circumstances sometimes lead to bad choices. Gemma did not know Isolde's true story. What had driven her to join Carter Holland's murder plot could only be guessed at. Had Isolde's life been so hard that she could be easily manipulated by Carter Holland? Or had Isolde been born like this?

'Do you have any further information on Isolde's true identity?' asked Gemma while still holding the photo.

'No. Not yet. But, with facial recognition software and other technology, I'm sure we will find her one day. Then, perhaps, we can get some answers… Perhaps…Perhaps,' replied the man in the dark blue suit.

It was at that moment that Gemma realized that the slightly younger man in the dark blue suit was the ranking officer in the room—not the older man in light grey and definitely not the young man in the charcoal grey wool suit. The man in the dark blue suit noticed that flicker of recognition in Gemma's eyes. Yes, The Honourable Gemma Ophelia Ripley was a very clever girl. Was Gemma Ripley hiding something? The man in the dark blue suit really couldn't tell.

At the end of the interview, the middle-aged man in the light grey suit thanked Gemma for coming in for another interview. They might need to interview her again. Gemma told them that that would be alright. She would be staying at Enoch Tara's house in Marble Arch from now on. (Enoch had insisted, though Gemma was staying in her own room. They wouldn't marry until June.)

Enoch had also assigned three bodyguards to Gemma who followed her around in a dark blue Audi A7. The same model of car (but a different color) that the man who had followed her that morning through Surrey had driven.

Gemma was buttoning her blue wool coat (with silver buttons) while walking down the hallway towards the elevator when she heard a voice behind her.

'Oh, Mrs Ripley?'

Gemma stopped, turned around, and saw the man in the dark blue suit standing in the corridor.

'Yes?'

'Mrs Ripley, if you do remember some detail of the man in the white motorcar, please contact us immediately. No detail is too small,' said the man in the dark blue suit from MI5.

'Alright,' replied Gemma quietly.

The elevator doors opened and Gemma stepped inside. The man from MI5 stood in the hallway and looked at Gemma with an unyielding gaze as the doors to the lift closed.

ST ALBANS

Gemma had driven to the small forgotten Anglican church in central London in her white Peugeot hatchback after leaving the Thames Building. It was here, in this small Victorian church built with the donations of British colonists in India during the Raj, that she had spent so much time in during her divorce and criminal trial, that Gemma could find solitude. Gemma could be alone and pray. She could speak with God and the departed amidst the Victorian box pews and grey stone pillars.

Gemma, in the pair of dark khaki cotton trousers, the white cotton blouse (with a large collar), and the brown leather Oxfords that she had purchased during her visit to Oxford University with Enoch last summer, unbuttoned her blue wool coat. She sat down in one of the ornate Victorian box pews. It was cold in the church. That was alright; Gemma liked the cold.

Gemma remembered her meeting here with Winter, Grey's friend from North Carolina. It was here that she had told Winter what Grey had done to her. It was here, in this forgotten church, that Winter had warned Gemma to have Freya and Louise escape from All Saints before Grey's men could get to them. It was in this church that Poppy had married Brian Atherton on a glorious day in June. And it was here that Gemma had found a place to hide during her ruinous divorce. Yes, St Albans was Gemma's hiding place.

Gemma leaned forward and clasped her small soft manicured hands in prayer. Gemma thanked God for everything good that had ever happened to her. There were so many good things to be thankful for in spite of all the bad things that had happened to her. It was only at times like this, when Gemma prayed, that she realized how blessed she had been. Gemma prayed for the safe escape of the unknown man in the dark blue overcoat behind the wheel of the white Audi A7. Gemma prayed that he would be alright. She prayed that, having found his humanity again, he would turn his life around and start over somehow and somewhere. Winter had escaped the icy river, why not this nondescript driver too?

Amen.

Gemma leaned back into the Victorian box pew. She stared at the church's stone altar.

'Mummy? I know you are here. I miss you. I know I have made a mess of so many things, but I am trying. I wish I had your wisdom. I know you would like Enoch. He is so sweet and kind. And good. I wish you had been able to meet Poppy, Gula, and Violet. I was happy at All Saints. I only missed you, Mummy. I know you are happy to be reunited with grandmother and grandfather. I miss them too. I still listen to the church bells on New Year's every year. Grandfather taught me a lot about bell ringing. Whenever I hear church bells, I always think of grandfather. Does Arthur ever talk to you? I know he was close to you. He's in Hong Kong. I never hear from him. I wish he would telephone me. I would like to hear his voice just more time. I understand him. I'm not upset with him. Maybe you can talk with him and convince him to telephone me? It would be nice to have a brother again. Oh, Mummy, Enoch gave me a kitten. He is a tiny baby and black as coal, so I named him Soot. He is really tiny and cute. He follows me around the house. He is my baby. I remember the kitties we had when we lived in London. I remember how much grandfather and grandmother loved your cats. After you passed away, everyone felt that they were a physical connection to you, somehow. I wanted a cat when I married George, but George wouldn't let me. He never liked animals. One day, I will see you all again in Heaven, Mummy. I'm looking forward to it. I don't expect it will be anytime soon, so please, visit me often and make yourself known.'

Gemma's face was wet with tears by the time she had stopped speaking. Gemma made no attempt to wipe away her tears.

One of the large wooden double doors to the church opened and a blast of cold air accompanied by a wave of natural light flooded into St Albans. Gemma turned around and saw Enoch standing in the doorway. His brown hair freshly cut like a City banker and wearing a charcoal grey wool suit, a white dress shirt (with a St James collar), and a dark grey tartan necktie. Enoch was handsome. He had unbuttoned his dark blue wool overcoat (with a light brown fur collar) before opening one of the wooden double doors to St Albans. Enoch stepped inside and carefully closed the doors behind him.

'I was worried about you, Gem. I'm sorry to bother you. I know you come here to find solitude. The security team told me that you had driven directly here after the meeting with MI5. Is everything alright?'

'Yes, I'm alright. Come and sit down with me,' said Gemma.

Enoch walked down the aisle of the church and sat down next to Gemma in the ornate Victorian box pew. He noticed that Gemma had been crying.

'What's wrong, Gemma?'

'I think too much,' said Gemma quietly.

Enoch noticed that Gemma was wearing the outfit she had bought last summer in Oxford. Yes, Enoch kept the two sets of dark khaki cotton trousers and two white, cotton, button-down, dress shirts he had purchased that weekend in a separate part of his wardrobe. Those three days in Oxford had changed everything.

'Thinking is a good thing, Gem. Most people don't really think much about anything anymore.'

'A lot has happened to me in the last few years, Enoch. When I think about it now, it seems like that life belongs to a stranger. Not my own life. Someone else's. I have just been observing it from a distance,' said Gemma quietly.

'I know your life has been difficult, Gemma. I can only imagine what you have been through, but I know I couldn't have survived it. I know that. You are strong, Gemma. I am blessed to have met you and blessed to be with you now. When I thought…I…had lost you…Nothing mattered anymore. I should have been more protective of you, but I know how much you value your independence. I didn't want to make a mistake and lose you. Being too cautious, I almost did. I thank God that you are safe and here with me now,' said Enoch quietly, his voice breaking with emotion.

'We are blessed, Enoch. I am blessed to have you. And I am blessed to have true friends—**true friends who have saved my life**.'

Gemma paused for moment. Yes, Enoch noticed.

'Gemma…is there something you want to tell me?'

'I'm worried about the man who spared my life. Whoever was driving that car saved my life. And now, I wonder, is he still alive? When I was driving down the road that morning, I was alone and the road was deserted. The map that Isolde gave me was part of the trap. It bothers me that someone I really liked and trusted so absolutely could betray me so horribly. If the driver had not had a change of heart, I would be dead. Enoch, I hope the driver can somehow escape.'

Enoch adjusted his dark blue wool overcoat. He was quiet for a moment.

'Yes, I have thought about him too. The photograph he sent me showed how close he actually was to you. Yes, he chose not to do what Carter Holland had sent him to do…. I have no doubt that he made a conscious decision and disobeyed Carter Holland's orders. The driver refused to do it, even at the risk of his own life,' said Enoch quietly.

'And now, mostly likely, he is dead,' replied Gemma quietly. 'He saved my life, Enoch. I have had others help me, some have even saved my life, and I have had the ability to help them in return. But this man, this unknown man, I cannot help. And he needs my help. It hurts me to think about him. A total stranger saved my life, and I have no way to help him,' said Gemma.

'Gemma, I feel the same. I truly wish that I could help him too. I can only imagine what kind of person would get tangled up with Carter Holland, but it's only my imagination. I don't know this man's story. I don't know what circumstances he faced that put him in that situation. How can we repay someone that we will never see again?' asked Enoch.

Gemma, kind, sensitive, and fragile, had no answer. No, wait. Maybe she did.

'I think this man knew exactly what he was doing all along. When I walked into the office, and Isolde saw me, she was absolutely shocked. Someone had told her I was dead. Was it Carter Holland? Perhaps. But, the more I think about it, the more I am convinced that the driver, this unknown and brave man, reported my death to Carter Holland after letting me go. He gave me time to escape. I hope he gave himself enough time to escape too.'

Enoch reached out and grasped Gemma's small soft hand.

'Gemma, it was God and this brave man who gave us a second chance. This man saved your life. He saved my life. I will always be grateful to him. I said a prayer for him that afternoon. For now, that's all we can do. Gemma, sometimes, there is no solution. Sometimes things end badly. It's not fair. We have both suffered unfairly. We know this is part of life. For now, until he reappears, we will remain grateful and indebted to this unknown man for this act of self-sacrifice. He didn't do what he did on that road because he expected a reward. At least not an Earthly one.'

Gemma nodded slightly and reflectively in agreement.

Enoch noticed that the skies had cleared completely and now bright sunshine flooded into through the church windows. It was a beautiful day. And they were both alive, and safe, and together. Enoch thanked God and said a silent prayer for the driver of the white car. Enoch prayed that the driver had somehow escaped.

Gemma brushed her soft, glossy, brown bangs away with one of her small manicured hands and said, 'I hope and pray that brave man has escaped. And if he has not, I pray he finds peace and Heaven awaiting him. I will pray for him. I will include him in all of my nightly prayers. For the rest of my life, I will pray for this man whose name I don't even know.'

Gemma stood up. She began to button her wool coat. 'It's time I get back to Millennium Investments. We are short staffed. The Singapore office is handling most of the work right now, but in a few days, the workload will shift back to London, and Alexa will need me more than ever.'

'Alexa is nice enough to let you bring part of the Household Security Unit with you to the office. I am grateful to her for that,' said Enoch.

'Alexa understands the situation, and she is my friend. And besides, Alexa told me she needed me to stay awhile longer. Just until we can find a suitable replacement,' said Gemma.

'How long do expect to stay at Millennium Investments, Gem?'

'Well, I would like to work until we get married in June. Then, we can pack up and move to the country, if you still want to do that,' replied Gemma.

'It's up to you, Gemma. As long as we are together: you, me, and baby Soot.'

Gemma smiled.

'I will miss working at Millennium Investments much more than I miss working at the magazine as an editor. Alexa gave me a chance. She believed in me. Alexa helped me when so few would. Millennium Investments changed my life. And I will always be grateful to the people there for helping me when I was at my lowest,' said Gemma quietly as tears started to well up in her eyes.

Gemma reached out and held Enoch's hand. Enoch felt a warmth move through him: love. And Gemma felt the same emotion moving through her.

'I think, for a while at least, we can split our time between London and the countryside. I am, and I always will be, a London girl,' said Gemma happily.

And Gemma smiled.

MAYFAIR

On New Year's Eve, the 4th Baron, Lord Maud, held an opulent and well attended party at his Grade I listed Georgian house in Mayfair. It was a spectacular white tie event for friends and family. The white plaster Mughal Gothic ballroom was crowded with people that freezing cold winter night.

Külli and Octavia—both absolutely poured into their dresses, had spent the evening dancing happily with everyone.

Freya, in a beaded white gown, and Louise, in blue velvet, had enjoyed talking about their future plans with anyone who would listen—which was everyone. Young people should all plan for a bright future—even if it seems that one, at that moment, is impossible. One never knows how one's life will turn out. Louise's father, Major Harold Percival, svelte, handsome, and dashing in white tie and tails, had happily listened to the girls—the new Bright Young Things of England—as they regaled everyone with their hopes and dreams. And yes, Freya still wanted to become a flight attendant, which Violet, blonde and radiantly beautiful in white satin, happily agreed would be a great way to see the world.

THE LAKE DISTRICT

Poppy, still safely and happily ensconced in the family pile in the Lake District, happily talked with everyone at the party through the camera in her smartphone—something which both the Barons Devereux and Maud found amazing. Poppy and Brian enjoyed introducing the twins to everyone over the phone camera. Poppy had also told everyone that she would be returning to London in the spring—with the twins, Waverly and Arthur. And Holly, the nanny, would be staying with them in Poppy's small Edwardian house in Covent Garden.

SURREY

Jinx (or Jane) had telephoned Freya from Surrey to wish her a Happy New Year. She had told Freya how blessed she felt to have roomed with her at Midlands-Hasegawa. She also thanked Freya for introducing her to the modeling agency. Jinx's family was now on a much better financial footing. Jinx also told her that she had won a Best Actress award at a film festival in Busan.

Louise had spoken with Jinx too (via online camera) and Jinx had been amazed by how beautiful Louise looked in her dark blue velvet dress. Freya and Louise both noticed how *ravishingly* beautiful the glossy, raven-haired, and blue-eyed Jinx was, even though she was spending the evening at home in Surrey with her family in a pair of khaki and blue tartan wool trousers and a white cotton blouse (with a large collar).

Jinx told the girls how happy she was to be at home with her Rhodesian grandparents. She had missed them all terribly while at boarding school in Wales and later at Midlands-Hasegawa. And Jinx knew that, at their age, they might not be here for much longer. The Christmas holidays had been a very happy one for her and her family.

Jinx had bought everyone in her family wonderful gifts of coats, velvet slippers, leather shoes, black rubber wellies, books, sweaters, and smartphones—which she was teaching her three grandparents how to use.

She had also enjoyed making all kinds of delicious food in the kitchen with her mother. Jinx had also bought her family a new set of white bone china dishes.

And Jinx had purchased her father several out-of-print books on the history of Rhodesia, which he loved and had spent the last few days reading.

Jinx had shyly told the girls that Rex and Jinx had decided to marry the week after graduation from university. Freya and Louise had both clapped happily at the news.

SOUTH WEST LONDON

Aurelia, speaking in front of a stainless steel refrigerator in her kitchen in London, had also spoken with the girls (including a telephone call to Jinx in Surrey) and told them how excited she was to be spending the rest of university with her dearest friends in the world in the alcove at Muddy Hills. Yes! Absolutely! They would rule Muddy Hills!

Louise told Aurelia that she had bought an automobile. Louise had found a 1958 'Bugeye' Sprite for sale online and purchased it. The Austin-Healey was not in running order. It would need a lot of work. It lacked an engine and needed to be completely restored, but Louise's father knew of a workshop in East Anglia that specialized in restoring classic British cars and he would see to it. Louise was going to have the car painted a glossy Baltic blue—the same color as Freya's Bristol Fighter. Hopefully, the Sprite would be delivered to her, completely restored, sometime in late February.

'So, you're going to learn how to drive a manual transmission? asked Aurelia.

Louise smiled impishly. 'No. I'm going to have it rebuilt with an automatic transmission.'

Aurelia laughed and said, 'Oh, good, then Freya will be able to drive it.'

Freya smiled. 'Louise has never driven a car before. I am going to teach her how to drive during the Hilary Term at Muddy Hills.'

'I read the review of **The Undaunted** in the Daily Telegraph,' said Aurelia. 'I am so proud you, Louise.'

'Thank you, Aurelia. I will give you a copy of my novel soon. I am expecting a box of books from the publishers to arrive in the next couple of days.'

'Thank you, Louise. I will buy a copy for my mother too,' said Aurelia.

'I hope she likes it,' said Louise.

'I'm sure she will. Mummy is wondering if she will be able to tell who you based the characters on,' said Aurelia laughingly. 'Tell me more about the Sprite,' said Aurelia.

'I used the advance for novel on the 'Bugeye' Sprite. The car didn't cost much. And buying the car with my book money makes this car really special,' said Louise happily.

'Yes, the 'Bugeye' Sprite. I have never seen such a wreck with such potential,' said Freya laughingly.

Freya and Louise, both in dresses and heels, went downstairs with their smartphones to the garage, pulled off the white tarp, and Louise happily explained to Aurelia that she was going to upholster the interior of the badly neglected Sprite in beige Connolly leather. She would also have the rotten wooden dash relaced with one of polished burl wood.

MERCIA

Wren, her honey blonde bangs partially obscuring her blue eyes, had telephoned Mayfair from Mercia, where her family was hosting a New Year's Eve party at the fortified manor house. Wren, strikingly beautiful in a white satin dress, had excitedly told everyone (via the camera of her phone) that the castle ruins would be open for tours in March. A film director had also signed a contract with the family to film some scenes for an American movie in February. Wren had helped her parents build an online store for the castle, and she was helping her father, the 23rd Baron, write a book on the baronial family history. Wren was also happy and excited about the Hilary Term at Midlands-Hasegawa. She would bring a box of potatoes from the garden to bake in the fireplace.

SURREY

Wallis adjusted her position in front of the smartphone screen. Wallis, her long, glossy blonde hair held in place with a white velvet headband, smiled.

Wallis was standing in an opulent looking drawing room in her house in Surrey. She was smiled happily. Wallis was standing in front of a smooth white plaster wall with Georgian plaster crown molding and a large gilt framed oil painting of the iron sail-powered, paddle wheel and screw propelled steamship SS Great Eastern. The gigantic ship's five funnels, six giant masts, and giant paddle wheels were propelling the great ship across a vast ocean. The painting had been painted in the 1871 and purchased by Wallis's great grandfather in 1913. The magnificent oil painting served as the backdrop for most of the phone call with Freya and Louise via the smartphone's camera. Wallis was clad in a pair of dark khaki wool trousers and a white cotton blouse with open cuffs and an open collar.

'Masako, don't be shy. Come over here and wish Freya and Louise a Happy New Year,' said Wallis laughingly. Masako, her long, glossy black hair piled onto her head with silver hair pins which revealed the smooth nape of her neck, stepped into the camera frame.

'Happy New Year, Freya. Happy New Year, Louise,' said Masako in her flawless and posh English. Masako, tall and slender, smiled shyly. The Japanese undergraduate, the descendent of Japanese daimyo, bowed slightly. Masako, in a pair of pale blue and dark blue tartan trousers and a white cotton blouse, looked like she had just emerged from the Scottish Highlands. 'I will have you over for tea in our rooms after you have settled into the alcove,' said Masako. 'I am looking forward to the Hilary Term with you, Louise.'

'Oh, thank you, Masako. I have heard such nice things about you from Freya. Yes, and I will have you over to our alcove for tea often,' said Louise happily.

'We're staying home with Mummy this New Year's. We've had a nice Christmas holiday. Masako and I went caroling with Mummy on Christmas Eve. We had a nice time. Afterwards, we went to a local pub and had dinner with some of the other carolers,' said Wallis in her posh and Sloaney intonation.

Yes, the Sloane Rangers would soon be regrouping at Midlands-Hasegawa

University. And there, safe from the societal ills of England's cities, the girls would be happy and safe from harm. For a while.

THE MUGHAL GOTHIC BALLROOM
The luminously beautiful Gemma, in a minimalist white satin dress of stylish design, and Enoch, extremely handsome in white tie and tails, stood near one of the tall windows of the crowded white walled ballroom. It was almost midnight. Gemma, shimmering in the incandescent light of one of the crystal chandeliers, smiled.

'How one's life can change so completely in a year,' said Gemma. 'I had almost given up on finding happiness and true love. If this is a dream, please don't ever wake me up, Enoch.'

Enoch smiled as he gently took Gemma's small soft hand in his. 'I'm happy to say that this is not a dream. You need not fear ever waking up from it. I am here, and we are together. And we always will be. I promise. I love you, Gemma Ophelia Ripley.'

'And I love you,' said Gemma gently, softly, in barely whisper, as she leaned forward and gently kissed Enoch, which made Enoch feel as if he were floating through the air.

'Gemmy!' said Külli excitedly. 'You look beautiful, as always!' Külli, her long, glossy brown hair framing her smooth face, in a light grey satin dress of minimalist design, and standing at nearly 6'3" in high heels, towered over the 5'3" Gemma. Külli smiled and said, 'I love you, Enoch.'

Enoch smiled. 'And I love you, Külli.'

'A moment alone, Gemma?' asked Külli.

Gemma smiled and Külli led Gemma a few steps away and they stood in front of another of the large white pane glass windows. Outside, beyond the low stone wall and the ornate iron railings, it was freezing cold and dark. Gemma and Külli were partially illuminated by the large crystal chandelier that hovered above the ballroom. Külli, at forty-one, was starkly beautiful and youthful. Yes, a lifetime of strict diets and exercise, and a strict regimen of skincare treatments, had left her looking much younger, perhaps ten years younger than her true age.

'I am so blessed to have met you, Gemma. I have made a lot of mistakes, especially with you, but you were kind enough and brave enough, to give me another chance, and I will always be grateful to you for that. I know that I can never get those twenty lost years back between us, and it hurts me. So much time that we should have spent together, Gemmy. I love you, Gemma. I love you. I am so happy that you found Enoch. I hope you are happy forever after because you deserve to be happy. I am happy. You gave me back my peace of mind. I will always be here for you, Gemma. I know we have talked about this before, but, here, now, I want to tell you all of this just one more time. Thank you, Gemma. Thank you for being you. Please never change,' said Külli, her voice breaking with emotion.

'Oh, Gula. Dear Gula. We all make mistakes. Please, never be sad again when you think about us. I love you. I always will. I am happy that you have found peace and Octavia—beautiful Octavia. And I am grateful to have you, my dear friend and confidant, back in my life. Forever,' said Gemma, her gentle voice a mixture of happiness and fragility.

The two Inseparables embraced in the shadowy incandescence near the window.

'All of this affection, and you did not invite me,' said Violet happily. Violet, slender, blonde, and beautiful, smiled. 'Our first day at All Saints seems like yesterday. How blessed we are to have met. How I wish we could all go back and relieve those glorious days in Sussex,' said Violet in her posh and Sloaney intonation.

'I love you, Vava,' said Gemma happily as she turned to look at Violet.

'I love you, too, Vava,' said Külli happily. 'Come hither, Vava. I need you.'

'I need you, too, Vava!' said Gemma happily.

Violet smiled and the three Inseparables embraced.

'If only Poppy were here,' said Violet. 'Then we would be complete.'

'She will return to London in a few months, and we will all be reunited, Vava,' said Gemma happily.

The three Inseparables, now in a circle and holding hands, radiated love and friendship.

'Whatever happens in the future, we will always have each other. If I have learned one thing in this life, it is that in the end, love is what really matters and love is all that remains,' said Gemma, her voice trembling with emotion.

The three girls gently squeezed each other's soft hands, and through tears, all of them smiled gently.

Suddenly, there was a commotion in the center of the crowded ballroom. The towering figure of Lord Maud, the white-haired 4th Baron, in white tie and tails, and standing directly under one of the large shimmering crystal chandeliers, smiled. Lord Maud, his white waistcoat practically glowing in the incandescent illumination, looked at his silver Asprey wrist watch and said, 'Ten! Nine! Eight!'

And all of the other party guest joined in.

'Seven! Six! Five! Four! Three! Two! One!

Happy New Year!'

10 KALLI YUGA

Gemma—An Invisible Fear—Jem

SURREY
January 10th, 2020
The last time The Revenant had contacted Jem (which had been via an encrypted smartphone), he had told Jem to assembly his unit (many of them former British Paras) and have them standby. The war would begin in less than two weeks. Be ready. That was over two weeks ago. The Revenant had gone silent.

Of course, Jem had been following the news. It had been just over a week since Carter Holland, facing imminent arrest, had disappeared, with Scotland Yard, MI5, and MI6 in tireless pursuit. And yet, Carter Holland, the subject of dozens of international arrest warrants, including one issued by INTERPOL, had seemingly vanished into thin air.

So had the Revenant.

What had gone wrong?

It was astounding really. How could someone, like Carter Holland, who was guilty of so much; who had stolen so much, and killed so many, have just disappeared? The whole world was looking for Carter, and yet, nothing. Had he been murdered; his corpse buried in concrete? No. **No, life doesn't work that way.** Carter Holland had escaped into exile.

Everyone in the Core Army had gone to ground. That hadn't been difficult. Only the Revenant knew everyone's identities, and he wasn't talking. The unit under Jem had been disbanded a few days earlier. Jem had offered no reasons. No one had asked. Everyone, as per the (strictly verbal) agreement, had been paid in full, in advance of the operation. That had meant at least £200,000 each. Senior ranks had received more. Jem had over £2,000,000 in gold bullion deposited two weeks ago in a bank vault in Switzerland. All of the men had been paid in gold. That was also part of the agreement.

Jem had been curious about what had gone wrong, and where the Revenant now was. It had never occurred to him, not really, that the Revenant could be dead. No, the Revenant was immortal. And Jem knew, he knew that the Revenant had unfinished business to attend to after the civil war was over. Jem suspected that the Revenant would return to his homeland and attempt to reclaim it. The Revenant had never told him that, but Jem could sense it. Yes, the Revenant was a deeply scarred man; only retribution and redress would free him. And Jem had told himself that when that day came, Jem would volunteer to return with him. Free of charge.

It was a telephone call early that morning at Jem's cottage in Surrey that had alerted him that something had happened to the Revenant. The Texan had telephoned and told him that he needed to see him that day. It was important. The Texan refused to answer any questions on the phone. He would explain everything in person. They had to meet somewhere private; a place that few, if any, ever frequented. Jem knew just such a place in his village.

THE ANGLICAN CHURCH

It was snowing when Jem reached the medieval ironstone rubble church in the center of the village. He looked around. No one was outside. The village was already blanketed in snow. As pretty as a postcard.

Jem breathed hard as stood before the church. Jem looked at his dive watch: 12:03pm. The Texan was already here. Jem was late. That morning had found Jem breathless. He often found himself trembling for no reason. Yes. Jem knew the second he had put down his smartphone that he would probably never see the Revenant again. Something had happened. But what? The last few hours had been an absolutely maddening mixture of anxiety, dread, and hope. Please, God. Please let the Revenant be alright.

The tall, muscular, and handsome Jem, in a pair of faded blue jeans, a button-down white Oxford dress shirt, a long dark grey wool coat (with a light brown fur collar), and a pair of brown leather Chelsea boots, entered the dimly lit church. It was cold inside. The church was usually left unheated, except on Sundays, when a dozen, mostly elderly locals would attend.

The church service was led by an elderly retired Anglican priest who had volunteered to come partially out of retirement and conduct services at three different churches in the area. All of the churches now had small congregations, the largest a dozen, the smallest, only five. The elderly vicar would drive from village to village in his small hatchback every Sunday. He was happy to do it. Now a widower, he lived alone. His daughter was now married and lived in America. She would telephone him and talk with him every day.

Monday through Saturday, the church was left unlocked from 9am till 10pm, at which time, a local volunteer would walk over to the church and lock the large double doors. Yes, this was the perfect meeting place.

A bright shaft of natural light flooded into the church as Jem pushed open one of the wooden double doors. Latin words, engraved in the stone walls, appeared. And then Jem closed the door and the words disappeared into the dim light provided by the wall mounted lamps (most of which had been switched off to save money). Jem looked around. No one. But, of course, Jem knew he wasn't alone. The Texan would not be so unwise as to present himself as an obvious target to anyone who might enter through the main doors.

'I'm over here, Jem,' said the Texan, as he took a step out from behind a stone pillar. He was clad in faded blue jeans, a white button-down Oxford dress shirt, a dark blue wool blazer, a light grey wool scarf, and pair of cowboy boots. The middle-aged American was holding a weathered cowboy hat in his hands. The slender Texan's chiseled handsome face was pale. Yes, the news would, undoubtably, be bad.

Jem and the Texan each took a seat in the last wooden pew near the entrance which was partially hidden behind a large pillar. If any of their enemies entered the church, the two would have the advantage of attacking unseen from behind. Jem, this time, was carrying a M57 Tokarev pistol in the inner pocket of his wool coat.

'What happened?' asked Jem apprehensively. He had been wanting to ask this question all morning, and now he was. And now he found himself really not wanting to know the answer.

The Texan would not keep Jem in anymore suspense. The cowboy from West Texas knew that Jem had been left agonizing over the fate of the Revenant all morning long. The Texan hadn't wanted that, but security was paramount.

'Yes. He's dead,' said the Texan quietly.

Jem felt a terrible shock rush through him and a burning sensation filled him. Yes. The Revenant was dead. Jem had known that all morning, but he didn't want to accept it. He held out hope that his friend had somehow managed to elude capture and was safe. Of course, Jem knew that's not what had happened, but still, he had told himself that it was possible. The news that the Texan was bringing him needn't be bad.

The powerfully built Jem clinched his iron like fists; he was trembling. He felt dizzy.

'I found out what happened early this morning from someone who knows someone who knows someone who was on the team which killed him,' said the Texan while slowly turning his weathered cowboy hat in his hands.

Jem steadied himself with his hands on the wooden pew in front of them.

'Carter Holland had him killed. I don't have all of the details, but from what I do know, Carter gave him one last assignment to do the same day he was scheduled to fly out of London. Enoch Tara has a fiancée. Carter had managed to have someone close to this woman place a tracking app on her phone. Carter wanted the General to abduct and murder her. This was supposed to throw Tara into such a paralyzing state of grief and shock that Carter would be able to easily rollover Tara and loot his holdings. Carter Holland, from what the General told me, was absolutely ruthless. This sounds like something Carter would do. And, it probably would have worked. However, Carter Holland did not anticipate that the General would balk at killing a defenseless and innocent woman. From what I was told this morning, the General had agreed to do it, but instead of killing her, as was the plan, he let her go.'

'Of course, he did,' said Jem. 'He wasn't the type of person to harm the innocent. The General was a true man's man. An honourable solider. That's why I always followed his orders. I knew he would never agree to harm innocents,' said Jem quietly in his West Country dialect.

'The way I figure it, the General went along with it because he knew that if he didn't agree to it, Carter Holland would find someone else who would,' said the American cowboy in his Texan drawl.

'Yes. You're right,' said Jem quietly.

'I was told that Carter's security team had placed a tracking device in the General's car before he had left the office and traced him to his house in the Midlands. I was told he lived outside of a small village. Lots of trees and snowy fields around the house. Before Carter Holland escaped into exile, he dispatched a three-man team to get him. They waited outside the house. Eventually, when the General came out and walked to his car, they shot him dead. The bullet shattered his jaw. He died instantly. I hope he did.'

Jem started to choke back tears.

'They left him where he fell. The police are investigating. There was a news report, but the name they gave was not the General's. Well, it wasn't one of the names he had ever given me. The General had a lot of different identities, passports, travel documents. As far as I can tell, they haven't connected the General to Carter Holland. I doubt they ever will. The General will just be another unsolved gangland murder in England,' said the Texan quietly.

'So that's it? This is how it ends?' asked Jem.

'I suppose so,' replied the Texan quietly.

The two comrades, friends, sat quietly in the wooden pew for a few minutes without speaking.

'Do you know what the General's real name was? Do you know where he was from?' asked the Texan.

'No. I met him almost twenty years ago, and in all those years since he had never told me his real name or where he from. I never asked. I didn't really want to know. I know he was a war refugee and that his family was dead. I could see in his face that they had suffered terrible deaths. So, I never asked. He said things sometimes which I later pieced together. I know he had a really terrible past. So, no, I never asked. I know he was a good person. A flawed, but good person,' replied Jem.

'Yes. He was a good person. I wish that he had contacted one of us before he drove off that day. If one of us had been with him, I think we could have helped him escape,' said the Texan.

'Yes. I think so too,' said Jem. 'He must have known that he would be killed for failing to murder that woman, but he drove off alone anyway. He didn't want to risk us. That's why he didn't contact us. He knew he would be killed, and he didn't want to risk either one of us,' said Jem.

The Texan nodded slowly. 'You know, I think you're right. I can feel that in my bones. Yes, the General knew that the game was up. That if Carter

Holland was ordering men to do things like that, Carter was best sabotaged.'

Jem exhaled. Yes, it had all become clear to them. The General had sacrificed himself, saved an innocent person's life, and derailed Carter Holland.

'I think the General was trying to redeem himself,' said the Texan. 'I know somethings were eating at him. I don't know what exactly was going through his mind that day; no one but the General and God knows that. But, in that moment, on that road, wherever it was, the General had a choicc. I think he chose right.'

Jem agreed, but showed no physical sign of it. He simply stared off into space, deep in thought.

'I am leaving England tonight. I have a plane to catch, Jem. I think it is best I get out the country while I still can. You never know what the police will find. I saw the police carrying box after box out of Carter Holland's offices in London on television this morning. I had never even heard of Carter Holland until all of this.'

Jem held his head in his hands for a moment. He was trying to collect his thoughts, control his emotions.

The Texan stood up and made his way to the center aisle of the church. He looked around. The Texan noticed the Latin letters carved into the Medieval stone. He read the Latin out loud.

'Do you understand Latin?' asked Jem.

'Nah. I wish I did though. I never went to college. I joined the Foreign Legion and learned how to speak French instead. Do you understand Latin?'

'Me? No. I joined the Paras. I barely got through the local comprehensive,' replied Jem.

Jem stood up and made his way between the wooden pews. When he reached the Texan, the Texan held out his right hand while grasping his hat in the other.

'Goodbye, Jem.'

Jem extended his hand and grasped the Texan's.

'I'll never see you again?' asked Jem.

'Not for a while. I don't know. I would like to say that I'll just go back to my ranch in Texas and live quietly, if not happily ever after. But, seeing how things are going in the States and the rest of the world, I don't think I'll be able to do that. I have always known that I would not die a peaceful death, Jem. I think the General knew that too. Right now, I just want to go home and try not to think about anything too much,' said the Texan in his West Texas drawl.

'I doubt things will stay quiet for long. And you're right. The General knew he would die a violent death. He knew. I just wish he was still here. Just for a little bit longer. I miss him. I have lost a lot of friends over the years, but this one hurts more than any of the others,' said Jem.

The Texan turned and faced the Medieval stone altar. 'I prayed for the General's soul this morning. I'm going to continue to pray for God's mercy. You know, I think God places us on the Earth as a test. A series of tests. And I think more times than not, we fail those tests. But I think, in the General's case, he passed the final test. I'm hoping that God will take that into consideration when judging him. I hope to pass the final test myself. I want to see the General again. I want to see him in Heaven. I want to see you in Heaven, too, Jem.'

Jem was a bit startled by the Texan's admission of faith. He had never heard him talk of religion. But the Texan was from the American South. Should the Texan's Christian faith really come as a surprise? The Texan was, after all, a hired gun. But, on second thought, the Texan had refused to work for bad characters in the past. **The Texan had fought against the Serbs and Montenegrins in Croatia and Bosnia**. He had fought shoulder to shoulder in the trenches against the Chetniks with Jem.

'I haven't prayed in a church since I was thirteen,' said Jem.

'But I bet you prayed to God every day in the trenches,' said the Texan, and he smiled.

Jem smiled. 'Yes, mate. I did. And I will.'

Jem, suddenly felt a rush of emotion, he took a step forward, and hugged his American friend. The Texan hugged back. When they parted, both men had tears in their eyes. The Texan then took a step back, pivoted on his heels, and started walking to the doors of the church. Jem stood in front of the stone altar in silence. The Texan pushed open one of the doors, a burst of natural light flooded into the church illuminating the interior and Jem.

The Texan put on his weathered cowboy hat as he stood in the open doorway. The Texan smiled.

'Say a prayer for me, too, Jem.'

The Texan then pulled the door shut. And just like that, the Texan was gone.

Jem now stood alone in the church. He turned and faced the altar. He began to pray, and then suddenly stopped. No. Do this right, Jem. Jem went down on his knees on the stone floor before God; he clasped his hands in prayer, just as his mother had taught him, closed his eyes, and prayed.

'Please, God. Have mercy on the soul on the General. Please, God, let the General be with his family in Heaven. Please, God, have mercy on a poor sinner. Please, God, have mercy on me and my mother. Dear God, have mercy on my American friend. Please, God. Have mercy on your children.

Made in the USA
Coppell, TX
16 January 2023

11172225R00233